FAMILY
AND FORTUNE

*Studies in Aristocratic Finance
in the Sixteenth and Seventeenth
Centuries*

FAMILY AND FORTUNE

Studies in Aristocratic Finance
in the Sixteenth and Seventeenth
Centuries

BY

LAWRENCE STONE
DODGE PROFESSOR OF HISTORY
AND DIRECTOR OF THE
SHELBY CULLOM DAVIS CENTER
FOR HISTORICAL STUDIES
PRINCETON UNIVERSITY

OXFORD
AT THE CLARENDON PRESS
1973

Oxford University Press, Ely House, London W. 1

GLASGOW   NEW YORK   TORONTO   MELBOURNE   WELLINGTON
CAPE TOWN   IBADAN   NAIROBI   DAR ES SALAAM   LUSAKA   ADDIS ABABA
DELHI   BOMBAY   CALCUTTA   MADRAS   KARACHI   LAHORE   DACCA
KUALA LUMPUR   SINGAPORE   HONG KONG   TOKYO

*Printed in Great Britain
at the University Press, Oxford
by Vivian Ridler
Printer to the University*

This book is dedicated to
the owners of private family archives
who have so generously made
them available to serious scholars

ACKNOWLEDGEMENTS

ALL of these essays are constructed on the foundation of private family papers generously made available to me by their owners. Part I, concerning the Cecils Earls of Salisbury, is based on the papers of the Marquis of Salisbury at Hatfield House. The chapter on the Manners Earls of Rutland is based on the papers of the Duke of Rutland at Belvoir Castle; that on the Wriothesleys Earls of Southampton on the Wriothesley papers deposited in the Hampshire Record Office; that on the Berkeleys Lords Berkeley in part on the papers at Berkeley Castle belonging to the Trustees of the will of the Right Honourable Randal Thomas Mowbray, Earl of Berkeley, deceased; and that on the Howards Earls of Suffolk in part on the papers of Lord Braybrooke, deposited in the Essex Record Office. To these and other owners of private archives who have given me access to their collections, I am profoundly grateful, since without their enlightened co-operation this book could not have been written.

Some parts of Chapter I were published in *Essays in the Economic and Social History of Tudor and Stuart England*, ed. F. J. Fisher, Cambridge University Press, 1961; versions of Chapter II and Chapter III, section ii, appeared in *Archaeological Journal*, cxii, 1956, and cxiv, 1959. For financial support in the preparation of this volume I am grateful to the Princeton University Research Fund and the National Science Foundation.

I am indebted to my wife for picking up many errors in the text and for her skill and patience in compiling the index.

ACKNOWLEDGEMENTS

ALL of these essays are constructed on the foundation of private family papers generously made available to me by their owners. Part I, concerning the Cecils Earls of Salisbury, is based on the papers of the Marquis of Salisbury at Hatfield House. The chapter on the Manners Earls of Rutland is based on the papers of the Duke of Rutland at Belvoir Castle; that on the Wriothesleys Earls of Southampton on the Wriothesley papers deposited in the Hampshire Record Office; that on the Berkeleys Lords Berkeley in part on the papers at Berkeley Castle belonging to the Trustees of the will of the Right Honourable Randal Thomas Mowbray, Earl of Berkeley, deceased; and that on the Howards Earls of Suffolk in part on the papers of Lord Braybrooke, deposited in the Essex Record Office. To these and other owners of private archives who have given me access to their collections, I am profoundly grateful, since without their enlightened co-operation this book could not have been written.

Some parts of Chapter I were published in *Essays in the Economic and Social History of Tudor and Stuart England*, ed. F. J. Fisher, Cambridge University Press, 1961; versions of Chapter II and Chapter III, section ii, appeared in *Archaeological Journal*, cxii, 1956, and cxiv, 1959. For financial support in the preparation of this volume I am grateful to the Princeton University Research Fund and the National Science Foundation.

I am indebted to my wife for picking up many errors in the text and for her skill and patience in compiling the index.

CONTENTS

PART ONE
THE CECILS EARLS OF SALISBURY, 1590–1733

PART TWO

OTHER FAMILIES

LIST OF ILLUSTRATIONS

ABBREVIATIONS

Arch. J.	*Archaeological Journal.*
Bodl.	Bodleian Library, Oxford.
B.M.	British Museum.
Cal. S.P. Dom.	*Calendar of State Papers Domestic.*
Econ. Hist. Rev.	*Economic History Review.*
Eng. Hist. Rev.	*English Historical Review.*
H.M.C.	*Historical Manuscripts Commission.*
P.C.C.	Prerogative Court of Canterbury: Wills in Somerset House.
P.R.O.	Public Record Office.
P.R.O., S.P. 12	Public Record Office, State Papers Domestic, Elizabeth.
,, S.P. 14	Public Record Office, State Papers Domestic, James I.
,, S.P. 16	Public Record Office, State Papers Domestic, Charles I.
T.R.H.S.	*Transactions of the Royal Historical Society.*

NOTE

TITLES of honour are given in accordance with sixteenth-century rather than twentieth-century conventions, except when more precise definitions are needed to avoid ambiguity. In quoting from original sources, spelling, punctuation, and the use of capital letters have been modernized, for I am now persuaded that the loss of flavour is more than compensated for in a work of this nature by the gain in ease of comprehension. Days of the month are old style, but the year is taken to begin on 1 January.

INTRODUCTION

EIGHT years ago I published a book entitled *The Crisis of the Aristocracy 1558–1641* (Oxford, 1965) in which, among other things, I analysed the various forces which were working to increase or diminish the financial resources of an aristocratic family. When the book was published, several critics complained of the absence of any detailed chronological studies of specific families by which it would be possible to trace the varying effects on these families of fertility, marriage, court service, conspicuous consumption, estate administration, debt, legal provisions, and industrial and commercial entrepreneurship. These case histories are an attempt to fill this gap and to provide detailed examples to demonstrate the practical working of the general theories advanced in the earlier book.

These studies range in time way beyond the limits imposed in the earlier book, but in other respects they are narrower in focus. In the first place, all the examples are drawn from the very topmost ranks of the aristocracy, an élite within an élite, members of a group which in France was known as 'Les Grands'. One compelling reason for this selection is that the records are more complete for these very great families, since their very size has tended to preserve them—and therefore their archives—down through the centuries to the present day. These particular families have been selected, not necessarily because of their typicality, but rather because of the wealth of surviving but unpublished documentation about them. The second reason for choosing members of this topmost level of society is that, because of their intimate connection with the Court, high office, and royal favour, the speed and the scale of the gains and the losses are at their most dramatic and the story is therefore more interesting than it would be for more modest aristocratic families less exposed both to opportunity and temptation. These are families living on a heroic scale, streaking up to the heights, and sometimes plunging down again with the spin of Fortune's wheel.

The second narrowing of focus concerns the subject-matter, which is almost exclusively financial history. The religious, political, and personal sides of the lives of the individuals in the story are mentioned only in so far as these things affect the fortune of the family. This book is fairly exclusively concerned with that mythic and rather dismal abstraction, *homo economicus*. The justification for such a limitation is that the central concern of the individuals under study was—or was supposed to be—the prosperity and continuity of the family, and that the preservation of the family as an entity from generation to generation is very strictly determined by economic and biological considerations. The prime responsibility of the current head of the family was to preserve, or perhaps increase, the family inheritance, and to ensure its continuity by producing a healthy male heir. It is no accident that contemporary family histories, like those of the Berkeleys Lords Berkeley, the Hastings Earls of Huntingdon, or the Wentworths Earls of Strafford, should concentrate so exclusively on economic matters, on the buying and selling of property, the rise and liquidation of debt, the burdens and rewards of office, the lottery of marriage with rich heiresses, and the number and sex of the surviving children as they affected the dispersal of the family fortunes.[1] This book must therefore be regarded as a coda to the 1965 volume, which now focuses exclusively upon financial history, and which organizes the material chronologically around individual families, rather than analytically around general themes.

This narrowing of focus should not be taken to mean that there is any underlying assumption about economic determinism as a controlling factor in influencing human behaviour. Indeed, if these stories carry any message, it is that the maximization of profits was far from being in the forefront of the minds of many of the leading members of this highly restricted group. They were, for the most part, more concerned with expenditure than with income, and it was only if the latter was failing in its duty to support the former that attention was shifted to means of increasing revenue. On the other hand, the family patrimony was the source of the social and political power and prestige of these great lords, and its history is therefore central to the study of the English ruling class over the last four centuries.

The case histories assembled here provide examples of most of the experiences to which a great family could be subjected at this time. The Berkeleys show how an ancient inheritance could be

---

[1] J. Smyth, *The Berkeley Manuscripts*, ed. J. Maclean, Gloucester, 1883–5. Bodl., Carte MSS. 78, ff. 410–17. Sheffield City Library, Wentworth Woodhouse MSS. Strafford MSS. 40/1.

dissipated by extravagantly conspicuous consumption, not compensated for by Court favour at the two critical periods of lavish
royal giving, 1536–52, when church property was being dispersed,
and 1603–29, when James and Buckingham were rewarding
favoured courtiers on a gigantic scale. The Wriothesleys were a
family created in the first wave of royal largesse, the Cecils and
Howards in the second. Both the latter were families whose fortunes were built on the massive spread of corruption in political
circles in the reign of King James, and yet both were threatened by
the consequences of a concurrent building spree of unprecedented
and illogical proportions. Both survived the fall from office, and
managed to liquidate the debt, but both were subsequently threatened by the excessive fertility of their wives, and by the excessive
devotion to all his children of the head of the family. The Cecils
survived these blows far better than the Howards, partly because
of better management, partly because of a more ruthlessly single-
minded search for rich heiresses to marry. The Wriothesleys and
the Manners demonstrate both the profits to be derived from industrial exploitation of the estate and the losses that could be
incurred by personal extravagance in the wild years of the 1590s.
The Cecils and the Wriothesleys show the profits to be made from
the development of urban property in London. The Cecils, the
Howards, and the Manners illustrate the Scylla and Charybdis of
producing too many or too few children: either could endanger the
ship.

These are the main threads which run through these stories and
whose varying combinations are the warp and the woof of the
fortunes of the individual family. None of these case histories suggests any necessity to revise the fundamental findings of the former
book. What they do is to provide illustrative detail, and to point up
the importance of sheer chance and individual personality as independent variables in their own right. So powerful are they that in
specific cases they seem almost entirely to obscure the broad trends,
which can only be detected by a careful statistical study of the group
as a whole. The parts are in general less than the whole, as one
would logically expect, and yet in some ways they are more, since
the peculiarities of the individual personality and the random un-
predictability of biological chance contrive to twist each case into
something of a sport. It is the quirky eccentricity of each family
that these case histories illustrate. They also enable us to watch the

working out of such general factors as patronage and primogeniture, a built-in tendency to excessive consumption, the profits and
the dangers of high political office, the declining cost of borrowing,
the general movement of rental income in relation to prices, and the
extraordinary importance of marriage and the number and sex of
the surviving children.

PART ONE

THE CECILS
EARLS OF SALISBURY
1590–1733

I

ACQUISITION
1590–1612[1]

I. NON-LANDED SOURCES OF INCOME, 1590–1608

ROBERT CECIL was the younger son, by a second wife, of William, first Lord Burghley.[2] In a long life spent in public office as Secretary of State, Lord Treasurer, and Master of the Court of Wards, his father had acquired a huge estate scattered over the home counties and the east midlands, and running up into Lincolnshire and Yorkshire. The custom of primogeniture made it inevitable that the lion's share of these lands should go to Robert's elder brother, Thomas. But it was not uncommon for a man whose wealth was the result of his own exertions rather than ancient inheritance to feel free to deal more generously than was usual with his younger children. Moreover, Lord Burghley had special reasons for dividing his estate. Thomas was a great disappointment to him, for it had early become clear that he had inherited none of his father's intelligence and ambition. An easy-going, unaspiring man, he was content to jog along in comfortable enjoyment of his inherited position as a leader of county society. Not for him the stresses, the toil, and the possible reward of an active political life. Burghley's hopes, therefor, centred upon Robert, and as soon as the young man's education had been completed by a stay in France, careful preparations were made to launch him on a political career. In 1589 he made a suitable

---

[1] Most of the documents used for this Part are preserved at Hatfield House, and I am deeply indebted to the Marquis of Salisbury for permission to examine them. The following abbreviations are used:

A.: Accounts
B.: Bills
D.: Deeds
F.P.: Family Papers
G.: General
L.: Legal
S.: Salisbury MSS. (bound volumes of official correspondence)
Box G, Q, U, V, S: Boxes of deeds and documents
Pet.: Petitions.

[2] See genealogical table no. 1.

marriage with Elizabeth, daughter of Lord Cobham, and in order to provide for her jointure Lord Burghley drew up his second and final settlement for dividing his estate after his death. On Thomas he settled the great country seat of Burghley House in Northampton-shire, the town house in London on the north side of the Strand, and all the estates outside the home counties. This left Robert with the reversion of the gigantic palace at Theobalds in Hertfordshire with the accompanying eight sub-manors, the five other manors in the same county, a manor and extensive farms and lands at Edmon-ton and Enfield in Middlesex, and the large manor of Essendine in Rutlandshire.[1] More lands were added to the settlement in the early 1590s as Lord Burghley became increasingly dependent on his son in his political activities.

What income this estate brought in to Robert Cecil when he inherited it in 1598 we do not know for certain. In 1609 the gross rental of all except the Theobalds group totalled £910,[2] which must mean an average income, including casualties, of well over £1,000 a year. Much of the Theobalds estate was given over to unprofitable deer-parks, and its rental seems to have been no more than about £700 a year, and may well have been rather less.[3] We should therefore be safe in assuming that Robert Cecil's inheritance in 1598 brought in about £1,800 a year, out of which he had to find the money to maintain the huge palace of Theobalds. This calculation is independently supported by the report that Cecil himself declared that 'his own part will not rise to £1,600 a year upon the rack'.[4] But this substantial inheritance was in prospect, not in possession, and so long as his father was alive Robert Cecil probably depended on an annuity in order to supplement the profits of office. As early as 1590, long before he obtained a major appointment, his close association with his aged father opened the way for a steady stream of bribes and gratuities from suitors seeking favours from the Lord Treasurer. In 1596 he was finally made Secretary of State, which gave him a secret-service allowance of £800 a year in addition to the official salary and fees. The next year he also acquired the Chancellorship of the Duchy of Lancaster, in 1598 he succeeded his father as Master of the Court of Wards, and

[1] D. 217. G. 39/3. F. Peck, *Desiderata Curiosa*, London, 1732, I, v, pp. 25–43.

[2] Box Q/2.

[3] The surviving records are confusing, but this seems to be the most likely figure (A. 6/16, 20, 36; 7/2).

[4] N. E. McClure, *Letters of John Chamberlain*, Philadelphia, Pa., 1939, i, p. 42.

in 1608 he won the highest and most lucrative office of all, the Lord Treasurership. These last two offices gave Cecil control of strategic economic decisions affecting large numbers of wealthy and influential people, who were prepared to conform to the custom of the times and offer 'gratuities' in order to influence policy. It is not surprising, therefore, to find him beginning to buy land very soon after he became Master of the Court of Wards. For the first ten years of the acquisitive phase, from 1598 to 1608, enough material has survived to enable the historian to offer some circumstantial evidence to flesh out Sir Fulke Greville's jocular comment: 'In the point of profit I perceive you resolve now to multiply yourself.'[1] After 1608 the process can be documented in embarrassing detail.

The last years of Elizabeth were a time when the standards of financial probity in public life seem to have been slipping. The giving and accepting of gratuities was part of the normal way of life in this period, as indeed in all patrimonial bureaucracies, and need not be taken too seriously by the historian. On the other hand, there is a good deal of evidence that contemporaries were aware of a deterioration of standards in the 1590s, under the continued pressures of fixed salaries, monetary inflation, increasing royal parsimony in the distribution of rewards, and the normal opportunities for fraud and profiteering that war inevitably offers.[2] An important addition to Cecil's political influence, but only a very minor addition to his income, was made by accumulating local offices from corporations and ecclesiastical authorities anxious to stand in well with the great court figure. The real importance of these offices lay in the influence they gave over borough elections and the granting of church leases, but the fees they brought with them were not entirely negligible. Though most of them were passed on to the Earl's servants, they at least relieved him of the necessity of increasing their wages. The boroughs of Totnes, Plymouth, Dartmouth, Exeter, and Gloucester paid him annuities; Doncaster, Hull, High Wycombe, Portsmouth, Winchester, and Exeter made him their High Steward. He was Steward of

[1] J. E. Neale, 'The Elizabethan Political Scene' in his *Essays in Elizabethan History*, London, 1958. *H.M.C. Salis. MSS.* xvi, p. 196. J. H. Hurstfield, *The Queen's Wards*, London, 1958, pp. 300-4.

[2] Neale, op. cit., *passim*. J. H. Hurstfield, 'Political Corruption in Modern England', *History*, lii, 1967, correctly points out that mild corruption was deeply, and indeed structurally, embedded in the social and political system. He is not convincing, however, in his argument that there was no deterioration in ethical standards at this time.

Cambridge University, Trinity College, and Eton. He drew an annuity from the Dean and Chapter of Windsor, was High Steward of the Deans and Chapters of Wells, Westminster, and Winchester, and Captain of the Liberties of Bath and Wells. He was made Steward by the Bishops of Oxford, Hereford, Worcester, and Rochester, Surveyor by Oxford and Norwich, Master of Game by Coventry, and Clerk by Salisbury. The total fees from these sources only came to about £150 a year.[1]

Like so many nobles of the period, Cecil could not resist the temptation of high-risk speculative ventures in such things as novel industrial developments and in privateering. With only one exception, however, investment in the former seems to have been uniformly unrewarding, despite the wide spread of activity.

In 1590 Cecil added to the family holdings by buying a $\frac{1}{48}$ share in the Mines Royal Company from Sir Thomas Smith, and in 1601 the Mineral and Battery Company gave him a share in their undertaking, presumably in return for political favour. Neither of these companies ever showed much of a profit and it is doubtful whether Cecil got anything from them. The joint purchase with the Earl of Cumberland in 1595 of a monopoly patent to manufacture iron, steel, and lead with either peat or coal must have been equally unfruitful, for it was not till many years later that the art of smelting iron with coal was mastered. Equally speculative, and equally unsuccessful, was the investment with Buckhurst and Shrewsbury in Bevis Bulmer's prospecting for minerals along the Scottish border.[2] More profitable, perhaps, was the acquisition in 1598 with Lord Buckhurst of Sir John Packington's eight-year monopoly patent for the manufacture of starch. This was an exceedingly complicated transaction and the details are obscure. Not surprisingly, the full weight of the Privy Council was put behind the enforcement of the monopoly, the official production figures rose sharply in 1599–1601, and there is every reason to suppose that the monopoly showed a profit, possibly a large one.[3]

But these tentative and mostly unhappy ventures into industry are overshadowed both in scale and in success by Cecil's investment in privateering during the interminable Anglo-Spanish war of 1585 to 1604. This time-honoured method of naval warfare cost the

[1] Box V/172. Box S/7. For a typed list of offices, see F.P. iv, p. 187.

[2] D. 45/2; 73/9; 94/8. College of Arms, Talbot MSS. i f. 266.

[3] *H.M.C. Salis. MSS.* viii, pp. 172, 233, 565; xiii, p. 559; xiv, pp. 59, 87, 102, 169; S. 204 f. 123.

Crown nothing, inflicted damage on the economic life of the enemy, and brought a fortune to the Lord Admiral, who took 10 per cent of all prizes. One of the hazards of the business, however, was the uncertain legal position over neutral goods and neutral shipping *en route* for enemy ports, and in practice the distinction between legitimate privateering and indiscriminate piracy was hard to draw, despite efforts by the Crown and the Court of Admiralty.[1]

It seems to have been the Lord Admiral, Lord Howard of Effingham, who first drew Cecil into this speculative business. It offered special attractions to both of them, since they could—and did—use their official positions to offset some of the costs. Cecil could use some of the secret-service money to fit out ships, on the grounds that one of their purposes was to hang about off the coast of Spain to pick up information about Spanish naval preparations; Effingham and Cecil between them could get ships put on the royal pay-roll and then use them for their private advantage.

Cecil's first venture was in the winter of 1595–6 when he joined Effingham in building the *Truelove*. The bare hull was said to have cost £800, but if other contractors were treated like the supplier of cordage, who had still not been paid his bill of £95 in 1603 and was by then in the Fleet for debt, the actual cost to the adventurers must have been much reduced.[2] At first it was intended to use her on the voyage of Kemys to Guiana to follow up Ralegh's first glowing account of the fabulous riches of that area, but in the end she went instead with Nottingham on the Cadiz Expedition. As Ralegh complained many years later, 'At sundry times Cecil seemed willing to embrace my project, yet always upon conclusion . . . he withdrew himself.'[3]

In March 1597 the *Truelove* at last set off a-privateering. Her instructions were to cruise down the Spanish coast to pick up intelligence, then pass on to Barbary with a commercial cargo. After the goods had been sold she was to sail northwards 'to seek adventures on the coast of Spain'. The voyage cost Cecil and Nottingham little since the *Truelove* was added to the pay-roll of the royal fleet for this spring. Since the fleet was only commissioned for three months it looked a little awkward to put the *Truelove*

[1] K. R. Andrews, *Elizabethan Privateering, 1585–1603*, Cambridge, 1964, Parts I, II.

[2] *H.M.C. Salis. MSS.* xv, p. 206. A. Collins, *Sydney Papers*, London, 1746, i, p. 377. M. Oppenheim, *The Naval Tracts of Sir William Monson (Navy Record Soc.)*, 1902, i, p. 358.

[3] E. Edwards, *The Life of Sir Walter Raleigh*, London, 1868, i, pp. 199–200.

down for six. This difficulty was overcome, however, by inflating the nominal muster of the crew, so that they were double victualled for three months, thus making the equivalent of the full six months. In June the *Truelove*'s captain could report the capture of a 160-ton Brazilman laden with £1,800 worth of sugar, Negroes, and cotton wool, the cargo of which was sold in Barbary, and a 120-ton flyboat with wine and sugar, which was dispatched to England under a prize crew. In addition the Brazilman took on a cargo in Barbary for a commercial voyage back to England. Although there was trouble over the flyboat, whose contents turned out to be Dutch-owned, the capture of the Brazilman, coupled with the fact that the Admiralty was bearing the costs of the voyage, must have brought substantial gains to Cecil and Effingham.[1]

Although Cecil talked of sending her to join one of Cumberland's large-scale privateering expeditions, in the end the *Truelove* set out on a similar half-commercial, half-privateering trip to Barbary in early 1598, again capturing a flyboat, the ownership of whose cargo was not altogether clear. By July she was back in England on royal service, she was with the fleet again in the summer of 1599, and some time after that Effingham and Cecil sold her to the Dutch.[2]

The *Truelove* was by no means the only ship in which Cecil had an interest during these years. He had a share in a pinnace called the *Darling* which in 1598 was meant to join a privateering squadron under Sir John Gilbert. In the same year it became urgent to obtain information about Spanish naval preparations. So Cecil and a London merchant Thomas Honiman hired a Dutch ship, the *Black Horseman*, filled her with banned goods, mostly naval stores, put an English spy on board disguised as a Dutch factor, and set her off on a smuggling voyage to Corunna. Both politically and financially it was a disaster, and Cecil lost his 500 ducats investment in the cargo, paid for out of the secret-service fund. Spanish suspicions were aroused, the spy confessed under torture and was then strangled, the ship and its goods were confiscated, and the unfortunate Dutch master, who was entirely innocent of any knowledge of the espionage, was condemned to eight years in the galleys.[3]

[1] *H.M.C. Salis. MSS.* vii, pp. 79, 82, 148, 277, 522, 538.

[2] *Cal. S.P. Dom., 1595–7,* p. 465; *1598–1601,* pp. 270, 285. *H.M.C. Salis. MSS.* viii, pp. 173, 236; ix, p. 331. M. Oppenheim, op. cit. i, p. 358, n. 1.

[3] P.R.O., S.P. 12/268/95. L. Stone, *An Elizabethan: Sir Horatio Palavicino*, Oxford, 1956, p. 326 *H.M.C. Salis. MSS.* xi, p. 576.

This experience seems to have deterred Cecil for a while, and he abandoned the sea during 1599. In 1600, however, he took the major share in setting out a large London ship, the *Lioness*, with over 100 men aboard on a privateering cruise in the Mediterranean. Of the original investment Cecil subscribed £743, Lord Howard of Effingham, now the Earl of Nottingham, £150, and Lords Cobham and Thomas Howard £100 each. Officially, the captain's instructions were to put down English pirates preying on French and Italian shipping, and to seek legitimate prizes, but there is no evidence of any effort to implement the former objective.[1] The voyage was a brilliant success, thanks to the capture in the Straits of Gibraltar in February 1601 of a large ship laden with sugar. The value of the prize turned out to be £10,915, and the total expenses, including customs payments, came to £1,734. Of this Cecil would have paid about £1,150, and since his share of the prize came to £7,189, his net profit must have been about £6,000. On the other hand, part of the goods proved to be owned by Dutch merchants and the captain of the *Lioness* (and presumably Cecil) had to pay £160 to settle all claims in the Court of Admiralty.[2]

In the summer of 1600 Cecil was also induced to go half shares with Lord Thomas Howard in fitting out for five months the *Lions Whelp*, a 100-ton pinnace owned by the Earl of Nottingham. She had been engaged in privateering or hired on royal service ever since 1592, but this is the first time that Cecil is recorded as taking a share in her. Although she managed to capture three Lubeckers full of naval stores, they were patently innocent neutrals, and the best that could be done was to extract £300 from the owners as a composition to avoid interminable litigation in the Court of Admiralty. As a result Cecil and Howard made a net loss of £41.[3]

Soon afterwards she was apparently sold by Nottingham to the Crown, and served in the Navy in the summer of 1601. This was a very convenient arrangement, for in the winter of 1601–2 she was fitted out, at the expense of the Crown and nominally as part of the Channel Guard, but in fact to be used on a privateering expedition

[1] A year before there had been strong protests against English piracy by the Duke of Tuscany, and all privateering in the Mediterranean had been forbidden by the Queen (N. E. McClure, *Letters of John Chamberlain*, Philadelphia, Pa., 1939, i, p. 66).

[2] H.M.C. *Salis. MSS.* x, pp. 392, 400, 424; xi, p. 177; xvi, p. 168. S. 87 f. 164; 142 f. 175. A. 6/9; 119/12. Essex R.O., D/DP, L. 38.

[3] H.M.C. *Salis. MSS.* x, pp. 194, 200, 347, 349, 350, 361–2, 370, 387; xiv, pp. 50, 135. M. Oppenheim, op. cit. i, pp. 281, 358.

of Cecil and Nottingham. This was one of the most ambitious projects they had yet embarked upon, and involved the use of a 300-ton London ship, the *Marigold*, carrying 100 men aboard her. Though there is reference to the 'excessive charges' to which the adventurers had been put, unless there were two London ships called the *Marigold*, she was certainly on the list of merchantmen hired by the Crown for operations at Kinsale in Ireland from October 1601 until January 1602. It looks as if Cecil and Nottingham had again managed to shift most of the cost of their expedition on to the Exchequer.

The instructions for the *Marigold* and the *Lions Whelp* were to attack English pirates in the Levant, and to intercept some of the Spanish merchant vessels plying between Barcelona and Alexandria with bullion on the outward journey and spices and oriental goods on the inward. How successful the voyage proved we do not know, the last report being of the capture off Sicily of a Hamburg flyboat, claimed as prize largely because it had the temerity to offer resistance, and of the intention to pursue an English pirate who had just taken 4,500 pieces of eight off a Genoese ship. One would hesitate to decide whether it was righteous indignation at the piracy or an eye for the pieces of eight that inspired this latter project.[1]

Meanwhile Cecil had made a far more fortunate investment in a privateer of Sir John Gilbert called the *Refusal*. He had had a 5 per cent share in her voyage in the summer of 1601, which was apparently moderately successful. For the next voyage to the Spanish coast, which set out in December, Cecil had a 50 per cent share in the victualling of the *Refusal* and the *Carvel* (captured on the previous voyage), the remainder of the cost being borne by Nottingham and Sir Walter Ralegh. To save expenses Gilbert suggested that he be empowered to impress the crew, while if Cecil wanted to reduce his adventure the captain when at sea could offer the men half of the victualler's thirds of the profits in return for surrender of half their pay. But fortunately for himself Cecil wanted to increase his investment rather than decrease it, and so while the ship was still at sea in March he bought a quarter share in her from Gilbert for £200. Less than a fortnight later the *Refusal* arrived in Plymouth with other English privateers and a rich haul of prizes.

[1] H.M.C. Salis. MSS. xi, pp. 408, 453–4, 457; xii, pp. 25, 549–51. M. Oppenheim, op. cit. ii pp. 126, 169, 170.

There was a 400-ton Portuguese ship bound for Venice with sugar and pepper, a Seville flyboat with 20,000 ducats worth of goods, and a third small vessel. First reports of the value of the prizes were so exaggerated that Lord Buckhurst, the Lord Treasurer, promptly appointed Commissioners to survey the cargo on behalf of the Queen. To Cecil and Nottingham's indignant protests at this meddlesome intrusion he retorted with the dubious doctrine that 'all great and royal prizes are due to the prince or state, but mean prizes are divisible among the adventurers by general toleration'. But in the end the value of the goods turned out to be only about £16,000 instead of the rumoured £100,000, and royal cupidity was soon diverted to the great carrack that was brought into Plymouth a few weeks later by Sir Richard Leveson. The share-out of the spoils was infinitely complicated by the fact that several ships had taken part, and several others had been within sight or had share agreements with the participants. As late as September the quarrel was still in full swing: 'There hath not one day passed without controversy, for most of these ships had private consortship with other ships unknown to us till the time we began to divide.' What with all their rival claims to be dealt with and the fact that part of the goods proved to belong to neutral Italians, the nominal value of Cecil's share only came to £1,851. But as the official concerned had cheated in the weighing in Cecil's favour, no doubt the goods in the end sold for rather more. In any case there seems little reason to doubt that his net profit was well over £1,000. Not surprisingly Cecil retained his quarter share for the next voyage, which again brought in a prize with large quantities of sugar aboard. The last that is heard of the *Refusal* is an inquiry by Sir John Gilbert whether Cecil wanted to adventure half the victualling in a third voyage in the spring of 1603.[1]

Yet another privateer in which Cecil had an interest was the *Fortune* of London. He and Nottingham both had shares in her when she sailed on a voyage to the Mediterranean in 1602. Unfortunately the captain disobeyed his instructions to confine himself to enemy shipping and instead seized some Dutch goods in French ships, claims for restitution of which were promptly made in the Court of Admiralty. The adventurers had to pay £522 to the Dutch to settle the matter, and as a result they lost on the voyage. Cecil

---

[1] H.M.C. *Salis. MSS.* xi, pp. 457, 528, 539; xii, *passim*. Box S/7 f. 13. For examination of some of the complexities of consortship see L. Stone, op. cit., pp. 215–19.

was very angry at being semi-publicly involved in open piracy, but it did not deter him from adventuring half the victualling costs for the next voyage, the remainder being apparently borne by Lord Cobham and Sir Walter Ralegh. This time he took care to impress on the captain the need to avoid these embarrassments, and also urged his co-adventurers to conceal their names, 'at least my name above all other'. The rigidity of the instructions wrecked the voyage. After a prolonged cruise off the Spanish coast Captain May brought the *Fortune* back to Weymouth in June and reported total failure. The ship proved too slow to catch such potential prizes as came in sight, and the only capture was a Frenchman whom the captain duly released, though he nearly provoked a mutiny among the crew by doing so.[1]

By now peace with Spain was imminent, and Cecil finally withdrew from the privateering business. There can be no doubt at all that over a period of eight years he had gained handsomely on his investments. He had been prudent enough to spread his capital over a number of ventures instead of staking all on a single voyage, and he had avoided those over-ambitious projects that were the undoing of Cumberland and Lord Thomas Howard. He had also contrived to shift part of the expenses on to the Navy or his own secret-service allowance. As a result his gains had far outweighed his losses, and in 1601–2 his share of the captures made by the *Lioness* and the *Refusal* must have brought him a net profit of about £7,000 which could be used for investment in land.

The only official reward for his services that Queen Elizabeth bestowed upon Cecil during these years was a grant of the farm of the customs on imported silks and satins—and even this was a concession which had the appearance of benefiting the Crown as much as the grantee. Under the pressure of an insatiable demand for luxury clothing by the upper classes, imports of silks, satins, and velvets were rising rapidly. Hitherto most of them came overland from Venice and were imported to England from the Low Countries. Although it was evident that the use of these rich textiles was growing in England, and thus that imports must be rising, the Customs figures actually showed a sharp fall in the late 1590s. There was good reason to believe that the cause of this was extensive smuggling in the Port of London, and the Exchequer officials finally decided that the only way to put a stop to it was to enlist the

[1] H.M.C. *Salis. MSS.* xii, pp. 357, 432, 467, 599, 625; xv, p. 127.

aid of the profit motive by leasing the silk customs to a contractor on a fixed rent.[1] There was a good precedent for this method both of producing a stable revenue and of rewarding deserving courtiers, for the Sweet Wine farm had for years been one of the financial supports first of the Earl of Leicester, and then of the Earl of Essex. There was therefore a long-standing precedent for Cecil's successful request for a ten-year lease from January 1601 of the silk customs at a rent of £8,882. This was £1,200 a year higher than the average for the previous seven years and the lease therefore involved the Crown in no financial loss. But in view of the fact that the average receipts for 1589–93 had been £9,675, it was clear that Cecil had only to reduce smuggling to its previous proportions to be able to make a handsome profit.[2]

For the first year Cecil worked by appointing his own collectors in the Customs House, and the results were not unsatisfactory. He admitted to making a profit of £200 over and above the increased rent payable to the Queen, which was evidence of a marked improvement, while another document suggests that in fact his profit came to £434.[3] But if really large sums were to be squeezed out of the farm, more drastic measures were necessary. In the first place the original patent had been badly drafted, and had omitted to include a number of the countless names of different varieties of silks. Although the previous seven-year average of these other silks came to £640, Cecil persuaded the royal officials, by means which can only be guessed at, to alter his patent to include them at an increased rent of less than £100, making a new total of £8,977. At the same time stringent orders were given to prevent unlading of ships from Amsterdam and Zeeland anywhere except at the London Customs House, and detailed checks of invoices were instituted.[4] The result was a marked improvement in receipts, shown in a sharp rise in the customs paid by the great London silk man Baptist Hicks. From April to November 1601 Hicks had paid £189, but in May to December 1602 £569. No wonder there were angry protests at the tightening up from him and other importers, under pressure of which Cecil temporarily compromised in 1603 and changed his collector.[5]

---

[1] *H.M.C. Salis. MSS.* xi, p. 1. B.M. Harl. MSS. 1878/59. *Cal. S.P. Dom., 1598–1601*, p. 499.
[2] *H.M.C. Salis. MSS.* xi, p. 1. L. 85/3.   [3] *Cal. S.P. Dom., 1601–3*, pp. 155, 188.
[4] *H.M.C. Salis. MSS.* xii, pp. 76, 77, 176. *Cal. S.P. Dom., 1598–1601*, p. 517 (wrongly dated); *1601–3*, pp. 163, 188. D. 133/8; 197/3.
[5] *H.M.C. Salis. MSS.* xv, pp. 22, 96, 115, 124.

With the accession to the throne of King James in 1603, the days of royal parsimony were over, and royal largesse was scattered throughout the Court on a scale not seen since the early years of the reign of Edward VI. James had particular cause for gratitude to Cecil, since the latter had been the principal planner of the brilliant political manœuvre which had resulted in a smooth and unchallenged succession. The first mark of royal gratitude was a pardon given to Cecil for almost a whole half-year's arrears of rent for 1602, which put £4,411 into his pocket. A year after the new reign began Salisbury (as he now was) obtained a very much larger favour, namely a new lease of the silk farm for the lengthy period of fifteen years with no increase of rent. This was a major concession, as is proved by the fact that Cecil promptly sublet the farm for six years to a merchant syndicate led by Francis Jones at a rent which guaranteed him a clear net profit of £1,333 a year. Moreover, in the same year the introduction of a new Rate Book enhanced the value of the farm, and this improvement Cecil sold to the subcontractors for an additional £3,286 in cash.[1] When this subcontract expired in 1610 Salisbury obtained from King James an even more staggering concession, a renewal of the main lease, still at the old 1601 rent, for no less than nineteen years. By now the value of the farm had enormously increased owing to the very rapid growth in imports of luxury silks. Consequently Salisbury was able to sublet the lease to merchant contractors on terms which guaranteed him the astonishing clear net income of £7,000 a year at no cost or trouble to himself.[2] If it had run its full course for nineteen years the single grant by King James to his Lord Treasurer (who was the man who was supposed to be watching over the financial interest of the Crown) would have been worth between $1\frac{1}{2}$ and 2 million pounds in money of 1971. The silk farm thus became Salisbury's most important single source of income. From it he gained £436 in 1601; £4,441 in unpaid rent in 1602–3; £3,286 in cash in 1606 for improved rates; £1,333 a year from 1604 to 1610, and £7,000 a year thereafter.

Nor were these Salisbury's only pickings from farms of the customs. In 1605 the Privy Council decided to lease the general body of the customs in a single 'Great Farm', and tenders were

---

[1] D. 209/2; 164/1. H.M.C. Sackville MSS. i, p. 122. S. 129 ff. 129, 133. Leeds City Library, Temple Newsam MSS., English Customs iv/1.

[2] D. 114/4, 8; 216/8.

invited. One of the competing syndicates of merchants rallied behind Cecil, who acted as their spokesman, though as Secretary he was also a leading member of the selection committee. After a struggle the contract was awarded to his syndicate (of which his silk farmer was a member), and he promptly sold his interest to the farmers for £6,000 down.[1] As so often happens, it is difficult here to be dogmatic about Salisbury's motives. He was probably genuinely anxious to provoke competition for the contract in order to get the best possible offer for the Exchequer. On the other hand, his public spirit—if such it was—was rewarded by a dubiously acquired £6,000.

II. INCOME AND EXPENDITURE, 1608–1612

In the spring of 1608 the Earl of Salisbury succeeded the Earl of Dorset as Lord Treasurer. In addition he retained both the Mastership of the Court of Wards and the Secretaryship of State, a unique combination of offices which put him in control of almost every aspect of domestic and foreign policy. Furthermore, the Mastership of the Court of Wards and the Lord Treasurership were notoriously two of the most lucrative offices in the state, the tenure of which had made the fortune of his father, Lord Burghley. It was widely believed that since that time standards of financial integrity in political circles had markedly deteriorated, and that even greater, if less reputable, profits were now being made. During the early Stuart period contemporary commentators kept up an unflagging stream of complaints and witticisms about the spread of corruption in high places, and in a number of instances this easy venality was used as a convenient means of destroying ministers by impeachment. In hardly any instance, however, have sufficient private papers been preserved to make it possible to reconstruct from the inside the finances of a great Jacobean political figure.

Thanks to the chance survival of his Receiver-General's accounts, one striking exception is the case of the Earl of Salisbury, whose finances can be examined in considerable detail for four years from Michaelmas 1608 to Michaelmas 1612, six months after his death.[2] The accounts throw light not merely on the career of the Earl of

---

[1] F. C. Dietz, *English Public Finance, 1558–1640*, New York, 1932, p. 332. A. P. Newton, 'The Establishment of the Great Farm of the English Customs', *T.R.H.S.*, 4th ser. i, 1918. *H.M.C. Sackville MSS.* i, p. 291.

[2] A. 160/1. Box G/13.

Salisbury himself, but also on the general problem of the scale and methods of political corruption at this stage in its development. As they stand, however, they do not tell the whole story. In the first place it is evident that fairly large sums of money were passing to and fro without being recorded in the accounts. In some years the receiver, Roger Houghton, paid nothing at all into the Earl's privy purse, which was evidently fed from elsewhere. Furthermore, from time to time Houghton records the receipt from the Earl, usually in gold, of large sums with which to make certain payments, while at other times he notes that money he has paid out is in addition to other payments made directly by Salisbury from his private reserves. For example, although the accounts for 1609–10 do not record the payment to the Earl of Cumberland of a marriage portion, Houghton mentions in passing that £2,000 in gold was in fact paid by Salisbury and that another £3,000 was advanced by Houghton from his own resources. Altogether Houghton notes £4,755 which Salisbury paid to him or to others over these years, in addition to which there must have been large sums paid in and out of this private account of which the Receiver-General had no knowledge or which he had no reason to record. For example, Houghton received all the official payments from the Exchequer for secret service, totalling over £5,500 over these four years, but he only made the most obvious and open payments, such as Charles Paget's annuity or the cost of a trip to Germany by Salisbury's secretary, Levinus Munck, the whole amounting to a mere £732. It would be quite false to assume, however, that Salisbury was making a profit by pocketing large balances on the secret-service account, for a memorandum, drawn up for purely internal purposes, observes that the money was 'nearly all spent'.[1] Evidently, therefore, the accounts do not cover all the sources of income of the Earl, nor do they include more than a small part of his secret-service payments, which must have been running at about £1,200 a year more than is accounted for. The Earl had very large private cash reserves, which were fed from sources unknown to the accountant.

Since so many thoroughly disreputable sources of income are recorded in the account, the problem remains, therefore, what other very large source of income is not accounted for. The answer is the pension from the King of Spain. It has long been known from

[1] Box Q/2.

Spanish official archive sources that at the time of the peace treaty with Spain in 1603 the Spanish King found it prudent to offer, and the leading members of the English Privy Council found it proper to accept, very large pensions in return for their goodwill and assistance. From that moment on, most of the leading Jacobean statesmen were on the pay-roll of a foreign power, a situation unique, so far as is known, in English history. As Secretary of State and the leading adviser of King James on foreign policy, Salisbury was a special recipient of favour, being offered bribes by the Dutch not to make peace with Spain, and large bribes by Spain to make peace. The degree to which this secret financial tie with Philip III influenced Salisbury's conduct of foreign policy is a disputed issue. There can be no doubt that after 1607 his policy became increasingly anti-Dutch if not pro-Spanish, but it is not so clear whether he reached these conclusions by a realistic appraisal of England's national security interests, or whether he was increasingly a prisoner in the financial net thrown around him by Philip III.[1]

The available evidence shows that Cecil in 1603 obtained a Spanish pension of 4,000 escudos, later increased to 6,000, which was the equivalent of £1,000 and £1,500 a year. How regularly it was paid, however, and how often it was supplemented by special gifts, is not so clear. In 1607 Cecil himself made discreet but clearly mercenary overtures to the Spanish Ambassador, as a result of which he certainly received no less than £12,500 before the summer of 1608, just before Houghton's account begins. The purpose of this gigantic bribe was to ensure English neutrality over the Dutch-Habsburg peace treaty, and to this extent it was a worthwhile investment. Next year Cecil's confidante, the Countess of Suffolk, was extremely importunate for money, and the Spanish Ambassador gave her £11,000, some of which was supposed to go to Salisbury. Further sums were given to the Countess in 1610, part of which may again have been for Salisbury. It seems that the pension had by now been abandoned, and thereafter the available evidence suggests that these occasional gifts also became rarer and less generous.[2] But at any rate up to 1610, we can now be certain that

---

[1] S. R. Gardiner, *History of England, 1603–16*, London, 1863, i, pp. 122–3; ii, App. III. A. J. Loomis, 'Sir Robert Cecil and the Spanish Embassy', *Bulletin of the Institute for Historical Research*, xlii, 1969.

[2] A. J. Loomis, op. cit., pp. 55–7. B.M., Add. MSS. 31111/10–11. Allegations of further large pensions from the Dutch and the French can hardly be true in view of the precarious state of Salisbury's finances at the time of his death.

an irregular but very substantial quantity of gold passed into Salisbury's private treasure chest in the form of bribes from Philip III of Spain.

Although Houghton's accounts are apparently unique in the degree to which they record illegal and quasi-legal sources of income, their value to the historian is diminished by some rather half-hearted efforts at concealment. Although in 1612 no politician had yet been prosecuted for peculation on the basis of impounded private papers, there was always a risk that this might happen, and Houghton was evidently instructed to be as discreet as he could without falsifying his accounts. He did his best. When he referred to the 'w. of one Ponies in Essex, £400', or 'of Lady Derby to your use for a certain w., £500', or 'the wardship of one L, £200', there is no doubt that he is talking about the unofficial sale of wardships for his private profit by the Master of the Court. But many very large payments are merely recorded with the name of the payee, and one can only guess at their true significance. It may be assumed that all payments by Exchequer officials are for the purchase of offices and for other perquisites at the disposal of the Lord Treasurer, and that all payments by Court of Wards officials are for the sale of wards. 'Mr. Wright for a certain quarter's pay £115', which recurs up to 1609 and then ceases, is perhaps the pension from the lessees of the Wine Licence which they had been paying Lord Treasurer Dorset for his goodwill up to his death in 1608, and which was presumably renewed for a time to his successor.[1] But when all these more or less identifiable items have been eliminated, there still remains a residue of unexplained receipts. And even on the payment side there are one or two mysterious items, such as 'to one at your Lordship's order £400', 'to the same party £200', and so on.

To make the most sense of these accounts, therefore, various things have first to be done to them. First of all the huge sums casually paid in have to be broken down into their component parts, in so far as this is possible. Houghton was not entirely consistent in his allocation of various items to their respective categories, and a certain amount of tidying up and reorganization is necessary. Interest payments must be separated from capital repayments. When there is evidence of payments from the Earl's private funds, when certain rents were paid directly to Lord Cranborne,

[1] *H.M.C. Sackville MSS.* i, p. 290.

when debts were liquidated by direct transfer of land, the amounts involved must be added to the account. After all this has been done, we are left with a set of figures which throw a good deal of light upon the gigantic but precarious finances of a great Jacobean courtier. We can begin to appreciate how men enjoying such truly staggering incomes could nevertheless contrive to run up equally staggering debts.

As we shall see, during the four years 1608 to 1612 Salisbury was involved in the liquidation of the lands acquired from the Crown in 1607 along with Hatfield in exchange for Theobalds, and also the lands of Charles Brooke, full possession of which was only obtained in 1610. At the same time he was buying fairly heavily in order to consolidate his holdings at Hatfield in Hertfordshire and around Cranborne in Dorset. As a result his landed estate was changing its composition with bewildering speed, which must have made administrative continuity extremely difficult. The accounts show that receipts from rents from this fluctuating body of land varied between £4,700 and £5,300 a year, together with a further £1,000 or so a year in fines and casualties. To this figure there must be added a £1,000 rent of the newly built multiple store in the Strand, the New Exchange, which did not enter into the accounts since it had been taken over by a syndicate of customs farmers as part of a complicated loan transaction which will be described later. Some of the rents from the Cranborne estate also failed to enter into the accounts, since they were retained on the spot to help pay for the building operations there. Consequently receipts of rents shown in the accounts are well below the true figures. A document of 1609 gives a gross rental, including woods, casualties, and the New Exchange, but excluding fines, of £7,121. This would suggest that the true gross profits from all the landed estates in town and country, including fines and casualties, came to well over £7,500 a year. This income, however, was not all derived from land in possession, for £1,500 of it came from leasehold property held from the Crown, a Cambridge college, and ecclesiastical authorities. The rents due to the landlords, together with certain fixed annuities, came to £719. Moreover some of the property in possession was ex-Crown land saddled with fee-farm rents, while there was a £300 a year annuity to Lord and Lady Hunsdon going out of Brigstock Parks, and a number of other similar charges. If all the existing annuities and fee-farm rents charged on the estate are included, the total fixed deductions to be made amount to over £2,000 a year, and the Earl's net rental in 1609 was therefore under £5,100. Alternatively, if only the fee-farm rents are deducted, the net rental came to over £6,200.[1]

The profits of political office, however, far exceeded the income of the landed estate, no matter how it is calculated. The official salary of the Lord Treasurer was no more than £366, together with about £30 from casual fees. The real income came from other unofficial sources, and for once it is possible to illustrate with concrete examples those rumours of corruption, pay-offs, kick-backs, free gifts, and gratuities which filled the Court correspondence of the day. First there was about £360 a year derived from the sale of the surplus plate, in addition to what was kept to add to the store, which was presented in New Year's gifts from Exchequer officials, suitors, courtiers, and other seekers after influential friends. By now these gifts were standardized levies upon suitors and officials, and can hardly be regarded as more than one of the customary perquisites of office. The £1,000 a year on yearly average paid in by Sir Walter Cope, Chamberlain of the Exchequer, may well be the profits from the sale of numerous lesser offices in the Treasurer's gift. But other sums have a more sinister flavour. What are we to make of the £2,400 paid into the Earl's account in 1608–9 by various tellers of the Exchequer? They are certainly not private loans, for they are not listed under that heading. They may be further receipts for the sale of offices, though there is no reason why they should pass through the hands of the tellers. A possible explanation is that they are raids on the royal Exchequer made by Salisbury to assist his own financial position. That this was a practice among Jacobean Lords Treasurer is known from the confession a few years later of the Earl of Suffolk, who admitted 'borrowing' money from the tellers for his own purposes, and retaining it, interest free, for over four years. Indeed he only repaid the money in a hurry after investigation into his peculations had already been opened.[2] It is more than likely that in this practice he was merely copying the habits of his predecessors.

Other items in the accounts are equally suspect. In 1608–9 the royal jeweller, Sir John Spilman, paid £1,581, and shortly afterwards obtained a warrant from Lord Treasurer Salisbury for the

[1] Box Q/2.
[2] Suffolk's confession is in Wilts. R.O., Suffolk and Berkshire MSS., Moore's Boxes 5/21.

repayment of heavy debts owed him by Queen Anne. The next year the royal goldsmith paid £762, and shortly afterwards obtained a warrant for the payment of Crown debts due to him. Suffolk later admitted that his wife took bribes to get warrants signed for the repayment of Crown debts, one such episode actually involving the same Sir John Spilman, and the close correlation of these payments with the issue of warrants is certainly very suggestive. Finally, there is a further £1,000 paid into Salisbury's account between 1608 and 1610 by Henry Spiller, an Exchequer official in charge of recusant fines.[1] If these are all accepted as probable fruits of office as Lord Treasurer, they come to about £2,800 a year, which is almost certainly an underestimate of the total receipts. In 1621 Montagu alleged that there were between 700 and 800 offices of which the Lord Treasurer had the nomination, which he valued at £1,000 a year. By the 1630s the income of a Lord Treasurer from more or less reputable sources was estimated at about £7,000 a year, while the irregular profits were guessed to amount to another £6,000 or £7,000 a year.[2] Even if these latter are regarded as the equivalent of Salisbury's income from the silk farm, and even if the rumours seriously exaggerated the total profits of a Lord Treasurer, the evidence of the accounts would suggest that Salisbury was exercising more discretion as Lord Treasurer than did his successors in that office, for the unidentified and unaccounted items can hardly have filled the gap between £2,800 and £7,000 a year. Had they done so, Salisbury would not have been obliged to run up such enormous debts as he in fact did. From this one could argue that the shadow of his father still placed some restraint on Salisbury's appetite for money, and that some vestiges of the more respectable mid-Elizabethan standards of public ethics still survived in official circles. And yet, as the Earl of Newcastle observed some forty years later; 'that profitable place is a great temptation to honesty, and, as the Earl of Strafford told me, that if the Lord Treasurer would stretch his conscience that he might get the Devil and all—and I never heard of any Lord Treasurer's conscience but was of stretching leather'.[3]

The full profits of the Mastership of the Court of Wards are even more difficult to estimate than those of the Lord Treasurership.

---

[1] *Cal. S.P. Dom., 1603–10*, pp. 574, 625, 377. P.R.O., Chancery Proc. Series I, Jas. I, S. 32/27.
[2] F. C. Dietz, *English Public Finance*, New York, 1932, p. 182. *Cal. S.P. Dom., 1635*, p. 120. *Clarendon State Papers*, i, pp. 158–9.
[3] S. A. Strong, *A Catalogue . . . of Documents at Welbeck*, London, 1903, p. 194.

Official fees for diet, and casual fees for the seal of the Court and
for the passing of liveries came to about £480 a year. Clearly
identifiable private sales of wards by the Master came to about
£1,400 a year, while at least another £700 may reasonably be
guessed as coming from the same source. It is likely therefore that
the total recorded income of the Master in these accounts is about
£2,600 a year. To this may probably be added some of the payments that otherwise cannot be explained, and certainly about
£2,000 of the debts noted as due to the Earl by others in 1612.[1]
We should not be far wrong in estimating Salisbury's total income
as Master as about £3,000 a year, the bulk of it derived from the
private sale of wards on his own account.

Even before his father's death and his appointment as Master in
1598, suitors were approaching Robert Cecil with offers of gratuities to obtain wardships.[2] Thereafter there is plenty of evidence
that Salisbury was carrying on his father's practice of granting or
selling wards for personal advantage. Nor is there any doubt that
he used his power to distribute wardships of wealthy minors in
order to reward friends and dependents. His architect Simon Basil,
his land-agent Thomas Treffry, his sister-in-law the Countess of
Kildare (who made a net profit of £900) were all grateful recipients
of wardships, which they resold at a profit to the highest bidder.[3]

More frequently, however, Salisbury reserved the profits for
himself. For example, in 1602 his secretary Michael Hicks asked
him for a ward, but was refused. Cecil explained that 'the Court is
absolutely full of importunity for it', and that he intended to profit
by this competition 'to draw some benefit to myself and yet not so
to appear to my Lord Cobham'.[4] With the help of the accounts, the
way the system worked can be traced in detail in one or two cases.
In 1612 the wardship of Edward Duke was sold to three family
trustees for a sum which could not have exceeded £150 or £200,
of which £50 was paid into the Court of Wards that year; and yet
on his death the trustees owed £500 to Salisbury's personal estate,
which proves that the private gratuity to the Master of the Court
was at least three times the size of the official sale price. Again in
1611 George Cowper paid £323 to the Court and £600 to Salisbury
privately for the wardship of John Cowper. Sir Henry Wallop paid

[1] A. 6/7.   [2] H.M.C. Salis. MSS. iv, p. 554; vi, pp. 363, 425; vii, p. 115.
[3] Ibid. xv, p. 265; xvi, p. 346; xvii, p. 176.
[4] B.M., Lansd. MSS. 88/45. See also H.M.C. Salis. MSS. x, p. 107; xii, p. 466.

£60 to the Court and £800 to Salisbury privately for the wardship of Gabriel Wright. John Gobert paid £370 to the Court and £1,400 to Salisbury privately for the wardship of John Jennings, son and heir of Sir John Jennings of Sandridge.

These transactions, in which the bribe paid to the Master of the Court for his favour exceeded the official sale price by a factor of up to ten or even more, go far to explain why the Court was incurring such intense hatred among the landed classes at this time, culminating in the prolonged debate over the 'Great Contract' for its abolition in 1610. It may perhaps not be altogether a coincidence that thirty years later the former ward, John Jennings, was one of the leading opposition M.P.s in the Long Parliament. On the other hand, we have no reason to think that these private bribes to the Master of the Court were more numerous or more extortionate than those negotiated by Lord Burghley in the 1590s.[1] There is no clear proof of any growth in the level of corruption in the Court of Wards under Salisbury, while there was certainly an increase in official receipts. This increase was mostly due to Salisbury's success in cutting down those middlemen's profits that had flourished so luxuriantly in the days of Burghley, a policy which included measures to protect the interests of the ward and his family. Another point in Salisbury's favour is his energy in promoting the Great Contract in 1610, by which the Crown was to surrender its rights of wardship in exchange for a fixed grant by Parliament.[2] Had it been accepted, it would have resulted in the abolition of the Court of Wards and the suppression of the office of Master. Salisbury could certainly have relied on receiving compensation for the loss of office, but it is more doubtful whether he could hope to obtain the full equivalent. It is possible, however, that the nineteen-year lease of the silk farm in 1610, which brought a clear profit of £7,000 a year, was meant to be such compensation.

Of the hard core of the unexplained payments, some £2,900 over the four years is recorded as being received from or on behalf of the Countess of Derby. Some of these may have been connected with her private estate, while others were undoubtedly gratuities passed to Salisbury via his favourite niece. Then there is a mysterious

[1] A. 6/7. P.R.O., Wards, Misc. Books, 408. M. F. Keeler, *The Long Parliament*, Philadelphia, Pa., 1954, pp. 233-4. J. H. Hurstfield, 'Lord Burghley as Master of the Court of Wards, 1561-98', *T.R.H.S.*, 4th ser. xxxi, 1949, p. 108. See also *Archaeological Journal*, viii, 1851, p. 180.

[2] J. H. Hurstfield, 'The Profits of Fiscal Feudalism, 1541-1602', *Econ. Hist. Rev.*, 2nd ser. viii, 1955, pp. 60-1.

£900 received on a warrant from the Attorney General in 1609, £1,320 from the jeweller and merchant Peter Vanlore in 1610–11, and £500 from a Mr. Morgan of the Temple in 1609–10—flotsam from transactions the nature and propriety of which we now have no means of discovering. Lastly there is the £4,755 paid over in gold from the Earl's private treasure chest. Since all other possibilities have been explored, one is forced to conclude that these reserves came mainly from the only source that seems to be unaccounted for, namely the very large occasional gifts from the Spanish Ambassador. Another possible source is gratuities for favourable treatment from newly founded trading companies. Whether the Spanish Company gave Salisbury anything we do not know, but it certainly offered his servant Richard Langley the sinecure office of Clerk at a fee of £66. 13s. 4d.[1] In 1609, when the French Company was being set up, 'a great sum' was said to have been given to a certain peer for his help, besides £300 to various secretaries. Since Salisbury was then Lord Treasurer and at the height of his influence with the King, he is the most probable recipient of the bribe.

More precise evidence is available for the income from the silk farm, of which the grant in 1601 and the subsequent vicissitudes have already been described. When the accounts open in 1608, Salisbury was drawing a regular £1,333 annuity from the farmers, who had made themselves fully responsible for the administration of the farm and the payment of the rent to the Crown. In 1610 he engineered a fresh grant of the farm from the Crown for nineteen years at the old rent, and relet it to the old syndicate at the enormous rent of £7,000 per annum clear.[2]

Apart from the £670 a year repayment of loans due to Salisbury from others, there only remain to be discussed the two truly extraordinary sources of revenue, namely the receipts from the sale of land, and the money borrowed to meet current expenditures. The former realized £57,100 over the four years, or an average of £14,270 a year. In the first two years the money came from selling off some of the outlying properties acquired from the Crown in exchange for the surrender of Theobalds. There was a lull in sales in 1610–11, but they picked up again in 1611–12, with over £20,000 realized from massive sales of the Brooke estates. Although these receipts from the sale of land amounted to more than double the receipts in

[1] G. 28/1.   [2] A. 10/14.

landed income of all kinds, they must be set off against the large sums concurrently spent on land purchase. Nearly £20,000 was recorded as spent on buying land over the four years, to which must be added the £32,000 in loans and obligations incurred in return for the acquisition of the Brooke estates. Sales therefore exceeded purchases by no more than £5,100, so that what we are seeing is a frantic process of buying here and selling there in order to establish a compact and suitably located estate for permanent retention, rather than any massive process of disinvestment.

The same favourable interpretation cannot be put on the even larger operations on the money market. In the four years from 1608 the accounts show that Salisbury borrowed a total of £61,000 and repaid £36,000. In fact, however, the situation was graver still, for in addition to the £61,000 borrowed on his own account he had also taken on £14,000 of Charles Brooke's debts, the repayment of some of which is included in the £36,000. The net increase in the Earl's indebtedness in the last four years of his life was therefore £39,000. Since he was already heavily in debt before 1608 it is not surprising to find that in July 1611, soon after taking over the Brooke inheritance, the Earl's total burden of bonded debt came to £49,461, to say nothing of another £3,506 of unpaid bills. A total debt load of £53,000 bearing upon a net landed income of about £6,200 was little short of terrifying. The huge profits derived from his official position, which alone allowed Salisbury to support so gigantic a burden, were entirely dependent on the accidents of good health and the personal favour of King James, and might be cut off at any moment. Things were indeed critical at this stage. Salisbury was already ill, and had never recovered politically from the disastrous attempt to steer the Great Contract through Parliament in 1610. James held him personally responsible for what he regarded as a misguided effort to come to terms with an irreconcilable opposition in the Commons, and his position was insecure.[1] During the last year of his life a determined policy of land sales was therefore undertaken in an effort to reduce the burden of debt. Nevertheless, as Salisbury lay on his death bed in April 1612 he was obliged to acknowledge in a shaky hand a list of debts which, excluding the £9,450 due to the customs farmers, still totalled £37,867.[2]

In all, Salisbury borrowed a total of £61,000 over the four years from a very diversified list of creditors. One group were household

[1] S. 134 f. 143; 147 f. 162.   [2] Box U/39. A. 10/6. S. 143 f. 146.

officials of the Earl himself, who put up £4,750; another were tellers in the Exchequer, who advanced £4,000, almost certainly from balances of Crown revenues left lying in their hands; a third were personal friends in the peerage, Lords Cavendish and Carew and the Countess of Derby, who lent £2,500; and a fourth were a large number of small capitalists, petty merchants, officials, lawyers, and widows, investing their savings through the good offices of two or three London scriveners who specialized in this proto-banking activity.

The great bulk of the money borrowed, however, amounting to £42,500, came from twenty-one great London merchants and finan-ciers. Most of the really important aldermen and tycoons of the age figure on the list of creditors. There was the professional financier Thomas Sutton, the great silk-merchant Sir Baptist Hicks, the great goldsmith Alexander Prescott, the Lord Mayor Sir Thomas Camp-bell, Aldermen Francis Jones, Thomas Bennett, John Eldred, Ralph Freeman, George Huxley, John Leman, and Stephen Slanye, and prominent members of the thriving foreign merchant com-munity in London like Sir Thomas Coteeles, Sir Peter Vanlore, and Moses Tryon. No less than £23,400 came from merchants engaged in one or other of the customs farms, the money presum-ably coming at least in part from customs revenue balances held by the farmers. Since it was Salisbury's duty as Lord Treasurer to keep a strict eye on the customs administration and to negotiate new leases on terms favourable to the Crown, these huge advances to bolster up the Earl's private finances were, to say the least of it, unfortunate. They open up disquieting vistas of private pressure upon the Lord Treasurer. The uneasiness is strengthened by the discovery that in 1611, while negotiations were proceeding for a new grant of the Great Farm of the customs, the farmers formally took over £20,000 of the Earl's debts, including £9,450 already due to themselves. The interest on the £9,450 was apparently secured by their taking over the management of the New Exchange at a rent of £1,000 a year, while the capital sum and new interest were to be paid off in five and a quarter years at £5,000 a year out of the profits of the silk farm, which Salisbury had previously sublet to the same syndicate.[1] As a result, the farmers only paid into

---

1 S. 141 f. 352. The rent of the New Exchange is not recorded in the accounts, and the building was certainly leased to the new silk farmers by 1612. Although there is no statement to link the lease with the interest on the debt, this seems the only reasonable explanation.

the account a little more than £5,000 the first year, and a mere £175 the second, although a leading farmer, Nicholas Salter, also paid over an unexplained £1,000. Here again it looks as if Salisbury, both in borrowing from the farmers and in accepting money from them, was anticipating practices which a few years later were to be the downfall of Suffolk when they were proved in open Court. This is the sort of transaction which twenty years later led Sir John Harrison to the conclusion that the personal financial interest in the customs farms of the current Lord Treasurer was one of the principal causes of their retention.[1]

Although these accounts for 1608–12 clearly do not record all the receipts and expenditures of Salisbury, they at least serve to give some idea of the order of magnitude. As they stand, after certain corrections, the accounts show total average receipts of about £49,800 a year. £15,300 of this came from loans and £14,300 from the sale of land. Of the remaining £20,200, £6,900 were certain or probable legal and illegal profits of the three offices of Lord Treasurer, Master of the Court of Wards, and Secretary of State. Other sources of income that derived ultimately from political office, the pension from the King of Spain, the annuity out of the silk farm, payments by the customs farmers, cash paid into the account by the Earl himself, and other unexplained payments together amount to about £5,200. Compared with these huge sums from official or semi-official sources, the receipts from land were relatively modest, amounting to just on £6,000. The remainder was made up of £700 from or for the Countess of Derby, which might be loans, purchases of wards, or receipts concerned with her estates, £700 from the repayment of money lent, and £600 from arrears and other miscellaneous payments.[2]

To appreciate the astonishing scale of these figures, it is necessary to put them in a comparative perspective. Even if the 'extra-ordinary' sources of revenue, like borrowing and the sale of land, are excluded, the fact remains that from all official, unofficial, and landed sources Salisbury in the last two years of his life, from 1610 to 1612, was receiving at least £25,000 a year. This was a time when the unskilled manual labourer could not hope to earn more than £10 or at most £15 a year, when the greatest landed income in the country was less than £8,000 a year, and when the 'ordinary'

[1] R. Ashton, *The Crown and the Money Market, 1603–1604*, Oxford, 1960, p. 98.
[2] See Appendix, p. 59.

revenue of the Crown itself only amounted to about £300,000.[1] Several of the overmighty subjects of the Middle Ages could boast of an annual income equal to one-twelfth of the recurrent revenues of the Crown. What makes the early seventeenth century different from the fifteenth is that this huge income now depended very largely on the profits of office, dependent in its turn on the whim of the King. Withdraw that favour, remove the profits of office, and the whole edifice would come tumbling down. What makes the early seventeenth century different from any which has come after it is that never again has the income of a private individual amounted to even one-hundredth that of the Crown itself, let alone one-twelfth.

Why was Salisbury obliged to accept these large and irregular sums from clerks and suitors, foreign powers, and domestic customs farmers, and why did he none the less contrive to run up such a terrifying load of debt? The answer, in brief, is that he found himself caught up in a world of fiercely competitive conspicuous consumption that reached its apogee during his time. As a leading figure in one of the most recklessly extravagant courts in Europe, he had little option but to compete in the race, although it can be argued that in one key aspect, that of building, he compulsively over-built on a scale that defies rational justification.

In the first place the Earl maintained a household establishment at Salisbury House on a most lavish scale. It is clear that in this great rambling building in the Strand he kept open house for the widespread political and personal 'connection' that he had built up around himself. Such open-handed ways were necessary for the maintenance of his position at Court, but they were not cheap. Including the running cost of the stables, the establishment at Court and at Hatfield Parsonage, all tradesmen's bills, and wages and liveries for the eighty domestic servants, the running cost of the household came to nearly £7,000 a year. This figure was swollen from time to time by the recurrent need to entertain royalty, as a means of winning and keeping the favour of the King. In 1606 the Earl had entertained James and the King of Denmark at Theobalds for five days, at a party which degenerated into a prolonged druken orgy that attracted a good deal of unfavourable comment from outsiders. Including presents to the royal guests,

[1] W. R. Scott, *Joint Stock Companies to 1720*, Cambridge, 1912, i, p. 135.

the bill came to no less than £1,180.[1] On 18 May 1608, Salisbury spent £100 on a banquet for the royal family at his town house in the Strand. In July the next year a politically strategic feast for the French Ambassador cost £132. In March 1611 Queen Anne was entertained at Salisbury House, at a cost of £45, and in July King James paid his first visit to the almost completed palace at Hatfield, and was treated to a dinner which cost his host £200.[2]

Salisbury was as lavish in expenditure on his person as he was on his guests. He spent over £600 a year on clothes for his own use, and drew some £400 a year more for personal out-of-pocket expenses. The great London mercers Baptist Hicks and Edward Barnes presented bills for Italian cloth of the richest quality: 36½ yards of rich crimson cloth of tissue at £4. 10s. a yard, £164. 5s.; 12 yards of rich black Florence veined velvet for a gown, £18; the mere embroidery of a suit and cloak for the installation of the Prince of Wales came to £79. 10s. Salisbury had a taste for exotic toys and novelties which he indulged to the full. He paid a Dutch merchant no less than £1,060 for a great organ for Hatfield House, 'a table of silver like a picture', 'a clock in the form of a tortoise', and other rareties. He bought a 'bird of Arabia in a cage' for £15. 10s. and a white parrot for £20. Indeed so great was his desire for strange birds and animals that in 1607 he sent a man out in a ship of the East India Company in order to collect parrots, monkeys, and marmosets. When living animals failed, he fell back on manufactured curiosities like 'little artificial parakeets in a cage of silver wire', or 'a castle upon a rock, made of the metals of the mines of Scotland'. Once he paid no less than £150 to Benedict Lamp 'a high German, for a coach of silver with a clock and other motions in it'. The Earl was passionately fond of music, and was the first patron of the distinguished musical family of Lanier. He employed John, Innocent, and Nicholas, the last of whom had a very distinguished future before him. Nicholas was a member of the household, and drew a pension of £20 a year, besides supplying the Earl with strings for his lutes, viols, and other instruments. The Earl was continually buying new instruments, like a 'portative organ', and kept in his household a young Dane who certainly played the viol and may have been a singer.[3]

[1] *H.M.C. Salis. MSS.* xviii, p. 237. The scene is described by John Harington, *Nugae Antiquae*, London, 1804, i, pp. 348–53.
[2] B. 22. A. 160/1.
[3] A. 7/16; 160/1. Box G/13. B. 29; 67B. *Cal. S.P. Colonial, East Indies, 1513–1616*, p. 146

As disease progressively undermined his constitution he spent more and more prodigally on doctors and medicine in a pathetic effort to purchase good health. In the last year of his life he spent no less than £1,500 and on an average over the four years about £500 a year. Of his three children the two eldest, Lord Cranborne and Lady Frances Cecil, had now reached an age when they were at their most expensive. The marriage preparations and feast for the latter cost over £1,300 and the marriage portion £6,000. Between 1608 and 1610 Lord Cranborne was on the Grand Tour, punctuated only by a brief return to England to get married. He was accompanied on the tour by his tutor, the future royal Master of Ceremonies Edward Finet, his doctor the celebrated Dr. Lister, his brewer, apparently to brew his beer,[1] and several footmen. The whole expedition cost no less than £8,500. Soon after his return in 1611 he set up house and was put on an allowance of £2,000 a year. Altogether his children cost Salisbury £24,000 during these four years.

Gifts and rewards to servants bringing presents, to friends, court officials, and political associates came to over £700 a year, a figure swollen by the £1,094 spent on a suit of hangings given to Queen Anne in 1610, presumably in the hope of winning her support to buttress his precarious standing with the King. Extraordinary payments, running at over £1,200 a year, covered a variety of mysterious items, the largest of which is £2,000 to the Earl of Dorset in the winter of 1608–9. The reason for the payment is entirely unknown, though it is presumably connected in some way with Salisbury's succession to Dorset's father in the Treasurership. Fixed charges on the estate, that is fee-farm rents to the Crown, rents to church authorities for leased lands, fees of bailiffs, and fixed annuities and rent-charges granted to servants and allies came to nearly £2,000 a year—a heavy burden on a gross landed income of only £7,100.

Compared with these vast sums, the amount given to charity and paid in taxation for the upkeep of state and church was pitiful indeed. Church dues amounted to £20 a year, taxes to £63, and regular alms to the poor to £60. This last includes £13 distributed at Christmas to the poor prisoners in the ten London prisons, and

---

[1] Good beer seems to have been unobtainable abroad. Thus a London brewer sent three tons of beer over to France in 1609, along with water dogs and hounds for Lord Cranborne's recreation (A. 160/1; B. 34A).

Christmas boxes of 4*d*. and a loaf of bread to sixty-five men and thirty-four widows at Hatfield.[1] In addition to these regular alms, special measures were taken in a bad year to create employment and to reduce hardship. In 1608 the harvest failed, food prices rocketed, and there were serious disturbances in the Midlands. Salisbury took steps to alleviate conditions near his own houses by buying 400 quarters of wheat and rye from Arthur Ingram at the market price of £846, and reselling at Westminster and Hatfield for £385, the difference of £461 coming from his own pocket. A perpetual rent-charge of £40 was settled on an almshouse at Cheshunt, where in 1605 the Earl also entered into a contract to set up and maintain a house for the instruction of forty poor boys in the art of pin making. Four years later he repeated this scheme by setting up a factory for new draperies in a farmstead at Hatfield. £60 was spent in bringing technicians over from Holland, a dye-house and fulling mill were built at a cost of £186, and the clothier Walter Morrell was given £100 a year annuity for nine years to get things going. Although Morrell employed fifty poor children at Hatfield for several years, by the end of James's reign he was heavily in debt, and it appears that the project collapsed in the early 1620s.[2]

Heavy though these household, courtly, and personal expenses were, they were certainly not crippling in view of the income at Salisbury's disposal. What was it that made the Earl, in a codicil to his will, recommend Sir John Daccombe to his son and heir saying 'in mine own estate I had been overthrown by large expense and lack of care, if he had not been'?[3] At the time of the Theobalds exchange, Ben Jonson had argued that Salisbury was not motivated by

> a vaine desire
> To frame new roofes or build his dwelling higher;
> He hath with mortar busied beene too much,
> That his affections should continue such.[4]

The poet could not have been more wrong, for the loss of Theobalds spurred Salisbury into the most astonishing building programme of the age, a programme so grandiose in its scope as to

[1] B. 34B.

[2] B.M., Sloane MSS. 3827 f. 189. A. 160/1; 161/4. Box Q/2. *H.M.C. Salis. MSS.* xvii, p. 623, P.R.O., Chancery Proc. Series I, Jas. I, M. 12/41.

[3] P.C.C., 49 Fenner.

[4] C. H. Herford and P. and E. Simpson (eds.), *Complete Works of Ben Jonson*, Oxford, 1941, vii, p. 156.

overstrain even his gigantic financial resources. At one time he was building simultaneously at two country houses, Hatfield House in Hertfordshire and Cranborne in Dorset, one town house, Salisbury House in the Strand, and one supermarket, the New Exchange, also in the Strand.[1] Easily the greatest expenditure was on Hatfield House, which cost some £40,000 between 1607 and 1612. The total expenditure on building in the last five years of the Earl's life came to over £63,000, the average from 1608 to 1612 being £13,500 a year. It was this fantastic orgy of building which caused the soaring debt, the mere interest charges on which were running at about £4,000 a year,[2] and which forced Salisbury to make overtures for rewards to the Spanish Ambassador and to entangle himself in the financial tentacles of the customs farmers. It was this that so alarmed his financial adviser John Daccombe, who by 1611 saw his master rushing headlong to financial disaster. 'I beseech your Lordship to forbear buildings', he wrote despairingly towards the end of 1611,[3] and it was his sense of urgency to reduce the debt to manageable proportions which forced the massive campaign of land sales which took place between 1611 and 1613. Although Salisbury House and the New Exchange have vanished entirely, Cranborne and Hatfield survive to this day to bear witness to the architectural ambitions and financial recklessness of the greatest builder of an age which itself was the greatest period of country-house building in English history. Fortunately for the Cecil family, the building programme was completed just in time. Salisbury lived just long enough to see it through and to make provision for the liquidation of the great burden of debt which he had consequently incurred.

III. CREATION OF THE LANDED ESTATE, 1598–1612

During the fourteen years from 1598 to his death in 1612 Cecil was engaged in a massive programme of land purchase which turned the modest inheritance from his father into one of the greatest estates in the kingdom. Year after year first the fruits of privateering and then the ever increasing profits of office were ploughed back into land. This process is a familiar one at all periods of English history, and particularly during the reign of James, but in no other

---

[1] See below, Ch. II. H. A. Tipping, 'Cranborne House' in *English Homes*, Period III, vol. ii, London, 1927, pp. 353–71. 'Salisbury House' in *L.C.C. Survey of London*, xviii, London, 1937, ch. 18.

[2] See App. I, p. 61 n. 1.   [3] G. 26/5. S. 196 f. 52.

contemporary case can the process be studied in such intimate and revealing detail.

During the 1590s Cecil lived in a house to the east of his father's London residence, Burghley House on the north side of the Strand, which he may have built for himself.[1] Although there is some evidence that he was buying and selling property on a small scale during these years, it was all for speculation rather than for permanent acquisition. Thus he had acquired a house in Holborn which he sold to Sir Matthew Arundel for £1,500 in 1594. In the same year he bought land in Lancashire for £1,750 only to resell it in 1598 for well over £2,000 to Nicholas Mosley, Alderman of London. And so it was not until 1597 that the first permanent acquisition was made, with the purchase for £200 from a cousin, William Cecil, of the little farm at Alltyrynys on the Welsh border in Herefordshire from which the family originated.[2] In the same year he acquired his first country seat. In 1595 the dowager Lady Dacre had died, leaving to Lord Burghley Beaufort House in Chelsea, the former home of Sir Thomas More. In 1597 Lord Burghley surrendered his rights to Robert Cecil, who at once bought out the lessee, took over possession, and had his first taste of the excitements and expenses of building by putting on a new front. No sooner had the work been completed, however, than he lost interest and began trying to resell the property. A smaller house in Chelsea was sold to the Countess of Huntingdon for £700. He offered the great mansion to Sir John Fortescue, who turned it down, and then persuaded the weak and unstable Earl of Lincoln to accept it for a £6,000 which he could not afford.[3] Lincoln was just then in great need of help in his many quarrels and lawsuits, and it was doubtless hopes of political favour that induced him so rashly to accept Cecil's invitation to buy the house at so very high a price. At any rate the bargain worsened Lincoln's financial difficulties, and quarrels about payment of the money dragged on over the next three or four years, as his plight became increasingly desperate. He offered to pay part of the price of the unwanted Chelsea house by surrendering his town house in Cannon Row or

[1] *H.M.C. Salis. MSS.* iv, pp. 292, 355; v, pp. 23, 391. *L.C.C. Survey of London,* xviii, 1937, p. 125.

[2] P.R.O., Close Rolls, 40 Eliz. pt. 1. G. 44/16. A. 13/34. A. L. Rowse, 'Alltyrynys and the Cecils', *Eng. Hist. Rev.* lxxv, 1960.

[3] P.R.O., Close Rolls, 42 Eliz. pt. 20; 41 Eliz., pt. 23. D. 117/5; 104/13; 102/13. A. W. Clapham and W. H. Godfrey, *Some Famous Buildings and their Story,* London, n.d., pp. 79–91. *H.M.C. Salis. MSS.* viii, p. 387.

by handing over some valuable pearls, but Cecil pressed him inexorably for the cash.[1]

The cause of Cecil's hasty sale of Chelsea was the decision to buy a site on the south side of the Strand on which to build a new town house in this fashionable area that would be worthy of his position as one of the leading courtiers of the day. Beginning in 1599 he therefore bought up property after property so that he finally managed to acquire a large building site in the choicest part of town, between the Strand and the river.[2]

Meanwhile, substantial acquisitions were being made in the country. In 1599 the appalling cost of the Irish war compelled the English Government to sell off in a hurry considerable quantities of Crown land. This was a decision in which Cecil must have participated—and it was also one from which he was apparently determined to profit. He began by paying £4,661 for a large and scattered range of properties in the west of England, including one-half of the great tithes of Martock rectory in Somerset, St. Michael's Mount in Cornwall, Cranborne and Cranborne Holwell manors and Cranborne Hundred in Dorset, and Warborough manor in Wiltshire. In gratitude for permission to make this purchase, Cecil presented the Queen with a ruby and topaz jewel, accompanied by the usual fulsome letter in praise of her matchless beauty. Since he raised £2,900 in fines alone from the property in the next few years, he had much to be grateful for.[3]

The Cranborne purchase, on which Cecil had had his eye since 1597, was of great significance for the subsequent history of the family since it has formed the centre of one of the main property holdings from that day to this. Once he had acquired the two manors in 1599 he proceeded methodically to consolidate his territorial position. At Cranborne itself the priory and rectory were bought in 1601 for £2,000 from Sir Ralph Horsey. This was a slightly complicated and murky transaction, as is so often the case with Cecil, since Sir Anthony Ashley, who apparently had a prior claim, waived his rights in return for Cecil's help in obtaining for him the restoration of royal favour. In 1602 he bought the third

---

[1] E. Lodge, *Illustrations of British History*, London, 1791, iii, p. 108. *H.M.C. Salis. MSS.* ix, pp. 75, 79; x, pp. 57, 117, 122, 305, 324; xi, pp. 127, 171, 211, 448; xv, p. 90. A few years later there developed another quarrel between Salisbury and Lincoln over a complicated transaction concerning Hyde Park (S.P. 14/35/20).

[2] For details of these transactions, and subsequent building activity, see below, pp. 92–3.

[3] G. 44/16. Box S/7 ff. 43ᵛ, 45, 67. Box S/8. A. 135/4. P.R.O., Land Revenue Office, Misc. Books, 72, 73. *Cal. S.P. Dom., 1601–3*, p. 260.

manor of Cranborne Alderholt for £500, the borough from the
Crown contractors for £129 in 1611, and various small holdings in
the village for £1,450. This agglomeration was further extended by
the purchase of the manors of Berwick Saint John, Bollesborough,
and Damerham from the Earl of Pembroke for £6,200 in 1608; of
Rushton manor from Sir Walter Vaughan for £2,400 and of farms
in Damerham and Wimborne All Hallows for £1,600 in 1611; by
a grant from King James of the castle and borough of Old Sarum
in 1606; and by the purchase for £172 from the Crown contractors
in 1612 of a miscellaneous rag-bag of medieval rights in Wiltshire
that belonged to the former honour of Gloucester.[1]

The tracing up to 1612 of the growth of the London and West
Country estates should not be allowed to conceal the extraordinary
scale of Cecil's land purchases all over the country in the last two
years of the Queen's life. Some of the acquisitions of these months
were designed to consolidate and extend existing properties. The
£2,660 spent on Cranborne and the £4,320 paid to Thomas Dacres
for Cheshunt rectory near Theobalds are obvious cases of this.
There were several minor purchases to increase existing estates
elsewhere, and an unknown sum was spent on enlarging the holding on the south side of the Strand for Salisbury House. The Earl
of Derby was just now selling off very large quantities of the ancient
Stanley estates in order to clear off old debts and make large settlements on the three heirs general, and Cecil saw his chance and
bought two outlying manors of Haselbury Plucknett in Somerset
and Great Gaddesdon in Hertfordshire for about £4,500. But this
seems to have been more for speculation than for investment, for
Great Gaddesdon was promptly resold to Sir Adolphus Cary for
£3,000 and Haselbury Plucknett went to Sir John Portman in
about 1606–7 for £3,800. The capital gain on this transaction was
£2,300, or over 50 per cent.[2]

The bulk of the purchases were from the Crown, which was
throwing large areas of its land on the market in order to pay for
the Irish war. In January 1602 Cecil paid £5,088 for a job lot of
Crown property ranging from Norfolk and Suffolk through
Huntingdonshire and Hertfordshire to Cornwall, an investment
that bore little relation to his existing holdings. In April he spent

[1] G. 71/27; 56/1. D. 201/18. L. 233/14. A. 112/6. Box S/7 ff. 66, 105. P.R.O., Close Rolls,
42 Eliz. pt. 10. H.M.C. Salis. MSS. vii, pp. 405, 434; x, p. 282; xi, p. 17.
[2] G. 44/16. Box S/7 ff. 95, 103, 105. D. 151/3; 238/1–6. A. 112/6. P.R.O., Close Rolls, 43 Eliz.
pt. 5.

a sum which can hardly have been less than £5,000 on a group of six Cornish manors; two months later he paid the Crown £6,839 for Temple Roydon manor and rectory and Roydon Hall manor and vicarage in Essex, and Worcesters manor in Enfield, Middlesex; and finally in the same year he paid 'a round sum of money' for Brigstock Parks in Northamptonshire.[1]

After spending over £5,600 on land purchases in 1599-1600 there can be little doubt that Cecil spent another £30,000 for the same purpose in 1601-2, besides completing the building of Salisbury House. That the Secretary of State should have had sums of this gigantic order at his disposal raises embarrassing questions about his financial integrity, even at this relatively early stage in his career. In fact the sources of a good deal of the money for this huge speculation in real estate can be accounted for. There was the £6,000 he had squeezed out of the Earl of Lincoln for Chelsea House. Between his father's death in 1598 and 1601 he raised £4,400 in fines for the renewal of leases and in profits from the sale of woods and stock on the Hertfordshire and Middlesex inherited estate. There were the unknown but possibly large profits from the starch patent, and the unknown but probably large profits from the private sale of wardships. Privateering paid off at this time, with a windfall of about £7,000 in 1601-2, while the silk farm showed a profit of £434 in 1601, and £4,441 in unpaid rents to the Crown in 1602. Yet all this was insufficient for Cecil's current needs together with his building activities and his land purchases, and in consequence his agents began to borrow heavily from London aldermen. To add to his worries one of these huge purchases turned out to have been a mistake. When it was surveyed the Cornish property was shown to hold little prospect of improvement. Cecil's faithful steward, Richard Percival, said he was not surprised and urged his master to resell at once. The details of the intrigue elude us, but the fact remains that Cecil succeeded in selling these unwanted estates back to the Crown early in 1603 for £5,200, which was probably what he paid for them.[2]

One would have thought that the manipulation of these complicated, multifarious, and often shady financial dealings would alone have been enough to occupy all Cecil's energies, but it must never be forgotten that he was one of the leading political figures

---

[1] P.R.O., Close Rolls, 44 Eliz. pt. 22. S. 204 f. 139. G. 44/16. P.R.O., Land Revenue Office, Misc. Books 73. *H.M.C. Salis. MSS.* xv, p. 361.   [2] Ibid. xi, p. 397; xii, pp. 289, 348, 408.

in the country, wholly absorbed at this very period first with destroying his rival the Earl of Essex and then with arranging (behind the back of the old Queen) for the peaceful succession of King James. Both politically and financially this was a time when Cecil was gambling for very high stakes indeed. The problem remains, however, of explaining this extraordinary outburst of investment in land. The obvious explanation is that, thanks to the series of fortunate accidents which have been described, he found himself with a lot of free capital to be invested, and that he viewed the Crown sales of land to pay for the Irish war as an excellent opportunity, which might never recur since the war was winding down, to make an investment in land at very cheap prices indeed. Cecil was among the half dozen largest purchasers in Crown lands at this period, his only serious rivals being one or two pure speculators buying for immediate resale, and Sir John Spencer, the great London merchant and money-lender, who was just now transferring his capital and putting it into land for the sake of his daughter and heiress, whom he had just succeeded in marrying into the peerage. There can be little doubt that Cecil's political position and official contacts gave him access to information, and even the power to influence decisions, which enabled him to make particularly advantageous purchases. To give one example, the purchase price of one piece of property was based on an official valuation made as long ago as 1514, since which time land values had risen about four times. And if things went wrong, Cecil even had sufficient pull in high places to get the Crown to buy the property back again.

It is possible, however, that there was another motive also at work to drive Cecil into this sudden outburst of land purchasing, for it must be remembered that he was borrowing money heavily, at the current rate of 10 per cent, to provide some of the purchase price. He had good reason to be uncertain about his political future, which depended on his success in weathering the coming crisis of the succession, and he may well have been trying to salt away the profits of office and thus protect the patrimony of his family in the future, while there was still time. Land safely conveyed to trustees for uses—and all this property was normally held by agents and servants on his behalf—was fairly immune from confiscation. Cecil may have thought that even if he was executed or imprisoned, his gains from office would pass safely on to his children.

It has been plausibly argued that just after the Dissolution of the Monasteries Crown land was being sold at something approaching its true market value. It is hardly possible, however, to maintain that this was still the case half a century later.[1] A striking example of the profits to be derived, admittedly by a well-placed politician with unusual knowledge and means of pressure, from buying Crown lands in the early seventeenth century is provided by the £5,088 purchase by Sir Robert Cecil in January 1602. He paid between thirty-six and forty years' purchase of the stated rentals, which might seem a very fair price. But one Norfolk estate, at Fitton, was bought for £327 and promptly resold for £600. Another, at Barton Bendish, was bought for £326 and sold eight years later for £1,800; Bungay Priory in Suffolk was bought for £1,596 and sold in 1608 to the Earl of Northampton for £1,800. Ripton Regis, Huntingdonshire, was bought for £748 and sold in 1618 for £1,400; Elinglas in Cornwall was bought for £480 and sold in 1608 for £800. Altogether, Cecil made a capital gain of 85 per cent on his investment, most of it within eight years.[2] Land values may have risen in the first decade of the seventeenth century, but certainly not at anything approaching this extent.

Early in 1603 Cecil bought from the Queen the Great and Little Parks of Brigstock, Northamptonshire, and followed this up two years later by the purchase of the manor and rectory.[3] His attention had first been drawn to this prize in 1601, when Sir Francis Carew told him that he was proposing to ask the Queen for a reversion of the parks after the death of the existing lessee, Lord Hunsdon, for which he was willing to pay £666. With a ruthlessness and duplicity that goes far to explain the popular hatred that surrounded him, Cecil promptly seized the opportunity to obtain the parks for himself, behind the back of Hunsdon, and without regard for the prior claims of Carew. He promptly had the parks surveyed by that elegant draughtsman Israel Amyce, a former servant of the Earl of

---

[1] A. 6/10, 16, 17. D. 5/20. H. J. Habakkuk, 'The Market for Monastic Property', *Econ. Hist. Rev.*, 2nd ser. x, 1958; R. B. Outhwaite, 'The Price of Crown Land at the Turn of the Sixteenth Century', *Econ. Hist. Rev.*, 2nd ser. xx, 1967.

[2] S. 204 f. 139. D. 102/4, 44. A. 112/6; 160/1. Blything Hundred, which was bought for £428 and immediately conveyed to Sir Edward Coke, has been disregarded in these calculations. It is possible that Coke did not pay for his acquisition, which may have been a reward from Cecil for his services as Attorney General in promoting the deal. If so, it should be set off against Cecil's profits.

[3] Box S/7 f. 99. D. 81/4; 181/10. P.R.O., Close Rolls, 2 Jas. I, pt. 19. *H.M.C. Salis. MSS.* xv, p. 361; xvi, p. 99.

Oxford who had passed into the service of the Cecils. He finally bought out Lord Hunsdon's interest in return for an annuity of £300 a year for himself and his wife, and by the early spring of 1603 he obtained full possession, though burdened with a fee-farm rent to the Crown of £67 per annum.[1]

During the last weeks of the old Queen's life Cecil's agents began a ruthless transformation of the property. Under the owner-ship of Lord Hunsdon the local inhabitants had exercised extensive rights of common over the parks, which were stocked with deer. The purpose of this old-fashioned, easy-going administration was not to maximize profits, but to balance off the needs of the rich for deer-parks for hunting, and the needs of the poor for fuel and grazing and a little surreptitious poaching. All this was now swept away, and parks transformed into a series of well-fenced private sheep pastures. Most of the trees were cut down, much of the timber was used to erect sturdy palings round the new enclosures and the rest carted off to be sold, and the deer were rounded up and driven out into the forest. The local inhabitants were enraged. As James came south in April he was presented with a petition urging him to stop the felling of the wood and the expulsion of the deer. Engineered, so Cecil suspected, by his enemies, including Sir Arthur Throckmorton, the petition had an immediate effect. As a passionate hunter James was indignant at the suggestion that the deer were to be replaced by sheep, and he issued peremptory orders for the process to stop. Cecil replied in a long evasive letter. He protested that he had paid a good price for the parks, which were now his private property. He alleged that except for his customs farm this was the only reward he had ever had from the Queen. He said that the trouble was due to encroachment upon the royal parks and chases by cottagers, who were complaining because their illegal usurpations were being curtailed. In the end the King and Cecil reached a compromise agreement at the expense of the local peasantry. Deer still roamed the Little Park, but all the Great Park was turned into enclosed sheep runs. As a result rioting broke out in May and had to be suppressed by force, and there seem to have been further disorders early next year.[2]

The property was resurveyed by John Norden—apparently not

[1] *H.M.C. Salis. MSS.* xi, p. 190; xv, p. 361; *H.M.C. Buccleuch (Whitehall) MSS.* i, p. 236. A. 160/9. S. 98 f. 177. B.M., Add. MSS. 38444 f. 8.
[2] *H.M.C. Salis. MSS.* xv, pp. 60, 71, 361; xvi, pp. 38, 266, 318.

very well—in the winter of 1603–4, but the document has not survived. A later survey in 1615 shows that the Great Park contained 1,149 acres of pasture and 327 acres of woods and the Little Park 567 acres of pasture and 171 acres of wood. In 1609 this great ranch was on lease to a large-scale grazier on payment of a fine of £2,000 and a rent which was to rise in 1612 to £1,209.[1] If Lord Hunsdon's annuity represents all he had been getting from the parks, there can be no doubt that enclosure and conversion to sheep pasture had resulted in a truly enormous increase in income.

Apart from the heavy expenditure on enlarging existing property around Cranborne, there were only two significant purchases over the next three years, a manor in Sussex, bought from the Earl of Nottingham for an unknown sum and sold again in 1610 for £7,000, and South Mimms manor in Middlesex, bought from Lord Windsor's executors for £5,500. In 1607 James rewarded Salisbury with the gift of a Gloucestershire manor, which was resold to Sir Thomas Roe six months later for £1,600.[2]

It was at this point, in 1607, that the emerging pattern of the Cecil estates was shattered by a wholly unexpected development. When Lord Burghley had finished improving and extending Theobalds between 1562 and 1585, it had become a gigantic palace more suitable for a monarch than a subject.[3] Indeed, apart from Westminster Palace and Hampton Court, it was the largest building in England. It had been inherited by Robert Cecil, who lost no time in putting it to its intended use as a residence in which to entertain the sovereign. Unfortunately, however, James began to take far too keen a liking to the place, and in 1607 Cecil thought it only prudent and tactful to offer it to the King. James was the most passionate royal hunter since the Angevins and the causes of his affection for Theobalds were clearly set out in the preamble to the deed of exchange. The King, it explained, had 'taken great liking to Theobalds house and two parks of the Earl of Salisbury's in the County of Hertford, the one replenished with red deer, the other with fallow deer, as most convenient for his princely sport and recreation, and commodious for his Highness' residence'. Nowhere else within such easy reach of London was to be found so large a palace with such ample provision for hunting—provision that was

---

[1] *H.M.C. Salis. MSS.* xvi, p. 451. A. 112/6; 133/1; 160/1. G. 11/22.

[2] A. 112/6. L. 233/4. D. 69/16. P.R.O., Close Rolls, 2 Jas. I., pt. 23; 4 Jas. I., pts. 26, 29. Wadham College MSS., Southrop, 9, 12.

[3] J. Summerson, 'The Building of Theobalds, 1564–1585', *Archaeologia*, xcvii, 1959.

immediately to be improved by massive additions to the parks. By the terms of the exchange, Cecil handed over all his property in Cheshunt, including eight manors and numerous farms, but excluding Cheshunt rectory which was intended for the endowment of a hospital for poor soldiers. The rental of this property was probably under £500 a year, to which must be added the capital value of the palace and the woods.

In return the King promised 'a Princely recompense', although on the face of it it seemed a trifle mean. It included the much smaller and older early Tudor palace of Hatfield, with its surrounding park, and manors, granges, and lands in ten other counties, the existing rental of which was probably about £780 a year. Since the property was burdened with a fee-farm rent to the Crown of £571 a year, the bargain appears a bad one. Salisbury had lost a modern and gigantic county house and land worth about £500 a year, in return for an out-of-date old palace and land the net rent of which, after deduction of overheads, was only about £210. But this calculation omits from the reckoning the habitual ways of early Stuart financial administration. In the first place Salisbury in his capacity as Lord Treasurer never dreamed of enforcing payment of the fee-farm rent from himself, and after his death his heir obtained a royal pardon for the arrears and for all future rent. Secondly, the land was let on old leases at unimproved rents, and therefore held the prospect of a very great increase in profits in the near future.[1]

More serious than any theoretical loss of net income, which in any case did not occur, was the loss of Theobalds itself. To replace it Salisbury promptly set to work to pull down most of Cardinal Morton's palace at Hatfield and build himself a new one in the latest style. On this undertaking he spent about £40,000 between 1607 and 1612, a sum which must be set off against the value of the lands exchanged. To cover this enormous expenditure a good deal of the newly granted property had to be sold off in the next few years. £16,600 was raised between 1608 and 1613, about £3,000 in 1618, and a further £5,400 in 1628. It is a significant commentary on the administration of Crown lands under Lord Burghley and his successor Lord Buckhurst that Salisbury managed to sell these lands for about fifty years' purchase of the existing rents. It is

---

[1] S. 143 f. 112; 98 f. 177. No rental for all the property exists. A rental of all except that which had already sold by 1609 is to be found in Box Q/2, and a rough estimate of the remainder can be obtained from the sale prices, which are known (A. 112/6; 160/1).

doubtful whether the Cecils lost very much in the long run by the Theobalds–Hatfield exchange, for they received about £25,000 in cash and a 1640 rental of £1,500 a year, whereas the Theobalds rental is very unlikely to have increased to this sum. They had also got rid of a house that was far too large for comfortable and economic occupation by a private individual. In the short run, however, the £40,000 needed for building the new house meant a terrifying rise in the load of debt, nearly all of it at 10 per cent interest. The real gain was in imponderables—in the continuing goodwill of King James, from whom still greater rewards might be expected. If the renewal of the silk farm is regarded as a by-product of the deal, as seems reasonable, there can be no doubt that it paid off handsomely.

The Hatfield grant involved a substantial shift in the existing pattern of the Cecil estates. It led to many new purchases to round off the new holdings, and also to sales of former property in order to pay for them. At Hatfield itself the rectory was bought from Sir Goddard Pemberton in 1608 for £6,000, and in the next few years woods, freeholds, and copyholds were bought piecemeal for £3,940 until the Earl obtained possession of almost all the village. To pay for this some earlier purchases had to be sold off. For example, Cheshunt rectory, which with the disposal of Theobalds to the Crown had now become an outlying property, was sold to the Earl's physician Dr. Atkins for £3,600.[1] The Sussex manor which had been bought from the Earl of Nottingham in 1607 was now sold for £7,000 to a London merchant. Two Gloucestershire manors which had been purchased in 1607 were resold within two years for £4,800 to Robert Delabere and Sir Thomas Roe, and two East Anglian manors granted by James in 1607 were sold within three years for £4,750 to Sir Henry Carey and Sir Robert Crane.[2] But when in 1610 James, under Salisbury's guidance as Lord Treasurer, started further extensive sales of Crown property, the temptation to buy again proved irresistible. Purchases, however, were now limited in scale and in purpose, being no more than a judicious rounding off of existing estates at a total cost of under £1,300. The precarious state of the Earl's finances would in any case have prohibited any repetition of the speculative orgy of 1602.

---

[1] A. 112/6. Cecil had paid £4,320 for the rectory in 1602, but it was now burdened with a rent charge for the upkeep of the hospital (G. 44/16; A. 121/16).

[2] A. 160/1; 112/6. Box U/19. D. 69/16; 114/1, 6. Wadham College MSS. 61/12, 19.

One might have supposed that the huge transaction of the Theobalds–Hatfield exchange, involving rapidly rising debt and the endless difficulties of finding buyers for the land, would have deterred Cecil from anything more than these limited purchases to consolidate the existing estate. In fact, however, he simultaneously involved himself in a series of very complicated transactions by which he acquired the bulk of the property of the attainted Lord Cobham. Cobham's sister had been Cecil's late wife and the mother of his children, and therefore the Brookes and Cecils were linked by intimate family ties.[1] But Cobham was an irascible and unattractive personality and his close association with Ralegh and his obvious ambitions made Cecil determined to exclude him from royal favour. This loss of favour tempted Cobham into treasonable speeches, and led to his arrest and condemnation in 1603. Cecil certainly laboured to save his life, although the dramatic last-minute reprieve at the scaffold of the three conspirators, Cobham, Grey, and Ralegh, is likely to have been the personal whim of the King himself. Thereafter Salisbury's attitude became more ambiguous, although Cobham continued to treat him as his leading advocate at Court. It could hardly fail to be noticed that, despite Salisbury's enormous influence over the King, Cobham continued to languish in prison in the Tower of London, while the remorseless carve-up of what was left of his ancestral estates made it plain that there were influential persons with a vested interest in his total ruin. Of those acquiring a stake in the dismembering of the Brooke estates, Salisbury soon became by far the most important. But the steps by which this hold was acquired are so involved and took place over so extensive a period that one cannot be sure that they were predetermined stages in a Machiavellian plot by Salisbury to dispossess his brother-in-law. It is perhaps more likely that Salisbury was at first torn between a desire to advance his own interests and a desire to come to the help of his afflicted relative, and that only at a later stage did he succumb to the temptation to take over the Brooke estates altogether for himself.

In 1602–3 Lord Cobham's net landed revenue came to about £3,450, together with a further £240 or so in rents in kind. Though the income was small in comparison with the huge sums at Salisbury's disposal by virtue of his official positions, this was nevertheless a very large landed estate, which put Cobham among the

---

[1] See genealogical table no. 2.

wealthier of the Elizabethan peerage.[1] Most of the estate was in Kent, but there were outliers in Essex, Bedfordshire, Gloucestershire, Leicestershire, and the West Country. About £650 of the income came from leases from the Crown and from ecclesiastical authorities, to whom rents of about £150 were due.[2] The title to all this land was very varied. By the conviction of Lord Cobham on a charge of treason there came into the hands of the Crown all his personal estate, including the leased lands, and all the land held in fee simple. The bulk of the property, however, was tied up in an entail of George Lord Cobham, the grandfather of the current Lord, and the Crown's interest was therefore limited to the lifetime of the latter. After his death without heirs the property, according to the entail, should descend to William the son of his brother George, who was executed after the plot in 1603, and if he in turn died without an heir male it would revert to Duke Brooke of Templecombe, a son of the current Lord's uncle George. There were therefore three persons with an interest in the inheritance: William, the infant son of George Brooke, Duke Brooke, and Lord Cobham's wife Frances, the dowager Countess of Kildare, who had claims for maintenance as long as her husband was alive, and for her jointure after his death.

Lady Kildare had long been on bad terms with her husband, and had no compunction in salvaging what she could for herself out of the wreckage of the Brooke fortunes. To help her in this task she turned to her brother-in-law the Earl of Salisbury; and it was in reward for the latter's services that in 1607 she sold him at a knock-down price of £1,000 her interest in the very valuable estate of Canterbury Park, which included the palace built by Henry VII in the ruins of St. Augustine's Abbey. As she bluntly put it to Salisbury, 'I know you have been . . . better to me than any commodity I should ever make out of Canterbury Park.'[3] Indeed she had reason to be thankful, for a private Act of Parliament of 1604 had assured her a present allowance of land valued at £481 a year, and a reversion after her husband's death of a further £501 a year.

---

[1] See L. Stone, *The Crisis of the Aristrocracy, 1558–1641*, Oxford, 1965, App. VIIIᴮ.

[2] S. 145 ff. 90–9. P.R.O., Exchequer, Declared Accts., Pipe Office, 412. In this year there was an additional £450 for fines for three new leases, which has been ignored as exceptional. In 1596 the net rental after deduction of rents due for leased lands came to about £3,100 (A. 154/1).

[3] *H.M.C. Salis. MSS.* xvii, p. 176. P.R.O., Close Rolls, 4 Jas. I, pt. 32.

The main problem was how to dispose of what was left. Despite the very doubtful title of the Crown because of the entail, King James had not hesitated to give a lot away to his courtiers. All the West Country property had gone to the Earl of Devonshire, the Gloucester estate to Walter Pye and Robert Beale, probably as trustees of Lord Compton, and the Leicestershire estate to Sir William Woodhouse.[1] To secure the title to these properties another Act was pushed through Parliament which declared the forfeiture of all the estates of Lord Cobham, George Brooke, and their heirs, and which confirmed the royal grants. The Lords put in a saving clause preserving Cooling manor and park, worth £420 a year, for Duke Brooke, but otherwise made no attempt to obstruct this high-handed legal robbery. This Act freed the Crown's title and therefore allowed it to sell to Duke Brooke all the remainder of the estate, valued at £962 a year, for £8,000 and a further £3,500 for the reversion of the Countess of Kildare's jointure lands.[2] The Brooke inheritance was thus transferred to the loyal branch of the family, and the Crown and several courtiers made a handsome profit. Among the profiteers was Salisbury himself, who in 1605 had been given the leased lands and the reversion of Canterbury Park, thus constituting his first personal stake in the Brooke estate.[3] As for the legal heirs of the traitor George Brooke, they were totally disinherited, and even when they were restored in blood by a private Act in 1610, the ever-watchful Salisbury and other beneficiaries saw to it that a proviso was inserted expressly excluding them from all rights and claims to the property of Lord Cobham.[4]

The only difficulty with these convenient arrangements was that Duke Brooke simply did not have the £11,500 with which to redeem the property from the Crown. He already owed £1,000 to the Lord Mayor of London—and he was obliged to borrow the money from the great London financiers, the first £5,000 being lent him by the goldsmith Alexander Prescott.[5] But since he now

[1] J. Hutchins, *History of Dorset*, Westminster, 1861–70, ii, pp. 82, 84, 111, 115. J. Collinson, *History of Somerset*, Bath, 1791, iii, pp. 303–4. T. D. Fosbrooke, *History of Gloucestershire*, Gloucester, 1807, i, p. 265. *Cal. S.P. Dom.*, *1603–10*, pp. 227, 169, 106. H.M.C. *Salis. MSS.* xvi, p. 352. There is no record of this grant among the Compton MSS. at Castle Ashby, Northants, but the Pyes were later certainly involved in the Compton affairs.

[2] H.M.C. *Salis. MSS.* xvi, p. 224. S. 145 f. 115. House of Lords MSS., 1 Jas. I, Cap. 50; 3 Jas. I, Cap. 33.

[3] P.R.O., Patent Rolls, 2 Jas. I, pts. 13, 27. *Cal. S.P. Dom.*, *1603–10*, p. 206. H.M.C. *Salis. MSS.* xvii, p. 628.

[4] House of Lords MSS. 7 Jas. I, Cap. 24.   [5] P.R.O., L.C. 4/195 ff. 343, 385, 403.

had a free title to the property, he was able to sell off parts of it in
order to repay the debts, which is what he proceeded to do. The
two Essex manors of Radwinter and Bendish Hall, which were sold
to his creditor Prescott, had a rental of £300 a year in 1602–3, and
their sale price probably covered the full value of the £5,000 loan
and interest.[1] The second instalment of the purchase price was
raised from the great London financier, Sir John Spencer, who was
paid by the sale of the Bedfordshire estate of Newnham priory and
rectory. This was reckoned to be worth £3,700, but whether
Spencer paid so much is uncertain.[2]

At this point Duke Brooke died and was succeeded as heir to
the estate by his brother Charles. Charles was evidently a wild and
extravagant young man, and within a year his position had become
desperate. It so happened that his principal friend and creditor was
John Daccombe, who was also Salisbury's solicitor and chief
financial adviser, and it is no doubt because of this link that he
began borrowing heavily from the Earl on the security of his
estate. This comprised the West Country property inherited from
his mother, the heiress of Richard Duke, including the huge estate
of Bishops Teignton, Devon, and other manors in Somerset and
Dorset, as well as the newly recovered Kent lands of Lord Cobham.
While borrowing from the Earl, he also plunged ever more deeply
into the toils of the leading London money-lenders, including Sir
John Spencer, Peter Vanlore, Thomas Sutton, Sir William Harvey,
and Alderman John Leman.[3] Gradually he found himself more and
more dependent on Salisbury to support his credit and to keep him
out of the Fleet prison, and gradually the Earl came to assume
control of more and more of his estate in return for taking on the
burden of his debts. In 1607 he lent Charles £1,800 free of interest
and borrowed another £4,600 for him. In return for this sum and
a further £1,200 which Salisbury paid the Crown as part of the last
instalment of the purchase price, the latter took over some of the
Kent estates, which he thus acquired at about nineteen years' purchase. On his behalf his Receiver-General, Roger Houghton,
advanced £3,000 to Brooke on the mortgage of one manor, and
another servant Henry Flint £1,100 on another. He himself bought
Bishops Teignton outright for £5,000, the reversionary interest in

---

[1] P. Morant, *History of Essex*, London, 1768, ii, pp. 535, 537. S. 145 ff. 90–9.

[2] *H.M.C. Salis. MSS.* xvii, pp. 119, 539.

[3] A. 7/13; 9/12; 128/1. S. 141 f. 352. P.R.O., L.C. 4/196 ff. 139, 151, 220, 242, 287, 332, 338, 362, 421; 197 ff. 13, 15. Charterhouse, Founder's Papers 1/14, 97, 123; 2/29; 11/11.

some of the Countess of Kildare's lands for £1,200, and took a mortgage on more of the Kent estate for £5,000. By April 1610, when Charles made his will, his position was hopeless. Ignoring the claims of his wife and child, he made Salisbury's two agents Daccombe and Houghton his executors, and left his whole personal and real estate to the Earl in return for the payment of his debts, those to others being scheduled at £14,000. And so for a total investment of £36,700 the Earl of Salisbury had acquired nearly all the Brooke estates, both in Kent and in the West, together with a personal estate in goods worth about £4,000.[1]

There are two possible explanations of these transactions. One is that Salisbury was merely extending a helping hand to relieve distant relatives of the consequences of their political and financial imprudence. The other is that, with deliberate calculation, he first destroyed the main branch of the family and then, using subtle baits like interest-free loans, he lured the heir to the family estates into a position from which there was no escape other than to turn them all over to him. But whatever the motives, there can be no doubt about the long-term consequences, which were financially extremely profitable to Salisbury, and extremely disadvantageous to Charles Brooke and his family. In the short run the benefits were more dubious, and the wisdom of floating this great venture concurrently with the Theobalds–Hatfield exchange and the building of Hatfield House seemed very much open to question. A consequence of running these two operations together was that at one point in July 1611 Salisbury's debts, including £5,176 taken over from Charles Brooke, rose to the truly terrifying figure of £52,968.[2] At a time when the interest rate was 10 per cent the strain placed by this debt load on the Earl's finances filled his advisers with alarm. The massive and rapid sale of both the Theobalds exchange lands and the Brooke estate was the only solution.

This undertaking was tackled with energy and success by the Earl's agents. Coming at the end of nearly a decade of post-war prosperity and during a period of rapidly rising rents, the time could hardly have been more favourable for such an operation. By December 1614 at least £56,000 had been raised by the sale of the bulk of the Brooke estates. The largest single sale was that to

[1] A. 9/4; 13/54; 112/6. L. 64/16. G. 56/16. S. 145 ff. 118, 128. P.C.C. 38 Wingfield. P.R.O., Close Rolls, 4 Jas. I, pts. 5, 29; 5 Jas. I, pt. 30. There are various estimates of the total cost, ranging from £30,740 to £37,700.
[2] Box U/39.

Lord Wotton for £12,260 of Canterbury Park. This was the property, her life interest in which the Countess of Kildare had surrendered to Salisbury for £1,000 as a bribe for his favour. The great Devon estate of Bishops Teignton was sold off piecemeal for about £10,000, and the Somerset estates for the same amount. A further £7,500 was raised by further sales between 1616 and 1623, and £6,100 in 1629–32 from the Kent lands of the Brookes which only came to the Cecils after the death of Lady Kildare in 1628.[1] In all the Cecils realized over £70,000 from the sale of the Brooke estate, plus £4,000 in goods, in return for a mere £36,700 advanced to Charles Brooke. But this apparent profit of 100 per cent takes no account either of the interest on the money borrowed to pay Charles which was paid between 1607 and 1612, or the £200 a year annuity provided for Charles's widow until her death in 1626.[2] But even if £10,000 is added to the investment to allow for these overheads, the net profit is still over 50 per cent. In this case, as with the Theobalds exchange land, most of the property was sold within six or seven years of the purchase, during which time land values had certainly not risen under the general inflationary pressure by more than 10 or 15 per cent at the very most. Was it this happy speculation in Brooke lands to which John Daccombe—Charles Brooke's 'friend'—was referring when he claimed in May 1612 to have gained for the late Earl £1,000 a year in rents and £35,000 in cash?[3]

Such were the methods by which in a mere fourteen years Salisbury built up a great landed estate which has remained the support of one of England's leading families from that day to this. It is evident that a crucial part was played by political influence. It was not merely that most of the money used for land purchases came

---

[1] The evidence for sales between 1612 and 1620 is incomplete, and the true figures may be slightly higher.

A. 12/7; 13/53; 112/6; 154/1; 157/3; 160/1, 5.

B. 109.

D. 40/10; 102/13, 19–23, 27, 28, 40; 125/31; 160/27.

L. 44/1.

Box G/13; N/3.

Not all the Brooke estates came into the hands of the Cecils. Lady Kildare's interest in the house at Cobham Hall and a number of other properties was granted in reversion to the Duke of Lennox in 1612, after having been refused by the scrupulous Somerset (*Archaeologia Cantiana*, xi, 1877, p. 218). *Egerton Papers* (*Camden Soc.*), 1840, p. 455.

[2] Box G/13. A. 133/1; 160/5, 6.

[3] G. 16/17. Daccombe ended up as the owner of some of the Devonshire property, so that his relationship to Charles Brooke as friend, executor, financial adviser of the principal creditor, and personal beneficiary from the dissolution of the estate, was, to say the least of it, equivocal (S.P. 14/95/53; P.C.C., 19 Meade).

from the profits of office. Other sources such as the windfalls from privateering or the annual income derived from the silk farm were ultimately derived from royal favour or political power. Part of the land was granted by the Crown as a reward for services; part of it was given in exchange for the surrender of Theobalds; most of that which was bought came from the Crown. Much of the rest came from fellow peers: extravagant fellow courtiers like the Earls of Nottingham and Pembroke, hard-pressed countrymen like the Earl of Derby and Lord Windsor selling up family estates to pay off debts and settlements. And finally there was the acquisition of the estates of the family of Brooke Lords Cobham, first broken by political folly and then ruined by personal extravagance. In every case it was his political position that gave Salisbury the necessary contacts and capital.

Though this picture of the conversion of political influence into landed property is a familiar one, certain features of Salisbury's career are very unusual. Few men can have bought and sold so much property in such a short space of time, and these massive sales make the story one of abnormal complexity. Broadly speaking, four main episodes stand out: the steady accumulation of property along the Strand and up St. Martin's Lane in London; the frenzied purchases of 1601–3, which created the Dorset group of estates centred around the secondary house at Cranborne; the Theobalds–Hatfield exchange, and the consolidation of estates around the main new house at Hatfield; and the investment in the estates of Lord Cobham and their subsequent liquidation. It was not until several years after the first Earl of Salisbury's death in 1612 that the sales to clear off the debt were completed and it becomes possible to see the permanent pattern of the estate which remained. By 1617, when most of the sales were over, the second Earl enjoyed a gross income from land of between £7,200 and £7,500 a year.[1] With prudent management and two large injections of additional property from the heiresses of City fortunes, this was an estate large enough to carry the Cecils comfortably through to the late twentieth century as one of England's greatest landed families. In fourteen frantic years of manic activity, the ethics of much of which do not stand up to very close scrutiny, Robert Cecil Earl of Salisbury had created something that was destined to last, and to influence English history, for centuries to come.

[1] A. 16/5; 160/5.

IV. DEATH, 1612

The death in office of a great political figure is always a peculiarly painful occasion. It means the premature termination of a career which, for good or ill, has made its impact on history. It marks the end of an epoch, the passing of power from one patronage group to another, and a consequent shift of political methods and objectives. For the individual concerned it means departure from a life that has given a satisfaction, in terms of power and wealth, which is denied to most human beings.

In 1610, two years before his death, Salisbury was at the height of his career. Ever since the execution of the Earl of Essex in 1601 he had been the leading minister of the Crown. He had skilfully engineered the peaceful accession of James in 1603 and had successfully weathered the critical transition to service under a new monarch. He had accumulated powers, offices, wealth—and hatred —as he went. In 1610 he staked his political career on an attempted political settlement with the Commons, by which the Crown would have traded in its ancient feudal rights of taxation in return for a permanent revenue granted by Parliament. James had always opposed the scheme, the Howards were waiting like vultures in the wings, and its failure marked the end of Salisbury's undisputed political hegemony. On the dissolution of Parliament James wrote Salisbury a blistering letter, blaming him for the whole enterprise, and from then onward the latter was fighting a slowly losing battle for both political power and physical health. The story of physical decay is uniquely documented for the age; its progress can be traced in the accounts of payments to doctors and apothecaries, in lengthy medical diagnoses by his professional consultants, and in eye-witness accounts from two of his closest attendants. Finally, the whole episode is spiced by the vicious comments of his innumerable enemies, which were widely circulated in manuscript.

Ever since 1609 Salisbury's health had been delicate, and it was evident that his hold on life was precarious. Though his mind was limited, it was clear and keen, and he was quick to see through intellectual frauds. He had no patience with the ridiculous genealogical researches that so delighted his father, however flattering they might be to the ego. When offered a pedigree which traced his ancestry back to Bleddyn, the most ancient of the five Princes of Wales, he refused the gift with the comment: 'I desire none of these vain toys, nor to hear of such absurdities.'[1] It is all the more tragic, therefore, that he should have placed such unquestioning faith in the ignorant and mischievous brutalities of contemporary medical practice. He consulted doctors, not singly but in dozens, and submitted to a terrifying regimen of purges, glisters, vomits, and electuaries. It is hard to avoid the suspicion, also voiced by contemporaries, that his doctors helped to kill him:

> Thus to king and state he was a great stay
> Till Poe with his syringe did squirt him away.[2]

As early as 1609 Stephen Higgins, the apothecary, was providing a huge list of remedies running from innocent cordials like rose-water, liquorice, Indian balsam, wormwood wine, and a tisane, through ambiguous prescriptions such as 'his lordship's posset drink', 'a liquor for broth with china roots', a diet drink by Dr. Paddy, another by Dr. Atkins, and distilled water by Dr. Poe, down to a straightforward glister and dangerous concoctions such as a 'litharge of gold in powder' and 'mercury sublimaticum'.[3]

By the summer of 1611 he was worse still, and the distinguished French physician Dr. Theodore Mayerne gave him a full medical check-up.[4] The result was not encouraging, 'this tender and delicate body being but a weak mansion for so noble a mind'. The Earl's stomach was cold, 'neither doth it perfectly concoct, but ingendreth crudities, suffers distentions by the variety of humors'. Evidently he had chronic digestive troubles. As for his liver, it was 'exceeding hot . . . which kindleth and nourisheth concupiscence in the natural parts and increaseth the animosity of the heart, from whence proceeds the natural propention to anger'. Here, as delicately as he could, Dr. Mayerne drew attention to the fact that Cecil was both lecherous and bad-tempered. There is a little evidence for the second fault, but it was widely believed that there was truth in the first. Salisbury's wife had died in 1597 and contemporary gossip had it that he subsequently found consolation elsewhere. D'Ewes speaks of 'his unparalleled lust and hunting after strange flesh', and the Master of Gray spread a story among his friends that they

---

[1] *H.M.C. Salis. MSS.* xvii, p. 595.

[2] Huntington Library MSS., HM 198/2 f. 125ᵛ (I owe this reference to Mr. Julian Mitchell).

[3] B. 34, 56.

[4] T. T. Mayerne, *Opera Medica*, ed. J. Browne, 1703, pp. 78–85. Quotations are taken from a contemporary version in English made by or for Dr. Henry Atkins (Herts .R.O. 65440). Mayerne's preliminary notes are printed in H. Ellis, *Original Letters*, 2nd ser. iii, p. 246.

first met in a brothel. A savage anonymous epitaph, combining illusions to his deformity and his lust, ran:

> Here lies Robert Cecil
> Composed of back and pizzle.

Francis Osborne and the anonymous libellers named Lady Audrey Walsingham and the Countess of Suffolk as among his numerous mistresses, an allegation which is perhaps lent some support by the frequent appearance of Lady Walsingham in the accounts, and the bequest to her of a life annuity of £160 a year. As for the Countess of Suffolk, we have seen how she shared with Salisbury the gratuities given by the Spanish Ambassador. It was widely alleged that his death was a direct result of these amorous adventures.

> Twixt Suffolk and Walsingham he often did journey
> To tilt in the one and in the other to tourney.
> In which hot incounters he got such a blow
> He could not be cured by Atkins and Poe.

Ralegh commented savagely that 'In spight of the tarbox he dyed of the shabbo', and another libeller that 'It was pity the pox did cozen the halter'. This widespread belief that Salisbury was killed by venereal disease, which is also mentioned by Manningham, Weldon, and Osborne, was apparently quite unfounded, for in his preliminary notes Dr. Mayerne expressly mentioned that there was 'Nihil unquam siphillicum'.[1]

He suffered, however, from almost all the other ills to which man is heir. Apart from poor digestion and constipation, he had a large tumour, probably cancerous, in the liver, a sore mouth, a tumour in the neck, piles, and other 'issues' about the body. The general recommendations for this condition were sensible enough, although quite futile to cure a cancer; a spare diet, fresh air, exercise, moderate sexual activity (despite his widower condition), plenty of sleep, the use of medicinal baths, and clarified whey and ass's milk to help the digestion. The chemical prescriptions, however, were less innocuous, for they emphasized the current obsession with destructively explosive laxatives. Among them were 'a glister', a 'purging syrop', 'a drink to open obstructions and prepare the

[1] *Autobiography and Correspondence of Sir Simonds D'Ewes*, London, 1845, i, p. 50. G. P. V. Akrigg, *Jacobean Pageant*, Cambridge, Mass., 1962, p. 107. F. Osborne, *Traditional Memoyres on the Reign of King James*, London, 1658, pp. 87–9. J. Aubrey, *Brief Lives*, ed. A. Powell, London, 1949, p. 327. Bodl., Malone MSS. 23/4. A. Weldon, *The Court and Character of King James*, London, 1651, p. 12. B.M., Harl. MSS. 5353 f. 44ᵛ. Huntington Library MSS. HM 198/2 f. 126.

humors', all prescribed with the vain assurance that 'by these remedies insuing so shall you thoroughly root out the cause and foundation of most infirmities'. However, it must be admitted that Dr. Mayerne advised against blood-letting, at any rate until matters became really desperate early in the new year.

By February 1612 the Earl was seriously ill, with swollen legs, distended stomach, and a red skin rash. He had difficulty in breathing, and was liable to intermittent fevers. This condition was diagnosed by Mayerne as 'une disposition à l'hydropsie compliquée avec le scorbut, lesquels sont deux mauvaises hostes en un corps faible et delicat'.[1] By now the doctors were crowding round in shoals, and every fashionable practitioner in London was called into consultation. There were Doctors Mayerne, Atkins, Poe, Lister, and Hamond, and Sergeant Goderous, four surgeons, and the faithful apothecary Mr. Higgins. They did not go unrewarded, for in his desperate search for relief the dying man was reckless in his generosity. In December £45 was distributed among them and in March over £350, £100 of which went to Dr. Mayerne. But it was all to no avail. Foreign doctors were consulted, a Frenchman and a certain Dr. Argente. An apothecary was sent specially to Dover to collect certain stones whose properties one of this milling horde had recommended, and others were sent hither and thither to bring in scurvy grass. More largesse was distributed in April, ranging from £15 for Watson the surgeon to £50 for Dr. Mayerne. At last in May, as the Earl became ever weaker, as his legs continued to swell and as sores broke out all over his body, it was decided to try the waters of Bath. In his journey from London he was attended by his chaplain, by one of the royal musicians, and by Drs. Atkins and Poe, two surgeons, and Sergeant Goderous, who despite his legal title appears to have been a doctor. The dying man was now in considerable pain from his body sores, and special preparations had to be made. Twenty-three pounds of down were used to make a bed in a coach, down pillows and stools were provided, the softest of Turkish leathers was prepared to lay under the Earl's back to make a horse-litter, a special wheel chair was built with heavily padded elbow rests and rests under the armpits to ease the weight of the body.[2]

---

[1] R. Winwood, *Memorials of Affairs of State* . . ., London, 1725, iii, pp. 332, 338. R. C. Bald, *Donne and the Drurys*, Cambridge, 1959, p. 99.

[2] *H.M.C. Rutland MSS.* i, pp. 434, 436. Box G/13. B. 76.

The sad cortege left London on 28 April and travelled by easy stages to Bath, which was reached six days later. The Earl was both irritable and in some discomfort on the journey, and at Reading cloth was bought to make a hand-litter, in the hopes that it would prove less painful than the coach or the horse-litter. At Bath men worked day and night to construct a carefully padded chair suspended from a pulley, in which Salisbury was gently lowered waist-deep into the water of the Cross-Bath. At first this treatment seemed to do some good, but he soon relapsed, and his body broke out in blue and livid spots. The doctors again intervened and cut an issue in the leg 'to drain the humors', with no appreciable result except to increase the weakness of the patient.[1]

Meanwhile, the Earl was a prey to spiritual fears. The long and wasting sickness had given him time to look back over his career, and what he saw was not encouraging. Anxiously he sought reassurance from his chaplain, Dr. Bowles, that however terrible had been his sins in the past, his faith in God and his sincere if tardy repentance could redeem them. Somewhat tactlessly, the chaplain pointed out how God had favoured him by allowing time for repentance, instead of cutting him off suddenly in full criminal career like King Herod. But Salisbury took no offence by the comparison, so full was he of the enormity of his past offences. What particularly preyed on his mind we do not know, though it is significant that in his last interview with his son he enjoined him earnestly: 'Take heed, by all means, of blood; whether in public or in private quarrel.' Was it the execution of Essex eleven years earlier that now lay uneasy on his conscience? Perhaps at times he even envied the swiftness of the block:

> to tumble
> From bed to bed, be massacred alive
> By some physicians, for a month or two,
> In hope of freedom from a fever's torments,
> Might stagger manhood; here the pain
> Is past ere sensibly 'tis felt.[2]

Dr. Bowles relates how he tried to comfort him by reciting the parables of the prodigal son and the lost sheep. '"Oh!" said my

---

[1] S. 129 f. 106. There are two accounts of the last journey to Bath. The first, by the chaplain, is in B.M., Add. MSS. 34218 ff. 125-8, and was printed by F. Peck, *Desiderata Curiosa*, London, 1732, lib. vi, pp. 8-15. The second, by John Finet, was printed in R. Winwood, op. cit. iii, pp. 367-8.

[2] John Ford, *Perkin Warbeck*, Act V, sc. iii.

Lord, "that sheep am I, that sheep am I!" Often ingeminating the speech, "that sheep am I!"' The next day there was a painful scene when

he leaned upon his crutches & lifted up his eyes to heaven. His gesture was in the likeness of a wrapt passion, his mouth smiling, his hands stretched out, and he uttered this saying, 'O Lord Jesus, now sweet Jesus, O Jesus now, O Jesus, let me join unto thee. My audit is made, Let me come now O Jesus, in the strength of my understanding, in the act of my memory. For if otherwise, what will the people say? But O Jesus, I care not, thy will be done, I am safe: I am safe;' & here the tears ran down from his eyes and stopped his speech.

Thus tormented in both body and spirit, the dying man set out once more for London, accompanied by doctors, clergy, household attendants, musicians, and a number of aristocratic friends. As he grew weaker, so his anxiety increased, particularly during the long watches of the night, until Dr. Bowles was obliged to set him at rest by asserting—perhaps over-confidently—'that God did certify him, by me, that he was in the estate of salvation'. The end came, without pain, at Marlborough, on 24 May 1612. The body was no doubt too decomposed to allow it to be successfully embalmed, and there had to be a relatively prompt funeral. The last remains were solemnly interred at Hatfield on 9 June at a cost, including the funeral feast, of nearly £2,000.[1] It was evidently a ceremony on a scale suitable to the occasion; it marked the close of the formative stage of the House of Cecil.

It is not the business of the historian to throw stones at the dead. And indeed, owing to his happy lack of personal experience, an Englishman living in the twentieth century is singularly unfitted to form a balanced judgement about corruption in public life. As Lord Keynes once remarked, in some societies corruption is the simplest and most convenient method of taxation. Under certain circumstances, and practised with moderation, it is not incompatible with a devotion to the public interest. 'I hope I may get nobly and honestly with profit to the King', confided Pepys to his diary as he negotiated to receive £300 a year for the award of the victualling contract for Tangier.[2] What is inadmissable is to apply modern standards of ethics to a patrimonial bureaucracy of premodern societies. Before the reform of the civil service in western

[1] S. 206 f. 60. B. 71, 72.   [2] S. Pepys, *Diary*, 2 July 1664.

countries in the middle of the nineteenth century, bureaucrats, politicians, and administration were not paid a living wage by the state, and were expected to obtain their financial compensation from gifts and payments from the members of the public whom they serviced, from the use for private gain of public money left lying in their hands, and from occasional extraordinary rewards from a grateful monarch. Modern standards of professional integrity and incompatability could not exist in such an atmosphere. Furthermore the ethics of the day still tended to place the interests of the family alongside if not superior to those of the state, so that nepotism was a moral duty rather than a vice.[1]

This does not mean, however, that the behaviour of public servants was wholly outside the moral code. There was a morality to which officials were expected to conform, even though it was very different from ours. There were limits, even if ill-defined and hazy, to what was considered permissible and respectable in the acceptance of gifts and in the manipulation of political power to acquire personal wealth. The question that must be asked, therefore, is whether the detailed evidence from the documents will support a charge that Salisbury exceeded the limits established by the conventional wisdom of the early seventeenth century. We have seen that as he lay dying a lingering and painful death in 1612, Salisbury himself was clearly consumed with doubts about how his career might be judged in another world. Many observers were also worried by the apparent spread of corruption throughout the central organs of government, a disease which they believed was getting noticeably worse. Letter writers like John Chamberlain filled their pages with rumours of financial scandals; in the 1620s two great public figures, Bacon and Cranfield, saw their careers blasted by well-founded charges of peculation, and a third, the Duke of Buckingham, was only saved by the hasty dissolution of Parliament. Time and time again the House of Commons came back to this theme of corruption at Court, as a principal cause of the wastage of the revenues of the State and of the inability of the King to live of his own. There is reason to believe that it was a powerful factor in turning the country gentry against the administration, and in the development of a group who called themselves 'the Country', or 'the Patriots', a new phenomenon of open political opposition to the Court and all it stood for. This suspicion of corruption goes

---

[1] J. Hurstfield, 'Political Corruption in Modern England', *History*, lii, 1967.

far to explain the obstinate refusal of Parliament to contribute to the burdens of government, a refusal which in turn made even more outrageous resort to corruption almost inevitable.

Sir John Neale has suggested that there was a substantial deterioration of financial probity among politicians in the 1590s, and much of his evidence for this deterioration comes from the correspondence of Robert Cecil and his secretary.[1] A careful examination of Cecil's private papers amply supports the contention that he used his official position for personal financial gain on a very large scale indeed. Moreover, a simple comparison with his father overwhelmingly supports the theory that there was a deterioration of public morality between the mid-Elizabethan and the Jacobean period. It took Burghley fifty years in high public office, twenty-eight of them as Lord Treasurer, to build three houses and acquire a very substantial estate. His son the Earl of Salisbury built up an even larger estate and built five houses in less than sixteen years, in only four of which he was Lord Treasurer. Since Burghley got far more land in free gifts from the Crown than did Salisbury, and also obtained the extensive property of the Lords Latimer by marrying his eldest son to the heiress, it seems clear that the annual profits derived from office by Burghley were less than those extracted by Salisbury by a factor of ten or more. The conclusion seems inescapable that Salisbury was infinitely more grasping than his father and that he must bear some personal responsibility for the decline in official morality that in the end was to have such serious political consequences.

In his handling of the Court of Wards there is nothing in the records to suggest that Salisbury was behaving very differently from his father. As Secretary of State, however, his approach to the Spanish Ambassador which resulted in a cash gift of £12,000—the modern equivalent of about a quarter of a million pounds—is surely without precedent. Even if it did not deflect English foreign policy from the pursuit of national self-interest, it must surely have made it difficult for Salisbury to break with Spain if ever he had decided that he should do so.[2] By any standards, at any time, the

---

[1] J. E. Neale, 'The Elizabethan Political Scene', in his *Essays in Elizabethan History*, London, 1958.

[2] One of Cecil's more devoted apologists has managed to convince himself that this extraordinary transaction 'may have contributed to the diplomatic flexibility with which the Secretary could serve the interests of King and country as Cecil saw those interests'! (T. M. Coakley, 'Robert Cecil in Power', in *Early Stuart Studies*, ed. H. S. Reinmuth, Minneapolis, Minn., 1970, p. 84.)

acceptance of a gift on such a scale from a foreign power by a Secretary of State would be thought highly scandalous. It is worth pointing out that this gift alone was sufficient to cover a quarter of the cost of building Hatfield House, and may well have been responsible for the decision to build on such a grand scale. The available evidence suggests that Spanish gold may have amounted in all to half the total cost of the building.

A number of transactions carried out by Salisbury in his capacity as Lord Treasurer seem to be equally indefensible by any standards of any age. One of the most sinister features of the early seventeenth century is the stranglehold obtained upon government finances by the customs farmers, and here Salisbury's personal financial dependence upon these predatory creatures is both new and alarming. When the Lord Treasurer is as deeply in their debt as Salisbury found himself by the end of 1611, it is vain to expect the cancellation of the system, the grant of the contract to a rival syndicate, or even the negotiating of a new lease of the farm on the most advantageous terms for the Crown. Here, at any rate, things had clearly gone downhill sharply during Salisbury's tenure of office.

On the other hand, it is quite wrong to suppose that Salisbury was merely the unscrupulous careerist described by his enemies. Unlike so many of his contemporaries in early Stuart politics, he was a shrewd and clear-headed statesman who worked actively to further what he conceived to be the best interests of his country. He greatly improved Crown revenues, both as Master of the Court of Wards and as Lord Treasurer. As Master he took novel—even revolutionary—steps to protect the interests of his charges. It cannot be proved that he allowed his Spanish pension to affect his judgement on foreign policy, and at least on one occasion, when he proposed the Great Contract, he was deliberately putting the public interest before his personal advantage.

In any society in which corruption of public officials is a way of life, most bribes are modest in scale, morally acceptable in nature, and designed to achieve negative rather than positive ends. The worst that can be said of Salisbury is that there are in his career one or two conspicuously scandalous exceptions to these norms, and that they contributed to the evident decline in standards which took place in his lifetime.

APPENDIX

The First Earl of Salisbury's Recorded Average Annual Income and Expenditure, 1608–1612[1]

(i) INCOME

		Average per annum to nearest £10	
Landed Income		£	£
Rents		5,090[2]	
Fines and casualties		990	
	TOTAL		6,080
Profits of Office (certain and probable)			
Master of the Court of Wards		2,590	
Lord Treasurer		2,780	
Secretary of State		1,490[3]	
	TOTAL		6,860
Profits of Patents and Receipts of Bribes and Gratuities			
Silk farm annuity		1,170	
Payments by customs farmers		1,560[4]	
Pension from French wine licencees (?)		140[5]	
Sales of surplus plate		250	
Unexplained payments		2,070[6]	
	TOTAL		5,190
Receipts from or for the Countess of Derby			720[7]
Money borrowed			15,260[8]
Repayment of money lent			670
Sales of land			14,270
Arrears, etc.			610[9]
	TOTAL		49,660

[1] These figures, which are based on A. 160/1 and Box G/13, are only approximate and have been adjusted and added to as explained on pp. 15–19. While all figures have been averaged over the four years, a number represent once-and-for-all items that were non-recurrent.

[2] To this should be added £1,000 a year for two years 1610–12 for the rent of the New Exchange, taken by the customs farmers.

[3] All but £100 of this was secret-service money, which was apparently nearly all spent, but not accounted for.

[4] This is the amount paid by the farmers after the beginning of the new lease of the silk farm in December 1610. The full rent was £7,000 a year, but most of this does not appear in the accounts since it was absorbed in debt and interest payments.

[5] This pension was for £230 a year, until it ceased at the end of 1609.

[6] This includes cash sums paid by Salisbury into the account, and also certain unexplained payments by others.

[*Footnotes 7, 8, and 9 on next page*

(ii) EXPENDITURE

		Average per annum to nearest £10	
Family and Personal		£	£
Cash paid to the Earl		390	
Apparel for the Earl		640	
Medicine and doctors' fees		510	
Expenses of the children		6,010	
	TOTAL		7,550
Household			
Household expenses		1,790	
Extra household expenses		330	
Expenses at Hatfield parsonage		260[1]	
Expenses at Court		1,050	
Stable expenses		1,100	
Tradesmen's bills		1,660	
	TOTAL		6,190
Wages			
Wages and liveries		620	
Board wages		140	
	TOTAL		760
Gifts and Rewards	TOTAL		720
Charity and Taxation			
The poor: alms		60	
Net loss on purchase and sale of corn in 1608		210	
Subsidies		60	
Church dues		20	
	TOTAL		350
Rents, fines for leases, annuities, and fees	TOTAL		1,950
Extraordinary payments	TOTAL		1,240[2]
Funerals and legacies	TOTAL		240
Secret service payments	TOTAL		180[3]

[7] This was probably partly connected with the administration of the Countess's estate, and perhaps partly receipts and gratuities received by the Countess on the Earl's behalf.

[8] In addition there was another £14,000, or £3,500 p.a., of Charles Brooke's debts which were taken over as part of the price of his land.

[9] The arrears are not true receipts, being merely the carry-over of the nominal surplus on the charge account from the previous year. This explains most of the discrepancy between receipt and expenditure.

[1] The Parsonage was used as a family residence while Hatfield House was building.

[2] This figure consists mostly of large unexplained payments, such as the mysterious £2,000 to the Earl of Dorset in 1608–9, probably connected with the Earl's dealings in patents and sales of offices.

[3] This does not represent more than a fraction of the payments for secret service, which apparently took up the full allowance.

Loans

Loans to others by the Earl	430	
Repayment of money borrowed from creditors	8,990	
Interest charges on money borrowed from creditors	2,000[1]	
TOTAL		11,420

Purchases of land   TOTAL   4,910[2]

Building

Hatfield House, Park, parsonage, and factory	8,910	
Cranborne House	880[3]	
Salisbury House and adjacent buildings	1,780	
The New Exchange	1,930	
TOTAL		13,500

Investment in Virginia Company   20

TOTAL   49,030

[1] To this should be added the interest on the £20,000 worth of debt taken over by the customs farmers, and presumably paid out of the rents of the New Exchange and the silk farm. This would mean that the total interest paid in 1611–12 was in fact more like £4,000 a year.

[2] To this should be added most of the £35,700 worth of cash payments, loans, and obligations assumed in return for the acquisition of Charles Brooke's land, only £3,700 of which are included in this item. The total amount spent on land purchase was therefore £19,655 + 35,700 − 3,700 = £51,655 which gives an average of £12,914.

[3] To this should be added unknown sums taken directly out of the Cranborne rents.

II

THE BUILDING OF HATFIELD HOUSE
1607–1612

OF all the great houses of the late sixteenth and early seventeenth centuries none is better documented than Hatfield House.[1] Hitherto, however, no attempt has been made to give a full account of the progress of the building in all its vicissitudes and, in consequence, a number of the most important architectural and economic problems have remained unexamined and even unnoticed. Unrivalled though they are in the wealth of information they provide, the surviving papers are unfortunately incomplete in one vital respect; not a single architectural plan or drawing has come down to us,[2] and as a result some of the most intriguing problems of responsibility still elude our grasp. Nor are there any weekly accounts of the clerk of the works, such as we possess for the contemporary building of Wadham College, by which progress can be followed almost day by day.[3] What there is, however, is vastly more than has survived for any other building of the age, about the construction of some of the most important of which, such as Audley End, we know virtually nothing. We have a series of letters to and from the principal officers in charge of the works, a number of contracts with the craftsmen, repeated surveys of the existing state of the building and estimates of the future programme, an almost complete series of six-monthly building accounts, and a very large number of detailed bills.

Right up to the last five years of his life the first Earl of Salisbury had no intention of building himself a great country seat, since he had inherited from his father that extraordinary Elizabethan showpiece, the house at Theobalds. With this huge palace, situated so close to London, he could easily fulfil his obligations to entertain

---

[1] The most comprehensive account is by H. A. Tipping, *English Homes, Period III*, vol. ii, London, 1922, pp. 305–52. Almost all the documents are preserved at Hatfield.

[2] In 1636, in the inner room of the 'Evidence House' at Salisbury House, there were still preserved one great plot on paper and seven other plots and rough drafts of the old and new houses at Hatfield (A. 160/9).

[3] T. G. Jackson, *Wadham College*, Oxford; 1893, chs. ii–iv.

his royal mistress or master. For it must be borne in mind that these enormous houses of the late sixteenth and early seventeenth century were based on the custom of the royal progress. The range of state apartments and the mass of subsidiary lodgings were designed for the accommodation of the court on one of its cere-monial summer tours. Some, such as Audley End, were vast enough to house most of the courtiers and civil servants, besides the prince and his personal attendants. Others, such as Hatfield, were limited to accommodation for royalty and the greater courtiers. In both cases, however, the scale of building was greatly in excess of the normal requirements of even the largest private household. Thus at Hatfield the family lived on the ground floor of the east wing, as they do to this day, while the first floor of the east wing con-tained the King's apartments and the west those of the Queen, the two linked by the Long Gallery.

If the royal progress dictated the design of these houses, their size reflects the spirit of emulation between courtiers and politicians jostling for prestige, position, and favour. As a result building activity tended to go in bursts, as one court faction succeeded another in favour and architectural display. In the first decade of the seventeenth century all the great court figures were building. The Howard clan set the pace with Northampton House at Charing Cross, Greenwich House, and Audley End in Essex, while the Earl of Dorset was building at Knole. But Robert Cecil was not far behind with Chelsea House, Salisbury House, and the New Ex-change in the Strand, Cranborne House in Dorset, and finally Hatfield House in Hertfordshire.

It is against this background of building activity that Hatfield House has to be seen. The son of Lord Burghley, who had built Burghley House, Theobalds, and Cecil House in the Strand, the brother-in-law of Lord Cobham, who had extended Cobham Hall and built Cobham College, the political friend and rival of the builders of Knole, Audley End, Northampton House, and Green-wich House, Cecil had from earliest childhood lived in an atmo-sphere of architectural ostentation and had personally begun building the moment opportunity offered. But it was not till 1607 that the possibility of really large-scale activity arose.

In that year James I's increasing predilection for Theobalds as a hunting-lodge made it prudent and, it was hoped, profitable, to offer the house and parks to the Crown. James was duly grateful and gave in exchange some seventeen manors spread over twelve counties, including the old royal palace and park of Hatfield.[1] Cecil might reasonably conclude that the sale value of the other properties would amply pay the cost of pulling down the old palace and building a new one near the old site, and this he immediately proceeded to do.

The first problem is to identify the architect of the new house. But the evidence makes it clear that there was no such person, in the sense of a single individual exclusively responsible for planning and design. Instead we have a confused picture of collaboration (or competition) between a number of people. The Surveyor of the King's Works, Simon Basil, was concerned with the Earl's other London buildings, and there is at least a presumption that he had some share in their design. It would therefore be only natural for Cecil to turn to him when considering his plans for the last and most ambitious of all his undertakings. It is not surprising, therefore, to find Basil mixed up with Hatfield from the beginning. In 1607, precisely when we do not know, he and the Earl's gardener, Mountain Jenings, visited Hatfield to look the site over. He was down once more in December 1608 to survey the state of the buildings and assess costs, and again in March 1609 to try to work out possible economies. A year later Cecil sent him down to survey progress and investigate the reasons for the ever-mounting costs that continued to soar far beyond the estimates. In January 1611 he was again at Hatfield to confer about future costs. And in that year his supervision of the work was so close that he personally appointed the joiner to do the wainscotting in the great chamber.[2]

From all these scraps it is clear that Basil was regularly used by the Earl in a consultative and even a supervisory capacity, but there is nothing to suggest that he took an active part in planning. On the other hand, the Earl was clearly in the habit of turning to him for expert advice, and it is more than likely that the designs were submitted to him.

The man who was primarily responsible for the original design can be proved to have been Robert Lemyinge (or Liming), a carpenter.[3] The evidence hardly leaves any room for doubt on this

---

[1] S. 143 f. 112.

[2] B. 21, 25, 27. S.P. Dom., Jas. I, 57/82; 53/65, 79; 63/88 (1).

[3] He usually signs his name Lemyinge, but he is often referred to by others as Liminge or Lyming, and his death is thus entered in the parish register of Blickling. Consequently he is usually known to modern writers as Liming.

subject. In November 1607, soon after work had begun, Cecil gave him £40 'in gift towards my charges about building and surveying of Hatfield'. The receipt is endorsed 'in surveying for and plotting of Hatfield houses', and it is probable that the surviving plan of the old palace is Liming's work.[1] Now this is a very large sum of money indeed (the modern equivalent, in so far as such a figure has any meaning, would be about £800), and not at all the sort of reward given to the ordinary land surveyor. The presumption, therefore, is that this huge gratuity was for his creative work in designing the house. Liming and the Earl's official, Thomas Wilson, together drew up the original estimate of costs, and in August 1607 there is a reference to Liming's 'plat for the point of the great chamber'.[2] Liming lived at Hatfield throughout the whole five years of the building operations, acting as clerk of the works in close supervision of the workmen at a wage of 12s. a week.[3] Letters of his in 1609 and 1610 prove conclusively that he regarded himself as the man responsible not merely for the soundness of the construction but also for the design. Of a drastic economy proposal of 1609 Liming commented that 'it will be very deformed for the uniform of the build, both within and without, which I will never agree to'.[4] A little later he wrote that he was 'about the drawing of an upright for the front of the gallery', he agreed with the chaplain about 'a mould of the lights of the chapel windows', and he drew up 'plots' of the gardens for Cecil's approval. Finally in October 1612, when the building was finished, the second Earl gave him a princely reward of £100 'in consideration of my pains about his Lordship's works at Hatfield'.[5]

Who was this Robert Liming, to whom the Earl of Salisbury entrusted the design of his greatest undertaking? Unfortunately the details of his earlier career elude us. We do not even know what part of the country he came from, though the fact that in 1612 there was a John Lyming living at Deene, in Northamptonshire, may be suggestive.[6] The Hatfield papers are very scanty before 1607, so we do not know when he first entered the Earl's employment; his earliest recorded work is some carpentry for Theobalds almshouses in 1607, and it is as a carpenter that he is still described at this stage. Indeed Wilson suggested that he should act as

[1] B. 14/4; 15.   [2] S. 143 ff. 114, 115.   [3] A. 160/1. Box G/13.
[4] S.P. Dom., Jas. I, 66/42; 45/69.   [5] Ibid. 66/42; 58/9; 67/62. B. 653.
[6] Brudenell MSS., O. xxii. 4. I am indebted to Mr. G. Brudenell for permission to examine his family papers.

contractor for the carpentry work at Hatfield, though in the end the idea was dropped. As late as December 1609 he is still described in the accounts as 'Mr. Liming the carpenter'.[1]

It is very strange that Salisbury, accustomed as he was to patronizing the most eminent London artists and craftsmen of the day, should have picked this apparently obscure carpenter for his architect. It is an odd choice, even if the latter was a qualified architect, and even if Liming's designs were submitted to the scrutiny of the more experienced Simon Basil. But Basil and Liming do not exhaust the range of participants in the original plans, much less the later alterations; there are also the patron himself, Robert Cecil, and his *homme d'affaires* Thomas Wilson. From the start Wilson was put in charge of the financial arrangement for the building. 'The expenses of Hatfield may lie entire upon me', he wrote in August 1607, after some bickering with the Earl's steward over responsibility, and thereafter, until he gave up the job in 1611, he remained in financial charge; he hired the workmen, signed the contracts, and paid the money. All bills were signed by Liming and his foreman, John Shawe, and they were then paid by Wilson. He lived in Salisbury House in the Strand, where he dealt with the shippers and contractors, and at regular intervals he rode down to Hatfield with money to pay the workmen. He was a party to every inquiry into costs and estimates, to every survey of work done, to every scheme for reduction of expenditure.[2]

Lastly there was Salisbury himself. The role of the patron in architectural planning naturally varies with the capacity and interests of the individual. There can be no doubt whatever that his father, Lord Burghley, played a very active part indeed in the development of both Burghley House and Theobalds, and the same is true of his friend the ninth Earl of Northumberland, the rebuilder of Syon House. Before the latter began he bought a 'Book of Architecture' for 30s. 6d. and made a tour of the most celebrated modern buildings. In 1603 he wrote to Salisbury that he was about to 'go and see Copthall, for now I am a builder I must borrow of my knowledge somewhat out of Theobalds, somewhat out of every place of mark where curiosities are used'.[3] It is certain that Salisbury's role, if not as decisive as that of Burghley and Northumberland, was a far from passive one, for we have ample evidence

---

[1] B. 21. A. 160/1. S. 143 f. 114.   [2] S. 143 f. 116. S.P. Dom., Jas. I, 57/82.
[3] *H.M.C. 6th Report*, p. 228. *H.M.C. Salis. MSS.* xv, pp. 382–3.

from the many letters to him from Wilson and others of his keen interest in his buildings. And when Arnold was planning the re-building of Cranborne House, we are told that he was closeted with the Earl for an hour every day.[1]

In April 1607 the Earl personally chose the site of the new house at Hatfield, on the highest point of ground to the south-east of the old palace. As he explained in a letter to Sir Thomas Lake, 'I . . . looked upon Hatfield, where it pleased my Lord Chamberlain [the Earl of Suffolk] my Lord of Worcester, and my Lord of South-ampton to be contented to view upon what part of ground I should place my habitation.'[2] There are repeated references to designs and proposals being referred to him for approval, and an excellent illus-tration of his role as final arbiter is to be found in Wilson's letter of 21 August 1607. 'Liming is confident in his plat for the point of the great chamber where he designed it, which we will dispute when your Lordship comes to Windsor.'[3] The series of letters which have survived makes it clear that Cecil closely scrutinized not merely the finances but also the design of the building. On occa-sions, as we shall see, decisions of his at a late stage caused radical alterations in the building programme and the design of the house, even involving considerable demolition.

Hatfield House emerged, therefore, through the interaction of the ideas and wills of four men: the designer and clerk of the works, Robert Liming; the eminent professional adviser, Simon Basil; the financial administrator, Thomas Wilson, with architectural opinions of his own; and lastly the patron himself, Robert Cecil, looking at Liming's drawings, listening attentively to all this advice, even calling in outside help, and then taking the ultimate decisions.

Before discussing the progress of the building and its architec-tural problems, it would be as well to explain the organization of supplies and workmen. In 1607 and 1609 Cecil was building actively in four places, at Cranborne, Salisbury House, the New Exchange, and Hatfield, and there was obvious need for some administrative centralization to ensure a smooth flow of supplies and men to all these sites. This was a time of tremendous building activity all over the south of England, and skilled workmen were

---

[1] Essex Record Office, Petre MSS., D/DP. Q 13/3/11 (I owe the reference to the kindness of Miss Nancy Briggs).

[2] S.P. Dom., Jas. I, 27/7.   [3] S. 143 f. 115.

very scarce. Cranborne, Salisbury House, and much of the New Exchange were built in stone, and serious difficulties were encountered in finding the necessary masons. In view of this shortage and of the great cost of building in stone it is hardly surprising that Cecil decided to copy Theobalds and use brick with stone dressings at Hatfield. He was not prepared to compete with Audley End.

No detailed accounts have survived to enable us to calculate the total labour force engaged at Hatfield, but there can be no doubt that it ran into hundreds. Only the unskilled labourers, engaged in digging foundations, pulling down the walls of the old palace, levelling the courts and gardens and so on, were recruited and paid directly. These were supervised by Liming's assistant John Shawe and by Liming himself, who also controlled all the other building operations. The rest of the work was done on a contract basis, with master craftsmen in charge who hired and paid their own workmen and presented their gross bills to Liming and Thomas Wilson. Thus all the masonry was carried out by Edward Collin, the carpentry by William Wode, the joinery by Jenever, and the bricklaying by Jeremy Talcot.[1] Of these leading craftsmen the most important were naturally Collin and Talcot, but there is nothing to suggest that either was more than an executant carrying out a contract job. Only Jenever had any share in design, for he was presumably responsible for the details of the joinery and he certainly drew 'plots' of the wooden chimney-pieces. Unlike the others, the joiners did not work on the site but in the London workshops, whence the finished articles were sent down to be fitted up. For example, the back panelling of the gallery was made in a hurry in 1612 by twelve London joiners working according to measurements supplied by Jenever.[2] In this respect they were more like the decorative trades than the other main building operatives.

In an enterprise of this scale, both speed and economy depend upon an even flow of materials to the site. Robert Cecil was therefore fortunate that the two main building materials, brick and timber, were obtainable from local sources. The theory that most of the brick was reused material from the old palace is not borne out by the documents. These old bricks were used for some of the garden walls and for rubble filling to level the courtyards and make the new approach road, but that was all.

[1] In 1609 Talcot was appointed Royal Bricklayer (B.M., Add. MSS. 33378).
[2] S.P. Dom., Jas. I, 52/17. S. 143 f. 122.

The bricks for the new building were made on or near the site at Hatfield itself, suitable clay being apparently readily available. The organization of this brick supply did not run too smoothly, owing to the enormous quantities involved. So far as we can tell, between one and three million bricks were used every year for at least four years.[1] The brickmaking season was fairly short, being confined to the summer months and ceasing in early October. For the first two years the brickmakers were direct employees, who were supplied with free fuel from Hatfield woods. In March 1609 Wilson decided that it would be cheaper to work on a contract basis, and Eustace Kellie was engaged to supply bricks at 11s. 6d. a thousand, paying 6s. 8d. a load for wood from Hatfield woods. The wood was to be cut by the Earl's workmen, but the brickmakers would have to fetch it.[2] Towards the end the brickmakers began using coal brought from London in order to save wood, and perhaps also costs.

Apart from the minor item of tiles, which came from Woodhall park at a cost of 11s. a thousand plus 3s. a load for transport, the only other locally supplied material was timber. Oak for the main timbering and for laths was mostly bought from Sir Robert Wroth at Westley wood and Tewin warren. Sir Robert sold the standing trees at over £1 each, leaving the Earl's men to cut and carry them to Hatfield.[3]

All the other materials for the building had to come from elsewhere, some of them hundreds and even thousands of miles away, and were funnelled through the great port of London. Unloaded at Tower wharf, Wiggins's quay, Chester's quay, Galley quay, and Cock's quay, they were taken to a yard and warehouse in Redcross Street, where a scrivener, Henry Doughty, was responsible for checking the goods in and out.[4] From there the materials, of which the most important in bulk were stone and coal for lime-burning, were sent down to Hatfield by local carriers. There were some dozen of these, each of whom in the busy season at the height of

---

[1] In October 1609 Liming said there were 1,100,000 bricks on hand which would last till the next year (S.P. Dom., Jas. I, 66/42). It was estimated that 2½ million more bricks were needed for the 1610 building season (S.P. Dom., Jas. I, 53/65) and between Christmas 1610 and October 1611 700,000 bricks were made (Box G. 13).

[2] Pet. 2418. S. 196 f. 130.

[3] B. 25, 36, 38, 69. A. 160/1. There is an early bill of £10 for charges for providing timber out of Ireland, but nothing seems to have come of this scheme, presumably because Sir Robert Wroth's timber became available soon after (B. 23).

[4] B. 28, 24. A. 160/1. Box G/13.

summer picked up a fresh load every two or three days. The loads were small, at most about $2\frac{1}{2}$ tons[1] or 20 sacks of coal, and it is a revealing commentary on the current state of the road from London to Hatfield that the average winter loads were not much more than half those carried in the dry season from June to August.

After brick, the most bulky and costly building material was naturally stone, which was needed for the dressings, paving, and south front at Hatfield, and also for the buildings in the Strand. In 1601 stone for Salisbury House had been obtained from a wide variety of sources, uncut stone from Oxford (presumably Headington) quarries, wrought Kentish stone from Lady Sidney at Penshurst, and Caen stone, which had been imported for repairs to old Saint Paul's, from the Bishop of London.[2] Even greater diversity of sources is found for the still more urgent operations of 1607 and after. A good deal of stone for all these buildings was reused material from the ruinous walls and gatehouse of the former monastery of Saint Augustine at Canterbury, which the Earl had acquired by grant and purchase between 1605 and 1607. Despite protests from the inhabitants, who were apparently resentful of the destruction, demolition went forward in the summer of 1608; 520 tons of stone were acquired in this manner and shipped to London via Sandwich.[3]

Apart from this Kentish supply, the bulk of the stone for all the buildings came from Normandy. The fine white stone from Caen had been used in England from the twelfth century onwards, and it is not surprising to find it still in high demand in the early seventeenth century. The contract for the stone was placed with a London merchant, Robert Bell, who merely between October 1606 and January 1608 delivered at Tower Wharf some 800 tons of stone at a gross cost of £640. This was a very high price and Bell felt a little nervous about presenting so stiff a bill. He explained that the stone would have been cheaper 'but that to make expedition to provide stone for your Honour's several buildings we were forced to buy a quarry & hire workmen to dig out the stone, which was very chargable, & also there was lost and spoilt at Caen [in] the last great frost about four score ton.'[4] Even so, the cost of the stone at the waterside was only £275, the remaining £365 being the

---

[1] B. 38.   [2] H.M.C. Salis. MSS. xi, 343, 358, 362.
[3] D. 102/40. S.P. Dom., Jas. I, 35/61; 36/12; 36/35. B. 29. S. 143 f. 115.
[4] A. 8/3.

freight costs to London. Between April 1609 and November 1610 another 995 tons were imported, the cost of the stone being £285 and the freight £462, besides an extra £13 for a horse presented to the governor of Caen to obtain his goodwill.[1] The stone was shipped in a host of small vessels carrying between 12 and 50 tons each, many of them owned by Dutchmen. Indeed the tiny scale and exorbitant costs of transport in the seventeenth century are vividly brought home in these accounts. Little or no technical or organizational improvements had been made since the Middle Ages, and the result was to impose a crippling burden on all economic activity.

Besides these two principal sources of supply, minor quantities of stone were obtained from a variety of other sources. Ancaster stone was provided by the Hatfield master-mason Edward Collin, which suggests that he may have been a Lincolnshire man.[2] Blue slates of the best quality were sent up from Plymouth by the local Admiralty official, James Bagg, and a good deal of Purbeck stone was quarried and sent to London for use in paving. Eighty-two very large slabs arrived in January 1609 and William Hammond wrote triumphantly of this conquest over transport difficulties: 'The carriage of them at this time of the year from the quarry to the waterside up the steep hills they were to pass, were held in the country from whence they came a difficulty (till it was done) not to have been overcome by the industry of man.' Even now transport troubles were not at an end. Though shipped on 4 December, the cargo was held up by bad weather and was not delivered in London till 25 January.[3] Other black paving stone came from near Berwick and was shipped ready squared and polished. It was got on the sea-shore below the tide line, and was carried to the ships on men's backs. There was some talk of using an agate-coloured stone from a newly discovered quarry in the Earl of Northumberland's lands, within three miles of a port, but it seems that nothing came of the suggestion.[4] An element of the exotic in the stone used at Hatfield is provided by the fine white marble used in the fireplaces. This came from the Carrara quarries in Italy and was shipped via Leghorn by an English merchant.[5]

[1] G. 12/11.   [2] S. 143 f. 115. B. 36.
[3] S.P. Dom., Jas. I, 36/39. S. 125 f. 19.
[4] S. 125 ff. 44, 51. Northumberland was getting building stone for Syon House from Brotherwick and Coquet Island, and paving stone from Walbottle (*Northumberland County History*, v, p. 323).
[5] B. 38. A. 160/1.

The only other materials of any significance were nails for the timbering and lead for the roof. The former came from the still flourishing Sussex iron industry, being bought from Robert Courtup, a blacksmith at Framfield,[1] and the latter from the Derbyshire mines. At first there was some uncertainty whether to use lead or copper. The sergeant plumber was consulted, who advised that copper would be 7*d.* a foot dearer, and so it was decided to use lead. Thomas Wilson advised the Earl to get his lead direct from Derbyshire and ship it himself, rather than to buy it from merchants in London. He suggested that the Theobalds plumber should go to Derbyshire to make the arrangements, and the Earl's friend, Sir Walter Cope, advised an approach to Lord Cavendish for help in making local contacts. By this means Wilson optimistically hoped to get the lead for £9. 10*s.* a fother instead of the £15 at which it was selling in London, but he never in fact achieved this figure. He managed a reduction to between £11. 2*s.* 6*d.* and £13. 10*s.*, plus the cost of carriage from the wharf to the warehouse in Redcross Street.[2]

It is clear from this account that the organization of supplies for the building of Hatfield House was one of considerable complexity. Materials had to be obtained from a very wide area and transported to London. There they had to be stored and fed to the building works as required. And it is a tribute to the efficiency with which Thomas Wilson organized this side of arrangements that in Liming's many letters only once does he complain of shortage of materials. This is in the autumn of 1610 as the south front was going up, when he made an urgent appeal for more stone to keep the masons employed. But the fault was hardly Wilson's since a sudden change of plan during the winter had made unexpected new demands on the supply of stone.[3] In general the documents illustrate the extreme difficulty of arranging a smooth flow of materials owing to the primitive nature of seventeenth-century transport, and prove the success with which the difficulties were overcome.

Both the plan and the elevation of Hatfield owe much to Lord Burghley's building at Theobalds.[4] The use of brick and stone dressings, the idea of big square blocks at the corners, joined by

[1] B. 24.   [2] G. 3/11. S. 143 f. 115. A. 160/1.
[3] S.P. Dom., Jas. I, 58/9; 53/79.
[4] J. Summerson, 'The Building of Theobalds 1564–1585', *Archaeologia*, xcvii, 1959.

a lower section, the entablature running round the first- and second-floor levels, the balustrade and the flat roofs, the little domed turrets and the gilded lions on the roof-line, the central clock tower and the open loggia, all derive from this earlier palace, where Liming had worked and the Earl of Salisbury had lived.

But even if these basic items were all agreed upon, it does not mean that the plans were rapidly approved. Although Cecil was busy choosing the site for his new house in April 1607, work did not start before August. And even then Liming and Wilson were still arguing over the ground plan, in particular over the site of the great chamber. The reference to this dispute is very obscure, for Wilson writes that pending a decision 'the foundations may go forwards for all the rest, and that (as a thing standing apart from all) may be added at any time if your Lordship shall so please'.[1] It is difficult to see how a great chamber could be tacked on to the existing structure without disfiguring the general appearance, and yet there is no great chamber on the ground floor. The best explanation, for which some additional evidence is available, is that the original plan of Hatfield lacked the great rambling extensions to the wings that give it its very peculiar ground plan, but that Liming envisaged some such extensions from the first.

Not very much was done in this first season's work other than to clear the site, dig out the cellars, and raise some of the foundations up to ground level. Next spring work went forward with fresh impetus, and the main and partition walls were erected up to or above the first floor. At the same time a large unskilled labour force was turned onto the task of pulling down the old palace to the west of the new buildings.[2] It was during this year that the first major change of plans took place. Unfortunately we have no correspondence for this period, so that it is very difficult to reconstruct precisely what happened. What the records tell us is that when the Earl was at Holdenby new plans were adopted which involved pulling down two main load-bearing walls each 58 feet long, one of which was already 27 feet and the other 14 feet high. At the same time a partition wall was pulled down 'whereas a pair of stairs came up near the old chapel'. The bricklayer's bill up to 1610 also included an item for making two chimneys and two doors in 'the new chapel' and 'working up a wall in the old chapel where a sumer lay'.[3] From these scraps of information it is certain

[1] S. 143 f. 115.   [2] Ibid., f. 117.   [3] B. 26, 27. A. 9/24.

that a major change of plans took place, involving the destruction of two main walls and an abandonment of the original site of the chapel. The references to an old and a new chapel in the bricklayer's accounts leave no room for doubt on this point, but it is far from clear where the 'old chapel' lay. The problem is complicated by the fact that a further alteration to the chapel was decided upon in the winter of 1609–10, and some of the undated entries in the bricklayers' accounts may refer to this second change of plan.

One possibility is that it was intended to preserve the former chapel of the old palace as a detached block, and that work was begun with this object in mind, but later abandoned. This theory is virtually disproved by the reference in the accounts to the work of labourers in January–April 1608 in pulling down the chapel.[1] There is, however, another explanation, though it must remain a mere hypothesis, which accords with these entries and also solves one of the architectural puzzles of Hatfield. The oddity about the ground plan lies in the expansion of the ends of the two wings into large oblong blocks three rooms deep (fig. 1). This expansion of the ends of the wings is unknown elsewhere. Not merely does it create an extraordinary irregularity of plan in the outer faces to east and west, but it also largely obscures the basic structure of the house, which consists of two high square blocks at either end, linked by a lower section in the centre and with wings running out at right angles. All this strongly suggests that the expansion of the wings was an afterthought (and not a very happy one at that), and that in the original design the wings were of the conventional narrow width (fig. 2), like those of Sir Thomas Cecil's house at Wimbledon, Surrey, begun in 1588[2]. If this is so, the 58 feet of destroyed main walls ran on the lines A–B in fig. 1, and the chapel may have been intended to be at the end of the east wing.[3] The new wall in the old chapel would be the present cross-wall C in fig. 1, below the 'sumer' or beam that was to support the cross-wall above the chapel on the first floor. It is extremely improbable that the twin towers at the

---

[1] B. 27.

[2] J. Summerson, *Architecture in Britain, 1530–1830*, fig. 7, pl. 22A.

[3] Sir John Summerson has suggested to me that the original walls may perhaps have been in line with the east and west walls of the two main blocks to the north, that is between the existing walls and those in fig. 2. I do not favour this view, partly because the length of destroyed wall would then only need to be 52 feet instead of 58, and partly because the increase of space in the new plan would hardly have been worth the trouble and expense of alteration.

The reference to the stairs near the old chapel remains a puzzle, since the existing stairs going up to the first floor in the middle of the wing are said to be a nineteenth-century addition.

ends of the wings were part of the original design, where they would have been much too close together. There may have been intended only a single tower at each side, towards the inner court, or more probably no tower at all but merely little turrets on the tops of the wings at the corners, as at Audley End.

The change in the site of the chapel can be attributed to a decision to leave the whole of the east wing clear for the private apartments, looking out over the terrace into the great ornamental garden. The new site was probably chosen in imitation of the plan of Wimbledon House. However, it is undeniably awkward, since access on both floors to the whole of the west wing is possible only by traversing the chapel. The desire for a general expansion of the size of the house probably arose out of the death on 19 April 1608 of the first Earl of Dorset from apoplexy at the Council table. Robert Cecil succeeded him in his most lucrative office of Lord Treasurer, and it was probably this unexpected accession of dignity and wealth that inspired the change, in the same way that Lord Burghley's accession to the Treasurership in 1572 had led to a similar expansion at Theobalds.[1] This hypothesis is supported by a letter written to Salisbury by the Earl of Shrewsbury after a visit to the site in October 1608, in which he remarks: 'We took it to be but a petty poor pile for a Lord Treasurer of England to build, only we found that you might hereafter at your pleasure double the platt divers times without disuniformity to that which shall be first erected.'[2]

After this alteration, building proceeded swiftly throughout 1608, and most of the walls were well beyond the first floor when winter put a stop to further activity. The works were covered with straw to protect them from the frost, and the Earl's advisers had time to straighten out the accounts.[3] In the spring of 1609, however, there arose a new crisis in the history of the building, this time due to a financial panic. What Cecil had been told about the probable cost of his enterprise we do not know, but he now realized that the expenses were soaring far in excess of estimates. Owing to a reckless indulgence in land purchase and building, the Earl's general expenditure was running far ahead of even his

---

[1] The Earl of Salisbury was appointed on 6 May. King James and the Court were at Holdenby in the second and third weeks in August, which must have been when the alterations were carried out (J. Nichols, *The Progresses of James I*, 1828, ii, p. 203). The huge £12,500 bribe from the King of Spain also took place at about this time, and may well have been an incentive to build on a grander scale (see above, p. 17).

[2] S.P. Dom., Jas. I, 37/27.   [3] B. 25.

enormous income. Venal though he was, he could not squeeze enough out of his official positions to stand the strain, and already his debts must have been approaching the £40,000 level that they were soon to reach.[1]

In March 1609 Simon Basil was sent down to Hatfield to suggest economies in the building, and on 25 May Liming drew up his estimate of possible savings on the official, and absurdly optimistic, estimate of £8,146 needed to finish the building.[2] Suggestions, all of which were evidently made with extreme reluctance, included omitting the entablature of stone designed to run twice round the inner court (Pl. I); the taffrails or open strapwork scrolls over the windows, and the lions holding vanes over the gable ends; and the Purbeck marble paving in the kitchen area. More serious were two other proposals, of which the first was to cut off the six towers on the north and south fronts and roof them over level with the rest of the house; it was of this proposal that Liming rightly remarked that it 'will be very deformed for the uniform of the build, both within & without, which I will never agree to'. The second was a suggestion for simplifying the ornament on the south front, the precise nature of which is not clear and which will be discussed in detail later on.

Four days later there was produced a final list of possible economies, drawn up after a general conference of the chief workmen before Simon Basil and the Earl's officers.[3] The suggestion about the towers was here dropped, no doubt owing to Liming's vigorous objections, and the chief savings were achieved in the works in the east garden and in the elaborate ancillary structures that had been designed to cover all approaches to the house. Nevertheless, the sides of the inner court were marked down for substantial alteration. The double entablatures were to go, as well as the taffrails over the windows, and £120 was to be saved in the 'garnishment of the front'. Inside the house the elaborate plaster ceilings were to be simplified, and expenditure on the wood-carving on the hall screen and elsewhere was to be halved. Meanwhile building was virtually at a standstill and all but twenty of the labourers were paid off. A fortnight later Robert Cecil himself came down to examine the position, but it was not until 28 July that the revised building

---

[1] In the year September 1608 to September 1609 his borrowings exceeded repayments by £15,400, and by 1610 his total indebtedness reached £42,395 (A. 160/1; S. 141 f. 352).

[2] S.P. Dom., Jas. I, 45/69.   [3] Ibid. 45/84.

programme was drawn up and signed. Unfortunately this document is missing, but we know from other evidence that it ordered
those economies in the stonework decoration of the inner court
which were mentioned in the earlier recommendations.[1]

Work began again at once in an attempt to make up for lost time.
Despite a lot of rain in August, Liming reported confidently in
October that he would be able to get most of the roof on before
the onset of winter.[2] By now, however, Robert Cecil had begun to
regret his cheese-paring of a few months before. By temperament
a spender, such economies did not come naturally to him, and by
October he had evidently begun to wonder whether he was not
spoiling the ship for a ha'p'orth of tar. At all events before next
April those economies so anxiously contrived in the spring and
early summer of 1609 had all been abandoned. The double entablatures, the taffrails over the windows, and the traceried gable-
ends were all restored, and the cuts in the internal carving and
joinery and in the terrace of the east garden were cancelled. In
addition, two new changes were decided upon. Major alterations
were ordered in the chapel and the chapel windows, costing
altogether no less than £200. There are certain hints to suggest
that these included redesigning the east window.[3] The tracery of
this window, with its round-headed lights, is quite unlike all the
other windows in the house, though it is similar to closely contemporary windows in the almshouses at Audley End and at Gosfield
Hall, Essex. It seems likely that originally there had been a bow
window to conform with the symmetry of the plan, and that the
projecting straight-sided window with its curious tracery was
substituted at this late stage.

The second change concerned the central feature of the whole
building, namely the south front, the complicated history of which
we must now examine in detail. As it stands today this front
presents a startling contrast with the rest of the building with its
bleak brick structure and fanciful strapwork decorations. In the
first place it is built entirely of stone, and in the second its style is
unlike that of the rest of the exterior. The classical frieze with its

---

[1] Ibid. 45/76; 47/53; 53/79.   [2] Ibid. 47/98; 66/42.
[3] The survey of joiners' work up to November 1610 included panelling 'in the passage
behind the chapel on the second storey . . . with that which was pulled down for the chapel
window' (S. 143 f. 118), and the survey of bricklayers' work for the same period included a
special item, additional to the main building, for 'the foundation of the chapel window'
(A. 9/24).

ox-skull and paterae metopes, the windows with their projecting corbelled sills and flattened mullions and transoms, quite unlike those anywhere else in the house, and the elegant pilasters between them give the first-floor gallery front a classical air that even the very Jacobean central porch and the strapwork and gable-ends above cannot altogether disguise (Pl. II). It is significant that none of these features appear in Liming's subsequent architectural venture at Blickling, though almost every other element in Hatfield's exterior can be found there.[1]

The inner court to the south, up to which ran the newly made approach road, was intended to be the principal feature of the house, and the original designs were probably made by Liming with Simon Basil's approval. From the first the ground floor of the south front seems to have been planned as an open loggia, a system becoming popular at just this period and here deriving directly from the four loggias at Theobalds. So far as we can gather from the evidence, the original design had a ground-floor decoration of pilasters, while at top and bottom of the first-floor gallery ran two stone bands of entablature that continued right round the inner court. Like the rest of the building, the first floor of the south front was to be principally built in brick with these decorative features in stone. All the brickwork of the south court was double pencilled, and the design was therefore a deliberate study in colour contrast of reddened brick and white Caen stone that is a characteristic of royal works of this period.[2] But this was not all. Liming's economy suggestions of May 1609 included the following proposal: 'If it may please his Lordship to let the front of the gallery to be built with pilasters as it is begun & leave out the columns, he may deduct out of the charge—120 *li.*'[3] From this it would appear that Liming had been planning a set of engaged or detached columns running up between the windows, and resting, presumably, on the pilastered piers of the ground-floor arches.[4] The idea of a pilastered (or pillared) first-floor front was thus

[1] Cf. respectively, Hatfield, E. side of S-W. wing (*Country Life*, lxi, 1927, p. 428, fig. 4), corner towers with two-storey bow windows (ibid.), and shape of gable-ends (ibid., fig. 3), with Blicking (ibid., lxvii, 1930, p. 817, figs. 8, 4, and 8). Where certain elements of the front are copied at Blicking, the work is coarse and the design is bungled. Compare the door spandrels in idid., lxi, 1927, p. 428, fig. 4, with ibid., lxvii, 1930, p. 814, fig. 8.

[2] E. Mercer, 'The Decoration of the Royal Palaces, 1553–1625', *Archaeological Journal*, cx 1953.

[3] S.P. Dom., Jas. I, 45/69.

[4] San Micheli's Palazzo Grimani of 1549 at Venice has this feature.

evidently part of the original Liming design, and must have been copied from the front of the New Exchange. The omission of this feature was endorsed in the official report four days later, when it was recommended that £120 be saved in 'garnishment of the front', and was most probably included in the new programme of 28 July.

On 9 October 1609 Liming wrote to Wilson to report progress. After explaining his hopes to have most of the building roofed before winter, he added 'I am about the drawing of an upright for the front of the gallery, which I can do little to but in the evenings by reason of giving order to the workmen . . . but the next week I will satisfy you at large the manner of it and what needful stones is to be provided for the performance of it.'[1]

But this measured drawing of Liming's was never executed. Some time during the winter Cecil had changed his mind again. By April 1610 the entablatures had been restored to the two sides of the court, and the main south front had been redesigned as a solid stone façade, at an estimated extra cost of £150.[2] Who then was responsible for the new design? It could, of course, have been Liming, though we have seen that there are stylistic grounds for thinking this unlikely. An alternative, and more exciting, hypothesis is that here we have the first known architectural achievement of Inigo Jones. The documents tell us that on 30 October, at the express orders of Robert Cecil, Thomas Wilson provided Inigo Jones with a horse from the Earl's stable and rode down to Hatfield with him. They spent two nights there and returned on 1 November. On 28 February 1610 the Earl's receiver-general entered in his accounts, *under the heading of expenses for Hatfield building:* 'To Inigo Jones, as your Honour's reward given him for drawing of some architecture £10-0-0.'[3] Now £10 is a large sum of money and would only be given for some outstanding service. For example, on the previous occasion when Cecil had employed Jones's services to design a masque to entertain the King at the official opening of the New Exchange in April 1609, he had only given him £13. 6s. 8d.[4] Though the wording of the entry is a little obscure—'some architecture' is a curious phrase to employ for what was usually described as a 'plot', an 'upright', or a 'model'—the conclusion seems inescapable that Inigo Jones did some architectural

---

[1] S.P. Dom., Jas. I, 66/42. Liming does not give the year, but from internal evidence the letter clearly dates from 1609, not 1611 as stated in the *Calendar of State Papers*.

[2] S.P. Dom., Jas. I, 53/79.   [3] Ibid. 57/82. A. 160/1.   [4] A. 160/1.

drawings for the Earl in connection with the building of Hatfield. His visit was carried out at the express orders of the Earl at just the moment when Liming's design for the south front came to the latter for final approval, and shortly before the design was radically altered. This certainly suggests that Jones was consulted about the new south front, though it does not mean that he must have designed the sculptured details, which may well have been left to the head carver. We cannot be sure who this carver was, but the payment to John Bucke of nearly £200 during 1611 may mean that he was responsible.[1]

The clock tower that dominates Hatfield (Pl. III) is also unlikely to have been designed by Liming.[2] These towers were present at Burghley, Theobalds, and Salisbury House, and it is only natural that there should have been one at Hatfield.[3] But its elegant simplicity of design forms a striking contrast with the earlier prototype at Burghley and with Liming's later tower at Blickling Hall, which is in the ponderous style of 'Artisan Mannerism'. Is it conceivable that the same architect, having designed the Hatfield tower, and having seen Jones's new building at Whitehall, whence he took the triangular pediments over doors and windows at Blickling, would have fallen back on this clumsy provincial contrivance? It seems likely, therefore, that Jones's 'drawing of some architecture' for Hatfield covered both the first-floor gallery front and the clock tower above it. Whether Jones also redesigned the central porch at the same time is more open to question, since there is little about it that could not have been contrived by Liming himself. Nor can we be sure what hand Simon Basil had in these alterations. He certainly carried out surveys of costs on 14 December 1609 and 4 April 1610 and his opinions must almost certainly have been sought on the new designs.[4]

It should be emphasized that the arguments in favour of Jones's responsibility for the clock tower and the south front do not depend on any hypothesis that at this stage, before the second Italian visit

[1] B. 58. A. 160/1. Box G/13.

[2] That the tower is not a subsequent addition is proved by references in accounts of 1611 to 'lead for the lantern' (S. 140 ff. 38–9) and to the painting of the great vane at the top and lions holding vanes standing about the lantern (B. 58); and by the fact that in the Receiver-General's accounts between 1620 and 1648, which are complete, there is no reference to any tower being added or rebuilt.

[3] The 'great lantern' at Salisbury House was finished in 1608. Its walls were painted by Rowland Bucket to resemble glass, and it bore two great dials; it resembled the Hatfield structure by being surrounded with lions bearing the Cecil arms and crest (B. 28).

[4] S.P. Dom., Jas. I, 57/82; 53/65, 79.

of 1613–14, Jones was necessarily working in the classical style for which he later became famous. All that is being put forward is that there are stylistic grounds for thinking that the south front and the clock tower are not the work of Liming, but that they are not impossible for one who had already visited Italy and seen something of architecture in a classical style. For a comparison of the south doorway at Hatfield with a similar doorway at Blickling, and of the clock tower at Hatfield with that at Blickling, shows an unmistakable coarsening of design and a retreat to a more insular Jacobean idiom. This serves to rule out Liming as the designer, unless we are to suppose his style actually retrogressed between 1610 and 1620. If Liming is therefore eliminated we are left with Jones, who we know was consulted at this time and was paid for some architectural drawings connected with the house, and with Basil, who was still acting in an advisory capacity. The latter, however, was never rewarded for any drawings.

It has always been realized that Jones must have done some designing of architecture as well as masque scenery before he was appointed Surveyor to Prince Henry in 1611. The problem has been to identify the building or buildings by which he had made his name. Nothing would be more likely than that in about 1609–10 Jones should have taken a hand in the design of a great house for one of the leading politicians of the day, and it now seems probable that in this south front at Hatfield we have Jones's earliest known architectural work, and the one which led directly to his first official appointment. Although the argument stands without any hypothetical conjectures about the sort of style in which Jones might have been working at this time, it should be pointed out that the Hatfield south front fits in very well with the scanty known facts of Jones's career. We have no idea in what style he was working at this date, except for a few sketches for masque scenery, and a drawing for a porch in a fairly conventional manner and dated 1616, *after* the second Italian tour.[1] But in 1609 he had been at least once to Italy, and had visited France that very summer. Now windows set between pilasters, with projecting corbelled sills and flattened mullions and transoms, are to be found in Philibert de L'Orme's book on architecture, published in 1567, and in a number of classically inspired sixteenth-century French chateaux. This type of window is, so far as I am aware, unique in English

[1] J. A. Gotch, *Inigo Jones*, 1928, pl. vi. J. Summerson, *Architecture in Britain, 1530–1830*, pl. 38.

architecture at this date.[1] On the other hand, the windows are not pedimented, there are Jacobean gables and strapwork above, and there is nothing very unusual about the porch. The front is in fact just what one might expect from a man still tied to the native idiom either by inclination or by the necessity of pleasing a very conservative patron, but already deeply interested by what he had seen abroad.

Work on the new design proceeded steadily throughout the summer of 1610, and by November Liming could report considerable progress. The bricklayers had virtually finished the work on the exterior, and the stone facing of the south front was completed up to the pedestals of the first-floor pilasters. No fewer than thirty masons were now at work on this front, and there was urgent need of more Caen stone to keep them busy during the winter in preparing the sculpture ready to be set up in the spring. At the same time the hall and tower roofs were leaded, all the stairs were finished up to the top of the house, the floors were boarded and joisted, the joiners were busy on panelling and chimney-pieces, some of the windows were glazed, and the mullions for the new chapel window were being made.[2]

By May 1611 the masons were busy on the chimneys, the openwork scroll taffrails that topped all the windows, and the balustrade that ran around the roof; the joiners were setting up the hall screen, and the plasterers' work was almost finished. In July the south porch was finished, apart from the coat of arms, and the scaffolding removed, and a sufficient number of rooms were matted and hung to enable King James and the Court to be entertained. By December the great lantern was leaded, the chapel was paved, the joiners and painters were busy with the interior of the house, and, by the winter of the next year, 1612, the whole house was ready for occupation.[3] But Salisbury had died in May, without having slept for more than a few days in the building on which he had lavished so much trouble and so much money.

Though the interior of Hatfield has undergone considerable changes since 1612, and though much of the west wing was gutted

---

[1] Philibert de l'Orme, *L'Architecture*, 1576, pp. 250–2. *Châteaux et manoirs de la France: La Loire*, ii, pl. 93. It should be emphasized that none of these are identical with the Hatfield windows, but they display the same basic elements. There *may* have been somewhat similar windows at the New Exchange but the Smithson drawing is not clear enough for one to be sure (*L.C.C. Survey of London*, xviii, 1937, pl. 58).

[2] S.P. Dom., Jas. I, 58/9. S. 143/118.

[3] B. 58. S.P. Dom., Jas. I, 63/88 (1); 65/3. S. 140 ff. 38, 39; 143 ff. 122, 123.

by fire in 1835, many of the principal decorative features of the house have survived. If the plaster ceilings by James Lee, the King's plasterer, have all disappeared, a good deal of the panelling and joiners' work executed under the direction of Jenever still remains.[1] Also preserved are the three stone fireplaces with their elaborate architectural settings. These fireplaces were the work of Maximilian Colt, the French *émigré* artist from Artois, who had just finished the tomb of Queen Elizabeth for Westminster Abbey. Much of the materials for these fireplaces, and for Robert Cecil's tomb which was commissioned at the same time in 1609, were provided by the Earl himself.[2] He supplied Colt with the Carrara marble, and exchanged more marble with another London tomb-maker, Cornelius Cure, for Purbeck marble and rance. Alabaster was bought by Colt and carried to his workshop, some from Islington and some from a warehouse by the Tower. The statue of King James for one of the fireplaces was executed in Caen stone by Colt and then painted to look like copper; the centre-piece of another was a mosaic portrait of Robert Cecil, executed by Venetian craftsmen under instructions from the English ambassador, Sir Henry Wotton, and based on a picture by John de Critz.[3]

The two masterpieces by the carver John Bucke, the screens for the hall and the carvings of the superb open-well staircase, have both survived. This type of staircase, which is closely modelled on that at Theobalds, may well have been designed by Liming, as it is repeated again in a more elaborate form at Blickling. The original appearance of screens and staircase was very different from today, for both were gaily painted. The year's work for 1611 by the painter Rowland Bucket included covering the screens with 'arms, gilding, & personages'. On the staircase he decorated the central pendant in white and gold and painted all the timber work, besides 'gilding & working of the naked boys and lions standing upon those stairs holding of instruments and his Lordshypps arms'. He even proposed to paint the walls of the stair-well, which in January

---

[1] The survey of joiners' work provides interesting specimens of the technical terminology of the day. For example, 'In the Queen's bedchamber one frize, Archi:, vaze, triddlefines (triglyphs), swellinge pannells, Cattooses, droppes, teeth and water crease, plantseare & oggeve' (S. 143 f. 118).

[2] B. 69. S. 143 f. 129. B. 35/2. Colt was also carving two statues in Burford stone for external niches in the New Exchange in the Strand (B. 29) and another fireplace for the Queen's closet in Salisbury House (S. 143 f. 129).

[3] L. Pearsall Smith, *Life and Letters of Sir Henry Wotton*, Oxford, 1907, i, pp. 452–3, 460. In Critz's bill of 1607 there is the item 'an other picture of your Lordship for the Ambassador of Venice, £4-0-0' (Box U/81).

1612 he was 'about a plot for'. In the Earl's bedroom the great bed, the chair, and the stools were also painted with 'flowers, birds, and personages'.[1] Everywhere, indeed, the interior was brilliant with colour. Wooden friezes and chimney-pieces in every principal room, the ceiling pendants and the huge organ installed in the great chamber, were all picked out in paint and gilding. This organ, or great wind instrument, was bought in 1609, along with other mechanical toys, from a Dutchman for the truly staggering sum of £1,060.[2]

The chief decorative effort, however, was reserved for the chapel, whose present sombre appearance is remote from its original condition. The plan of the chapel with its upper floor seems to have been copied from the slightly earlier chapel at Salisbury House, where there was also a 'room over the Chapel where my Lord goeth to prayers'.[3] In 1612 Bucket painted two canvases for the west end, one of the Annunciation and one of the angel appearing to the shepherds, and gilded frames for the total of eight pictures that hung around the lower chapel. Around the windows ran a broad band of gold, and between the pictures the walls were 'wrought with figures of the small prophets and with borders and scrolls gilded about them and very much other work'. The roofs of both upper and lower chapel were heavily gilt, the fireplace of the upper chapel was painted black and gold, and the soffits of the arches supporting the upper chapel were gilt and worked. In addition Bucket painted a big picture of Christ and the Apostles. It is difficult to exaggerate the importance in contemporary eyes of all this painting. Both inside and out the house was intended to be ablaze with gilt and gaudy colours, and no expense was spared to achieve this effect. Owing partly to the cost of the heavy gold leaf so lavishly employed, Bucket's bills were very high. For the nine and a half months from January to November 1611 he was paid no less than £577, a very large sum for that time.[4]

The stained glass in the east window of the Chapel is usually described as of Flemish workmanship. The architectural backgrounds, however, are French rather than Flemish, and the bills

---

[1] B. 36.

[2] B. 58, 77. S. 143 ff. 122. A. 160/1. It seems to have been quite common to have organs in living rooms at this time. For example, in 1613 the Earl of Arundel had his organ at Greenwich moved to the lower dining-room (M. F. S. Hervey, *The Life, Correspondence, and Collections of Thomas Howard, Earl of Arundel*, Cambridge, 1921, p. 93).

[3] B. 28.   [4] B. 58, 77. S. 143 f. 123. Box G/13.

and accounts prove that they were designed by a Frenchman, 'Lewis Dolphin' (presumably Louis Dauphin). But, as so often at Hatfield, the story is not a simple one. In October 1609 Dolphin was paid £8 for 'painting certain pictures' for the chapel window. He spent three days at Hatfield in March 1610 and throughout the year was paid various sums for 'pictures made in glass' for the chapel, finishing up with a large payment of £62 'to discharge Lewis Dolphin's works'.[1] But in January of that year there is a note by Thomas Wilson that a Martin van Benthem had made three pictures in colours for the chapel glass, for which he asked £6. Wilson suggested to the Earl that he be paid £3 for the lot and 6s. 8d. for pasting the pictures on cloth and for a tin case in which to send them to France. And on 3 January van Benthem was duly paid £3. 6s. 8d.[2] From this it seems clear that three of the windows were to have been designed by van Benthem and executed by a French glazier. But nothing more appears in the accounts either of van Benthem or of payments to a French glazier, and it seems certain that this project was abandoned. The heavy payments throughout the year to Lewis Dolphin, totalling some £90, can only mean that he actually supplied the glass himself, as well as designing it. But he was not the only glazier to be employed, for Richard Butler of Southwark certainly designed and made the Jonah window, and was paid a further £30 'towards making of the painted glass for the Chapel windows'.[3]

Contrary to general belief, the external appearance of Hatfield has probably been changed more radically than the interior over the past 350 years. Were Robert Cecil and Liming, Simon Basil and Wilson, to return today, what would shock them most would unquestionably be the present practice of approaching the house by what was intended to be the base court in the rear (Pl. IV). The whole building was carefully designed to look south, upon which face all the really lavish architectural and decorative effort was concentrated. A new road was specially built to lead up to the inner court to the south, and only the more inquisitive of visitors or guests making their way to the stables would see the north front.

Nor was the house itself as austere and self-contained as it appears today. When Evelyn visited Audley End he commented

[1] A. 160/1. S.P. Dom., Jas. I, 57/82.   [2] G. 12/21. A. 160/1.
[3] B. 38. A. 160/1. Box G/13. In 1611–12 Butler made the windows for the chapel at Salisbury House (Box G/13).

that it 'shows without like a diadem, by the decoration of the cupolas and other ornaments on the pavilions'.[1] Both Theobalds and Audley End proliferated in domed turrets, and Hatfield was not far behind. Besides the numerous lodges, pavilions, and gateways that surrounded the house on all sides, many with their own little domes and cupolas, the roof-line was originally enlivened with eight little turrets with their 'Dutch types' or leaded domes, in addition to the four existing turrets at the south ends of the wings and the two towers to the north. These eight turrets were placed at the corners of the two square projecting blocks at either end of the main building. Reference to 'the two great towers . . . and the gable ends belonging to the said towers' suggests that the presented truncated appearance of the tops of the towers is not original. Thus in 1612 this north front, topped by four little turrets and two ornamental gables, a great painted taffrail of timber above the central porch, and the eight lions glittering with gilt and holding gilded escutcheons with the Cecil arms,[2] was very different from its present condition of oppressive simplicity (Pl. IV). Even the south front was more ornate than it is today. All the fifty-four lions about the house were gilded and carried their gay little armorial vanes, every window was topped with its taffrail of open strapwork arabesques, the tall lantern was bright 'with fair colour', and the lions around it and the great vane were picked out in dazzling gilt.

Though the exterior of the house has become more drab over the centuries, even more radical changes have taken place in its surroundings. A great Jacobean house was not intended to be burst upon unheralded, and much pains were taken in planning the approaches.[3] Visitors came up to the house from the south along the newly constructed road. They passed first into an outer court and then through a gate in the curtain wall, flanked by two porters' lodges topped by painted castellations, into the paved and turfed inner court. The gateway itself was decorated with pilasters, architrave, frieze, and cornice, the walls were 'garnished' in stone, and there were two domed houses over doorways leading to the east and west gardens. In the base court at the back there was another elaborate gateway, and two little circular buildings at the corners;

---

[1] *Diary of John Evelyn*, ed. W. Bray and H. B. Wheatley, 1879, ii, p. 73.

[2] B. 77. A. 9/24.

[3] A good idea of the care expended on outbuildings can be obtained at Hampstead Marshall, Berks., where Lord Craven's great house has gone but some of the elaborate gateways survive, scattered about in the fields in bewildering profusion.

the west garden had two substantial banqueting houses, decorated with pilasters and an entablature, and topped by taffrails; and the principal garden to the east had further little buildings intended to conceal water cisterns.[1] From every angle, therefore, the house was surrounded by curtain walls, courtyards, and a protective cluster of little domed pavilions.

If a good deal of trouble was taken over these outworks, even more detailed care went into the planning of the gardens. This was a feature of particular interest to the seventeenth century, and many of Cecil's friends, relations, and neighbours, notably Lord Burghley, the Earl of Northumberland, Sir Thomas Fanshawe, and Lord Cobham, had distinguished themselves in this field. When Evelyn visited Hatfield in 1643 he observed that 'the more considerable rarity besides the house (inferior to few then in England for its architecture) was the garden and vineyard, rarely well watered and planted'.[2] Of these gardens so admired by Evelyn virtually nothing remains today, but from the documents it is possible to reconstruct something of their history and appearance.

It has been seen that the story of the house itself is a complicated one, involving many hands and numerous changes in design, and it is not surprising to find the same features repeated over the gardens. The first plans for the garden were drawn up in September 1609 by Mountain Jenings, the Earl's gardener, who was probably taken over from Theobalds and who later returned there to look after King James's silkworms.[3] He was assisted by Robert Bell, the London merchant who handled the import of Caen stone and other transactions with France on the Earl's behalf. Bell seems to have been something of a connoisseur of gardens. He told Wilson that he had tried to persuade one 'Bartholomew the gardener' to go and take over at Hatfield, but he had refused because he was too old. However, Bartholomew offered to visit Hatfield from time to time and to order plants from the Low Countries. Bell then reported that he and Bartholomew had conferred with Jenings, whom they found 'very sufficient'. 'We did determine of a plot to be drawn to be shewed unto my lord, which I think will do very well, & after may be changed or altered at my lord's pleasure.' But Cecil must have had doubts about Jenings's capacity, and another gardener, Thomas Chaundler, was also taken

[1] A. 9/24. S.P. Dom., Jas. I, 63/88 (1).   [2] *Diary of John Evelyn*, i, p. 39.
[3] F. Devon, *Issues of the Exchequer . . . during the Reign of James I*, London, 1836, p. 288.

on. Chaundler made 'many plots' of the gardens and in return for £55 supervised the layout of the principal show-piece, the east garden. Soon after this yet another gardener, John Tradescant, was employed to buy the necessary trees and plants, for which purpose he made several journeys both to Flanders and to France.[1]

The garden plans thus went ahead during 1609, 1610, and 1611 under the confused direction of three men—Jenings, Chaundler, and Tradescant—with Robert Cecil as the ultimate authority. And in January 1611 the waterworks for the Chaundler plans of the east garden were begun by a hydraulic engineer, Simon Sturtevant, presumably a Dutchman. But in November Thomas Wilson became dissatisfied with this project and sent down Prince Henry's engineer, the Frenchman Salomon de Caux. Though by now pipes had been laid, cisterns built, and substantial progress made with the 'works and devices about the fountains', de Caux ruthlessly recommended scrapping the whole hydraulic system and beginning again.[2] No wonder poor Cecil, tied to London by the pressure of work and the ravages of an increasingly painful illness, complained bitterly that 'every journey brings new designs'. De Caux promised to provide 'models' of his scheme, rough drafts of which have been preserved, and Liming was drawn into garden planning to make fresh 'plots'. Despite the heavy expense involved, Cecil accepted these proposals, Chaundler and Sturtevant were sacked, and Jenings entrusted with the responsibility of finishing the east garden according to the new designs of de Caux and Liming. And so it was not till January 1612 that the situation became clear and Jenings could draw 'a plot of all the garden' to show to the Earl.[3]

The layout comprised a kitchen garden to the north-west, with herbs, roots, artichokes, cabbages, etc., a west garden, with walks, trees, and hedges, a huge orchard, a vineyard some way to the east, and a large and ornamental east garden, the lower half of which was filled with raspberries and strawberries, roses and flowers. On his purchasing expeditions on the Continent, whence came most of the plants for the new garden, Tradescant spared no pains to make Hatfield the leading centre of English horticulture, and brought back with him a number of varieties unknown to Lord Burghley's gardener, John Gerard.[4] Tradescant was evidently an

[1] Box U/72. B. 35/6. A. 160/1. G. 11/25. B. 58.
[2] S.P. Dom., Jas. I, 61/37; 57/82; 63/88 (1). B. 58.
[3] S.P. Dom., Jas. I, 67/62. Box G/13. S. 143/122.
[4] J. Gerard, *The Herball*, London, 1597.

optimist, and hopefully transplanted to this dreary English climate such southern exotics as oleanders, myrtles, figs, oranges, aubergines, and no fewer than 206 cypresses. Already he was collecting curiosities, though at this time on his master's behalf, and his bills include the purchase of such things as 'one great buffalo's horn' and 'one artificial bird', perhaps intended as garden ornaments.[1] The vineyard was a very ambitious undertaking, stocked with 30,000 French vines presented by Madame de la Boderie, and tended by two French gardeners specially brought over for the purpose. Even here, however, the experts were not altogether trusted, and Cecil persuaded the Earl of Exeter's gardener to go down twice to Hatfield to plant vines himself, in order to see the difference between his method and that of the Frenchmen. The result is celebrated in a remarkably purple passage by Thomas Fuller. For the orchard, large quantities of pears, peaches, plums, mulberries, cherries, nectarines, and quinces were bought, mostly abroad, and to this was added in 1611 a present of 500 fruit trees from the French Queen.[2]

The greatest attention, however, was paid to the ornamental east garden, running down the hill to a stream in the valley below. This was surrounded by brick walls and divided into two halves, laid out in the usual formal manner with red brick-dust paths and grassy knots bordered by pinks. Immediately outside the house was the terrace, with painted wooden rails decorated with 'French terms' and cup-shaped finials. From the terrace stairs descended to the main garden, lined by twenty-four painted and gilded wooden lions. The central feature of the garden was the waterworks, which were subject to considerable alterations. As has been seen, the first works were designed by Simon Sturtevant and Jenings. The water was contained in two cisterns at the upper end of the garden and ran into a great cistern in the centre, in which were painted artificial rocks and a painted statue of Neptune. A great deal of trouble was taken over this cistern, especially for King James's visit in the summer of 1611, and Jenings was paid £13. 3s. 'upon his bill for altering a rock twice in the east garden'.[3]

All this was altered during the winter of 1611–12 in accordance with the new plans of de Caux, who designed a grand new central

[1] G. 11/25. B. 58, 69.
[2] S.P. Dom., Jas. I, 61/50; 57/82; 67/62. B. 58, 59, 24. T. Fuller, *The Worthies of England*, London, 1662, pt. ii, p. 17.
[3] B. 58, 77. A. 160/1.

fountain. In the huge marble basin, made by the Dutch tomb-carver, Garrett Johnson, was a great artificial rock on an ironwork core. On this stood a metal statue, cast by another Dutch tomb-carver, Garret Christmas, and painted to resemble copper by Rowland Bucket.[1] From this elaborate centre-piece ran a shallow meandering little river, in imitation of one at the Earl of Exeter's (presumably at Burghley House). This item also gave a good deal of trouble, and was altered several times. The bottom of the winding stream was paved with coloured pebbles and sea-shells. Winkles and stones were collected in England, and Tradescant shipped back from Paris one chest and eight boxes of shells. In addition, little leaden leaves, snakes, and fishes were scattered about the face of the rock and the bottom of the stream.[2] All this sounds very much like earlier work in some of the great French gardens, for example, those of Bernard Palissy at the Tuileries and Thomas Francini at Saint-Germain-en-Laye, and it is from these that de Caux most probably drew his inspiration.[3]

At the bottom of the garden the stream that ran through the valley was partially dammed and an artificial island, which still exists, was created in the centre. This island was linked to the mainland by two painted wooden bridges and its walks were planted with white-thorn, sweetbriar, and osiers. Down-stream, probably on the site of the existing lake, was a 'dell' with a water pump, fountains, and a large wooden 'standing' or first-floor erection over the stream. A rough sketch of this standing, perhaps by de Caux, has survived to give us some idea of its appearance.[4] Like the island, the walks of the dell were also closely planted with whitethorn and sweetbriar.

There are a number of general conclusions to be drawn from this detailed study of the building of Hatfield House. In the first place it shows once again the radical difference between the role of the architect in the early seventeenth century and today. His position was then very much humbler, and his reward for archi-tectural designs was very much less substantial than today. In consequence it was not thought at all improper for the plans of one architect to be criticized and altered by others, so that a building like Hatfield has not one designer but several.

---

[1] It took 2,500 pounds of plaster to make the mould, and 300 pounds of 'solder' for the casting. But the most expensive item was the marble basin, for which Johnson charged £70 (B. 69, 77; Box U/90, 92).   [2] S. 143 f. 122. Box G/15. B. 58, 69.

[3] Cf. Ernest de Gany, *Les Jardins de France*, Paris, 1949, pp. 48–9, 53.

[4] B. 77. Box G/13. A. H. Tipping, *English Homes, Period III*, vol. ii, fig. 410.

Secondly, we find that even a fairly symmetrical house, erected in a hurry within the space of a few years, has an extraordinarily complicated history, with frequent demolitions and changes of plan taking place all the time that building operations were actually in progress. No doubt such chopping and changing and such a wide range of consultants were unusual for any except one of the houses of the great courtiers. But if such practices were at all common in the case of these outstanding buildings, it would seem that very great caution should be exercised in asserting architectural responsibility except where the documentary evidence is more or less complete.

It should be noted that the cost of a house the size of Hatfield put such an undertaking far outside the reach of a private person, and indeed came near to ruining the greatest of public officials. Including the work on, and improvements to, the park and gardens, between September 1607 and September 1612 the recorded expenditure on Hatfield is no less than £38,848.[1] On all his buildings, at Cranborne, the New Exchange, Salisbury House, Hatfield, and Hatfield parsonage, the Earl of Salisbury in these five years spent about £60,000. Such was the cost of being one of the greatest architectural patrons of the early seventeenth century.

Lastly, the all-pervasive influence of foreign artists and foreign imports on early Jacobean decorative and luxury trades is very striking. From the Netherlands came plants, trees, and shrubs for the garden, a few Flanders bricks and tiles, and the organ for the great chamber. The fountain was the work of Garret Johnson and Garret Christmas, Jenever the joiner was probably also Dutch, and a design for the chapel window was made by Martin van Benthem. It was even planned to import Dutch workmen to Hatfield to weave tapestries to decorate the interior. From France came plants, fruit trees, and vines. The chapel windows were designed by Lewis Dolphin, the fireplace by Maximilian Colt, and the fountain and waterworks by Salomon de Caux, while at Salisbury House the principal carver was one 'John de Booke'.[2] In some cases even the current terminology is foreign, for example, 'French terms' and 'Dutch types'. Rarely has English decoration been so wide open to foreign influences.

---

[1] A. 9/5; 160/1. Box G/13. A contemporary estimate puts the cost as high as £43,000, but this possibly includes expenditure on buying land to enlarge the park (A. 112/6).

[2] B. 27, 28. Box G/13. The John Bucke who did the carving at Hatfield may well be the same person.

III

URBAN DEVELOPMENT IN LONDON
1599–1720

In the course of the seventeenth century the Cecils, Earls of Salisbury, succeeded in acquiring and developing urban property to the west of the Old City of London which in time came to play a very important part indeed in the finances of the family. The story of both its successes and its failures is illustrative of broader trends in urban planning and urban development in the area, and is therefore worthy of careful study. The period of acquisition was complete by 1612, by which time the first Earl had obtained his three London properties, the sites for Great and Little Salisbury Houses and the New Exchange on the south side of the Strand, and a strip of land along the west side of St. Martin's Lane.

I. SALISBURY HOUSE

Since his father's town palace, Burghley House, to the north of the Strand, went with the bulk of the estate to his elder brother, Sir Robert Cecil's first preoccupation was to obtain a suitable site for a large town house of his own. The most desirable area was on the south side of the Strand between the street and the river, but unfortunately the whole waterfront was already filled by a line of palaces, most of which had formerly belonged to the Church but had by now been absorbed by the great Court aristocracy. But his chance came in 1599 when he persuaded Henry Lord Herbert, son of the Earl of Worcester, to sell him for £1,000 a house which had formerly been the town residence of the Bishops of Carlisle. The house was on a narrow site, squeezed in between Russell House, the great palace of the Earls of Bedford, on the east, and Ivy Lane, an alley leading down to the river, on the west. Here Cecil immediately proceeded to pull down the old house and build a new one, apparently designed by the Comptroller of the King's Works, Simon Basil.[1] At the same time he rapidly extended his holdings

[1] *L.C.C. Survey of London*, xviii, 1937, ch. 18. P.R.O. Close Rolls, 44 Eliz. pt. 8. *H.M.C. Salis. MSS.* xi, pp. 343, 349, 358, 367, 397.

near the site by buying up tenement after tenement, so that he soon owned all the buildings down the west side of Ivy Lane, known as Durham Rents.

To the west of Durham Rents his path was blocked by the huge area of Durham House with its courtyard, garden, and out-buildings, the London palace of the Bishops of Durham, most of which was now occupied on lease by Sir Walter Ralegh. On 24 March 1603 Queen Elizabeth died and James was proclaimed King of England, events which involved not only a change of dynasty but also a shift in political power. In 1600–1 three groups had joined to bring down Essex. They were Sir Robert Cecil and Lord Buckhurst, the Howards, and Essex's great enemies, Ralegh, Cobham, and Grey of Wilton. Of the three, the first two had spent the last two years in preparing for the peaceful accession of James, the perpetuation of their own authority, and the destruction of the third group. And so the breath was hardly out of the Queen's body before Cecil wrote to the Bishop of Durham, urging him to eject Ralegh from his town house in the Strand where for twenty years he had lived rent free under the Queen's protection. A couple of months later Ralegh was abruptly and discourteously thrown out into the street, a dramatic example of the treatment he might expect under the new regime. The next step was to persuade the Bishop to surrender his rights. First a lease of part of the garden was obtained in 1604, followed by an Act of Parliament securing sur-render of the freehold in exchange for other property nominally of equal value. Under the same Act Cecil obtained permission to shift Ivy Lane bodily westward, thus widening the frontage of his own house.[1] In this enlarged area building began again in 1605 and con-tinued till 1607–8, resulting in the imposing pile of Great Salisbury House on the east and Little Salisbury House on the west. Though a late-comer on the scene, Cecil's skilful and persistent efforts had secured him a large site for a town house in this highly coveted area, at the expense of the Bishop of Durham, the former lessee Sir Walter Ralegh, and Lord Herbert.

After the first Earl's death in 1612, however, the owner of this double palace was no longer the leading minister of the Crown, besieged by suitors, officials, and servants, and the need for so enormous a town house disappeared. And so the second Earl

---

[1] Ibid. xv, pp. 37, 111. E. Edwards, *Life of Sir Walter Ralegh,* London, 1868, ii, pp. 262–5. L. 67/24. D. 183/14; 3 Jas. I, Private Acts, cap. 1.

retained Great Salisbury House for his own use, and regularly let out Little Salisbury House to members of the Court peerage who lacked a London residence in this favoured quarter. But in 1672 the third Earl tore down Little Salisbury House altogether, created a new street, Salisbury Street, running down to the river, and erected two rows of eight houses on either side. Behind one row on the top floor was a bazaar with sixty shops, called the Middle Exchange, stretching over a long covered area running right back to the river. Nor did this exhaust the Earl's entrepreneurial energies, for he inserted six apartments below the Middle Exchange, and also cut up the rambling old palace of Great Salisbury House into twelve substantial self-contained houses, reserving for himself only one wing.[1] To place this activity in context, it must be explained that all up and down the Strand the same thing was happening. As the noblemen moved north and west, they pulled down their Strand palaces and split the sites and grounds into building lots. It was the end of the aristocratic age of the Strand.[2]

How all this development by the third Earl of Salisbury was financed and what it cost we do not know, but the results in terms of gross annual revenue were quite striking. In 1671 the Salisbury House complex had been bringing in a revenue of only £300 a year, paid by the single noble tenant of Little Salisbury House; in 1674, a mere three years later, the total rent had risen to £1,400, paid by thirty-four tenants of apartments and houses and sixty tenants of shops in the Middle Exchange. But 1674 saw the peak of the area's prosperity, the brief moment when a nice balance had been struck between rising population pressures and declining social status and property values. Within ten years there were signs that some of the ventures were beginning to fail, the first to falter being the Middle Exchange, which was facing competition not only from Salisbury's own New Exchange but from the Exeter Exchange, launched by the Earl of Exeter in 1676. By 1680 only a few shops close to the Strand were still occupied, and the rent was down to £34 a year. When the third Earl died in 1683 he left irrecoverable debts owing to him by departed shopkeepers of over £900 in unpaid rents and fines. Throughout the 1680s the Middle Exchange sank lower and lower, in both prosperity and reputation, acquired the unfortunate nickname of 'the Whores' Nest', and finally

[1] A. 133/1, 6; 161/4; 162/1, 3; 160/5; 163/1; 61/5. Box O/3, 5, 6, 8, 9.
[2] L. Stone, *The Crisis of the Aristocracy, 1558–1641*, pp. 395–6.

expired in 1694.[1] Nor was the Salisbury Street venture as successful as was hoped. Owing to the constricted nature of the site, the street was little more than a narrow alley and the houses were mean and crowded, squeezed between the street on one side and the Middle Exchange on the other.

It was not until after the death in 1694 of the fourth Earl (leaving enormous debts), that the executors and trustees embarked upon a final and large-scale reorganization designed both to bring in more revenue and to arrest the social deterioration of the quarter. The collapse of the Middle Exchange had left the Earl with an unoccupied building on his hands. Furthermore the drift of high society to the west and north made Great Salisbury House an unsuitable area for the town residence of a nobleman. So in the 1690s the Earl completed the development of the site by another major transformation. Great Salisbury House and the now derelict Middle Exchange were pulled down and a new street of houses erected on the site. This time the mistakes of the Salisbury Street venture of 1672 were avoided. Cecil Street was a spacious roadway and the buildings on either side were now 'very good houses for persons of repute'. The Earls had saved the Strand as an area of diversified occupation with mean tenements and small shops side by side with substantial middle-class housing. In doing so they had succeeded in raising the rental income of the property to no less than £1,363 a year by 1720.[2]

II. THE NEW EXCHANGE

In 1606–7 the first Earl of Salisbury conceived of a novel scheme for the development of the area immediately to the west of Salisbury House. By a series of most complicated transactions, he proceeded to acquire control of part of the Strand frontage of Durham House, including the gatehouse and the old stables to the west of it (fig. 3).[3] In 1607 he bought out Dudley Carleton's interest in an eighty-year lease, and the next year obtained full possession of the lease from Toby Matthew, the late Bishop's son, in return for £1,200. In 1609 he extracted from the Bishop a lease of the court-yard behind the frontage, and in the Parliament of 1610 he secured

[1] A. 133/5, 9, 14; 136/20; 55/5; 154/3; 165/1; 62/7. *L.C.C. Survey of London*, xviii, pp. 122, 125.
[2] Ibid., pp. 122–3. See Appendix.
[3] The stables and gatehouse are clearly visible on Norden's map of 1593 (ibid., pl. Ib). The site, which has recently been levelled for road-widening, lies to the east of Charing Cross Station, between the Strand and Durham House Street.

his title by an Act which transferred this property to him in perpetuity in return for a rent of £40 a year.[1] The Bishop was extremely anxious to avoid any appearance of surrendering the patrimony of the see under political pressure, and he repeatedly emphasized that both parties to the agreement were above reproach. Indeed, Salisbury treated him with scrupulous fairness, connecting new drains to Durham House and building a new stable for the Bishop's horses in Saint Martin's Lane.[2]

This additional Strand frontage was not acquired for any further extension of Salisbury House, but for a novel commercial venture, the erection of a 'New Exchange' as a West End rival to Gresham's famous building in the City. As in the latter, space under an arcade was provided for the general assembly of merchants and citizens, acting as a sort of stock exchange and estate agency. Within were rows of small shops on two floors, a kind of bazaar for the upperclass clientele which normally passed along the Strand between the Law Courts and the Royal Palace of Westminster, and the Inns of Court and the City to the east. It is impossible to say whether the original idea came from the Earl himself or from his *homme d'affaires*, Thomas Wilson, who was certainly immediately involved in all stages of its early history. There can be no doubt, however, that the Earl took up the idea with enthusiasm. His motives were probably mixed. No doubt he hoped it would be a profitable investment, and that the rent would provide a fair interest on the capital. It would also add greatly to his reputation. On both architectural and economic grounds it was bound to attract attention, particularly as the expected customers would be drawn from the influential classes rather than mere merchants and shopkeepers. Cecil could hope to achieve even greater renown than the building of the Royal Exchange had already conferred on Sir Thomas Gresham.

He was therefore entirely unmoved by the indignant protests of the shopkeepers of the Royal Exchange, who were naturally afraid of this new competitor. Their appeal to abandon the project was supported by the Lord Mayor, who feared a general westward drift of business:

It is generally conceived that if such a work be erected, the situation of the place respected, being near unto the Court of Whitehall in the midst of the Nobility and where much of the Gentry lodge and reside, as also in the high way by which all Termers pass to Westminster, it will have such

---

[1] D. 226/14; 111/18. A. 112/6. L233/14.   [2] S. 126 ff. 83, 129.

advantages of our Exchange as will make it of no use for salesmen at all, besides a greater inconvenience to this City. For a Pawn being there erected and put into a prime course of trade, will take all resort from this place and put by that recourse from the City which occasions much profit to all sorts of retailers in other places leading to the Exchange, and in time will draw Mercers, Goldsmiths and all other chief traders to settle themselves out of the City in those parts, for the supply of Termers and such as reside thereabouts, to the great decay of the trade within the City. . . .

Cecil's reply was tactful but firm. He repudiated any wish or intention to harm the interests of the Londoners, doubted whether there would be any serious competition between the two Exchanges, and reminded the City that it should not begrudge sharing some of its prosperity with others. 'When I balance London with Westminster, Middlesex, or rather with all England, then I must conclude that London might suffer . . . some little quill of profit to pass by their main pipe.' In conclusion he expressed his determination to leave to the present and future inhabitants of Westminster 'some such Monument as may adorn the place, and happily derive some effect of present benefit and future charity to the whole Liberty'.[1] In other words, he was hoping to stimulate the economic growth of the West End, even if this meant drawing a certain amount of business away from the City.

There is reason to believe that before he finally decided on the design, Salisbury approached Inigo Jones for advice.[2] Jones produced an elevation which shows a remarkable grasp of Italianate style, and was far in advance of anything which had yet been built in England. But unfortunately the design was not accepted, probably because Salisbury's essential conservatism revolted against so un-Jacobean a project. Indeed, his insular and cautious temperament must have been very frustrating for Jones, for whom the cosmopolitan and classically minded Earl of Arundel was to be a much more congenial patron. Nevertheless, the rejected drawing may well have had its effect upon the accepted design, about the authorship of which it is impossible to be certain.

The man in charge of erecting the building was Simon Basil, the holder of the most important architectural post in the country, the Surveyorship of the King's Works. From the moment he first

[1] S. 195 ff. 24, 30. City of London Record Office, Remembrancia, ii ff. 323, 355.
[2] For the arguments for the date and authorship of the unexecuted drawing, see L. Stone, 'Inigo Jones and the New Exchange', *Archaeological Journal*, cxiv, 1959, pp. 108–11.

began building, Cecil had been employing officials of royal works. Some plans for the major alteration of his house in Chelsea in 1597 had been made by William Spicer, Surveyor of the Queen's Works; Simon Basil, then Comptroller of the Works, was certainly employed on Salisbury House in 1601, being rewarded for his services through Cecil's control of patronage of wards. Though he had picked on an unknown carpenter, Robert Liming, as the architect of his great house at Hatfield, the latter was evidently advised at all stages by Basil. At the New Exchange, Basil's control was more direct. He signed all the bills, even of the most trivial nature, and helped to recruit the workmen. The accounts, which unfortunately only begin in Michaelmas 1608, do not record any other architect being concerned with the actual building. The clerk of the works and principal mason was a William Southes (Southeast, Suthes, or Soothes), who was already employed under the Crown, and was to end his days as Master Mason at Windsor Castle. He was evidently in full charge on the site and his expense account included such items as 'Small whipcord to set out the work and to make lines, levels and plumb rules', and 'for planing and shooting of boards at sundry times to make moulds and templates'.[1] There is nothing to suggest, however, that Southes was anything more than the executant of the designs of others.

It is impossible to be absolutely certain about the precise appearance of the Exchange as it stood on completion in 1609. The Earl of Shrewsbury had commented in 1608, 'And for your range in the Strand, we trust it will far exceed the fair long shop in Cheapside, though it hold that form.' Indeed the plan of the Exchange was certainly very similar to that of any one wing of its rival.[2] Facing the street there was a long covered arcade 201 feet long, 17 feet high, and 21 feet deep, while within was a narrow corridor 10 feet wide flanked on either side by rows of small booths no more than $5\frac{1}{2}$ feet deep. Below there was a range of cellars, and above, reached by stairs at either end, were two corridors with more rows of shops running out over the ground-floor arcade.

The southern façade, looking out on a passage leading to the river and beyond on the outer court of Durham House, seems to have been a very simple affair with rows of rectangular mullioned windows below a gabled and battlemented roof. This is how it is shown both in the rough sketch map of 1626, and in the Hollar

[1] B. 29.   [2] S.P. Dom., Jas. I, 37/27.

drawing of about 1635.[1] More intriguing, and more difficult to
determine, is the appearance of the main front facing on to the
Strand. The only evidence available is a drawing by John Smythson
in about 1618–19, and a late seventeenth- or early eighteenth-
century engraving by John Harris, after considerable alterations
had taken place (Pl. V, VI). Smythson is unfortunately a somewhat
untrustworthy authority, who appears to have done much of his
work from memory, supplemented by imagination, at his drawing-
board at home.[2] It will be noticed that while the general appearance
of the ground and first floors is more or less the same in both
drawings, Smythson's shows pilasters between the windows which
are omitted by Harris. Now a pilastered first floor was present at
the Royal Exchange,[3] and this may have played tricks with Smythson's memory; alternatively, of course, it is equally possible that
the pilasters were removed in subsequent alterations. Both show
medallions or circular openings between the windows, and a pair
of niches flanking the central porch on the first floor. The Smythson
drawing indicates that the building had a total of twelve niches on
the ground and first floors and it seems likely that the intention,
which perhaps was executed, was to fill all twelve with statuary.
Certainly the Royal Exchange was lavishly adorned with statues
all round the first floor, and Salisbury may have wished to emulate
this example. At all events in August Wilson reported that 'I have
according to your lordship's command in this last letter set Colt
awork with one of the Apostles, and of all 12 I have got the true
portraits.' Maximilian Colt was the 'Court' sculptor of the day,
who had just finished the tomb of Queen Elizabeth, and he was
therefore an obvious choice. And he certainly did one or two statues,
for two large blocks of Gloucestershire stone were delivered 'for
Colt to make figure to stand in the niche'. Over ten other carvers
were fully employed on the site from the end of August till April
1609—indeed, in September there were no fewer than fifteen—but
there was a great deal of decorative stonework to be carved, and it
is very doubtful whether they could have completed another eleven
statues in the time.[4]

There is one unusual feature about the building of the New
Exchange, and this is the astonishing speed with which it was

[1] T. N. Brushfield, 'Britain's Burse, or the New Exchange', *British Archaeological Association Journal*, n.s. ix, 1903, p. 34 and plan facing p. 33.

[2] I owe this warning to Sir John Summerson.

[3] A. M. Hind, *Wenceslaus Hollar*, London, 1922, pl. xxxii.   [4] B. 29.

erected. The first stone was laid on 10 June 1608, by July it was progressing fast, and by the end of August all the arches of the main arcade were already up. The normal custom of abandoning work during the winter was evidently not observed, and by 11 April 1609 the building and interior fittings were sufficiently advanced to be ready to receive King James at a formal opening ceremony. By the autumn the shopkeepers were installed and business had begun.

The reasons for this extraordinary speed can only be guessed at. Of course, the building was a commercial venture, and the sooner it was finished and occupied the sooner a fair return would be obtained on the capital invested. On the other hand, the hasty mobilization of men and materials must have added substantially to the initial cost, and the financial motive can therefore hardly have been decisive. The most important reason must have been the wish to reduce to a minimum the opposition of the City.[1] So long as building was proceeding and the Exchange was not actually in operation, the City would probably maintain its agitation. It must be remembered that on 28 July 1608 Salisbury had introduced the New Impositions, which substantially raised the customs duties on imports.[2] All in all, Lord Treasurer Salisbury cannot have been a popular figure in City circles this year, and he probably thought it wise to press on with the building as fast as possible, so as to minimize the period of agitation against the idea of a new exchange.

This decision to push on with the maximum speed put a very severe strain on the organization of men and materials. The business arrangements for all Cecil's buildings were in the very competent hands of Thomas Wilson, who lived next door to the site, at Salisbury House. The first problem was to muster the necessary manpower. Though most of the building was of brick, the whole of the street front was faced in stone,[3] which meant that very large numbers of masons were required. At the beginning of July Basil, Wilson, and Southes made a journey into Oxfordshire, Gloucestershire, and parts of Warwickshire and Northamptonshire 'for the providing of forty masons'. But this was still not enough and at about the end of the month Southes set off on another recruiting

[1] J. Stowe, *Survey of London*, London, 1633, p. 494. N. E. McClure, *Letters of John Chamberlain*, i, p. 259. S. 195 f. 40.

[2] S. R. Gardiner, *History of England, 1603–1616*, London, 1863, i, p. 439.

[3] B. 29, 40. See also Count Magalotti's description in 1669; L. Magalotti, *Travels of Cosmo III*, London, 1821, pp. 295–6.

drive into Berkshire, Oxfordshire, Gloucestershire, Worcestershire, and Warwickshire. By now he was drawing heavily on the available skilled labour in the area, and he had some difficulty in reaching his target. He found himself obliged to take the risk of distributing small advances 'to some of the masons which were stubborn'.[1] The result was a dramatic rise of the labour force. Work began in June with 43 masons and 9 labourers in addition to an unknown but very large number of bricklayers employed on contract. The total force was probably at least 100. By early August the number of masons had risen to 64, working six days a week with two hours a day overtime 'for the more expedition of the work'. By the 11th the 40 Cotswold recruits had arrived and there were 108 masons at work, while by the end of the month the second group had swollen the numbers to the extraordinary figure of 124, a level which was maintained at least till the end of September. It looks as if a fair proportion of the skilled masons of the west midlands had been mustered, presumably at the cost of current projects at Oxford and elsewhere.

These masons were supported by large numbers of labourers, while the elaborate sculpture of the street frontage demanded a small group of highly skilled carvers. In August and September 1608 there were 175 workers on time-rates on the site, together with an unknown number of bricklayers and about a dozen joiners on contract. The total labour force at the peak period must have been about 250 in all. The most highly paid were, of course, the two leading carvers, John de Beeke (de Book or Book), who had done a lot of work at Salisbury House, and the Dutch tomb-carver, Garett Christmas, who was fully employed on the sculpture of the Exchange from the end of August until April of the next year. They received 3s. a day, their subordinate John Barker 2s. 8d., the masons between 1s. 8d. and 2s., and the totally unskilled labourers 1s. The variation in wage-rate between the least and the most skilled was therefore as much as 300 per cent.[2]

Having recruited so large a force of men, the next problem was to provide them with sufficient building stone to keep them employed. There was no chance of obtaining in a hurry sufficient quantities of a single type, and as a result a wide range of sources had to be drawn upon. The greatest reliance was placed on the monastic buildings of Saint Augustine's, Canterbury, which Cecil

[1] B. 29.   [2] B. 29, 40.

had recently acquired as a bribe for favourable treatment from the wife of the attainted Lord Cobham, the Countess of Kildare.[1] Basil, Wilson, and Southes went to inspect the site, and a demolition contractor was put in charge, with orders to pull down the buildings. The stone was sent by lighter to Sandwich whence small ships of twenty to twenty-four tons brought it to Tower Wharf in London. There it was again transhipped and sent by lighter up river to Durham House stairs. Demolition went forward rapidly, in spite of considerable opposition from the inhabitants to the destruction of the monastic gateway, and despite a shortage of money to pay the workmen due to failure to sell stone locally to cover the costs. As has already been mentioned, in the summer of 1608 520 tons of stone were obtained from this source to be used at the Exchange and at Hatfield.[2]

But this was nothing like enough. The pillars for the arcade came from Buxted, and window stone from Shadwell. This Sussex stone was sent overland by cart to Vauxhall or Lambeth, and then taken across the river to Durham House stairs by barge. More hardstone for windows and steps came from a quarry at Boughton Monchelsea, near Maidstone, and ordinary ashlar from Kent, Oxfordshire, and Yorkshire. One pillar for the arcade came from Plymouth, while Caen stone for the sculpture was bought from the royal master mason Cornelius Cure—or rather from his executors.[3] Marble for the black and white paving of the arcade gave particular trouble. Not enough Purbeck marble could be obtained quickly, despite heroic efforts to overcome transport difficulties in winter.[4] Some came from Berwick, but it still was not enough, and in October Cecil appealed urgently to his old friend Gilbert, Earl of Shrewsbury, asking him to inquire about developing a quarry in Derbyshire. Shrewsbury did his best, though the results were not very encouraging. In November he told Cecil that 'as many hands is working at the blackstone quarry in the Peak as can possibly work together, which are but a few, and so soon as is possible it shall be sent to London.'[5]

Despite all these difficulties the building was ready for the formal opening ten months after the laying of the first stone. The occasion was marked by a state visit by the royal family and the Court: 'On

[1] D. 102/40. *H.M.C. Salis. MSS.* xvii, p. 176.

[2] S.P. Dom., Jas. I, 35/35, 61; 36/12, 35. B. 29. S. 143 f. 115.   [3] B. 29, 40. A. 160/1.

[4] See above, p. 71.   [5] S.P. Dom., Jas. I, 37/27, 64.

Tuesday being the 10th day of April . . . divers of the upper shops were adorned in rich and beautiful manner, with wares most curious to please the eye. . . . On the day following it pleased his Highness, with the Queen, Prince, the Duke of York, & the Lady Elizabeth, to come thither, attended on by many great lords and choice ladies.'[1] On arrival they were presented with some of the rarities from India and China that were on display, and were entertained with a show. The text was by Ben Jonson, the scenery by Inigo Jones, and the whole entertainment cost £179.

The script of the show has not survived, but we have an outline by Thomas Wilson of the proposed programme. After a fanfare of cornets and other loud instruments an actor emerged, who represented the keeper, grumbling to himself and defending the Exchange from its many traducers. The two other actors, of whom one was masked, began to play their 'mountebank tricks'. In due course 'he shall unmask as a merchant that sells not *merces adulterinas*' and the show ended with a presentation by him of the rarities.[2]

James's chief responsibility on this occasion was to give the building a name. There had already been some discussion, and Wilson had sent Cecil a mock-serious essay on the subject. After canvassing various alternatives, such as 'Cecil Castle', 'Bell Arma', 'Salisbury Plain', and 'English Rialto', Wilson finally recommended 'The Mercurial, because Mercury is the god of merchants and of craft and cunning'. But when he arrived on 11 April James firmly baptized it Britain's Burse, a name whose overtones of Anglo-Scottish unity in one realm suggest that it was the choice of the king himself.[3]

By the summer of 1609 the finishing touches had been put to the building. The footpath of the Strand in front of the building had been paved, the joiners had built the shops, Richard Butler the glazier had made and set up five large windows, with the arms of the King, the King and Queen, the Prince of Wales, and two of Salisbury himself, and the fashionable interior decorator Rowland Bucket had given the right air of opulence to what was hoped to be one of the more attractive features of the building, an insurance office run by Wilson.[4]

Wilson, who was building himself a house abutting on the south-west corner of the Exchange, was at first in full managerial control of this commercial venture. One of his first concerns was to draw up elaborate regulations governing the shopkeepers. Leases were to be granted only to traders in clothes, books, fancy goods, perfumes, and other personal articles likely to be in high demand by an upper-class clientele. Holidays and opening hours were regulated and elaborate provisions made to prevent disputes and brawling. After only a month or two's experience Wilson had discovered the unruly nature of seventeenth-century shop-assistants and apprentices, who created disorder by 'hunting of dogs with great noise & howling, playing of foils and cudgels, striking the ball (which breaketh the windows), buffetting and fighting one with another'. These were to be punished by corporal punishment, while stocks were provided for pilferers. One of the most intractable problems was sanitation, even though a 'pissing place' had been provided and linked by a sewer to the river. Under pain of 1s. a time, traders were forbidden to 'throw or pour out into the walk or range or out at any of the windows any piss or other noisesome thing', and the porter or housekeeper was enjoined 'not to suffer pissing or other filthy thing about the house'.[1]

It was one thing to draw up regulations, another to attract the shopkeepers. John Donne might well ask

> Whether the Britains Burse did fill apace
> And likely were to give the Exchange disgrace.[2]

The shops were offered on eleven-year leases at £30 fine and £10 a year rent. This was not cheap, and from the first some difficulty was experienced in filling up the vacancies. By the autumn some twenty-seven leases had been taken up, mostly by milliners, linen-drapers, and haberdashers, but as there were something like one hundred shops altogether, this was not very encouraging. In November the resourceful Wilson analysed the causes of the trouble:

1. Want of houses to dwell in for the shopkeepers
2. The small circuit of inhabitants for buying about the place, being but one street
3. The want of stowage in their shops for their wares, the shops being as it were small chests rather than shops
4. The malice of the confederate Londoners to keep out those that would come.

---

[1] S.P. Dom., Jas. I, 49/5.
[2] H. J. C. Grierson (ed.), *The Poems of John Donne*, London, 1912, i, p. 106.

Even its author regarded the proposed solution as somewhat bold: 'haply your Lordship will smile at it as a folly'. It was to buy up the whole site of Durham House behind the Exchange, pull down the old palace, and erect 100 houses, at an estimated cost of £20,000.[1] Salisbury was already cautiously developing the west side of Saint Martin's Lane as a residential area, but he was in no position to finance so gigantic an undertaking on top of all his other building commitments. Nevertheless, he was evidently tempted by the idea of exploiting and encouraging residential building in the area, and, no doubt as an alternative to Wilson's scheme, he approached the Earl of Bedford early the next spring with a request to buy Covent Garden. Bedford had led a riotous youth and had dissipated part of his estate some time before. But his relatives and heirs had obliged him to give a series of huge bonds not to disperse any more of the entailed estate, and the Earl had therefore to tell Salisbury that it was beyond his power to meet his request.[2] So died a suggestion which might radically have altered the fortunes of the Russells and the Cecils from that day to this.

The total cost of building the New Exchange had been £10,760, to say nothing of the £1,200 paid to Toby Matthew for his lease. Since the current interest rate was 10 per cent and there were the normal costs of upkeep to be met, it was necessary for the Earls to achieve an annual income from the shopkeepers of at least £1,200 a year if they were to obtain a reasonable return on their investment. The nearest they came to achieving this figure was in the first years of the Burse's life, between 1611 and 1617. During this period direct management of the concern had been leased for £1,000 a year to a merchant syndicate of customs farmers. This was part of a very complicated transaction by which the farmers had taken over £20,000 worth of the first Earl's debts, and much of this £1,000 a year was used to cover part of the interest payment.[3]

This arrangement broke down in 1616, when the farmers of the Exchange had to have their rent reduced to £700 and Salisbury again took direct control of part of the building. Nevertheless, the gross rental seems to have remained at about £1,000 till 1620-1, when the eleven-year leases of 1609-10 all ran out. The expiry of the leases coincided with the most serious trade depression of the

[1] S.P. Dom., Jas. I, 49/6.
[2] S.P. Dom., Jas. I, 53/127; 26/34. P.R.O., L.C. 4/192, p. 385; 193, p. 327; 195, p. 201; 196, p. 143.
[3] S. 141 f. 352. Box G/13. Box S/7 f. 49. A. 128/1. D. 216/8; 244/13; 46/25.

century and the result was that new tenants could be found for
only about half the shops. The rents received in 1621 were only
£361 and although the rental crept up slowly in the next few years,
it had still not risen above £415 in 1627.[1] It is clear that the position
caused the gravest anxiety to the Earl and his advisers. In 1623 it
was reported that he had sold for £6,000 the whole of the first
floor to Lady Hatton, Sir Edward Coke's formidable and affluent
wife, to be converted into her town house.[2] But the project fell
through and it looks as if most of the upper floor remained un-
tenanted during the 1620s. And so in 1627 it was decided that
drastic measures were necessary. 'Surveys and plots' were made by
a carpenter-architect, one Thomas Avys, and the next year the
work was carried out under the direction, and presumably in
accordance with the design of, a Mr. Carter, 'the Surveyor of the
Burse building'.[3] This was probably Francis Carter, who was asso-
ciated with Inigo Jones in 1611-12, made estimates for the Banqueting House in 1619, and died in about 1630 a Chief Clerk of the
Rolls.[4] The shops were ripped out and sixteen small flats were
created. Although wash-houses were provided below, sanitation
again proved a difficult problem. The best that could be done was
to bind the tenants in their leases not to let filth or urine seep
through on to the heads of the shopkeepers below, and to institute
a 10s. fine for emptying slops out of the windows. On the whole
the operation seems to have been a fair success. This was a time of
tremendous pressure for residential housing in this area—Covent
Garden, Drury Lane, and Lincoln's Inn Fields were all being
developed just now—and within three years all sixteen of these
rather inconvenient dwellings were occupied. They were let on
twenty-one-year leases at rents of £12 to £15 a year each, with fines
varying inversely between £20 and £10, though it is noticeable that
the fines had to be waived in order to fill the last tenancies.[5] As
a result, by 1631 the Burse was showing a rental of £387 for the
ground floor and £205 for the flats.[6]

In the 1630s, however, the economic climate changed again and
the shops in the Burse began to prosper. There was no difficulty
about renewing the eleven-year leases of the shops in 1633, and by
now the outer arcade had been filled with two rows of small

[1] B. 108. A. 160/5; 17/8; 20/8; 133/1.   [2] McClure, op. cit. ii, p. 535.
[3] A. 160/6; 157/3.
[4] I owe this information about Carter to Sir John Summerson.   [5] Box S/8.
[6] A. 29/1.

wooden booths, thirty in all. Though a third less valuable than the shops in the inner walk, they nevertheless added to the total rental.[1] This revival of the Burse as a fashionable shopping centre in itself might have tempted the Earl to buy out the lessees of the flats and to reconvert the first floor back into shops. In 1638, however, there was added the pressure of royal authority. For years the Crown had been trying to control building in central London, so as to prevent insanitary overcrowding and the growth of liability to epidemics and disastrous fires. New houses had to obtain a royal licence, but this was a formality with which Salisbury had failed to comply when he built his tenements in 1628. In the 1630s the desire to raise revenue by fines for non-compliance and the determination of a strong paternalist government to enforce measures that it deemed socially desirable led to a tightening up of the regulations, and on 4 May 1638 the Privy Council ordered Salisbury to clear out the inmates of his tenements forthwith.[2] Since these official instructions were not in conflict with the economic interests of the landlord, Salisbury carried them out with a promptitude that must have astonished authorities used to more dilatory tactics. The work, which was done between Michaelmas 1638 and Michaelmas 1639, was described as 'the altering of the upper part of Britain's Burse and reducing it unto Shops', and the result is shown in Harris's engraving (Pl. VI). It cost the large sum of £1,030, all of which was spent on purely structural items, since the partitions and fittings for the shops themselves were built by the tenants in return for being given twenty-one-year leases for low fines. The alterations included the central balcony on the first floor with its large new window, and also a complete reroofing. The Jacobean gable-ends on the street were removed and there were inserted rows of simple pedimented dormers.[3] Although there is no mention of any reward to an architect, it should be noted that the carpenter employed was Richard Rider, probably the father of Captain Richard Rider, who was later to emerge as an architect in his own right.

This reconstruction of the Burse was a great success. The upper floor was rapidly occupied and rents rose from £600 to £897. Though naturally affected by the outbreak of war in 1642, rents were back to £840 by 1647 and to £890 by 1661.[4] The next twenty

[1] Box R/5.   [2] Cal. S.P. Dom., 1637–8, p. 402.   [3] A. 157/3; 135/4; 162/1.
[4] A. 161/2; 40/1; 44/1; 50/1.

years saw the Burse at the peak of its prosperity. The surrounding area was now fully built over, but was still one of the most fashionable residential areas in London. As Pepys's diary shows, the Burse became the Bond Street of post-Restoration London, with a milk-bar in the cellar frequented by lawyers on their way to Westminster Hall, and in the arcades above the smartest emporia for gloves, stockings, garters, lace, and other finery.[1] Of the 109 shopkeepers in 1657 there were 42 milliners, 32 sempsters, and 8 tiremakers.[2]

The result of this increase of business was that the profits of the Burse rose steeply. No attempt was made to raise rents, which remained fixed at 12s. to 13s. 4d. a foot frontage, but larger and larger entry fines were charged at each eleven-year renewal of the leases. In 1647–8 the fines were set at one to one and a half years of the old rent, in 1658 they were three to three and a quarter years, and by 1681 they had risen to ten or more years. About £6,000 was received in fines in 1675 and £4,700 in 1681.[3] Between 1660 and 1680 the annual average return from the Burse increased by over 50 per cent.

Soon after, however, the Burse went into a slow decline. In the first place it had to face increasing competition from the Middle Exchange between 1672 and 1694.[4] A more fundamental cause of the decay of the prosperity of the Burse than competition from its rivals was the social deterioration of the neighbourhood due to the steady westward shift of the fashionable quarter. By now the nobility and the rich professional classes had moved on to Saint James's Square and beyond, and with their departure went the economic foundation of the Burse.

As the social standing of the customers went down, the shopkeepers resorted to more dubious advertising stunts, which in the long run did more harm than good. From the start one of the attractions of the Burse had been the physical appearance of the shop-girls. As early as 1619 it was observed that

> ... thy shops with pretty wenches swarm,
> Which for thy custom are a kind of charm
> To idle gallants.[5]

---

[1] *Diary of Samuel Pepys, passim*; for the milk bar, see iii, pp. 150, 261; iv, pp. 120, 177, 241, 427; v, p. 332. The bar consisted of a series of small wainscoted rooms with benches round the walls, a store-room, a kitchen, and a scullery with sink and running water (Deeds, 203/33).
[2] A. 162/3.   [3] A. 47 A/14; 162/3; 57/12; 136/14; 136/22; 61/2.
[4] See above, p. 94.
[5] Pasquin's *Palinodia*, London, 1619, quoted in Brushfield, op. cit., p. 45.

In 1666 Pepys 'walked up and down to see handsome faces, and did see several', and he succeeded in striking up a more intimate acquaintance with one or two of them.[1] By 1699 the reputation of these shop-girls seems to have become more doubtful. Admittedly Ned Ward was a professional pornographer, but his description of his visit does not inspire confidence. 'We came to the New Exchange,' he begins, 'into which seraglio of fair ladies we made our entrance, to take a pleasing view of the cherubimical lasses, who I suppose had drest themselves up for sale to the best advantage, as well as the fripperies and toys they deal in.'[2]

What with the unsavoury reputation of the place, and the steady social decline of the neighbourhood, the Burse in the early eighteenth century fell upon evil days. Tenants could not be found for the shops, and more and more of them fell empty. The rental, which had been £936 in 1687, fell to £553 in 1721 and £495 in 1731, while fines must have dwindled away to nothing.[3] At last, in 1737, the end came: the New Exchange was pulled down, and eleven houses built on the site.[4]

The story of the New Exchange in its 130 years of existence is of considerable interest both to the architectural and the economic historian. It was the cause of the first known architectural design by Inigo Jones, which on any assessment is of great importance. And it is probable that in the more conventional building as executed we have a collaborative effort of Jones and Basil, of which the south front at Hatfield seems to provide another example. The fluctuating fortunes of the building, its optimistic beginning in 1608, its early years of prosperity, the slump of 1621, the revival in the 1630s, the mild set-back in the 1640s, the boom of the 1660s and 1670s, and the subsequent slow decay till 1737, are all closely linked with the changing economic climate of west central London. The rise and fall of the New Exchange is an illuminating episode in the steady westward drift of the world of fashion.

III. ST. MARTIN'S LANE

The third piece of urban property that the Cecils owned was some nine acres along the west side of St. Martin's Lane, which had been bought up piecemeal for under £500 by the first Earl in

---

[1] *Diary of Samuel Pepys*, iv, p. 9; vi, pp. 40, 318; vii, p. 119; viii, pp. 220, 286.
[2] Edward Ward, *The London Spy*, July 1699, p. 10.   [3] A. 138/5; 90/6.
[4] *L.C.C. Survey of London*, xviii, p. 96.

1609-10. The intention was to develop the area for residential building, and the usual policy was adopted of letting the property on building leases, which in this case ran for thirty-one years at the modest rent of 1*s*. a foot frontage. The plots were nearly all between 30 and 60 feet in width and all ran back to a depth of 220 feet. The tenants contracted to build on the sites, without restriction on size, planning, materials, or aesthetic appearance. But in order to maintain the residential character of the area, the tenant was made to promise not to practice a trade or occupation and not to set up an inn, alehouse, or stables.[1] Though there were one or two men of some distinction among the original lessees, the majority seem to have been substantial tradesmen, and it was not till the 1620s that the social status of the lane began to rise. The second Earl and his advisers were quick to encourage this trend. In the new leases clauses were inserted obliging the lessees to spend substantial sums, ranging from £50 to £400, on building in brick. As a result a fairly imposing row of town houses sprang up, and this became the most fashionable side of a fashionable street—'many genteel fair houses in a row' as they were described by James Howel in 1657.[2] To improve further the value and attractiveness of the property, in 1632-4 the Earl joined with the other aristocratic landlords of the area, the Earls of Bedford, Suffolk, and Leicester, in supplying piped water via an 'aqueduct' and a 'waterworks house' containing a cistern, and in laying a sewer to carry the dirty water along the lane and down to the Thames. His share in the undertaking came to £525.[3]

This west side of the street, with its substantial houses with modern plumbing, set back from the street by small plots of ground and each with its own garden, coach-house, and stable at the back, formed a striking contrast with the east side, which was being developed at the same time by the Earl of Bedford, where the houses were crowded, narrow, and without gardens.[4] By the 1630s the Earl of Salisbury's houses were peopled with politicians and courtiers like the Earl of Annandale, Sir James Levingston, Groom of the Bedchamber, Sir John Finett, Master of Ceremonies, Sir John Bankes, Attorney General, Sir Henry Knollys, Clerk of the Green Cloth; wealthy squires like Sir George Fane, Sir Thomas

---

[1] *L.C.C. Survey of London* xx, 1940, pp. 4–5. Box S/8. A. 160/1.
[2] J. Howel, *Londinopolis*, London, 1657, p. 350.
[3] A. 157/3; 35/2; 137/7. *L.C.C. Survey of London*, xviii, p. 25.
[4] A. B. Grosart, *Lismore Papers*, 2nd ser. iv, p. 152.

Rowe, and Sir William Ashton; and top-flight professional men
like the doctor Sir Theodore Mayerne, the painter Daniel Mytens,
and the interior decorator Rowland Buckett.

So long as the original thirty-one-year building leases lasted,
however, the Earl gained little by the prosperity of Saint Martin's
Lane. His rental for the original leases in 1612 was £40, rising to
£53 in 1617, and £108 after the new leases of 1624.[1] The 1611-12
leases all ran out in about 1642, and in 1638 the Earl's officers began
to examine the problem. They reckoned that the full rack rent from
twenty-two tenants would be over £1,000 a year by 1643. In addition there were a further eleven leases for years or lives that on
expiry would be worth another £950 or so a year.[2] In fact this
estimate was over-optimistic, partly because some of the improvement was taken in fines, or in obligations to spend considerable
sums on new building, instead of in rent, and partly because of the
depressing consequences of the outbreak of war in 1642. Although
£1,700 were taken in fines for new twenty-one-year leases, and the
rental rose to over £720 by 1643, it remained at or below this figure
until 1651. However, it had jumped to £850 by 1656 and reached
a peak of £950 in 1662.[3]

The first and second Earls and their advisors can take a good deal
of credit for this development. From the very first they had decided
that it was an upper-class housing quarter that they wanted; they
had split up the area accordingly, allowing a decent frontage for
each house and a space for gardens and stables behind; and they
had later prescribed building in brick. They and the neighbouring
aristocratic landlords had had the foresight to lay on piped water
and drainage in 1632-4 at considerable expense to themselves, and
they had further encouraged substantial building by foregoing
fines for new leases in return for expenditure on the houses in 1642.

As soon as London showed signs of recovering its role as a
great social centre after the end of the civil wars, the second Earl
was inspired by the financial success of these earlier developments
to promote further building. In 1651 he took a ninety-nine-year
lease of Waller's Building to the north of his Saint Martin's Lane
site on payment of a fine which seems to have been over £1,200.[4]
In two stages, in 1653 and 1657, the existing tenements were leased
to a building contractor, Captain Richard Rider, for a term which

[1] S. 143/f. 147. B. 108. A. 17/8; 35/2; 40/1; 150/7; 161/5; Box O/4, 5.   [2] A. 35/2.
[3] Box O/4, 5. A. 401/1; 150/7; 161/5.   [4] A. 162/2; 124/9.

was finally extended from forty-one to fifty years. Under the first agreement Rider was to improve four houses and totally rebuild two so as to make them as attractive as any 20-foot frontage house in Covent Garden—interesting evidence of the crucial role of Covent Garden in dictating standards of residential housing in mid seventeenth-century London. Rider did better than he had promised, for within four years he had pulled down all but one house and built nine new ones, and he now undertook to rebuild a further seven in substantial brick.

As a result of this project Salisbury extended his holding along Newport Street, and added an additional £72 a year to his income.[1] As with his father's initial investment in the lane, the full profit of the venture would not be reaped till the expiry of the building leases, now postponed into the next century. By 1720, however, the rental of Saint Martin's Lane and Newport Street had risen to £1,347 a year.[2]

IV. CONCLUSION

These three London properties of the Earls of Salisbury provide an illuminating example of the trends in urban development in west central London in the seventeenth century. In the reign of James I it was an area of opulent palaces of great magnates, together with some new residential housing for rich courtiers and professional men and one bazaar for luxury goods for this élite clientele. As the century progressed the fashionable centre of London moved further west, and it was necessary to adapt the accommodation in the area to the needs of lower-middle-class people. And so the great palaces were pulled down to make way for modest housing in the late seventeenth century, and the bazaar went the same way in the early eighteenth. The well-to-do houses up Saint Martin's Lane retained their opulent comfort, but lost their fashionable residents as they drifted westward to Saint James's Square and north-west to Southampton Square.

Generally speaking, the response of the Salisburys and their advisers to this rapidly changing situation was shrewd and far-sighted. Apart from the New Exchange venture, they mostly avoided putting their own capital into development. But they saw to it that the social and economic standing of the district was so

---

[1] A. 162/3; 165/1. Box O/8, 9, 10.   [2] See Appendix, p. 114.

far as possible maintained, while adjusting steadily to the changing demand. As a result the proportion of the gross family income derived from urban housing rose fairly steadily from about 10 per cent before the Civil War to 37 per cent in 1720. The London property was of critical importance in pulling the Salisburys through their prolonged financial crisis, since, unlike that of the rural estates, the income derived from it went on growing right into the early eighteenth century.

APPENDIX

London Rentals of the Earls of Salisbury

	1612 £	1625 £	1639 £	1648 £	1677 £	1685 £	1720 £	1765 £
The New Exchange	1,040	438	897	842	893[1]	893[1]		553
Great and Little Salisbury House (later Cecil Street and the Strand)	..	100	..	105	795	710	1,107	
The Middle Exchange	..	..	..	..	410	134		
Salisbury Street	..	..	..	..	255	262	256	
St. Martin's Lane	37	108	215	682	690[2]	855	–,347	
Newport Street	..	..	..	..	72	72		
Total London rental	1,077	646	1,112	1,629	3,115	2,970	3,263	2,419
Total gross landed rental	7,313	7,221	9,942	10,257	10,491	10,591	8,715	
London rental as percentage of the total	15	9	11	16	30	28	37	
References	G.11/22	A.17/8	A.36/1	A.44/1	A.55/5	A.165/1	A.90/6	A.148/16, 19

[1] Much of the increased value of the New Exchange was taken in entry fines for new leases rather than in higher rents. Between 1675 and 1681 the Earl received £10,700 in fines (A. 47a/14; 162/3; 57/12; 136/14, 22; 61/2) so that in fact gross profits from the New Exchange increased by about 50 per cent between 1648 and 1685.

[2] The rental rose as high as £950 a year in 1662, but subsequently fell away (see p. 111).

IV

CONSOLIDATION
1612–1642

WHEN Robert Cecil died in 1612, his son and heir William was twenty-one years old. He had completed his education and the Grand Tour, and had already been married for four years. He was therefore ready to take up the financial and political heritage left him by his father. For the next thirty years, until the outbreak of the Civil War in 1642, he proceeded to live the life of a great nobleman. He was neither an intellectual nor a very forceful personality, but his relative failure in the world of politics should not be attributed exclusively to these factors. For the whole of these thirty years he was fairly assiduous in his attendance at Court. He performed in the stately and expensive rituals of masque and tilt, he repeatedly entertained the royal family at Cranborne and at Hatfield, but he never managed to secure for himself any of the great offices of state.[1] In the early years the reason for this exclusion was undoubtedly a reflection of the odium in which his father was now almost universally held, and the determination of the latter's old allies the Howards to exclude the son from power. Even the fact that he was married to a daughter of the Earl of Suffolk does not seem to have helped.

A more important reason may well have been that Salisbury's religious views gradually came to differ more and more from the increasingly High-Church leanings of the Court. He had been brought up a staunch Protestant of the Elizabethan school and as he grew older his opinions seem to have hardened in a Puritan direction. He supported divinity lecturers at Hatfield and Saint Martin-in-the-Fields who certainly held radical views, and his purse was ever open to preachers, whether at the Italian church in London, at Covent Garden Church, or at Saint John's College, Cambridge. He patronized young Calybute Downing, who was to become a prominent Puritan divine in the early 1640s, he was a

[1] McClure, *Letters of John Chamberlain*, i, pp. 487, 496; ii, pp. 10, 195, 298. J. Nichols, *Progresses of James I*, iii, p. 491; iv, pp. 888, 902.

regular visitor to the pious Lord Montagu at Boughton, and his purchase of books included works like a *History of the Antinomians in New England*, and John Knox's *History of the Reformation of Religion in Scotland*.[1] By 1640 his Chaplain was John Wincop, a future member of the Westminster Assembly.

The third reason for his political failure, which may well have been partly caused by the second, was that he repeatedly managed to arouse the antagonism of powerful enemies. He was bitterly opposed by Queen Anne in 1617, and he quarrelled with Pembroke in 1621 over electoral control of the pocket borough of Old Sarum. He opposed the Duke of Buckingham in the middle twenties, and in the 1630s he quarrelled with the Queen's protégé Holland and openly sided with the Earl of Cork in his battle with Wentworth as Lord Deputy of Ireland.[2]

The Earl's first serious attempt to obtain office was in 1617, when Viscount Fenton was prepared to sell the Captainship of the Guard. There were two suitors, Sir Henry Rich, who offered 5,000 guineas, and Salisbury who outbid him by offering 6,000. Fenton declared himself satisfied with the offer, but insisted that the King's permission should first be obtained. It seems that James was agreeable and the new favourite George Villiers raised no objection, but Queen Anne threw herself violently into the fray in bitter opposition. Fenton, who was anxious not to give offence to anyone, at once withdrew his offer and announced that he would retain the office. But Salisbury did not despair, hoping to exercise pressure via Villiers, who gave him every encouragement. James and the Court had now set off on a state visit to Scotland, and Villiers urged Salisbury to join them at once in the north to press his suit in person. But Salisbury stayed at home, alleging urgent legal business, his wife's imminent confinement, and his own ill health. As a result Villiers clearly lost interest, and after maintaining his suit all the summer Salisbury finally gave way to the inevitable and surrendered his claim to Sir Henry Rich.[3]

Thereafter Salisbury's relations with Buckingham cooled as fast as the latter's influence increased, and he therefore had to be

[1] A. 128/1; 157/3; 160/5; 160/6; 161/5. *Cal. S.P. Dom., 1640–1*, p. 212. P. Seaver, *The Puritan Lectureships*, Stanford, Cal., 1970, p. 272.

[2] L. Stone, 'The Electoral Influence of the Second Earl of Salisbury', *Eng. Hist. Rev.*, lxxi, 1956, pp. 395–6. P. Warwick, *Memoirs*, London, 1701, p. 5. A. B. Grosart, *Lismore Papers*, London, 1886–8, 1st ser., iv, p. 125; v, pp. 115, 190. W. Knowler, *Strafforde Letters*, London, 1739, ii, pp. 87, 124.

[3] McClure, op. cit. ii, p. 58. Box V/2, 139, 160. S. 129 ff. 134–43; 130 f. 168; 197 f. 124.

content with such ceremonial appointments as one of the welcoming committee for the expected arrival of the Infanta in 1624, and as the recipient of a K.G. in 1625. But his popularity with Charles was evidently considerable, and he was made a Privy Councillor in 1626, despite his association with the anti-Buckingham faction in the peerage and his refusal to execute minor requests of the all-powerful favourite.[1] With the murder of Buckingham in 1628 Salisbury's chances improved, and in 1630 he obtained both a verbal and a written promise from King Charles of the reversion of his father's old office as Master of the Court of Wards.[2] But in the end he was disappointed even in this hope. The aged Master, Sir Robert Naunton, persisted in clinging on to life and office, and in the end Salisbury was obliged to settle for something else. In 1635 he received compensation for nearly a quarter of a century of assiduous attendance at Court by the appointment as Captain of the Gentlemen Pensioners. This was an office of only modest power, status, and rewards. It carried with it a salary of £360, but in addition there were the profits to be made from selling offices of Gentlemen Pensioners as they fell vacant, the current price paid to the Captain for one of which in 1624 had been £350.[3] The very detailed accounts between 1637 and 1640 contain no direct reference to such sales, but they suggest that Salisbury may have been making a profit of £500 a year or so from them, the total fruits of office therefore amounting to not far short of £900 a year.[4]

There can be little doubt that in 1642 Salisbury was a disappointed man. For thirty years he had pursued power and office at Court, but the rewards had been both tardy and meagre. In one other respect, however, he had derived substantial benefit from his influential contacts. It will be remembered that the first Earl died in 1612 leaving to his heirs a lease of the Farm of Silk Customs that still had seventeen years to run, though terminable on the death of the King, and which was sublet for six years for no less than £7,000 a year clear. It looks as if this rent was more than the business would bear, for although Salisbury seems to have been paid fairly regularly, the farm passed rapidly from syndicate to syndicate of London financiers amid cries of anguish and woe, and to the accompaniment of embittered litigation by frustrated middlemen and intermediaries.[5]

---

[1] *Cal. S.P. Dom., 1627–8*, p. 63. McClure, op. cit., ii, pp. 589, 591, 595.
[2] *Cal. S.P. Dom., 1629–31*, pp. 312, 317, 330.   [3] Bodl. North MSS. b. 24, f. 35.
[4] A. 157/3.   [5] P.R.O., Chancery Proc., Series II, Jas. I, F 6/70.

Meanwhile the Exchequer was being run by a Commission, headed by the Earl of Northampton, who, on the principle of setting a thief to catch a thief, had enlisted as his private adviser an experienced ex-customs farmer, Lionel Cranfield. Cranfield soon pointed out that very heavy losses indeed were being sustained by the Crown by the system of farming out the customs in parcels to various peers, and in 1613 there was a general forced resumption of these concessions in return for fixed annuities. And so in October of that year Salisbury was deprived of his farm and compensated with a twenty-one-year annuity of £3,000 a year.[1]

In view of the precarious state of royal finances after the failure of the Addled Parliament in 1614, it was evident that these annuities were none too secure. This consideration, and the pressing need to raise ready cash to pay off the huge debt of the first Earl, induced Salisbury to sell £2,000 and reassign £200 of his £3,000 a year.[2] When Cranfield became Lord Treasurer in 1621 and at once began a rigorous pruning of royal expenses, including a general suspension of pensions, Salisbury must have been profoundly thankful that he had already capitalized all but £800 of his annuity. All the same, the suspension was still a very serious blow indeed, and he pulled every string he knew to get Cranfield to relent. He obtained the support of the King, but Cranfield obstinately resisted, asking whether a family who had already received over £69,000 from the silk farm should be preferred to poor tradesmen who were starving in debtors' prisons for want of payment by the Crown.[3] The fall of Cranfield in 1624 resulted in a thaw in this 'frost in the Exchequer' and a new agreement was made with Salisbury. Two thousand pounds were accepted in full settlement of the arrears from the three years of frost, and the annuity for the remaining twelve years was transferred to the more reliable revenues of the Court of Wards.[4] As a result of this transfer and of Salisbury's improving position at Court, the pension continued to be paid, though often not in full, and the arrears were finally all discharged in 1638.

The full profit of the silk farm to the Earls of Salisbury from the first grant in 1601 to the extinction of the annuity in 1638 must

---

[1] *H.M.C. Sackville MSS.* i, pp. 290, 268 (this last in fact dates from September 1613). D. 216/8; 244/13. L. 33/3. Box R/4. In 1615 Salisbury obtained an additional £1,000 a year for three years, but this was apparently part of a complicated transaction relating to the repayment by the Crown of advances made on James's behalf by the first Earl to Lord Hay, to enable the latter to pay off some of his debts (G. 27/26; D. 176/10).

[2] D. 126/13, 18; 106/2. Box R/4. *H.M.C. 4th Rep.*, App. p. 255.

[3] S. 130 f. 35. G. 82/6. *H.M.C. 4th Rep.*, App., p. 300.   [4] Box R/4. D. 164/4; 126/3.

have amounted to at least £90,000. This is a striking but by no means unique example of the way in which so many of the early Stuart peerage were in one way or another becoming royal pensioners battening upon a feeble monarch and a corrupt administration. As Cranfield realized, it was this kind of parasitism that caused Parliament to refuse to vote taxes, and led to the emergence of a self-conscious country party in revolt against the system.

Salisbury's relations with the Crown were not merely those of a frustrated place-seeker and a satisfied pensioner. Several aspects of royal financial policy threatened direct harm to his interests. Thanks to the grotesque under-assessment of his property, he, like other large landowners, was virtually immune from the incidence of parliamentary taxation. His contribution by way of subsidies to the war effort between 1624 and 1629 came to no more than £775, or a mere £130 a year. On the other hand, his status and position made him an easy victim of non-parliamentary financial exactions. In 1626 he contributed £350 to the forced loan, not a penny of which was ever repaid, and worse was to follow in the period of absolute government in the 1630s. Cut off from parliamentary supplies, the Crown ransacked its armoury of rusty weapons left over from the Middle Ages. Careful combing of the records enabled it to mulct the Earl £100 in 1636 for a relief due on his father's creation as Earl in 1605. Between 1635 and 1640 he paid £309 in ship-money.

The worst blow fell in 1636 when the Royal Commissioner, the Earl of Holland, perhaps partly in pursuit of a private vendetta, found that all the ancient Rockingham Forest was still under forest law, and fined Salisbury £20,000 for his father's enclosures at Brigstock Park, carried out in good faith thirty-four years before. This ferocious judgement was evidently largely *in terrorem*, like a Star Chamber fine, and vigorous legal counter-measures and political lobbying at once began. The original patent from the Crown was formally enrolled before a justice in Eyre, a plea for a full pardon was drawn up, and a galaxy of legal talent was hired, headed by the Recorder of London and including Sergeant Hendon and the well-known Presbyterian lawyer John Maynard. Ten pounds were spent in searching the official records in the Tower and the Exchequer for legal ammunition, apparently in vain. It was less the arguments of the lawyers than considerations of political expediency which induced Charles in 1638 to mitigate the fine to £3,000 in return for a patent giving full powers of dis-afforestation. Only £1,000 of this fine had been paid by the time royal government collapsed in 1640, but to this figure must be added £77 in legal expenses in fighting the case, and £88 paid in fees to various officials at the Attorney General's office, the Privy Seal, and the Great Seal to get the patent prepared and passed.

Nor was this the end of Salisbury's contribution to the cost of absolute government. Both as tenant in chief summoned to accompany his sovereign and as Captain of the Gentlemen Pensioners, he was obliged to go in person with a considerable retinue on the two Scottish expeditions of 1639 and 1640. The cost of these expeditions, on the second of which he was accompanied by Lord Cranborne and sixteen mounted troopers equipped and paid at his own expense, amounted to nearly £4,000, of which the Crown only paid £1,500.[1] Finally, when in 1640 the Exchequer was exhausted and Charles agreed to summon Parliament and at the same time appealed to peers for loans to enable government to be carried on, Salisbury advanced £10,000, secured on the revenues of the Forest of Dean. Of this sum only £5,000 of the capital and £300 interest had been repaid before war broke out in 1642; but his position as an influential leader on the winning side enabled the Earl to extract the remaining £8,989 of capital and interest from the parliamentary financial authorities between 1645 and 1652.[2] In this he was far luckier than most of his fellow peers.

These various charges do not exhaust the demands made on Salisbury's finances by the King. His constant attendance at Court, which was essential for the pursuit of his political ambitions, forced him into a way of life which was far more extravagant than that of a nobleman who lived—on however opulent a scale—in his country seat. On the maintenance of establishment, that is food, clothes, wages, transport, purchase of necessary supplies, and normal repairs of buildings, Salisbury was spending an average of £5,100 a year in the 1620s and £5,600 in the 1630s (Appendix II). In 1635, when expenditure had been exceeding income for several years, plans were drawn up to save £800 a year by a variety of economies, such as sending the left-overs from the lord's table to be eaten at the steward's table.[3] But nothing seems to have come of it, and things went on much as before.

---

[1] A. 157/3. Knowler, op. cit. ii, p. 124. Bodl., Banks MSS. 47/15.
[2] A. 157/3; 161/5; 139/4, 5, 7, 9; 124/9. Box N/10.   [3] A. 32/6.

It is impossible to estimate how much of these huge expenditures can be directly attributed to life at Court, but the cost could hardly have been less than £1,500 a year, and may well have been as high as £2,500. Certain special occasions were particularly expensive. Salisbury spent no less than £978 in 1625 to fit out himself and his servants for the occasion of his installation as Knight of the Garter, the embroiderer's bill alone coming to £350. When he accompanied King Charles on his visit to Scotland in 1633, he spent £80 on a coach and wagon, £70 on clothing for his three footmen, and £114 on 'a mouse-coloured suit and cloak of double satin laced within and without with rich gold and silver lace' for himself. In all, the trip cost him £740. On balance, therefore, the second Earl's dealings with the Crown achieved no more than the maintenance of a rough equilibrium. The silk farm annuity and the profits of office were probably just sufficient to cover the costs of life at Court and the demands of government finance. The real gain from nearly thirty years' attendance on King James and King Charles was the financial capacity to maintain over a long period a style of living more sumptuous than even his ample private revenues could have supported.

The second great charge on the Earl's resources during these years was provision for his growing family. He himself drew for private expenses sums varying from £200 to £800 each year, while the Countess had an allowance for pin money of £600 a year, which was cut in 1631 to £400. In addition there were life annuities left by his father of £400 a year to his sister Lady Clifford, and £200 a year to his cousin Sir Edward Cecil Viscount Wimbledon. While they were still young, his children cost relatively little, and the annual expense of their upkeep was not more than £200 or £300 at most. But as they grew up and as the Countess added almost annually to their number, the problem became more serious. By the late 1620s six boys and four girls had been born, of whom only one boy had died. The first to reach maturity was the eldest daughter, Anne, who was only eleven when in 1623 Salisbury arranged to marry her with a portion of £5,000 to the son and heir of his Hertfordshire neighbour, Sir Arthur Capel. After a good deal of haggling the terms were agreed and a contract drawn up for the marriage to take place in three years time, when Anne reached the legal age of consent of fourteen. But for some reason or other, perhaps because Anne raised personal objections, perhaps because the Earl himself decided to aim higher than the squirearchy, the contract was never fulfilled.[1] Instead, in 1628 Anne became engaged to Lord Percy, son and heir of the old Earl of Northumberland. The latter, who had spent many years in the Tower thanks, so he believed, to the political intrigues of the first Earl of Salisbury, was furious when he heard of this engagement. Though Northumberland was eventually induced to give his grudging consent, in order to secure this most eligible husband for his favourite daughter, Salisbury had to pay a marriage portion of no less than £12,000, the equivalent of one and a half years of gross landed income.[2]

In the late 1630s Salisbury's sons were rapidly growing up. First they were sent to Westminster School under the care of Dr. Busby, then they spent a year or two at Cambridge, followed by a prolonged Grand Tour. The eldest son, Charles Lord Cranborne, was at Cambridge in 1634-5, at a cost of £280, and then left for three years on the Continent, during which he contrived to spend £3,150. Meanwhile his two younger brothers had also set off on their Tour, which cost over £1,500 in the next two years. The two youngest boys were fortunately still at Westminster, where Dr. Busby was charging no more than £83 a year all found for the two of them. At this rather critical moment, when the Earl's resources were fully extended, the time came to marry his second daughter Elizabeth, who was contracted to the Earl of Devonshire with a marriage portion of £10,000. Salisbury had no hope of finding such a sum out of current income or from savings, but was enabled to pay it at once by arranging a marriage for his son and heir, Lord Cranborne. He was sold to Diana, the daughter and coheiress of a Scottish courtier, James Maxwell, Groom of the Chamber, in return for the huge cash portion of £18,000 and the future prospect of considerable landed inheritance in England and Scotland. Though he had to grant an annuity of £1,000 a year to the couple for present maintenance, this windfall enabled Salisbury to pay his daughter's portion and cover the other expenses of family and politics in 1638-40. This marriage was criticized by contemporaries for its very mercenary nature, but it is difficult to see how else the Earl could have solved his financial problems during these years.[3]

[1] D. 217/5. B.M., Add. MSS. 40631 B, f. 38.   [2] Box V/11, 16, 92. S. 126 ff. 168-9.
[3] A. 157/3; 41/1. *Cal. S.P. Dom., 1638-9*, p. 622.

It should be pointed out that the advantages derived from the marriage lay not merely in the size of the portion but also in the extremely favourable terms on which it was obtained. The match was unquestionably a mean one for the Cecils, and in return for their condescension they imposed severe conditions. In return for the £18,000 portion the jointure assured to Lady Diana was no more than £2,000 a year. The ratio of portion to jointure was therefore nine to one. The contemporary value of the jointure assured to Elizabeth Cecil on her marriage the same year to the Earl of Devonshire is not known, but she was left £2,500 a year in 1683.[1] It is therefore very unlikely to have been less than £2,000, making a ratio of five to one. That is to say, the terms on which Salisbury received the £18,000 were probably nearly twice as favourable as those agreed the same year with the Earl of Devonshire for the payment of the £10,000.

There is therefore some poetic justice in the fact that in the long run the marriage was a financial and perhaps also a personal disaster. Lady Diana was recklessly extravagant and in eighteen months succeeded in running up debts of £4,000 or £5,000 in excess of her allowance of £400 a year.[2] Not merely did Lord Cranborne continue to live in a state of chronic insolvency, but also in the end the Cecils seem to have failed entirely in their attempt to obtain some portion of the Maxwell inheritance.[3] The first of the attempts to capture an heiress made by the Earls of Salisbury was not an unqualified success.

Compared with maintenance of establishment and the cost of the family, the other expenditure of the Earl was of relatively minor significance. The largest individual item were life annuities, which were running at about £1,600 a year in the early 1620s. These were partly bequests by the first Earl to old servants and friends, and partly new annuities deliberately sold by the second Earl in order to raise money to pay off the load of inherited debt. This was a very expensive way of raising money, and in about 1623 the Earl was advised to strengthen his financial position by buying back some £1,100 worth of annuities at a cost which it was hoped would be no more than £3,690. The capital for this undertaking was to come from the sale of some leasehold property, the granting of

<hr />

[1] A. 135/4. Savernake House, Ailesbury MSS. 382.
[2] B.M., Add. MSS. 11045, f. 140.
[3] A. 48/12; 49/1. L. 88/18. *Calendar of the Commission for Compounding, 1643–60*, p. 2427. L. 110/12. D. 227/17.

new leases for large fines, and the sale of wood. Some such policy was in fact embarked upon, and £245 of life annuities and their arrears were redeemed at about four years' purchase. This eased the burden, which was reduced still further by the redemption of another £200 annuity at six years' purchase in 1633. However, in the mid thirties the Earl's general expenditure was rising and, in order to keep afloat in 1636–7, he sold annuities worth £700 a year, two for one life at six years' purchase, and one for twenty-one years at nine.[1] As a result, despite substantial erosion by death, the burden of annuities in 1642 was still nearly £1,000 a year. Other fixed charges, like rent for leased land, and general administrative costs about the estate tended to rise fairly fast, from under £800 a year in the 1620s to over £1,300 in the 1630s.

The first and most critical problem faced by the young Earl in 1612 was how to deal with the debts and legacies left by the first Earl on his death. As has been explained, a vigorous policy of sale of land and annuities, and the capitalization of much of the silk farm annuity, had reduced the problem to manageable proportions by the 1620s. From £45,000 in 1612 the debt had been brought down to under £11,000 by 1616. But £20,300 spent on buying more land in Hertfordshire in 1617–18 raised it again to £14,400, a figure that could only be reduced by further sales for about £12,000 in 1617–19. By 1623, however, the bonded debt had been brought down to the very manageable level of £5,500.[2] The difficulty was to hold it there. To find the £12,000 portion of Lady Anne in 1628–9 meant temporarily raising the level of bonded debt to £11,750. Some of this was cleared by the sale of more land, most of it recently inherited from the Countess of Kildare, for £13,600 between 1628 and 1630. Nevertheless, the very high current expenditure of the Earl in the 1630s meant that he could never quite balance his accounts. The load of bonded debt crept up slowly from £7,150 in 1630 to £11,200 in 1636, and there was no prospect of paying it off until some large fines from new leases and the sale of annuities in that year enabled the bulk of it to be cleared. Two years later the huge portion from James Maxwell for once converted the Earl from a borrower to a lender. But the surplus was soon soaked up by the marriage portion of Lady

[1] G. 139/6. A. 160/5; 157/3.
[2] G. 11/22; 12/7; 139/6. A. 12/16; 14/2; 16/6; 26/7. B. 109; 110. Box S/7 f. 43. N/3. U/57. S. 143 f. 146.

Elizabeth and the £10,000 loan to the Crown, to raise part of which about £5,000 of new debt had to be incurred.[1]

It is clear that the Earl used his great powers of borrowing to give flexibility to his finances. They helped him to buy land whenever a tempting opportunity arose, allowed him to even out the violent fluctuations in his expenditure due to special demands upon his purse, and in the early 1630s enabled him to live above his income for a few years in anticipation of windfall profits from fines for new leases. Loans therefore played a useful, indeed an essential, part in maintaining the equilibrium of his finances. But they had to be paid for. After things settled down in 1620, the Earl never resorted to mortgages to secure long-term loans. So far as he was concerned, the potentialities of development of the equity of redemption firmly secured in the Court of Chancery were never exploited at all, a fact which suggests that a mortgage was still looked upon by landowners as an undesirable necessity to be avoided whenever possible. Instead, Salisbury borrowed on bonds for short terms of six months or a year, despite the trouble of frequent renewals and a constantly changing list of creditors. The lenders fall into three groups: great London financiers; friends and relatives, mostly from the upper gentry; and his own officials and servants. The interest charged was almost invariably at the statutory rate of 10 per cent before 1624, and 8 per cent thereafter, though in 1636 a neighbour, Sir Thomas Dacres, was persuaded to lend £5,000 at $7\frac{1}{3}$ per cent. As a result he found himself paying in interest the not inconsiderable sums of an average of £385 a year in the 1620s and £542 in the 1630s. In Salisbury's case this fluctuating burden of debt was supportable, and indeed positively useful, but only because it was handled with discretion and care. As soon as it rose to the equivalent of a year's landed income, it was rapidly reduced, if necessary by sale of land or rent-charges; it was mostly used to finance special operations rather than to support conspicuous consumption in excess of normal income; the burden of interest was kept down to about 5 per cent of average landed receipts; and the position was carefully checked every year with a full statement of debits and credits and the resulting balance.[2] Under these

[1] A. 27/11; 28/18; 29/1; 31/1; 32/1; 33/1; 35/1; 160/6; 157/3.

[2] These statements survive for almost every year from 1612 to 1618, 1623 to 1642, and 1651 to 1668. A. 10/6; 12/33; 14/5; 16/6; 18/6, 8; 21/2; 27/29, 11; 28/18; 29/1; 29A/1; 31/1; 32/1; 33/1; 35/1; 36/1; 37/1; 38/1; 39/1; 41/1; 47A/1; 48/1, 2; 49/5, 7; 51/10; 52/3; 53/3; 54/4; 55/1; 139/12. G. 139/6. B. 107, 109.

conditions, and given a rapidly rising landed income, borrowing could be a useful weapon in the landowner's financial armoury. But it should be borne in mind that over the twenty-one years the Earl paid nearly £10,000 in interest on loans. Any relaxation of the strict auditing, any willingness to allow the debt load to creep up above one year's income, any cessation of the upward movement of income might have led to very serious consequences.

Salisbury's success in living for thirty years the life of a great courtier and yet more or less within his income was due in considerable measure to the growth of his landed revenues. It is to the administration of the estates that we must therefore turn. The organization of staff to run his estates and household did not differ materially from that of other noblemen of the day. In charge of income was a Receiver-General, through whose hands passed all receipts except those which were paid directly into the hands of the Earl. He in turn made advances to the heads of the various spending departments, who accounted separately. These were the Steward, responsible for the household; the Clerk of the Kitchen, sometimes directly dependent on the Receiver-General for his money, and sometimes on the Steward; the Gentleman of the Horse, who accounted for all stable charges; the Gentleman of the Chamber, who paid for the privy purse expenditure of the Earl himself; and the Steward of the West Country property round Cranborne. Apart from these permanent officers in full employment, there was an auditor, who carried out an annual check of the accounts; a solicitor, who managed the numerous lawsuits that dogged all seventeenth-century magnates; and occasionally a secretary or general surveyor.

The personnel who staffed these offices were men of education and breeding, and it is clear that the fortunes of a nobleman largely depended on the wisdom with which they were selected. We have already referred to the first Earl's revealing remarks in his will, referring to his solicitor and adviser Sir John Daccombe:[1] 'In mine own estate I had been overthrown ... if he had not been.' The importance of choosing these officials carefully, and the opportunities for extortion which lay open to them, are both illustrated by the affair of the Sherfield brothers. In 1617 a prominent Salisbury lawyer, Henry Sherfield, was appointed Steward and Surveyor of the Earl's

---

[1] P.C.C., 49 Fenner (see *supra*, p. 31).

West Country lands. Henry made his brother Richard Deputy-Steward with responsibility for day-to-day running of the estates, and the two no doubt looked forward confidently to a long and profitable tenure of office. But unfortunately for them they ran across a powerful local squire, Thomas Hooper of Boveridge, who was the lessee of much of the Cranborne demesnes. In 1624 Hooper accused Sherfield of oppression of copyholders and tenants by unjust and corrupt manipulation of the manorial court. Faced with these accusations against an apparently efficient servant, Salisbury appointed a commission of three local squires to investigate the business. It is significant of the contemporary attitude towards estate management that although they could not find that his activities were against the financial interests of the Earl, they nevertheless condemned Sherfield. 'We find Mr. Richard Sherfield his courses and carriage so directly opposite to your truly noble disposition by enforcing such strict penalties and law quirks that he hath justly drawn on him the hate and ill opinion of that part of the country and will not be a fit man for you to continue as understeward, as we conceive.' The Earl accepted the recommendation, dismissed Richard Sherfield, and appointed a solicitor from Blandford in his place. Sherfield's only defender was his patron and brother Henry, who was also soon at loggerheads with the Earl, and was later to get into serious trouble by an act of fanatical puritan image-breaking at Salisbury. If Richard shared his beliefs, here is an instance of a fanaticism in religion combined with a ruthlessness in economics that were both of them at variance with the normal standards of contemporary society.[1]

The succession of an heir to the estates almost always meant a fairly drastic turnover within the administration, if only to give the new lord a chance to impose his own will without interference from his father's nominees. As a result there was considerable job mobility among these officials, and there can be little doubt that a systematic collection of the names of officers in noble households at this period would reveal a good deal of coming and going from one family to another. Thus Salisbury's future Receiver-General, John Southworth, first appears in the service of Charles Brooke, who had probably inherited him from Lord Cobham; again when his old friend the Earl of Pembroke died in 1650, Salisbury took on

---

[1] G. 71/29, 32; 81/5; 82/15; 83/6, 10, 13, 27. L. 62/11. Box S/7 f. 8; see L. Stone, *Eng. Hist. Rev.*, lxxi, 1956, pp. 395–6.

in the same capacity his Gentleman of the Chamber, Edward Jolly.[1] Other officials seem to have moved in and out of government service. The first Earl's solicitor and adviser on estate matters, Sir John Daccombe, ended up as Chancellor of the Duchy of Lancaster, while one of his agents in charge of estate management was a feodary in the Court of Wards. A more interesting appointment was that of Arthur Squibb as the second Earl's Receiver-General from 1647 to 1650. Squibb was the son of a teller in the Exchequer, had obtained the reversion of a teller's place in 1640, and had been Clerk of the Pells since 1643. After the three-year interlude in the private service of Salisbury, he moved back again to government office in 1650 as one of the Commissioners for Compounding with Royalist Delinquents. He was a man of advanced religious and political opinions and later got into trouble for his opposition to the Protectorate of Oliver Cromwell.[2]

Auditors, of course, worked for several masters, since their responsibilities were limited to a few months a year. For example, in the 1630s William Collins served as auditor for the Earl of Salisbury, the Earl of Northampton, and the Duchy of Lancaster. By the mid 1640s he was also working for the Earl of Suffolk and for Parliament.[3] The connection between the royal administration and that of the greater private estates of men holding influential political office was evidently a close one. Most of the permanent officials of the second Earl of Salisbury, however, worked their way up the ladder of promotion within the family. John Southworth began in the Earl's service as Gentleman of the Chamber in 1612, and after thirteen years was promoted to Receiver-General; Robert Forest began as Gentleman of the Horse in 1617 and became Steward of the Household in 1624; Samuel Percival began as Gentleman of the Chamber in 1644, was promoted to Steward in 1650, and finally rose to Receiver-General in 1663. In this family administration, as in the royal service, there are some signs of a growth of hereditary tenure in the seventeenth century. They are, however, remarkably few, and it is clear that the paths were kept deliberately open to outside talent. The only striking case of hereditary office-holding was that of the Stillingfleet family. In 1612 Samuel Stillingfleet entered the Earl's service as Clerk of the

---

[1] A. 162/1; 168/2.

[2] J. H. Hurstfield, *The Queen's Wards*, London, 1958, p. 236 (John Budden). *H.M.C. 5th Rep.*, App., p. 85. *Cal. S.P. Dom., 1654*, p. 272; *1663–4*, pp. 121, 582. A. 139/4, 5, 7, 9.

[3] Cambridge University Library, Dd, IX, 48.

Kitchen. By 1602 he was housekeeper at Cranborne, eventually rising to the post of Steward of the West Country estates, which he held until his death in 1661. The father of Edward Stillingfleet, the distinguished Bishop of Worcester, Samuel was the first of a long line of the same name that continued to fill offices in the service of the Earls of Salisbury in the administration of their West Country estates right up to the nineteenth century.[1]

The rewards offered to the more important of these professional servants were substantial. They claimed for all expenses, and of course obtained free board and lodging, and probably personal service as well. In addition, there were the wages paid in cash. The Receiver-General had an annuity of £60 a year in 1614, which rose in 1628 to £100. In 1650 the auditor and the Receiver-General were both paid £60 a year, the Steward of the Household £40, and the rest of the officers £20 each. Finally, some of the more favoured officers, usually the Receivers-General, were given leases on the Earl's estates, presumably on deliberately favourable terms. John Daccombe held Pyms farm in Edmonton on a lease for three lives at 1s. a year rent. Keighley held South Mimms rectory and a farm in Broxbourne; John Southworth Royden Hall manor house; and Roger Kirkham an estate in Bermondsey. Samuel Stillingfleet, the Cranborne baliff, was granted first the Priory House and later the Market House there, and ended by farming the Cranborne and Holwell tithes as well. Other officers like John Thornhill, the Gentleman of the Horse from 1640 to 1651, were sometimes retired on pensions equal to the previous full salary.[2] Although great wealth could not be amassed by professional service of the aristocracy, except by corrupt means, there can be little doubt that the sum of the emoluments was sufficient to keep these men in considerable comfort, while their possession of leases and life annuities gave them security in case of the death of their employer. There were few more attractive openings for men of small means and considerable ability in the early seventeenth century.

On the spending side the most important official was usually the Steward, who was responsible for the upkeep of the household. Between 1612 and 1623, however, the office was vacant, the Countess managing affairs in person with a budget of £1,600.

---

[1] A. 165/3; 149/18. E. B. Clarke, 'The Economic Changes in the manor of Cranborne, 1500–1652' (unpublished B.Litt. thesis, Oxford, 1939), p. 42.

[2] A. 160/5, 6, 9; 157/3; 127/11; 162/1, 2; 133/1; 135/4. Box S/8.

Thereafter the practice was dropped, and a Steward was appointed, who accounted for nearly all household expenditure. But after two years the system was again modified, and minor officers, especially the Clerk of the Kitchen, began accounting directly for expenditure in their departments, the role of the Steward being reduced to that of the advancement of imprests. The key figure in the whole system was the Receiver-General, whose control of income put him in a commanding position. For the first two years, from 1612 to 1614, this office was in the hands of an inexperienced friend of the young Earl, Captain Brett, whose untidy and scrappy jottings show clearly his unfitness to cope with the tremendous problems with which he was faced. And so in 1614 he was replaced by Christopher Keighley (or Keightley) whose first appearance was as amanuensis to the Receiver-General in 1610. It was the administrative ability of this devoted servant which was the principal cause of the Earl's stable finances and buoyant income for the next twenty years. His value was soon recognized by his master, as is proved by the £15 spent on two of the best doctors in London who were sent to attend him when he fell ill in 1618.[1] Salisbury evidently trusted him completely and gave him a very free hand. By 1624 he had got the accounting system running smoothly, but there was an obvious need to increase revenues to meet rising expenditure. He therefore withdrew from day-to-day accounting responsibility and became the Earl's secretary, with a roving commission to visit and survey estates and suggest improvements and higher rents. These duties he performed for seven years before returning to his old job as Receiver-General for the last two years of his life. The result was that when he died in 1633 the machine he had created could continue to move smoothly forward under its own impetus.

Keighley's principal achievement was to centralize the whole financial system under his own direction, and to begin new forms of accounting control. Great aristocratic estates were usually administered on a decentralized basis, with particular receivers in charge of substantial receipts and expenditure, which never passed through the central accounting machines. As a result, it was very difficult to estimate the over-all financial position at any given time, a dangerous situation could easily develop unnoticed, and peculation by officials was very hard to check. Keighley's achievement of full central control was made possible by the geographical situation of the Earl's estates. Since most of them were in the home counties there was no necessity for a separate London agent, as was the case with northern magnates like Rutland or Devonshire. Of the Earl's four houses, three of them, Salisbury House in the Strand, Hatfield and Quixwood in Hertfordshire, were sufficiently close together and to London for their households to be administered as one. All that was required for full control, therefore, was to insist that the West Country estates should be accountable to the Receiver-General, and not to a particular receiver at the fourth seat at Cranborne. As a result there was achieved a degree of central control, which may well have been unique among great estates at this period. The bailiff at Cranborne was allowed to make deductions for bare working expenses of £100 or £200 a year, but otherwise every penny was accountable to the Receiver-General.

To exploit the possibilities of this centralization, a remarkable system of book-keeping was set up. The Receiver-General's annual accounts, which comprised virtually the whole income and expenditure of the Earl, were copied into stout volumes covering several years at a time. Summary budgets were drawn up forecasting the probable income and expenditure for the next six months, and a yearly statement was made of the debt position. In addition, general reports on the financial situation and prospects together with recommendations for action were prepared from time to time. On the landed revenue side, a rental was drawn up every year, any changes with the previous year were noted, and the figures were checked against the receipts recorded in the Receiver-General's accounts. New leases were entered into lease-books so that a check could be kept on changes in the terms of letting for every piece of property.

Particular attention was paid to accurate surveying and up-to-date valuations, which were the basis of efficient land administration. This fact had been realized by the first Earl, whose experience in the surveying and mapping of his own estates by recognized specialists like John Norden and Israel Amyce[1] led to the inauguration of a similar general survey of all Crown lands as soon as he became Lord Treasurer. This is a striking example of the application to the administration of the State of lessons learned in the handling of big private estates. Complete surveys of the whole Cecil estate were carried out four times in the seventeenth century, in 1609,

[1] A. 160/9; H.M.C. Salis. MSS. xvi, p. 58. B.M., Add. MSS. 38444.

1618, 1642, and 1674,[1] in addition to which particular valuations of individual properties were continually being made to serve as a guide to determining leasing policy. For example, in 1625 Keighley surveyed Hatfield Woods and Redrith; in 1626 he was measuring Bermondsey with a chain; in the same year he travelled down to the West Country and inspected the Dorset and Cornwall estates; those in Suffolk were surveyed in 1627, and in 1638 two whole months were spent in going over the Cornish property. Bermondsey, Redrith, Ruislip, and Brigstock were surveyed in 1632–4, Hadham in 1638, and Ruislip again in 1642.[2]

The second basis for efficient estate management, particularly in an age of confused land tenures and dubious copyhold rights, was the keeping of efficient records, particularly court rolls and other evidences of tenure. Money was spent on making careful investigations of official public records, and on taking copies. We find the Exchequer being searched in 1629, and the Tower of London in 1631. In 1632 the Auditor, Collins, was searching the Tower, the Exchequer, and the Augmentations Office. Once discovered, the evidence was carefully recorded. In 1621–3 there was being compiled a 'book of tenures for his Lordship' and 'a book of the most part of his Lordship's estates'.[3] In 1624 a clerk was making an abstract of Court Rolls, and in 1632 some were being engrossed. In 1635 Collins was transcribing an old survey of Cranborne on to parchment for its better preservation. Nor was all this information allowed to accumulate haphazardly in the muniment room at Salisbury House. In 1633 and 1634 Collins spent the whole of the two long vacations in sorting them out and arranging them; in 1636 more papers were transferred from the Earl's solicitor's office, and in that year a handlist was drawn up as a guide to the whole collection.[4] Within the limits set by the contemporary system of accounting, there can be little doubt that the finances of the second Earl of Salisbury were administered with the greatest possible efficiency. They were certainly among the very best-run aristocratic estates in England.

One would have supposed that in this inflationary period so efficient an organization would have made every effort to supply the needs of the kitchen so far as possible from the Earl's own

---

[1] Box Q/2. Box S/7 ff. 41–2. A. 160/1; 128/1; 133/1; 135/4; 133/5. The purchase in 1686 by the Cranborne agent of a theodolite and other modern surveying instruments must have led to still greater accuracy (G. 92/36).

[2] A. 160/5, 6; 157/3.   [3] This must be Box S/7.   [4] A. 160/9.

estates. This could be done by taking tithes in kind, by leasing near-by farms in return for rents in kind, or by running a large home farm. The second of these alternatives was never adopted by Salisbury and he seems rarely to have adopted the first. The corn tithes of Hatfield, which amounted to up to £400 a year in value, were usually either sold on the ground, or threshed and then sold. There remained the home-farms, which were operated at Quixwood and at Hatfield. At Hatfield in 1625 there were kept about 150 sheep, and the value of the crop was about £500. At Quixwood nearly 200 acres were under the plough, and some 350 sheep were kept.[1] But these farms were too small to contribute more than a modest proportion of the considerable needs of the Clerk of the Kitchen. Consumption was running at up to 50 beeves and 600 muttons a year, and correspondingly large quantities of other foods, but it was only in corn and hops from the Hatfield hop-yard that supply from the home-farm played a substantial part. As a result, the average value of home-grown provisions used by the kitchen between 1628 and 1639 was only £218, or under 10 per cent of the total expenditure on food.[2] But the home-farms also provided the feeding stuff for the horses, the value of which rose from about £60 a year in the early 1630s to over £200 in the late 1630s and 1640s, the fuel and straw for the hounds, amounting to between £20 and £40 a year, and £50 worth of hay and straw for the wagon team at Hatfield. The total value of the provisions in kind thus came to about £500 a year in the late 1630s (together with about £160 worth of wood for fuel), against which must be set the £250 spent on husbandry on the home-farms. But the wisdom of continuing this practice was seriously questioned, for in 1642 it was proposed to sell the stock and let Quixwood for twenty-one years, a project that was actually put into operation in 1649.[3] The evidence would suggest, therefore, that the home-farms at Hatfield and Quixwood supplied a good deal of the needs of the household in hops, corn, hay, and straw, though at all times this only formed a small proportion of the total expenditure on food-stuffs.

Since demesnes played so modest a part in the finances of the second Earl of Salisbury, it is evident that the main emphasis in estate management lay in leasing policy. The picture is a compli-cated one, however, since a very important section of the Earl's

[1] A. 47A/18; 18/4, 17; 21/3; 45/8.   [2] B. 110. A. 27/23; 29A/1; 30/1; 157/3; 162/2.
[3] A. 157/3; 161/4, 5; 35/1; 41/1; 44/13; 135/4.

landed income came from two highly specialized types of property: two blocks of urban housing, and two large pasture ranches, one for sheep and the other for cattle. The detailed history of the former has been told above and need not detain us here.[1] Suffice it to say that it contributed an increasingly important share in Salisbury's landed revenues, the proportionate share of net rental rising from 16 per cent in 1612 to 29 per cent in 1683.[2]

Year	Total net rental	Urban rental	Per cent of total
	£	£	
1612	6,716	1,080	16
1643	9,971	1,747	18
1666	9,706	2,162	22
1683	10,155	2,902	29

The first of the two great pasture ranches was Brigstock Parks in Northamptonshire. It has already been explained how the first Earl acquired the property from the Crown and ruthlessly enclosed it in the face of bitter local opposition.[3] In 1612 all the 2,200 acres were let for twenty-four years to come to a single tenant at a rent of £1,209 a year.[4] When this lease expired in 1636 a new policy was adopted. As early as 1632–3 a complete new survey was made and a map drawn, and when the lease expired £380 was spent on fresh enclosures dividing up the old closes. Thanks to the survey it was possible to vary the rent according to the quality of the ground, and a mass of new twenty-one-year leases were made for the individual closes, at rents that ranged from 12s. to 22s. an acre. Although a number of the closes were now let to small men, several were taken on by a local gentleman, Laurence Maidwell of Geddington, and many by a single great sheep-farmer, Nicholas Jackson. £1,267 were levied in fines, and the gross rental was raised to £1,830, but this high figure could only be achieved at the cost of certain concessions. This was the heyday of prerogative rule, with the Crown straining every nerve to raise non-parliamentary taxes, and Salisbury only succeeded in getting these high rents by guaranteeing the tenants immunity from ship-money, forest fines, reliefs, and all other taxes except parliamentary subsidies.[5] By this clause the landlord was given a direct financial incentive to work

---

[1] See above Ch. III.   [2] G. 11/22. A. 40/1; 54/6; 59/1. See Appendix I.
[3] See above pp. 38–40.   [4] A. 133/1.   [5] A. 135/4; 157/3; 161/1, 2, 4.

for the restoration of parliamentary control of taxation, and it would be interesting to know how widespread was this device. It was a concession well worth making, for royal rule collapsed four years later, and it helped to achieve an increase of rent of about 50 per cent. In 1643 Brigstock represented nearly 18 per cent of the total net rental.[1]

The second great block of pasture land owned by the Earl was at Bermondsey and Redrith, on the river-side flats along the Surrey bank of the Thames. This valuable property was part of the Theobalds exchange grant, but its immediate value was very limited since in 1587 Queen Elizabeth had granted a reversionary lease of twenty-one years after 1615 to Sir William Gardiner at a rent of £68 a year.[2] Already by 1612 the Earl's surveyors reckoned that the property was worth no less than £932 a year more than the rent, which is some indication of the astonishing ineptitude—or generosity—in the administration of Crown lands as conducted by Lord Burghley. In 1636, half a century after the Elizabethan grant, the lease at last expired and Salisbury was free to develop the property and to demand a realistic rent. As usual, careful surveys were made, and as a result £2,672 was taken in fines, and the rental rose overnight from £68 to £1,071. Along the river bank were a series of wharfs and tenements, all of which were now relet on thirty-one-year leases with obligation to rebuild or new build. The main income, however, came from the pastures, which were let out for twenty-one years to big London graziers and butchers. The value of these pastures as holding areas for fattening cattle for the London meat trade may be gauged by the fact that they were rented at between £2 and £3 an acre, together with fines that amounted to nearly two years' rent.[3]

It is clear that the Earl's policy towards his two great ranches was both far-sighted and shrewd. He had assured future growth by avoiding the temptations to reap immediate cash profits in very large fines at the expense of rental income, while careful surveying enabled him to extract the highest possible rent. As a result, in 1643 the rental of the London estate and of these two great pasture areas amounted to £4,606, or nearly half the total rental, to say nothing of the substantial sums that were periodically being collected in the form of fines for new leases.

---

[1] See Appendix I.   [2] L. 233/14. A. 133/1.
[3] G. 11/22. A. 161/2, 4; 157/3; 36/1; 135/4.

The remainder of the estate was fairly sharply divided into two groups: those in the east, mainly in Hertfordshire and Essex; and those in the west, mainly in Dorset and Wiltshire. The former were intensively cultivated, many of them had been enclosed long ago, and many of the copyholders had by now been transformed into leaseholders; the latter were still largely unenclosed, and copyholders predominated. Fortunately for the Earl, the custom of the manor on all of these estates left fines for new copyholds subject to negotiation. The type of lease current in the two areas differed completely, leases for years, usually twenty-one, being almost universal in the east, and leases for lives, usually three, in the west. As Samuel Stillingfleet wrote to Auditor Collins in 1634 'here with us lives are esteemed better than lease'.[1] This conservatism in the west powerfully affected the landlord's freedom of action and as a result the profits from the estate had to be taken far more in increased fines than in increased rents. Moreover, the convention that three lives was the equivalent of only twenty-one years was certainly not true by the early seventeenth century, so that the effective length of leases tended to be longer in the west than in the east and the calculation of the fine was based on a false premise. Owing to this difference in leasing policy and the variations between the relative importance of fines and rents, no precise calculation of the increased returns of the various properties is possible. It seems likely, however, that the upward movement in the west was rather slower than in the east. Excluding the special cases of Brigstock, Bermondsey, and London, on those individual properties in the east for which records have survived, rents on leases set in 1640–55 were 45 per cent more than the rents on leases set in 1610–25, whereas in the west the difference was only 5 per cent.[2]

Although this discrepancy was compensated for in part by increased fines, it is improbable that they fully bridged the gap. Moreover the difference between rents and real value in the western lands was widening steadily under the inflationary pressures of the age, which meant that the proportion of income received in fines grew steadily larger. Only a determined effort begun by Keighley in the early 1630s to change copyholds into leaseholds made it possible to begin to redress the balance.[3] An-

[1] G. 89/20.
[2] The evidence for the individual leases comes from A. 133/1; 160/9; 161/4; 162/1, 3, 4. Box S/8. By 1648 the Earl's officers were apparently reckoning three lives to be the equivalent of thirty-one years (A. 135/4).   [3] E. B. Clarke, op. cit., pp. 101, 107.

other consequence of the traditions of the west was that holdings hardly ever fell vacant, as it was normal practice to exchange old lives for new or grant new lives to add to existing ones, whereas in the east the leases were usually allowed to run their course. Only at Ruislip, where leases in the 1630s were made for no more than twelve or thirteen years at a time, was it customary to negotiate for renewal three or four years before the expiry of the old lease.

Surveying notes suggest that in the bargaining that preceded any agreement, the landlord by no means always had it his own way and was usually obliged to accept a fine somewhere between the one demanded and the one offered by the tenant.[1] There is reason to believe that on these estates fines were already being calculated in a scientific way. Certainly valuations were regularly made and the fine worked out in terms of years' purchase of the difference between value and rent. In the east, for example at Roydon in 1638, or Bermondsey in 1657, the practice was to increase rents rather than exact larger fines. Where the fines were raised, however, the Steward was probably using one of the books of tables based on varying rates of interest that were now coming on the market. Indeed the first of these tables ever published, which came out in 1622, specifically stated that the recommendations therein contained were already being used by the Earl of Salisbury in managing his estate. And so we find him asking a four years' purchase for a reversion of thirteen years after two at Ruislip in 1633, and ten years' purchase for twenty-one years at Bermondsey in 1657.[2]

There is no evidence whatever of any striking innovations introduced by Salisbury into his agricultural estates, no large-scale conversion to pasture, no throwing together of holdings, no evictions. From first to last he seems to have been concerned to extract the utmost that was his due without involving himself in any major capital expenditure and without disturbing the existing social framework. Standard provisions were drawn up for leases, which made the tenant responsible for all repairs to buildings, and for hedging and ditching. The fertility of the soil was safeguarded by clauses enforcing the use of all dung and the folding of sheep on the property itself, and prescribing one year fallow in every three. Moreover the tenant was prevented from ploughing up pasture to

[1] Box R/5.
[2] T. Clay, *Briefe Easie and Necessary Tables*, London, 1622. A. 47A/14; 48/11, 112/8. Box R/5.

reap a quick profit at the expense of the long-term values.[1] When capital investment was needed, usually for new farm buildings but occasionally for new enclosures, the tenant was made responsible for carrying out the work, in return for the waiving of part or all of the fine. As a result overheads were negligible, the cost of improvements being concealed in a reduction of casual profits.[2]

The policy of adjusting rents wherever possible, and of avoiding capital commitments by reducing fines instead, meant that the balance of income between rents and fines was kept at a reasonable level. Between 1629 and 1635 casualties, which included substantial sums for the sale of woods, amounted to $14\frac{1}{2}$ per cent of total landed receipts; between 1636 and 1642 they rose to 25 per cent owing to the exceptional circumstances of 1636-7 when in order to clear off debts the renewal of leases at Brigstock, Bermondsey, and for some tithes in Cornwall was made to bring in over £6,000; but between 1650 and 1656 they were back again to 14 per cent.[3]

Years	Duration years	Rents due	Casualties due	Total receipts	Casualties as per cent of total receipts due
		£	£	£	
1629–35	7	51,882	8,838	60,720	14·5
1636–42	6	60,419	20,056	80,475	25·0
1650–6	7	73,185	11,812	84,999	14·0

The extraordinary fluctuations in the level of fines, not merely from year to year but even from seven years to seven years, and even on a particularly well-managed estate, is evidence of the impossibility of making any precise calculation of the movement of land yields in a period of beneficial leases, and of the unreliability as a guide to income either of the bare rental or a single year's receipts.

A final aspect of the Earl's administration of his agricultural land before the Civil War is the increased attention paid to semi-obsolete feudal dues. In the same way that the House of Commons was using antiquarian lawyers to delve into medieval records to supply ammunition with which to assault the prerogative, and that the

---

[1] 'Observations in all my Lorde's leases' (S.P.15/39/140). The lease-books prove that these clauses were in fact used.

[2] This device was employed, for example, at Hatfield, Essendon, Hoddesdon, Little Hadham, Redrith, Bermondsea, Cranborne, Rockborne, Brownsea Island, and St. Michael's Mount (A. 160/9; 161/4; 162/1, 3; 135/4; Box S/8). The only important exception was the enclosing and subdivision of Brigstock Park (see above, pp. 39-40).

[3] A. 157/3; 161/5. Box N/10. A. 124/6, 9; 162/2; 48/1, 2.

Crown was also using the same methods to rebut the charges and to devise novel forms of taxation, so some private landowners in turn became aware of the potential value of such researches for increasing income from their tenants. The first hint of this new approach appears in 1625 when the Cranborne tenants were instructed to grind all their corn in the lord's mill. But in 1627, when Keighley had leisure to look around him and inqure into details of the Earl's estates, his attention was drawn to the Honour of Gloucester. This was a rag-bag of feudal rights attached to the medieval Honour, which had come into royal hands via Edward IV, and which had been sold by the Crown in 1610–12. The Earl of Salisbury bought the rights in Dorset, Wiltshire, and Somerset, which in 1627 were on long lease to the ubiquitous Henry Sherfield. Sherfield was therefore bought out for £200, and in 1629 researches were carried out in the royal archives in the Exchequer and the Tower to find out exactly what was involved. It appeared from the medieval records that on land held of the Honour as fragments of Knights' Fees the Earl could exercise the powers of wardship and could levy a relief at every death. Armed with copies of these records, Keighley promptly began to reassert these long-forgotten rights over some of the gentry of the west, including men as influential as Sir John Strangways, Sir Thomas Trenchard, and the Earl of Suffolk. As a result, the receipts from this source over a period of six years from 1631 to 1637 suddenly rose from about £20 a year to nearly £80 a year. But after 1637 receipts fell back to their former level, possibly in response to rising public indignation at the exploitation of similar ancient rights by the Crown.[1]

Profits from this enterprise were therefore both insignificant and impermanent, and hardly compensated for the political opprobrium they aroused or the research and administrative time they consumed. On the other hand, the process provides an interesting example of the way private landowners in the 1630s were imitating the Crown in trying to revive long obsolete medieval precedents in order to increase current income.

What was the net result of all this activity in terms of increase of receipts from land between 1620, when the pattern of the estate at last stabilized, and 1640? The issue is complicated by a certain

---

[1] G. 56/1. A. 160/5, 6, 10; 157/3; 161/4; 162/1; 135/41. Box N/10. Box S/8. Even in the 1650s the Earl continued to extract as reliefs from hundreds of individuals petty sums ranging from 1d. to 2s. 6d. (A. 46/1).

amount of buying and selling that went on spasmodically throughout the 1620s and 1630s. £3,000 was raised from land sales in
1622–4, no less than £15,000 in 1627–30, a good deal of it for land
just inherited from the Countess of Kildare, and another £2,000
for Saint Michael's Mount in 1640. On the other hand, there was
a trickle of minor purchases in the 1620s to round off existing properties or to buy in leases; £740 was spent on a wood at Hatfield
in 1637, and in 1641–3 three Hertfordshire manors were bought for
£7,300. On balance, between 1625 and 1643, about £200 a year
more land was sold than was bought. Nevertheless the gross rental
between these years rose from £7,221 to £10,486, an increase
which, allowing for this £200 a year, amounts to just on 40 per cent.[1]
Since fines formed a larger proportion of income in the 1630s than
in the 1620s, it is evident that this figure underestimates the full
rise, which may well have been of the order of 50 per cent or so.
Although one-third of the increase was due to the abnormal circumstances of the Crown lease of Bermondsey, the remainder was
the result of steady administrative pressure to increase the yield
wherever possible. As a result, the average gross income from land
was over one-third higher in the 1630s than it had been in the
1620s.[2] For the efficient but not oppressive landlord—and Salisbury
was unquestionably that—the generation before the Civil War was
a period of growing prosperity.

    This pressure in the period before the war to increase landlord
profits at the expense of the tenants nevertheless carried with it
certain dangers, of which the greatest was that the latter might be
forced into a position in which in bad years they would be unable
to pay the rent. There is some evidence to suggest that this was
happening. How far the appalling year 1619–20 affected arrears we
cannot tell, since a new set of accounts with a clean sheet was
begun in 1621. Between 1621 and 1625 arrears were running at a
mere £467 a year, which is only about 6 per cent of gross receipts.
None had to be written off as irrecoverable, and all were collected
within the next accounting year. It was not until the bad harvest
of 1629 that the problem of arrears began to get serious. Arrears
of £311 from the previous year were still unpaid, to which was
added a further £532 for the current year. By 1630 the total arrears
amounted to £1,344, and it was never again possible to reduce
them to the previous level. The 1630s were generally years of poor

[1] See Appendix I.   [2] See Appendix II.

harvests and high prices, which seem to have benefited the farmer as little as the consumer.[1] Arrears now dragged on and on, a steady £100 or so had to be written off every year, and yet still the totals mounted. From 1629 to 1638 they were running at an accumulated rate at the year's end of £1,195 or 12 per cent of gross receipts. This may be partly due to delay in paying the heavy fines levied during these years, but the still more dramatic rise in the next three years is not open to such explanation. Although over £250 was written off every year, the accumulated arrears still shot up from £1,272 in 1638 to £3,301 in 1641, so that in the last year before the outbreak of war accumulated arrears amounted to 30 per cent of gross receipts, and the arrears for that year alone to 20 per cent.

The contraction of business activity in the City, the hoarding of money during the growing political crisis, the slump in the cloth trade, and the fall in the price of wool all had their effect on the income of farmers. Moreover, the collapse of central government in 1640 meant a slackening of social control in the countryside, expressed most dramatically in enclosure riots, and perhaps more effectively by a growing refusal to pay full rents, as on the Salisbury estates. The second Earl and his advisers had created a strikingly efficient system of accounting, and had succeeded in significantly increasing the return on the property. They had refrained from socially destructive actions such as large-scale enclosure and eviction, they had even removed effective but extortionate officials like Sherfield, but in the end the weight of such efficiency seems to have been pressing too hard on the tenants. During and after the war, the latter were to take their revenge.

[1] B. Supple, *Commercial Crisis and Change in England, 1600-1642*, Cambridge, 1960, pp. 125-31.

APPENDIX I

Rentals of the Estates of the Earls of Salisbury

	G. 11/22 1612	A. 17/8 1625	A. 40/1 1643	A. 54/6 1666–7	A. 165/1 1683–4
	£	£	£	£	£
Hertfordshire	1,664	1,935	2,335	2,429	2,914
The West Country	647	1,081	1,267	1,235	1,161
Northamptonshire (Brigstock)	1,200	1,209	1,787	1,327	1,405
Surrey (Bermondsey, Redrith)	68	68	1,071	903	902
Rutland (Essendine)	204	281	321	309	269
Essex	214	495	588	606	578
Middlesex	1,513	935	931	985	393
Kent	545	306	436	450	..
Suffolk	78	260	3	3	..
Lancashire and Derbyshire	101	..	..	..	..
London	1,077	651	1,747	2,162	2,962
Total gross rental	7,311	7,221	10,486	10,409	10,584
Fee-farm rents and rents due for land held on lease	597	?	515	703	429
Total net rental	6,714	..	9,971	9,706	10,155
Value of lands in hand	..	..	..	..	629
Casualties	..	..	..	1,000+	1,119
Total net landed income	..	..	..	..	11,903

APPENDIX II

Receipts and Expenditure of the Second Earl of Salisbury, 1621–1641

(*A. 160/5, 6; 157/3; Box N/10*)

i. RECEIPTS[1]

	(10 years) 1621–30 average p.a. (to nearest £10)	(10¾ years) 1630–41 average p.a. (to nearest £10)
	£	£
Landed rents and casualties due	7,870	10,580
Annuity (in lieu of silk farm)	680[2]	600[3]
Sale of land	1,780	190
Sale of annuities	. .	510
Sale of plate, stock, and wood	100	160
Repayment of debts due and interest	60	1,010[4]
Marriage portions	. .	1,790[5]
Payment by Crown for the Scottish expedition	. .	90[6]
Borrowed on bond	2,660	3,070
Cash received from the Earl	. .	130
Miscellaneous	110	160
Total receipts in the year	13,260	18,290

[1] With one important exception these are actual receipts during the year and ignore the cash balances in the accountant's hands and the arrears carried over from year to year, which swell the nominal total under the system of 'charge and discharge'. These arrears are accounted for in different ways in the different account books and great care is necessary in order to separate them. The exception is that these figures represent rents *due* in these years, and not current rents received plus arrears paid in from the previous year. Thus any rise in arrears, such as occurred from 1627 to 1630 and 1638 to 1641, is effectively concealed. Owing to the rise in the level of arrears from £353 in 1621 to £3,015 in 1640 actual cash receipts were rather less than here stated.

[2] The £2,000 paid in discharge of arrears in 1625 does not appear in the accounts, but has been added in.

[3] The £660 which was satisfied by remission of debt to the Crown in 1636 does not appear in the accounts, but has been added in.

[4] This consists of the repayment of loans made in 1639 to the Crown and to others out of the Maxwell marriage portion.

[5] This figure is made up of £2,000 repaid by the Earl of Northumberland in 1632, and £17,050 paid by James Maxwell in 1639.

[6] £981 paid in 1638–9.

ii. EXPENDITURE

	(10 years) 1621–30 average p.a. (to nearest £10)	(10¾ years) 1630–41 average p.a. (to nearest £10)
	£	£
Maintenance of establishment		
(Household, chamber, kitchen, stable, purchase of necessaries, wages, and upkeep of houses)	5,080	5,620
Maintenance of family		
Cash drawn by Earl	340	260[2]
Allowance to the Countess	600	380[3]
Education and maintenance of children	120	730[4]
Marriage portions	1,200[1]	900[5]
Annuities to Lady Clifford and Viscount Wimbledon and daughters	560	590
Total family expenditure	2,820	2,860
Rents for lands on lease	400	500
Management costs of estate (fees, costs of court-keeping and litigation, and repairs)	370[6]	820[6]
Costs of demesne farming		210
Annuities	111	640
Legal and illegal taxes and exactions	80	170
Loans to the Crown	40	930
Scottish journey, 1638–9		370[7]
Repayment of loans	2,110	3,140
Interest	390	540
Loans to others		600[8]
Purchase of land or annuities, and fines for new leases	340	610
Miscellaneous (gifts, rewards, charity, sport, debts to officers, etc.)	540	560
Total	12,280	17,570

[1] £12,000 in 1638–9 for Anne Cecil on her marriage with the Earl of Northumberland.

[2] After 1635 these advances ceased since the Earl received personally his fees and the other profits of his office as Captain of the Gentlemen Pensioners.

[3] The allowance was reduced to £400 in 1631, and was not paid regularly.

[4] The true figure is rather greater, since between 1631 and 1633 this item is concealed in the figure for the household.

[5] £9,736 in 1638–9 for Elizabeth Cecil, being her portion of £10,000, less rebate of interest for payment in advance.

[6] To this figure should be added an extra £100 a year or so, which was deducted at source by the bailiff at Cranborne. It includes the cost of remodelling the New Exchange in 1628–9 and 1638–9. The 1621–30 figure is incomplete, since some of the farming costs were paid by the Steward of the Household.

[7] £3,957 in 1638–40.

[8] £6,500 in 1638–9.

V

DECAY
1642–1733

I. CIVIL WAR, 1642–1660

DESPITE the ominous rumblings, in 1640 the financial situation of the Earls of Salisbury had never been better. The second Earl's income was now so large as to be amply sufficient for his current needs, while his official position defrayed most of the extraordinary expenses involved in life at Court. With the collapse of authoritarian monarchy in 1640, however, his political position became increasingly embarrassing. As a moderate puritan he must have detested the Laudian movement, and as a property-owner and a conspicuous victim he was glad to see an end of such arbitrary taxation devices as forest fines. On the other hand, as Privy Councillor, courtier, and office-holder, he had intimate ties with King Charles. As extremist opinion forced Crown and Parliament further and further apart, the dilemma of the moderates became increasingly acute. The hope of using Bedford as a compromise leader collapsed with his death, after which the Commons twice asked the King to make Salisbury Lord Treasurer. But there is little to show that the latter was a man of sufficient calibre for the delicate task of reconciling the nation and averting civil war, and in any case the King refused. As the political crisis deepened Salisbury seemed to be continuing to side with the opposition, while so many other moderate Parliamentarians were swinging back to the King. He even voted with the opposition on the critical issue of control of the militia.[1]

But in the spring of 1642, when Charles left London for York and began preparations for open war with Parliament, Salisbury still did not know which way to turn. Loyalty to a monarch he had served for seventeen years, fear of loss of an office on the acquisition of which he had spent a lifetime of intrigue, and doubts about the extremist views of the Commons leaders drew him to

---

[1] *H.M.C. Buccleuch (Whitehall) MSS.* i, p. 287. *Journals of the House of Commons*, ii, pp. 248, 326.

York. His old resentment at failing to get the Mastership of the
Court of Wards, his growing Puritan sympathies, his dislike of
Charles's Catholic supporters, the pressure of his closest friends,
particularly his son-in-law, the Earl of Northumberland, the brutal
fact that the bulk of his revenue came from the Home Counties
which Parliament would probably control, all tended to keep him
in London. And so he dithered. At the summons of the King he
secretly deserted Parliament and fled north. But his reception was
not very warm, he found himself in doubtful company, and he was
bombarded with letters from Northumberland, who had firmly
decided to throw in his lot with Parliament. On 31 May the latter
bluntly told Salisbury that 'the only way to redeem what you have
lost is to do all good offices whilst you stay at York, and to return
hither again with all convenient speed'. A week later he warned
him that unless he returned promptly he would render himself liable
to severe censure from Parliament. Working busily behind the
scenes, he arranged for the peaceful return of the prodigal. 'If your
Lordship will speedily return I dare confidently say that you shall
not suffer any kind of censure from our House for what is past.'
A few days later he could promise 'a very hearty welcome both
from Parliament and from your own particular friends'.[1] Reassured
by these messages, Salisbury slipped quietly away from York and
galloped south again, announcing to the world that he set his
conscience above his office.[2] Soon after his arrival in London he
received a letter from the Earl of Dorset in York, written in a far
less ebullient tone than those of Northumberland. Dorset begged
him to remain neutral and to do his best to patch up a settlement.
'This fatal fire once kindled, who knows how to quench the flames,
or when or whether the conflagration may extend? . . . Men only
either of desperate fames or fortunes can promise themselves any
amelioration of condition by such broken and distract ways.'[3]

Though high in Parliamentary counsels by reason of his rank
and position, and though one of the commissioners in all peace
negotiations, there is little evidence to show that Salisbury exercised much influence over events. Nevertheless, he was one of the
few peers who played the Parliamentary game to the bitter end.
He even conformed sartorially to the fashions of the time, all the
suits he bought in 1646-7 being 'sad-coloured'. The decision to

---

[1] S. 131 ff. 176-81.   [2] H.M.C. Buccleuch (Whitehall) MSS., i, p. 305.
[3] S. 131 f. 182.

put on trial and to execute the King was too much for most moderate Parliamentarian noblemen to swallow, and they prudently withdrew to their country seats. But Salisbury actually got himself elected to the Rump in 1649 after the abolition of the House of Lords. His persistent service of the regicide regime is either evidence of a time-saving desire to retain political influence at all costs or of a growing religious fanaticism. In any case, so committed had he been to the Parliamentarian cause that it was only with a good deal of difficulty that in 1660 he managed to avoid being specifically exempted from the Act of Oblivion.[1] He was lucky to survive the political storms of the mid century.

Having finally chosen his side in 1642, Salisbury stuck grimly to it throughout the war and the Interregnum. What good did it do him? He certainly enjoyed all the excitement and prestige of being at the centre of the political scene throughout the whole of the 1640s. In 1645 the Commons decided to ask the King to make him a Marquis for his pains, but the request was turned down, and the family had to wait nearly 150 years before the chance came again. In terms of money, he persuaded the Rump to pay him £2,150 as war-time arrears of his fee as Captain of the Gentleman Pensioners of a King against whom he was fighting. He also extracted a promise, which the Protectorate failed to honour, of £5,361 in compensation for certain residual rights still claimed concerning the Theobalds exchange of 1609.[2] And he was sufficiently well placed to see that he received from Parliament the whole of the £10,000 loan made to the King in 1640, plus the accumulated interest. Perhaps equally important were the negative gains, the avoidance of the kind of misfortunes which happened to so many of his fellow peers. He was not liable to a heavy fine as a Royalist delinquent, and he could do something to protect his property from the casual depredations of the Parliamentary troops. He fended off an attempt by Sir William Brooke, George Brooke's son and heir, to seize by force some of the ex-Brooke estates in Kent; he got his parks in Hertfordshire freed from the monthly assessment, he fought for immunity from assessments for setting forth soldiers and finding arms, he protested at free quartering of soldiers on his estates.[3]

[1] H.M.C. 5th Rep., App., pp. 194, 207.
[2] Journals of the House of Commons, vi, pp. 57, 466.
[3] Journals of the House of Lords, passim.

Despite these advantages, the financial and social consequences of war were extremely severe. In the first place the pre-war social world collapsed overnight. There was an abrupt end to the round of the familiar great country houses, to the annual jaunts to Newmarket for the races, to Boughton, Petworth, Syon, and Chatsworth to see his friends, to Theobalds, Windsor, Oatlands, and Hampton Court to attend the Court. There was an end to the pleasures of the race-track, the hunting-field, and the bowling-green. Before the war, Salisbury had been a very keen falconer—'I hear you overfly all England', remarked the Earl of Rutland some years later—and had kept a string of race-horses which competed regularly in the main sporting events of the Midlands, at Newmarket, Royston, Brackley, Baldock, Lincoln, Carshalton, and Winchester.[1] Although he managed to hang on to his hawks and spaniels, his greyhounds, and his twenty-six couple of hounds, the racing stable was closed for the duration, the horses being sold abroad to the Duke of Vendôme for £300.

The number of household servants was sharply reduced from the pre-war level of sixty-four, and there were still only forty-nine in 1650. Reduced entertaining made the accumulation of gold and silver plate superfluous, and 7,000 ounces were sold to a London goldsmith for £1,734. At Hatfield the house was stripped and the contents sent up to London for safety, leaving a skeleton staff equipped with pikes and 'thunderbusses' to defend themselves and the house from marauders. By 1643–4 the annual expenditure on food and servants' wages was less than half the pre-war level.[2]

Although Hatfield escaped the ravages of war, Cranborne in Dorset was not so lucky, for it lay in the direct path of rival armies marching and counter-marching to and from the West Country. On 8 May 1643 the Earl of Hertford and Prince Maurice brought a Royalist army through Cranborne *en route* for Cornwall. Several hundred disorderly troops of Prince Maurice burst into the house, and thoroughly sacked it, carrying off anything valuable, and smashing the rest. It is interesting to note how hints of a class war can be seen in the countryside as law and order broke down. In the wake of the soldiery came the local tenantry, who poured into the gutted and undefended house of Cranborne and made straight for

---

[1] Box V/72. A/157/3. *Memoirs of the Verney Family*, London, 1892, i. p. 185. *Journals of the House of Commons*, iv, p. 361.

[2] A. 161/5, 2; 127/11; 41/1. In 1625 the full roll of servants in employment at all the Earl's houses had totalled 102 persons(B. 117/1).

the muniment room. They seized, scattered, and destroyed the Court Rolls containing the records of their copy-hold tenures, some of which were later bought back from the villagers by the Earl's local agent.[1]

To make matters worse, the area remained under royal control for some time, and orders were issued by the local military commander, Lord Hopton, forbidding the tenants to pay their rents to their rebel landlord. The tenants were naturally only too pleased to obey, to the exasperation of the Earl's local officials, who tended to see political motivation behind the refusal to pay. One of the officials described the tenants as 'a company of atheistical clowns, and all malignants or neuters'.[2] Even after the Royalists had been forced to withdraw, however, disorder continued, and rents could hardly be collected. At Cranborne, only £39 was received of £360 due in rent for some coppices from 1643 to 1646. The explanation of the tenants for their delinquency was that, 'The poorer sort of people carried away what they pleased out of the wood; and many who bought wood durst not come with their carts to fetch it for fear of losing their horses by the soldiers, and for my self and my man who sold the wood, we durst not oppose them for fear of losing our lives, which they did threaten.' Similarly at Martock, two years' tithes were forcibly seized by the poor.[3]

If the poor were helping themselves in these distracted times, it was partly from necessity, for it is clear that many tenants were utterly ruined by pillage and free quarters from the predatory soldiery of both sides. Despair eventually seized some of the peasantry and they ceased to till the ground since they could never retain the harvest. At Blagdon in Somerset 100 acres were untilled, and the rest much spoilt by soldiers' horses, while the stocks of grain in the barns were plundered.[4] The most graphic picture of the impact of war upon the helpless and indifferent peasantry comes from a letter of appeal from the tenant of a three-acre plot at Tarrant Rushton in Dorset to the Earl's agent:

Kind sir, after my service remembered unto you, these are to certify you that I have had so many soldiers that I am not able to pay the rent that is past, for I have had one and twenty that have been sent unto me with tickets,[5] besides many others. I have paid Contribution money ever since

[1] G. 72/12. B. 254/16. A. 161/5.   [2] G. 90/17; Cranborne accounts to 1649.
[3] A. 43/1; 161/5.   [4] B. 254/7.
[5] A ticket was a billeting order, which could theoretically be redeemed for cash at a later date, but which under the stress of war was often worthless.

the Wars begun, at the first two pence the week and then one penny, and
since Michaelmas one halfpenny the week; besides, there was never no
gathering for oats, hay or anything whatsoever I must be sure to pay.
They eat up my corn [so] that I was enforced to buy my seed of Mr. Cheine;
this is truth and nothing but the truth. Loving sir, you know that I have
but iii acres of ground which I pay as much as it is worth, with no apurte-
nance unto it. I pray you sir, aquaint my Lord with it and I hope my Lord
will be so honourable that he will grant a poor man's request, otherwise
I shall not be able to pay. And so trusting unto Almighty God that you
are in good health, I rest and remain,

yours at your Command,
John Couridge[1]

Whether this moving request had any effect, we do not know, but
at least the local agent passed it on to his superiors in London,
since it found its way into the Cecil archives.

If this was the situation in the west, things were little better
elsewhere. At the great pasture ranch at Brigstock in Northamptonshire there was no looting of cattle, but by 1644 no fewer than
680 acres had been abandoned altogether by the tenants. Of the
land still in occupation, some of it had been ploughed up without
permission, thus drastically reducing its rental value, and even that
which remained in pasture had lost value, and had to be let at a
reduced rent. Moreover, such tenants as were left were burdened
with contributions to pay for the garrisons at Northampton and
Rockingham, for the armies of Fairfax and the Scots, and for that
in Ireland.[2] These were blows from which the Brigstock estate
never really recovered. By 1660 new tenants had been found and
rents were more or less back to the pre-war level, but this position
could not be maintained. A rent reduction of £350 had to be
granted in 1666, and there was still land of a rental value of £150
for which a tenant could not be found. In 1685 the rent was 25 per
cent below the pre-war figure.

In London the houses occupied by royalists like the Earl of
Annandale stood empty, with the fines and rents unpaid; at the
New Exchange the shopkeepers were ruined by the flight of many
of their clients to the Court and the army, and they fell more and
more in arrears with their rent. At Bermondsey a large area of the
rich pastures was ruined by the building of a fort for the defence of
London and by the deliberate flooding of its surroundings. It was

<hr>

[1] G. 90/20.   [2] A. 38/1; 61/5; 41/9; 161/5; 161/4. Box R/5.

not till 1649 that all the land could be leased out again, the tenant undertaking to level the fort in return for the waiving of an entry fine. Everywhere else tenants complained of plundering, destruction of crops, and free quarters by ill-disciplined soldiery of both sides.[1]

The full effect of all this on Salisbury's income is difficult to assess. The nominal rental fell about 10 per cent between 1642 and 1644, and fines were lower still, so that the total of assessed rents and casualties fell from £12,972 in 1641-2 to £10,966 in 1644-5, or about 15 per cent. But the full effect of the wars can only be judged when one looks at the mounting flood of arrears. We have seen that the level was already rising fast from 1639 to 1641, when they amounted to £3,301. But the isolation of the West Country estates, and the general reluctance to pay rent even on the estates which were still under control, brought about a rapid increase in arrears, so that by 1644-5 they had reached £12,187. Nor does this fully convey the seriousness of the position, since large sums were already being written off as irrecoverable. £1,136 worth of arrears were cancelled in 1639-43, £5,719 in 1643-8, and another £2,836 in 1648-56, making a total of £9,691, most of which can be directly attributed to the consequences of war. Nor was it ever possible to revert to the pre-war level of arrears. Up to 1639 arrears carried over from earlier years never exceeded £550, and arrears on the current year never exceeded £1,000. By 1644-5, however, the former rose to £6,000, and the latter to £5,800. Even as late as 1661 the total arrears were still running at over £6,000, despite intensive efforts to compel the tenants to fulfil their obligations.[2] In 1652-3 no fewer than forty tenants were being hounded through the courts for arrears of rent, and in 1658-9 there were still eighteen.[3]

These difficulties in collecting the rent were only one aspect of the impact of war on the great landowner. For one thing, Salisbury had to spend between £2,000 and £3,000 between 1644 and 1653 in abnormal repairs on the estates to make good war damage, besides another £900 to repair and extend Cranborne House. For another, there were new taxes to be paid. Under the pressure of necessity and backed by force of arms, property-owners were at last made to contribute their fair share to state expenditure, and the result was a dramatic rise in the tax burden. The monthly

[1] A. 161/5. For London see above Ch. III.   [2] See Appendix I.
[3] A. 161/5; 162/2; 49/7.

assessments were levied directly upon the tenants, who claimed a rebate on their rents from the landlord, and by 1645 this rebate was costing Salisbury £1,100 a year, or about 10 per cent of his theoretical gross landed income. Taking into account reduction in rents, remission of fines, arrears written off, the permanent rise in the level of arrears, extraordinary repairs, and rebates to tenants for taxes, contributions and free quarter, between 1642 and 1650 alone the war must have cost the Earl nearly £30,000, or the equivalent of three years' income at the pre-war level. This evidence strongly suggests that the economic dislocation and damage caused by the war was far more serious than is generally supposed. If this was the cost to one of the leaders on the winning side, most of whose estates lay in areas immune from the ravages of actual fighting, the losses suffered by others less fortunately placed must have been very much more severe. If the long-term effect on family fortunes was generally slight, it was because a by-product of war was the collapse of the Court and Court life and a general reduction of conspicuous consumption. As a result, most great families managed to live on their reduced incomes without undue discomfort or even loss of status. As usual, it was the poor, like John Couridge, who were the principal sufferers.

II. FAMILY CRISIS, 1660–1733

After the Restoration, English price levels, and rent levels, entered upon a long period of stability or even decline, and it was only in the London property that entrepreneurial and administrative efficiency offered prospects of significant increases of income. The fortunes of the Earls of Salisbury were therefore determined not by movements in income but by changes in expenditure. The root problem of the Cecils in the late seventeenth century was how to provide for widows and the horde of younger children produced by three generations of exceptionally fertile wives. Earl William had eight sons and five daughters, of whom only three sons and one daughter died young. Family pride dictated that good marriages into the aristocracy had to be provided for the four daughters, regardless of the cost. Anne was married in 1628 to the Earl of Northumberland with £12,000; Elizabeth in 1639 to the Earl of Devonshire with £10,000, and Katherine in 1645 to Viscount Lisle, son and heir of the Earl of Leicester, with £6,000. In about 1653

the last unmarried daughter, Mary, contracted a run-away marriage
with Lord Sandys, without parental consent. As a result Salisbury
refused to supply a marriage portion, and it was only after Mary
had been brought to bed—somewhat inopportunely, in a sedan-
chair—that the Earl relented, and began paying her odd sums and
eventually a small allowance of £100 a year.[1] Most of the younger
sons eventually married, the Earl receiving £3,300 as the marriage
portion of William's wife in 1650 and £3,000 as that of Algernon's
in 1659. But in return he was obliged to settle life annuities on these
younger sons, amounting to £820 for four of them. The fifth,
William, received special favour and was given land in possession
and reversion worth about £380 a year, to be held by him and his
heirs male.[2]

After his marriage in 1639 his son and heir, Charles Lord Cranborne, was given an allowance of £800 a year, while his wife, Lady
Diana, was given an additional £400. No doubt partly because of
Lady Diana's fecklessness the pair were quite unable to live within
their combined income of £1,200 a year, creditors became increasingly importunate during the 1650s, and by 1658 Lord Cranborne's
debts had risen to £15,200.[3] His death the next year in Montpellier,
whither he had fled to avoid the duns and bailiffs, actually increased
the burden on the Earl since Lady Diana's jointure took the form
of an annuity of £1,800 a year. On this, and her inherited estates,
she had to maintain herself and clear off her husband's debts, a task
she was singularly unsuccessful in performing. In 1667 her coach
and horses were arrested by a creditor, and in 1674 she was still in
desperate trouble, 'my creditors . . . every day dunning me that I
scarce can support living in my own house'.[4]

But there is no sign that the Earls took any further responsibility
for her, and it was her children, four daughters and seven sons,
who now threatened to become the main problem. Once again
the infant mortality rate was low, for only one daughter and two
sons died young. One daughter died before marriage, and two
others were married off cheaply with a promise of £2,000 each. The
son and heir was married in 1661 at the age of fifteen to Margaret,
daughter of the Earl of Rutland, who brought with her the very

[1] A. 157/3. D. 22/4. A. 151/10; 129/4; 140/6; 162/2. B.M. Harl. MSS. 991. In a draft settlement of 1659 which was later revoked, the Earl so far relented as to make provision for the
payment to Lady Sandys of £3,000 as a portion (D. 135/3).   [2] 162/1; 53/5. D. 135/2.
[3] A. 18/32; 48/12; 49/1; 114/10. L. 88/18; 90/15, 16; 91/15; 95/3; 96/5, 8. D. 71/7; 186/21;
178/8; 224/29.   [4] G. 29/22. Box V/94. D. 220/9.

handsome portion of £11,000. All four surviving younger sons
remained unmarried, presumably because of poverty, though in a
draft settlement drawn up in 1659 the Earl left three of them £300
a year each and the fourth £100, to commence after his death. The
net result was that by 1667 the Salisbury estate was burdened with
£400 pin-money to the Countess, £1,800 annuity to Diana Dowager
Lady Cranborne, £920 to the younger children (now including
£100 to Lady Sandys), and £300 pin-money to Margaret Lady
Cranborne. The annual cost of supporting the family had risen to
£3,420 out of a gross income of under £12,500.[1] When in 1668
it cost £1,200 to get Viscount Cranborne elected as member of
Parliament for Hertfordshire it is hardly surprising that his grandfather was hard put to it to raise the cash.[2]

The death of the aged Earl William in 1668 made matters worse
still, since his widow, the Countess Katherine, was now entitled to
her jointure. And so there were two jointures going out of the
estate until her death in 1673 and one till Lady Diana's death two
years later, the two amounting to approximately £4,000 a year.
In addition the Earl died owing £18,840, £4,000 of which was due
to his daughters for their portions. Rents were running over £8,000
in arrears, so that things were not quite as serious as they seemed.
All the same, new borrowings of £14,000, mostly from Sir Robert
Atkins and the Duke of Albemarle, had to be made to cover the
situation.[3] To pay off these debts, the late Earl had allocated his
leases at Ruislip and in Kent, which were apparently sold, thus
reducing the gross rental by over £900 a year.[4] The third Earl's net
income was therefore seriously reduced, indeed drastically so until
the death of the last of the dowagers in 1675. But he continued to
live the life of an active Whig politician, flinging himself eagerly
into the battle to exclude the Duke of York from the throne, being
made a Knight of the Garter in 1680, and enjoying a seat on the
Privy Council during the height of the exclusion struggle from
1679 to 1681. He even embarked on a major land purchase in
Hertfordshire for £15,614 in about 1680–2, paid for partly by
selling some of the Brigstock estate for £4,000, and partly by
running up fresh debts.[5]

[1] A. 54/6; 129/12; 162/7. Box V/69.   [2] See above, p. 116 n. 2.
[3] A. 52/3; 54/4, 6; 55/1; 61/14; 133/6; 150/7.
[4] L. 108/10. Of course the rents for the leases to King's College, Cambridge, and the Dean
and Chapter of Canterbury also ceased, so that the net loss of income was less.
[5] A. 111/2. L. 128/8. G. 65/18. D. 151.

It was the death of the Earl James in 1683 and the revelation of the provisions of his will that provoked the great family crisis. Under the terms of the strict settlement drawn up at his marriage, Earl William had given his grandson permission to raise money to provide for his children by settling estates in a trust.[1] His Countess had given Earl James five sons and five daughters, of all of whom he appears to have been inordinately fond. In his first will of 1675 he left £10,000 to his Countess in augmentation of her jointure, £7,000 each to the five daughters and £5,000 each to the four younger sons. In addition he gave his daughters annuities of £150 a year each until marriage or the age of eighteen, and to his younger sons £300 a year each for life. In 1680 he altered the youngest sons' annuities into cash bequests of £2,600 each, and in 1683 he raised the legacies to each daughter to £10,000 and those to each son to £6,500. He also granted miscellaneous life annuities totalling £350 a year, and three others of £200 a year each to the three trustees— one of them Dr. Tillotson, the future Archbishop of Canterbury— to whom he assigned the responsibility of fulfilling the terms of the will.[2]

Thanks to the unprecedented generosity of Earl James towards his daughters and younger sons, the trustees were faced with an extraordinarily difficult situation. The gross annual income of the Salisbury estate amounted to £12,200 a year, of which about £1,100 came in the form of casualties, and £650 from land kept in hand and farmed directly. Out of the rental of £10,500, no less that £6,100 was turned over to the trustees, part of it for ten years to pay off the personal debt, part for ninety-nine years to raise the money for the children. The only thing which mitigated the gloom was the death of the Countess the year before, which saved her legacy of £10,000 in cash, and her jointure of £1,500 a year for life. The personal debts of the late Earl on mortgage, bonds and trades-men's bills amounted to £33,918 against which could be set personal assets, including stock for husbandry, the value of leased lands, and £4,360 of arrears of rent, of only £11,090.[3] In view of this situation it is hardly surprising that the trustees shuffled Earl James into the ground for a paltry £236, which must have been one of the meanest funerals ever accorded to a seventeenth-century Earl.

What filled the trustees and their advisers with gloom, however, was the cash legacies due to the children, which amounted to the

---

[1] L. 104/13.   [2] L. 133/1; 155/6.   [3] A. 136/20, 22; 165/1.

staggering figure of £78,600, as well as the £2,600 a year in annuities to them and others, only £750 of which would cease when the daughters came of age and received their legacies. It was estimated that the personal assets of the late Earl and the capital value of the ten-year and the ninety-nine-year trusts fell short of the charges by some £18,000, so that some of the fee simple estate would have to be set aside to meet them, thus further reducing the Earl's current income, which in any case was too small to maintain him in the style of an Earl.[1] Under these circumstances it was clear that some drastic action was necessary, and the only obvious way out was to trade the title and birth of the seventeen-year-old Earl in marriage to lower-class wealth. The choice fell on Frances Bennett, a multiple coheiress. Her great-grandfather had been Lord Mayor of London, her father had inherited the property of both his father and his uncle and had amassed a substantial fortune of his own in Mediterranean trade, besides marrying the coheiress of another Londoner.[2] Although two sons and five daughters were born, only three daughters survived into adolescence, and the death of the heir male in 1675 at once turned the girls into very attractive prizes. The eldest was snapped up by the son and heir of the Duke of Leeds, but died without children in 1680, which eliminated one claimant. The next married, against her father's will, a certain John Bennett of Abington, perhaps a distant relative, and in 1683 there remained the third, still only a girl of thirteen. She was the immediate heir to a landed estate of over £1,500 a year and to a portion of £20,000 left her by her father out of his personal estate. The only drawback was that her father had stipulated in his will that if she married before the age of sixteen she was only to get £10,000. But Salisbury's advisers could not afford to wait. They therefore persuaded the mother and guardians of the child to consent to an immediate marriage, on condition that its consummation be deferred until Frances was sixteen, and got John Bennett to promise not to contest the payment of the full £20,000.[3] As soon as the marriage ceremony was performed, the young man set off for the Continent, leaving his child-wife to her own devices, and his administrative officers and the trustees to cope with the problems of marrying his sisters, clearing off the debts and legacies, and

---

[1] See Appendix II. A. 63/5; 161/5; 137/10; 112/10. By 1690 the estimated deficit had risen to £22,660 (A. 67/7).

[2] For the Bennett Genealogy see G. Baker, *History of Northamptonshire*, London, ii, 1841, p. 342.   [3] L. 184/6.

fighting John Bennett, who had now gone back on his word and was contesting the Earl's right to the second £10,000.

By all accounts the fourth Earl of Salisbury was a fool. Even with his wife's land and her portion it was clear that he would have to live modestly for some years if he were to avoid piling up still more debts. Including his wife's income of £1,500 or more, he enjoyed a gross revenue of about £5,000 a year in the late 1680s, exclusive of the lands in the two trusts.[1] Out of this he had to provide for maintenance of a suitable establishment, repairs to houses, an allowance to his countess, and after 1689 a land-tax. But the reasonable economy that should have been exercised to deal with this situation was quite beyond the Earl. A gross and sensual glutton, he gambled his way about the Continent until he fell into the clutches of the friars. He then returned home as a distinguished Catholic convert in time to witness the ejection of James II and to be indicted for popery. As a result of his recusancy, he found himself paying the land-tax at the double rate of 8s. in the £1, which meant a burden of £1,400 a year after 1689.[2] He spent the next few years in and out of the Tower of London on suspicion of conspiracy, until finally he died in 1694, to the universal relief of all who knew him. But at least he had done his duty by the family in one essential respect since he had consummated his loveless marriage to the Bennett heiress sufficiently to beget a three-year-old son and heir.

His epitaph was written by the faithful Steward Samuel Percival in a letter to his friend George Stillingfleet, the agent at Cranborne, 'An unhappy self-willed man, [who] has put fair to undo himself, his relations, friends, all that had to do with him or for him.'[3]

By 1694 the financial situation was even worse than it had been eleven years before, at the death of Earl James. It was estimated that between his accession in 1683 and his death in 1694 the fourth Earl had been living at a rate of £9,700 a year on a disposable income of only about £4,000 a year. Some £117,000 of the old debts and legacies had admittedly been paid off, but much of it had come from windfalls. The £17,000 of the Bennett portion and £36,000 received for sale of land[4] had all gone to paying the legacies, in addition to the revenues from the land in the two

---

[1] A. 67/5. Another estimate in about 1686 puts it at about £6,000 (G. 103/11).
[2] A. 71/6; 154/3.   [3] G. 131/21.
[4] The chief sales were of Roydon and Temple Roydon, Essex, to Sir Joshua Child for £17,000 and of the recently bought Hertfordshire estate for £17,291 to Sir Edmund Desbouveries (A. 158/2; L. 187/7; 201/9).

trusts. Because of his extravagance, the Earl died leaving debts of
£52,000, which now had to be paid off. But the value of the estate
was shrinking, partly because of sales, partly because of declining
rents in a period of recession and cheap food prices.[1] The Bennett
estate passed to the dowager Countess for her life, and the gross
income of the Salisbury estate was now down to £10,000. Out of
this reduced income no less than £7,760 had to be spent on fixed
charges, £2,210 to the dowager Countess as her jointure, £1,810
in annuities, mainly to the family, £1,440 in land taxes, and £2,600
in interest on the debts.[2] Thus only £2,240 was left on which
to maintain the household and pay off over £50,000 worth of
debts.

It took the family half a century to recover from the effects of the
excessive family affection of the third Earl and the excessive folly
and imprudence of the fourth. Salvation came, slowly, in three
ways, the most important of which was sheer chance. In the first
place the fact that the fifth Earl was only three years old when his
father died meant that there was a long period of a minority when
the household could be reduced to a minimum, surplus houses shut
up, and expenditure kept at a very low level indeed.[3] Secondly,
a lot more land had to be sold once the Earl reached his majority,
£53,000 coming from this source between 1711 and 1716. Among
the sales were the two great grazing grounds at Brigstock and
Bermondsey, which sold for £27,000 and £20,000 respectively.[4]
Further sales for £17,000 took place after 1738, so that by 1755
£108,000 had been raised altogether since 1683 by the sale of some
40 per cent of the land included in the rental of that year. This huge
disinvestment certainly succeeded in reducing the load of debt and
interest, but only at the cost of a further permanent reduction in the
capital assets of the estate. These assets received an unexpected and
most welcome increase in 1733, however, when the third of the
Bennett daughters died intestate, thus bringing to the Cecils the
whole £5,865 a year of the Bennett estate. This huge windfall,
together with general improvement in rents, meant that the sixth
Earl's gross income was raised to nearly £16,000.

---

[1] The only improvement in the estate was the conversion of the whole of Salisbury House
into tenements (see above p. 94).

[2] A. 71/6. There are various calculations giving different results, many of them with palpable
errors of logic and accounting, and this is no more than a reasonable approximation of the
situation.   [3] See A. 132/20 for expenses 1713–23.

[4] D. 98. There were further sales for £17,000 between 1738 and 1746 (A. 148/16, 19;
149/18).

The sixth Earl was not yet out of the wood, however, since the Bennett estate was saddled with mortgages of £46,000, so that the full debt load in 1733 was still £81,000. Consequently between 1740 and 1755 we find that out of a gross income of £70,860, £35,400— or just half—was consumed by interest payments, and only £5,500 went to repay capital.[1] Under these circumstances the sixth Earl's decision to marry the impoverished daughter of the local rector of Hatfield was a courageous act of defiance of the conventional values of his class. The Salisburys certainly re-entered Court politics in the 1780s, and like all landlords they profited from the rocketing rents of the period of the Napoleon war, but the family finances were only fully stabilized again with the marriage to the heiress of the great Gascoigne inheritance in Liverpool in 1823. This second massive injection of mercantile wealth and genes meant that the Cecils were once more one of England's greatest families, with the resources—and the talents—necessary to play a prominent role on the political stage.

The story of the Cecil fortunes in the seventeenth century is one of dramatic changes dependent largely on personal character and biological accident. The great estate was built up by the first Earl, in ways that do not bear too close inspection, as a direct by-product of his political position. Unfortunately he was also obsessed by a consuming passion for building, and his premature death in 1612 left the estate very heavily encumbered. No doubt he had hoped to live and retain office for another five or six years, by which time he might reasonably have expected to have paid off the debts caused by the building programme of 1607–12. As it was, however, his tenure of office was becoming shaky after 1610, and he died just at the moment when the buildings were finished.

As a result, the rump of the estate left to his son after the inevitable sales had taken place was very large indeed but not in the really first rank. A second successful political career was needed to push the family right to the top, but the second Earl was consistently baulked in this objective. Instead he fell back, with remarkable success, on extracting as much from his tenants in rents and fines as could be done without attacking the existing social pattern in his villages. By 1642 this policy, together with the marriage of his son to a promising heiress, looked as if it would suffice to hoist the

[1] A. 91/5.

Cecils the last step up the ladder. But the marriage was a disappointment, the Civil War, heavy taxation, and the levelling off of rents
put a check to the growth of net income, and the Earl's position at
his death in 1668 was no better than it had been twenty years before.

The philoprogenitiveness and paternal generosity of the third
Earl, followed by eleven years of dissipation by the fourth, seriously
threatened the whole position of the family. Only marriage to a
low-born heiress and the early death of the fourth Earl saved the
situation, but even so it was half a century before anything like
equilibrium could be restored. The story illustrates the extreme
difficulty, despite all the talent and devotion of lawyers and agents,
of preserving a family fortune in the face of personal whims and
follies, and uncontrolled fertility. It was weakness of character,
made more serious by the presence of unlimited idleness; or
strength of virility, made more serious by the absence of contra-
ceptive measures; or total sterility, made more serious by the low
reproduction rate of younger brothers, which sapped the foundations of a family fortune. It was the strict settlement; efficient but
conservative estate administration; a subordination of personal
choice to financial advantage in the selection of marriage partners;
avoidance of addiction to horses, cards, dice, and women; and a
prudent policy of family limitation, which preserved it.

APPENDIX I

The Cost of Civil War

(A. 161/5; 139/4, 5, 7, 9, 17; 124/6, 9; 162/2; 48/1, 2; 51/1)

	Rents and Casualties due	Arrears		Rebate to tenants for contributions and assessments[1]	Misc. costs
		Total unpaid	Of which cancelled		
	£	£	£	£	£
1640–1	11,226	3,301	286	..	..
1641–2	12,972	4,516	382	11	..
1642–3	11,957	6,090	149	410	..
1643–4	11,645	9,619	1,157	695	..
1644–5	10,966	12,187	388	1,107	..
1645–6	12,495	10,879	553	1,335	238[2]
1646–7	14,242	9,889	1,800	1,307	300[3]
1647–8	14,191	9,126	1,821	732	716[4]
1648–9	9,321	?	?	801	..
1649–50	9,775	?	?	?	..
1650–1	12,314	7,285	865	997	..
1651–2	13,045	6,306	632	1,295	..
1652–3	11,841	5,543	..	1,046	..
1653–4	11,287	6,378	419	1,285	..
1654–5	12,346	7,109	706	947	..
1655–6	11,973	6,064	114	696	..
1656–7	14,502	6,688	..	749	..
1657–8	?	?	?	555	..
1658–9	?	?	?	?	..
1659–60	?	?	?	759	..
1660–1	12,463	6,238	119	775	..

[1] The monthly assessments were levied on the tenants but paid by the landlord.

[2] This was money paid to the Cranborne bailiff in recompense for losses and expenses resulting from the sacking of Cranborne House.

[3] Of this £203 was spent on rebuilding Cranborne House, and £97 paid the farmer at Brigstock in recompense for provisions and horses commandeered for the army by the Earl of Manchester and Sir William Waller.

[4] This was spent on rebuilding Cranborne House.

APPENDIX II

Summary of the Situation in 1683

(A. 137/10; 112/10; 115/13; L. 200/5)

		£	£
I. *Assets*: (1) Gross annual income			c. 12,200 p.a
(2) Personal estate of late Earl			11,093
II. *Debits*:			
(1) Annuities: 3 younger sons		900	
5 daughters		750	
3 overseers of the will		600	
others		350	
		——	2,600 p.a.
(2) Interest payments on debts and legacies			c. 2,000 p.a.[1]
		Total	4,600 p.a.
(3) Debts and legacies: Personal debts		33,918	
Legacies to 5 daughters		50,000	
Legacies to 4 sons		26,000	
Additional legacy to George Cecil		2,600	
		———	112,518

[1] This is the average figure given for 1683–94 in A. 71/6.

PART TWO

OTHER FAMILIES

VI

THE MANNERS EARLS OF RUTLAND
1460-1660

I. THE FIRST EARL THOMAS AND HIS PREDECESSORS,
1460-1543

AFTER over 200 years as relatively inconspicuous Northumberland knights and squires, the Manners family rose suddenly in the late fifteenth and early sixteenth centuries to become one of the leading members of the country's great landed aristocracy.[1] If the machinery by which this meteoric rise was achieved was the marriage alliance, the basic cause was a shrewd political sense that kept three successive generations of the family riding high on the fluctuating and dangerous currents of civil war, dynastic revolution, and religious reformation. It seems to have been favour with the great Earl of Warwick which in 1469 obtained for Sir Robert Manners the hand of Eleanor, sister and coheir of Edmund Lord Roos of Hamlake. In the end this single marriage, coupled with the fortunate death without heirs of Eleanor's sister, Isabel, brought with it the huge Roos inheritance, including Belvoir Castle in Lincolnshire and the extensive estate centred on Helmsley Castle in Yorkshire. Thus were the Manners transformed from remote Northumbrian squires to landed magnates of the north-east midlands. Next Sir Robert married his son, George Lord Roos, to the niece of Edward IV, to which was due the beginning of royal favour under Henry VIII. A further windfall was the bequest to George's son Thomas Lord

---

In this chapter the following abbreviations are used:

B/A	Belvoir Castle, Rutland MSS., Accounts			
B/BSA	,,	,,	,,	,,	Brief Statements of Accounts
B/C	,,	,,	,,	,,	Charters
B/G	,,	,,	,,	,,	Grants
B/L	,,	,,	,,	,,	Letters
B/M	,,	,,	,,	,,	Miscellaneous
B/S	,,	,,	,,	,,	Settlements
B/W	,,	,,	,,	,,	Wills

I am very grateful to the Duke of Rutland for permission to examine these manuscripts.

[1] See genealogical table no. 3.

Roos in 1522 by his wife's uncle Sir Thomas Lovell of some valuable property in Middlesex.[1]

From the beginning of the reign Thomas Lord Roos was an assiduous courtier of the young Henry VIII and was soon to reap the rewards. In 1525 he was made a Knight of the Garter and given the Earldom of Rutland. In the thirties his support of the breach with Rome, his zeal in crushing the Pilgrimage of Grace, and his readiness to vote the death-penalty in the succession of spectacular treason trials that punctuated Henry's erratic matrimonial progress made him an obvious candidate for grants of monastic property. Though he was described by a contemporary as of 'small wit and little discretion', the success of his career in a very dangerous and unstable political situation would suggest that in fact he was both astute and prudent, although probably time-serving and unprincipled.[2]

First he engineered an exchange of the Lovell property in Middlesex and Chilham Castle, Kent, for Rievaulx Abbey and surrounding property in Yorkshire and the fourteen manors in Leicester, Lincolnshire, and Northamptonshire that had belonged to Croxton Abbey. Although these were charged with a fee-farm rent to the Crown of £297 and although the exchanged property was no doubt of considerable value, there can be little doubt that the Earl gained enormously by the transaction. He would not have spent the large sum of £66. 13s. 4d. on gratuities to the Chancellor of the Court of Augmentations and other officials for their 'trouble' if it had not been worth his while. The net rental of the property after deduction of the fee-farm rent was £289.[3] Next he obtained by grant or purchase the reversion in fee and the reserved rent of the estates of Warter Priory in Yorkshire, the grant of which in tail he had obtained in 1536, and which included seven manors.[4] Then in quick succession in 1541 he made a series of gigantic speculations in the monastic lands that were then being rapidly thrown on the market to pay for the defence preparations against France. For £4,683 he bought fifteen manors formerly of Garendon Abbey, Leicestershire, and another block of twelve scattered manors, while in exchange for some Essex property and some cash he obtained the site of the Eagle Commandery and Belvoir Priory

[1] N. H. Nicholas, *Testamenta Vetusta*, London, 1826, p. 641.
[2] *Letters and Papers of Henry VIII*, 13, pt. 2, no. 732.
[3] Ibid., 14, pt. 1, no. 651 (43). B/A 14, 676.
[4] Ibid. 11, no. 510 (1); 16, no. (678) 6.

in Lincolnshire.[1] The result of these gigantic investments in real estate was to make the Manners family a major social and political force both in the north midlands, in Leicestershire, Nottinghamshire, and Lincolnshire, and also in the north, in Yorkshire. They established the dominant geographical characteristics of the family for the next hundred years.

The death of Earl Thomas in 1543 could hardly have come at a more inopportune moment, for his heir, Henry, was still a minor, and the family finances were in a critical and unstable condition. The most serious blow was the removal of the firm hand of Earl Thomas at a moment when his surveyors, agents, and bailiffs were still struggling to digest the huge increases of property which had fallen to them to administer within the last year or two. Moreover, the Earl had not yet paid the very large sums due to the Court of Augmentations for the property he had bought, nor three years' arrears of fee-farm rents of £553 a year charged on the newly purchased estates, while there was still a £332 fine for livery to be paid to the Crown when the heir attained his majority. Earl Thomas's second wife outlived him and so enjoyed as jointure until her death a substantial portion of the estate, the nominal rent of which amounted to £714. Finally, the late Earl still owed £533 of the £2,000 portion for the marriage of his eldest daughter Gertrude to the Earl of Shrewsbury, and in his will he had charged his estate with portions of £1,000 each to his three younger daughters, who were still unmarried.[2] At his death, therefore, the Earl left debts and legacies totalling about £8,400 and a gross income of at most about £2,600.[3] But this situation was by no means as serious as it might appear, because of the enormous potential value of the newly acquired monastic property. Within four years the executors raised over £10,000, of which £8,351 came from the sale of land, and the remainder from rents and the sale of woods on the monastic estates. With these sums they paid off many of the outstanding debts, including over £6,000 to the Crown for fee-farm rents and the purchase price of land.[4]

II. THE SECOND EARL HENRY, 1543–1563

When Earl Henry came of age in 1547 the worst of the problems left by his father were over. The legacy of the past, however, still

[1] Ibid. 16, no. 678 (7); 947 (11); 1056 (78).
[2] *North Country Wills*, Surtees Society, 116, 1908, p. 89. B/G 529. B/A 847, 676, 1153.
[3] B/A 27, 1137, 1141.   [4] B/A 26A, 29, 1153.

weighed heavily on him. In 1536, when he was ten years old, his father had married him to a girl little older than himself, Margaret, the daughter of the Earl of Westmorland. This child-marriage had not yet been consummated in 1542[1] and there is little evidence that it subsequently gave the Earl much satisfaction. At all events he only waited four months after Margaret's death in 1559 to marry again. The other obligation imposed on Earl Henry by his father was that of following the family tradition as courtier and soldier. And so at the first opportunity his mother launched him into royal service in the wars. He was present at the siege of Boulogne in 1544, accompanied an embassy to France two years later, and in 1547 was appointed Lieutenant of the English army against the Scots. The next year he foolishly got himself vaguely mixed up in Lord Admiral Seymour's inept conspiracy against Protector Somerset, but he was shipped off to the north out of harm's way without any damage to his career. Despite his inexperience and his youth, from 1549 to 1551 he served as Warden of the East and Middle Marches, and during 1551 he was a member of an embassy to France. These were time-consuming and very expensive offices which for long periods kept the Earl far from London, where the great share-out of royal money and property was proceeding. Whether or not this was intended by Somerset and Northumberland, the only financial result of his services was a mounting tide of debt.[2] With some of his father's debts still to be repaid, his sisters to be married off, and with his mother's jointure still going out of the estate, he had been advised to live in retirement for a while, exercising the utmost economy.[3] Instead he had chosen to plunge into political and military life, but he had failed to reap any reward to help pay for his expenses, and so towards the end of Edward's reign his debts mounted steadily. By 1552 he owed £1,257 in London of which £766 was due before Christmas.[4]

In 1553 things rapidly went from bad to worse when the Earl again broke the long family tradition of successful adjustment to changing political circumstances by backing Northumberland's abortive attempt to place Lady Jane Grey on the throne. Although there is evidence to suggest that he held firm Protestant views, he was clearly considered merely young and foolish, and Mary treated

---

[1] *North Country Wills*, Surtees Society, 116, 1908, p. 188.

[2] S. Haynes, *Burghley Papers*, London, 1740, p. 81. *H.M.C. Rutland MSS.* i, p. 32; iv, pp. 197, 201.

[3] Ibid. i, p. 32.   [4] B/A 711. P.R.O., L.C. 4/188, pp. 4, 47.

him with great leniency. He suffered a brief spell in the Tower, but was then released after payment of the costs of his apprehension and a fine of £666. However, the full restoration of royal favour was not an unmixed blessing, for it kept him at Court and involved him in the heavy expenses of participation in the festivities that celebrated the arrival of Philip of Spain. All this provoked mounting debts in London, and land sales in the country. He had borrowed money both to pay his fine and to finance his current expenditure, so that by 1554 he owed some £6,000 on bonds, mortgages, and bills to London tradesmen and financiers, and he was busy selling off some of the more scattered elements of his estates, one of which alone realized £3,700.[1]

At this point someone—either a family friend or a trusted servant—took alarm and addressed a long memorandum of advice to the young Earl.[2] He advised drastic measures both to reduce the debt and to live within income. The first step was to discover how much was owing. Revenue was then to be set aside to pay it off by degrees, while more money was to be made out of sale of woods, estimated to be worth over £6,600. This was a much better policy than selling land outright, for either the wood could be left for sixteen years to grow again, or else the land could be converted to pasture. If necessary, money could be raised from the sale of some plate and furniture, and finally, if the worst came to the worst, £100 a year of the worst ex-monastic property could be sold with the express proviso that the equivalent should be bought back in due course. There was recommended a reduction of the household to forty persons (that of the first Earl in 1543 had been no fewer than ninety-four)[3] and domestic expenditure was to be limited to £500 a year for the household, and £200 each for my Lord and my Lady for personal needs. The remainder was to be devoted to repayment of current debts and the legacies and portions left by the Earl's father by will. To carry out this plan a proper accounting system would have to be introduced. All the Earl's officers were to be given books in which to keep their accounts; the Comptroller was to be put in sole charge of the whole running of the household; cash was to be kept in labelled bags, a note was to be taken of all issues, and the Earl was to check it in person every week. These recommendations suggest that control of both income and

---

[1] B/A 55. *Cal. Pat. Rolls, 1554–5*, pp. 134, 210, 230; *1555–7*, p. 209. Rockingham Castle, Watson MSS. B/2, 3.   [2] B/C 7569.   [3] B/A 29.

expenditure had become very slack. There was, it would appear, some justification for the stern warning that 'if in time my Lord be not ordered by reason to be concluded by him & his witty loving council, his lands, his woods, his plate, my lady's jewels, his household stuff, his stocks and stores will be utterly consumed'. Indeed, 'my Lord so selling land every year . . . shall not be able to live and so by little and little shall consume all his lands, and so he and his posterity shall be utterly destroyed'.

Evidence has not survived to show whether Earl Henry heeded this powerful and disturbing memorandum and allowed his finances to be handled in future by his 'witty loving council'. Nor do we know the composition of this typically late medieval body. Certainly his affairs showed little sign of improvement, largely because he continued to accept expensive military offices without reward. He sold a great deal more land, and yet became more and more entangled with London aldermen and goldsmiths, to whom he was obliged to mortgage some of his estates. The accession of Elizabeth brought him increased royal favour and appointment to the very responsible position of President of the Council of the North. But this involved a heavy initial outlay and in 1560–3 he is found mortgaging some more of his manors and trying, with moderate success, to levy a benevolence of £700 from his tenants, presumably as an alternative to the less accommodating Londoners.[1] When he died in 1563 after fifteen years' continuous service to the Crown, the only benefit he seems to have derived from his efforts was the grant of the Crown interest in some ex-Roos estates in the West Country in 1554. In 1562 he bought from the Crown for £894 the Leicestershire manor of Shepeshead, but since the price was about thirty years' purchase of the rental, this was no more than a normal commercial transaction.[2] The Earl certainly did not take service with the Crown for financial reasons, but rather from a desire to exercise authority and be kept busy in responsible and prestigious positions. These things he enjoyed as long as he lived, but the financial cost to the family was a heavy one, and his career provides a classic example of the burden of unrequited public office.

[1] L.C. 4/188, pp. 153, 176, 202, 204, 369, 395, 397, 427, 429, 466, 498. B/L iii ff. 75, 96. *Cal. Pat. Rolls, 1560–3*, pp. 145, 581.

[2] B/G 67, 69. *Cal. Pat. Rolls, 1554–5*, p. 177; *1560–3*, p. 354. P.R.O. Rentals and Surveys, Portfolio 22/36. It is not at all clear what happened to these ex-Roos estates. They do not appear in any account or rental, and the Earl seems to have alienated his rights within the next few years (P.R.O., Chancery Proc. Ser. I, Eliz. K4/53, R1/56).

The situation on Earl Henry's death in 1563 was not unlike what it had been twenty years before, except that this time there were no huge capital gains to be realized from the sale of newly acquired monastic lands and woods. There were heavy debts to London merchants, to whom land rented at £95 a year was mortgaged, the heir was a minor and therefore one-third of the property passed temporarily into the hands of the Crown for wardship, and there was a £600 jointure for the widow to be paid out of the remainder of the estate. In addition to this handsome jointure the late Earl had left the Countess Bridget £500 in cash and the wardship and marriage of Henry Vernon, reckoned to be worth another £400.[1]

What with this jointure, the mortgages, the wardship obligations, and the settlement of other property on uncles and younger brothers, the estate of the young Earl Edward was much diminished. A Crown survey, which admittedly may omit a few items, and probably undervalues those it includes, shows that out of the very large nominal rental of £2,485 a year, there was due £553 a year in rents to the Crown. £423 was in the hands of uncles or brothers for life, £95 was mortgaged to London merchants, and £142 extended for nine years to pay off old debts due to the Crown. The net disposable rental was therefore only £1,226, and of this £483 fell to the Crown for wardship for seven years and some of the rest was in possession of the widow as jointure.[2]

III. THE THIRD AND FOURTH EARLS EDWARD AND JOHN, 1563–1588

Such was the position when Sir William Cecil, the Secretary of State, stepped in to take up what was to become his familiar role as guardian angel to the Elizabethan aristocracy. As he explained to the Earl of Shrewsbury, he was actuated by 'the reverence I owe to the maintenance of all such noble family'. He evidently distrusted the young dowager step-mother, and at once took control both of the boy's education and of the administration of the estate. His first care was to clear off the mortgages to the Londoners. The land was in theory already forfeited for non-payment of debt of £1,800 but as it was close to the two seats of Belvoir and Helmsley,

[1] B/S 360, 52.
[2] P.R.O. Rentals and Surveys, Portfolio 22/36. SP 12/44/58; Hatfield House, Salis. MSS., Petitions 2407. The remainder of the £600 jointure was presumably taken in the form of an annuity, which was a further charge on the estate.

Cecil redeemed it by borrowing the money from the Crown, to be repaid during the minority. Next he had the young Earl removed from the doubtful care of his step-mother, and sent down to London to his own house, where there was already another young aristocratic ward, the Earl of Oxford.[1]

It seems likely that one of Cecil's objects in exercising this paternal vigilance was to train up aristocratic heirs to take over high political offices and therefore help to hold back the tide of social change. One of Cecil's most severe problems, as became clear at the time of the rebellion of the northern Earls in 1569, was to reconcile the older aristocracy to the rule of an upstart like himself. No doubt he hoped—mostly vainly, as it turned out—that his aristocratic young wards would be grateful to their anxious guardian and that when they grew up and took office they would prove loyal to him. At all events the greatest possible care was taken with their education. Rutland spent the next few years at Oxford, Cambridge, and possibly Lincoln's Inn. He then had a brief experience of military service in the army assembled to put down the northern rebellion of 1569, before being launched on a tour of France, for which he was supplied with a long letter of instructions from Cecil. In this the young man's duties were clearly set out. Above all he was to continue in the worship and fear of God. He was to keep a diary in which he was to set down a wide range of information: the fortifications, garrisons, and governors of towns; the administrative and judicial systems; the state of the court with the characters and ages of the leading courtiers; the state of royal finances; details of the monetary system, the university, and the estates, finances, and administrative arrangements of the nobility. Nor was he to forget to make a note of such Roman antiquities or natural phenomena as he might come across. But this alarming catalogue of requirements concluded with a remark that revealed Cecil's dogged nationalism and fundamental suspicion of all things foreign. 'And so to end I trust none of all these things above-said shall more content you than the state of your native country if the same were only revealed and known to you.'[2] Surprisingly enough, the young man heeded his mentor's advice and actually made notes of matters of political or military interest that he observed on his journey. Indeed, unlike nearly all Burghley's

---

[1] Lambeth Palace MSS. 697, F. 31, 35. *H.M.C. Rutland MSS.* i, p. 89.
[2] P.R.O., S.P. 12/77/6.

other young wards, Rutland seems to have been genuinely grateful for the trouble taken over his education, for he possessed the qualities of intellect needed to profit by it.[1]

Nor did he suffer from the less attractive side of his guardian's ambitions. Though Cecil at one time had hopes of getting him to marry his daughter, the young man apparently evaded the offer without too much difficulty.[2] The reason for his reluctance was that he had already set his heart on Isabel, daughter of Sir Thomas Holcroft of Vale Royal and his wife Julian, the daughter and heiress of a London alderman. There can be little doubt that this must have been considered by many to be a *mésalliance* for one of the greatest Earls in England, and the disapproval must have been increased if it was true, as Lady Holcroft alleged, that the Earl was so deeply in love that he was willing to marry the girl even without a marriage portion.[3] No marriage contract has in fact survived, so that there is no means of knowing whether or not the Earl obtained a substantial cash sum on his marriage with Isabel in 1573.

For the remaining fourteen years of his short life Earl Edward lived in considerable splendour both at Court and in the country. He maintained his intellectual interests and became, according to Camden, 'a profound lawyer', so much so that the Queen had already decided to appoint him Lord Chancellor at the time of his sudden death in April 1587.[4] While studying the law, fulfilling a wide range of official duties, and waiting for this rich prize, he did not neglect either the management of his estates or the lighter side of aristocratic activities. He lived at Belvoir in great style, dispensing lavish hospitality. Years later Gervase Holles described him as 'the magnificent Earl who kept an house like a Prince's Court' and lamented that his Gentleman of the Horse, John Kingston, ruined himself in the attempt to live up to the same opulent standard. He was also keenly interested in field sports, and his correspondence provides a very early example of the familiar English obsession with dogs. In October 1575 a neighbour Anthony Thorold wrote to him:

My dogs are all unbreathed. For this fortnight I have kept my house, and have not been able to go forth of my house before this day. Neither have I seen any of my dogs run since Michaelmas last; so that they will

[1] *H.M.C. Rutland MSS.* i, p. 91. *Cal. S.P. Dom. Add., 1566–79*, p. 180.
[2] *H.M.C. Rutland MSS.* i, p. 95.   [3] Ibid., p. 97.
[4] W. Camden, *Annales*, London, 1635, p. 356.

not be in any good temper so soon. My brother Rigges is gone this day towards London, but I hope to borrow his dog off my sister. In what case he is I know not. The best dog I had was strained at a course about Mayday. If I like the day I will wait on you tomorrow at Belvoir.[1]

The study of the law was clearly not the only preoccupation of the third Earl of Rutland.

Despite his medieval style of living at Belvoir, the Earl paid close attention to the administration of his estate, and was careful to live within his income. After his death Sir Gervase Clifton told his brother and heir to reflect on 'how barely he was left and how well he has left you, having so little in hand during his mother-in-law's life'. Nor was this encomium unjustified. His step-mother, Countess Bridget, now remarried to the Earl of Bedford, outlived him and continued to draw her substantial jointure. There is not sufficient evidence to show how far he succeeded in increasing the gross income of what remained. But it is clear that he exercised the most intimate control over every detail of the management of the property that he farmed directly, and that he was responsible for the modernization and re-equipping of the Rievaulx ironworks, which was later to become so important an addition to the family income. Although he lived in such a princely style, he nevertheless saved enough out of current income to buy some five manors in Yorkshire and a rectory in Leicestershire in 1575–7, three more manors in the early 1580s, one of which cost him £2,000, and many copyholds on his existing estates. He also took a lease of Newark and Mansfield and so obtained a residence in Nottinghamshire, much to the irritation of the Markhams, who had hitherto dominated the district and were resentful of the competition.[2]

The great disappointment of his life must have been that he and his wife were the first to show signs of that infertility which was to dog the Manners family for the next half-century. They failed to produce a male heir, and he died leaving an only daughter, Elizabeth. Since the barony of Roos passed through the female line to Elizabeth, Edward decided to endow her with a substantial portion

[1] *H.M.C. Rutland MSS.* i, pp. 106, 169, 211. A. C. Wood, *Memorials of the Holles Family* (Camden Soc., 3rd ser., lv), 1937, p. 215.

[2] *H.M.C. Rutland MSS.* i, pp. 214, 111, 137–8, 145, 202–3. *V.C.H. Yorkshire, N.R.* ii, pp. 41, 42, 291, 432. B/W 22. B/L, vi ff. 32, 89; vii f. 189. For the ironworks, see below p. 190. *H.M.C. Salis. MSS.* ii, p. 227. P.R.O., S.P. 12/106/51. *Cal. S.P. Dom., 1581–90*, p. 218. On the fall of the Duke of Norfolk in 1547 Rutland had been one of the first to join in the scramble for the spoils, and had been told by a servant that in view of the distribution of power in the neighbouring counties 'there is but Nottinghamshire for you' (*H.M.C. Rutland MSS.* i, p. 32).

of the family estates. He left Elizabeth all the 1538 grant of Warter Priory and its possessions, all his purchases of 1575–7, and some former estates in Yorkshire and Essex, a total of some seventeen manors, two rectories, and a London house in Saint Andrew's Undershaft. Judging by the 1563 survey, this property must have amounted to about one-quarter of the total estate. This bequest was not to take effect 'if the said Elizabeth my daughter do marry or take to husband any person other than a Baron or heir apparent of a Baron . . . or a gentleman having land . . . of the yearly value of one thousand pounds', or if she tried to upset the will by claiming more of the former Roos inheritance.[1] The purpose of the first of these provisos was to ensure that Elizabeth would carry the estates and the Roos barony to someone who would add to them, in order to establish a major aristocratic family; and second was to try to avoid getting the family tangled up in an interminable and enormously costly lawsuit about the distribution of the property.

The heir to the three-quarters of the property which did not pass to Elizabeth was the Earl's younger brother John. He was not a scholar or a statesman, but a bluff, simple country gentleman suddenly elevated to a position of great authority. He was also very hot-tempered. As he admitted to Robert Cecil, 'Hasty I am and quick of conceit . . . I have a great mind and cannot disguise injuries. Plain I am and cannot abide to be cunningly dealt with . . . I am the most cholerick of men.'[2] This uncertain temper led at once into an open quarrel with his sister-in-law, the late Earl's widow. By the terms of the will Earl Edward plainly intended her to have the lease of Newark Castle and demesnes, and other property, free of any incumbrances. But Earl John claimed that all the debts and the charges of the enormously lavish funeral—for which the black draperies and clothing alone came to £898—should be paid before Isabel received her legacies, and as a result he found himself sued in Chancery. In the end the matter was submitted to the arbitration of Burghley and Walsingham, who ordered her own inheritance from her mother of Frodsham parsonage to be given to Lady Isabel at once and the Newark lease to be handed over only if the late Earl's personal estate would otherwise suffice to pay the debt.[3] Earl John's revenge for this quarrel was to appeal to the Queen to

[1] B/W 22.   [2] H.M.C. Rutland MSS. i, pp. 218–19.
[3] Ibid., pp. 216, 219, 223. P.R.O., Chancery Proc. Ser. I, Eliz. R6/56. P.R.O., SP12/201/58; 202/21. B/M 43.

remove from her mother's care the young Elizabeth, who was a royal ward, on the grounds that Lady Isabel was not a reliable person to be entrusted with the education of a great lady owing to 'the disposition she takes from her own mother'—a malicious allusion to the Countess's bourgeois ancestry. He even asked for the custody of the child for himself, despite the obvious impropriety of putting her in the care of one who stood to gain so much from her death.[1]

In the middle of these family quarrels and intrigues Earl John suddenly fell ill and died in February 1588, after holding the title for no more than ten months. During this short period, both in his own right as Earl and as executor of his brother he had received £6,766 from the estate. Three thousand of this came from the rents of lands owned and leased, and £515 from fines. The remaining £3,240 came from the sale of produce, £1,840 from cattle, sheep, and wool, £860 from corn and grass, £280 from wood, and £80 from iron. These huge sums were undoubtedly in excess of the normal annual profits of husbandry and must have been derived from the sale of the late Earl's personal estate. Even so, there was barely enough to spare to begin to pay part of the funeral cost of Earl Edward and some of his debts.[2] A second death within a year therefore created a temporary but acute shortage of ready money with which to pay for a second funeral, a second accumulation of debts, and a second list of legacies. These last included £1,000 portions to each of his three daughters, £3,000 to pay his debts, and one year's wages for all his servants. In addition the estate was further reduced by life grants of some Yorkshire properties to his three younger sons and the settlement on the widow for jointure of the very valuable manors of Helmsley and Rievaulx.[3]

IV. THE FIFTH EARL ROGER, 1588–1612

Earl John appointed the Earls of Leicester and Lord Burghley as supervisors of his will and as a result the latter for the second time in his life took control of the fortunes of the Manners family. In view of the urgent need for retrenchment he ordered the funeral to be carried out as economically as possible, a directive which still left room for the use of about 700 yards of black cloth.[4] It is fairly clear that the next six months saw a struggle at Court between

[1] *H.M.C. Rutland MSS.* i, pp. 219, 220.   [2] B/A 77.   [3] B/W 24.
[4] *H.M.C. Rutland MSS.* i, pp. 241–3. But the quality of the cloth was very poor, 'meaner than has been at any funeral for many years'.

Leicester and Burghley for the grant of the wardship of the heiress Elizabeth and of the young Earl Roger, both of whom were under age. Leicester had a strong tactical asset in the favour of the dowager Countess, Elizabeth, but Burghley was strategically well placed as Master of the Court of Wards. The prize was worth fighting for, since Elizabeth's future husband and Earl Roger would one day be in a position to exercise considerable political weight. Neither Burghley nor Leicester wanted this weight to be thrown against them in the continuing struggle for influence in Court and country.

Though both contestants were distracted by the political and military crisis of the Armada campaign, they still found time to continue jockeying for position. Burghley won the first round, directing the dowager Lady Elizabeth to return young Roger to the care of his tutors at Queens' College, Cambridge. Elizabeth riposted by sending her eldest daughter Bridget up to Court under the care of the Countess of Bedford, who was of the Leicester party.[1] Leicester was apparently on the verge of winning the main battle for Roger's wardship when he died suddenly in September. As a result Burghley, as Master of the Court of Wards, was entrusted by the Queen with the custody of the young Earl and took over the responsibility for his education.

So close was Burghley's control that the young man did not even dare to accept an invitation to visit his mother without obtaining Burghley's prior consent. Meanwhile the heiress Elizabeth, who was also a royal ward, was suing the dowager Countess Elizabeth for her inheritance in the Court of Wards, and the Countess was appealing to the Lord Chief Justice to obtain the lands due to come under her charge as her husband's executor.[2] These strained relations between Burghley and the Countess must have been gravely exacerbated when in 1589 the former, presumably by exercise of his powers as Master of the Court of Wards, and no doubt with Lady Isabel's consent, married Elizabeth to his grandson and heir in tail, William Cecil. When Elizabeth and her husband pursued their lawsuit against the Countess in Chancery and the Court of Wards, it is not surprising that it was reported that the Chancellor was under heavy pressure from 'great personages' to give a favourable verdict.[3] Though there is no hard evidence to

[1] Ibid., pp. 246, 250.   [2] Ibid., pp. 260-9, 274, 283.
[3] Ibid., pp. 277, 287, 292, 297.

prove that Burghley was anything but impartial in his judicial dealings, there was a clear conflict of interest between his role as guardian of minors for the Crown as Master of the Court of Wards, and his other roles as active politician seeking useful allies, and as scheming parent anxious to provide good marriages for his children. His manœuvre in capturing the rich heiress Elizabeth in marriage to his grandson, his close supervision of Earl Roger as guardian, and his official role as judge and arbitrator in all the family disputes, inevitably gave rise to a feeling of resentment at this stifling grip over the house of Manners. Although relations always remained polite, the duel between the dowager Countess Elizabeth and Lord Burghley continued for many years, sometimes openly, sometimes in more devious forms. For example, when in 1592 Burghley tried to catch the Earl of Northumberland as a husband for his grand-daughter, but was thwarted by the latter's assertion that 'she can not fancy him', it was promptly suggested to the Countess that negotiations should be opened for him to marry her daughter, Lady Bridget Manners.[1]

Meanwhile Earl Roger at Cambridge was torn between his guardian and his mother. The latter took him off on gay hunting parties at Belvoir, the former lectured him sententiously about his duties, urging that 'your learning do not diminish . . . for learning will increase if it be cherished, and cannot be lost but by negligence, and beside that, learning will serve you in all ages, and in all places and fortunes. But I must add to you that this learning wherof I write must be governed always with a knowledge and fear of God, for otherwise it will prove but for a vanity and lead you to folly.'[2] These ponderous moral lessons fell on deaf ears, and Earl Roger never showed any very marked interest in scholarship, nor more than average conformity to the religious practices of the age. Worse still, as early as 1591 he was beginning to show signs of that reckless temper which was to cost him so dear later on.[3]

Early in 1595 the Countess Elizabeth died, thus reducing the jointures charged on the estate from three to two, and Earl Roger, though still a minor for another two years, came into his own. The next five years were spent in a headlong orgy of dissipation and military adventure that is exactly paralleled by that of his crony Southampton. His mother's death interrupted his plans for the Grand Tour and for the next few months he was busy arranging

[1] H.M.C. *Rutland MSS*. i, pp. 298, 300, 301.   [2] Ibid., p. 274.   [3] Ibid., p. 296.

the funeral, clearing off the debts of about £1,500, paying £1,300 of the £2,500 portion of his sister Bridget on her marriage with Robert Tyrwhitt, continuing the everlasting lawsuit with his aunt the Countess Isabel and the Cecils, and running horse-races for high stakes at Galterby Moor.[1] But before the end of the year he was off to the Continent, where for the next two years he roamed through France, Switzerland, north Italy, and Germany. He fell seriously ill in Venice, but by the summer of 1597 was fully re-covered and was back in Paris, where he learned of the Earl of Essex's expedition to the Azores. Ignoring pleas to return home to manage his estate, he promptly rushed off to join it.

From now on he was swept up into the Essex following, with its open-handed reckless ways and its frank defiance of the Cecil faction. He spent much time and energy at cards and dice and in playing tennis, often at Essex House, though it must be admitted that there are a few signs of more cultivated interests, such as the purchase of a viola da gamba for £5, and Aristotle's *Physics*, *Rhetoric*, and *Ethics* for 12s. 4d. His purchase of the *Arcadia* in 1599 was hardly to be avoided if he was to be able to make proper suit to the author's daughter. Though he did buy a Livy, it is noticeable that it was in translation, and his very limited expenditure on books suggest a young man of some natural intelligence but who had failed to master the classics and whose main interests lay elsewhere.[2] In 1599 he reaffirmed his anti-Cecil alignments by marrying Eliza-beth, the daughter and heiress of Sir Philip Sidney, and by accept-ing the post of Colonel of Foot in the expeditionary force to Ireland under Essex. The next year, during Essex's period of disgrace after his return from Ireland, he filled in time by serving with Dutch troops in the Low Countries, but he was unfortunately back in London at the New Year. Early in the morning of 8 February 1601 he was roused and informed that Essex's life was in danger from his enemies, and was asked to rally to his aid. Without stopping to inquire the circumstances or calculate the consequences, he rushed out into the streets in defence of his chief, and found himself involved in the abortive *coup d'état* of the Essex Revolt.[3] For the second time in fifty years an Earl of Rutland had taken part in un-successful rebellion. Although he was imprisoned in the Tower of London, his life was never in serious danger. It very soon became

---

[1] B/A 378. *H.M.C. Rutland MSS.* iv, p. 410.
[2] B/A 97, 100. *H.M.C. Rutland MSS.* i, p. 339.   [3] Ibid., p. 366.

clear that he had had nothing to do with the preliminary plotting, and had acted merely from youthful folly and misplaced loyalty to a friend. Moreover, he did not lack well-placed friends, such as three influential maids of honour, Lady Walsingham, Lady Newton, and Mrs. Ratcliffe, to whom he had just sent New Year's gifts.[1]

Kicking his heels in the cold and draughty chambers of the Tower, and waiting to know the size of the fine the Queen would impose upon him, Earl Roger had time, if he cared to use it, to reflect on the course of his life over the last five years. Owing to the decentralized nature of the accounting system, he can have had no very clear idea of just what he had spent or how it had been paid for. It is possible, however, to combine the accounts to form a rough picture of what had happened. During the years of foreign travel from 1595 to 1597 expenditure was running at between £6,000 and £7,000 a year, but thereafter it rose dramatically to over £11,000 in 1598, and mounted to a crescendo of about £12,400 in 1600–1.[2] This rate of expenditure was almost certainly higher than that of any other private individual in the country, exceeded only by that of one or two of the great courtiers and officials dependent on royal favours for their support. There is no simple explanation of where the money went, except in terms of an all-embracing extravagance of scale. Even when he was abroad, the cost of upkeep of the household and establishment at Belvoir was at least £800 a year, a figure which had almost doubled by 1601. Fee-farm rents and leasehold rents due to the Crown were paid irregularly, but should have amounted to over £400 a year, while legal charges normally exceeded £200. The education and maintenance of his three younger brothers and two unmarried sisters rose rapidly from £470 to £1,640 as they grew older. Productive investment was not entirely absent, for the Earl spent altogether some £2,000 between 1596 and 1602 in consolidating and extending his existing holdings near Belvoir and in renewing expired leases from the Crown.

The bulk of the expenditure, however, went on maintaining a large establishment and an extravagant personal expenditure abroad, in London, or in Ireland. Huge sums, ranging from £1,100 to £2,300 were paid to the Earl each year for his personal use. Some of it was used to maintain himself on the Grand Tour or in Ireland or France, and some of it went in gambling. In addition, his expenditure on clothes and jewels for his own person was on a

---

[1] B/A 312.   [2] B/A 378, 90, 309, 310, 95, 97, 100, 312.

staggering scale, often amounting to over £1,000 a year, and rising to £2,600 in the year of his marriage. The mere embroidery of a suit with flames of gold and silver cost £60, while five pairs of silk hose—olive, silver, pearl, sky, and black—cost £11. The fitting up of a new coach in 1598–9 cost over £70, together with a further £64 for embroidering the crimson sumpter cloths with peacocks and the Manners arms. Everything he did was on the same princely scale. The man who opened the park gates at Rockingham as he passed through received a tip of 1s., the equivalent of two days' wages. The impression is one of absurdly conspicuous expenditure, undertaken not from a sense of what was becoming to one of his rank and wealth, but for sheer pleasure of spending.

Where did the money come from to pay for this extraordinary style of living? The bare rental of the Earl's estates amounted to £3,100, rising steadily to £3,500. In addition there were demesnes kept in hand around Belvoir, and Helmsley, the net profits from which on the average amounted to about £700 a year. Minor non-recurrent sources of income were an aid, levied in good medieval fashion on his tenants to support their lord in the Irish wars under Essex, which brought in £256; £666 squeezed out of the Countess Isabel after the interminable and very expensive lawsuit; and a cash portion of £4,000 with his wife Elizabeth Sidney. Of the recurrent sources, the net profits of the Rievaulx ironworks fluctuated wildly at this period, falling from over £1,000 in 1595 to nothing at all in 1598 and 1599. In 1600, however, steps were taken to open up a larger and more reliable market by selling some 80 tons a year to London merchants. As a result net profits of the works this year came to £380 and the way was opened for further substantial receipts in subsequent years.[1]

The most important source of all, however, remains to be discussed. During the years of the minority, before 1597, fines for new leases remained low, averaging no more than £200 a year. But in 1598 the Earl came of age, and since the trustees of the estate had been unable to renew leases for longer than the minority he found himself in a position to levy fines for new twenty-one-year leases on the greater part of his vast property. This undertaking was promptly put in hand and in the next four years produced nearly £14,600. Basically it was this huge windfall that allowed Earl Roger

---

[1] For the Sidney portion see F. Grose, *Antiquarian Repertory*, London, i, 1809, p. 275. For details of the ironworks see below, pp. 190–4.

to maintain without royal support a standard of living as opulent as that of any man in England.

But these fines and ironworks profits were not enough to save Earl Roger from running into debt, which he was first obliged to do on any scale in 1599, in order to finance his venture to Ireland under Essex. In that year he borrowed £2,800 in London, and from then until he was put in the Tower his debt burden rose yearly till it reached £4,991.[1] In view of the Earl's enormous resources that was a relatively minor burden, yet it is significant of the lack of confidence that his prodigality inspired, that he was forced by his London creditors to pay an extra 2 or 3 per cent in the form of gifts of plate over and above the statutory maximum interest rate of 10 per cent, besides giving bonds from his leading servants, for which he was obliged to issue counter-bonds in his own name.[2]

Despite his phenomenal rate of expenditure over the past five years, it is clear that Earl Roger's financial position was still basically secure. Thanks to his huge rental, to the great windfall of the fines for new leases, and to the now rising profits from the sales of iron, he ended this orgiastic period with a load of debt that was less than one year's ordinary income. But he could not have carried on for much longer. There were no more fines to be collected from his tenants, and the debt load was mounting swiftly. He still owed £1,000 to his brother-in-law as part of the portion of one sister, and there was £4,000 to be found very soon to marry off the other two. Even without the abrupt psychological jolt of rebellion and imprisonment, he would have been obliged before long drastically to alter his way of life. No wonder his friends, like the Earl of Southampton and Lord Compton, trying to live up to this rate without these extraordinary resources, found themselves in a desperate plight on the day of the rebellion.

In May 1601 Earl Roger was summoned before the Privy Council and fined the crippling sum of £30,000, while his two brothers, whom he had drawn with him into the Essex revolt, were fined another £2,666 each. But in fact things were not quite as black as they seemed, for these punishments were more in the nature of a public example than a real threat. Sir Robert Cecil obtained a grant from the Crown of the fines of the two brothers, and it was

[1] Hatfield House, Salis. MSS. 77 f. 68.
[2] H.M.C. Rutland MSS. iv, pp. 416, 418. B/C 246, 247, 253, 6245, 7143.

thought that he would let them off with little or nothing.[1] As for the Earl himself, there was every hope that the Queen would reduce his fine, a hope diligently nourished by a very dishonest statement of his financial plight that was forwarded to Sir Robert Cecil in order to soften the Queen's heart. In it he had the effrontery to pretend that his rental before his grandmother's death early in 1601 had been only a mere £2,410 a year, whereas in fact we know it was nearer £3,500, to say nothing of casualties, profits of demesne farming, and receipts from the sales of iron.[2] The result of this document and of influential pressure was to reduce the fine to £18,000, payable in instalments over the eighteen months before November 1602. To secure payment the Crown took a mortgage on some of the Earl's property. It is perfectly clear, however, that there was collusion in the Exchequer. The total receipts from the mortgaged property in 1603–4 were under £600 a year, which means that their capital value was at most only £12,000. Furthermore, although the Earl made no attempt to pay his fine, no steps were taken to foreclose on the mortgage, and hardly had King James reached London in 1603 than he issued instructions for its cancellation. In the end, therefore, Rutland's participation in the Essex revolt cost him nothing. This treatment was not unusual for the Essex conspirators—Lords Cromwell and Mounteagle fared exactly the same—but with Rutland a far larger sum was at stake.[3] It seems very unlikely that the aged Queen was aware that the fines were not being paid, and one may conclude that Buckhurst, the Lord Treasurer, was treading delicately in the knowledge that before very long James would be on the throne, and that the conspirators might once more be back in high favour at Court.

It was lucky indeed for Rutland that he was able to evade this huge fine. In addition to his existing debts to his sisters and to creditors, it would have imposed a burden that could only have been shaken off by the sale of not far short of a quarter of his landed estates. As it was, however, he was not obliged to do more than sell three manors for about £8,700—and one of them belonged to his wife.[4] He also imposed a benevolence on his long-suffering tenants in order to help pay the hypothetical fine to the Queen. In this he was surprisingly successful, obtaining no less than £625

---

[1] H.M.C. *Rutland MSS.* i, pp. 375, 377.   [2] Hatfield House, Salis. MSS. 77 f. 68.
[3] P.R.O., Close Rolls, 1 J.1, pts. 5, 8, 10.
[4] B/A 104, 374. H.M.C. *Salis. MSS.* xi, p. 396. P.R.O., Close Rolls, 1 J.1, pt. 14; 2 J.1, pt. 6.

in cash and promises. Out of 142 tenants listed in Yorkshire only twenty-five refused outright, the centre of disaffection being the village of Pockley, where all six tenants remained obdurate.[1]

The year 1601 saw the lowest point in the fortunes of Earl Roger. The accession of James in 1603 restored him to royal favour, which brought substantial rewards in addition to the remission of his fine. Although this Court favour involved him in an expensive embassy to Denmark which must have cost far more than the £825 he received from the Exchequer, it also meant that his request for help, 'especially seeing the weakness of my estate and greatness of my debts', did not go unanswered. In 1605 he obtained a grant of ten recusants with whom he was free to compound for his own profit in return for their release from the penalties attached to Catholic worship. The next year he was given a life annuity of £424 a year so as to cancel the fee-farm rents due to the Crown, and in 1607 the renewal for forty years of the lease of Long Bennington, Lincolnshire, at a rent of £36, which two years later was bringing in a gross rent of £83.[2]

It was not until 1606, however, that Earl Roger was able to free himself from the burden of debt that he had created by his youthful folly. He borrowed again heavily in 1602–3, some of it on mort-gage,[3] and it was only the sale of a very large quantity of iron to London merchants in 1606 for £4,200 that enabled the Earl to clear off the worst of the debt to individual creditors. Though there is no evidence that he had yet paid all the £5,000 due as marriage portions to his three sisters—he was paying £300 to Lord Scroope in 1605–6 as interest on Elizabeth's unpaid portion—the finances of the Manners were now at last back on an even keel.[4] After the grant of his pension in 1606 Earl Roger seems to have withdrawn from Court life to rural pursuits and local administration at Belvoir, and no further Crown bounty came his way before his death in 1612.

V. THE ADMINISTRATION OF THE ESTATE, 1560–1641

Before examining the later history of the family, we should first describe the way in which the property was managed during the eighty years from 1560 to 1640. Hardly any accounts have survived before 1587 and it is only after this that we can fitfully reconstruct

---

[1] B/A 794, 851, 852.   [2] H.M.C. Salis. MSS. xvii, pp. 6, 194. B/G 169, 617.
[3] B/A 104. P.R.O., Close Rolls 1 J.1, pt. 1.   [4] B/A 110.

the nature of the administration. The accounting system changed hardly at all over these fifty years. Although all records were kept in English, roman numerals were used right up to 1640 for the final accounts. By 1613, however, most working drafts were kept in arabic numerals, which proves that the book-keepers were by now thinking and calculating in arabic. Although the first drafts of the accounts were throughout kept in paper books, the final copies for preservation were made out on membranes of vellum sewn together at the top and done up into rolls—a manner of keeping accounts that went back to the Middle Ages. There are signs, however, that these final rolls were already obsolescent. The signature of the auditor often appears on the books, which seem to have provided the basis for his work and the fair vellum copies, though also signed by the auditor, often contain transcription errors, and have evidently not been used nor even checked with much care. Until 1600 the accounting year ran from December to December, but in that year it changed to August and later still it shifted back to July. All accounts were kept in the old charge and discharge system by which an accountant dealt not with the actual cash he received during the year, but with the sums he ought to have received together with arrears due on his account from previous years.

For the fifty years between 1590 and the eve of the Civil War, the Earls of Rutland were predominantly courtiers, and spent most of their time in London. They were therefore faced with the problem of handling an income derived from estates in widely separated rural areas and an expenditure that was concentrated largely on London. This difficulty was surmounted by instituting a decentralized system by which separate accountants paid money to and fro between them, as the need arose. This provided great flexibility, though it made any proper assessment of the annual balance of income and expenditure exceedingly difficult.

Thus between 1599 and 1601 there were bailiffs of the three principal demesne holdings, at Belvoir, Helmsley, and Garendon, and there was a clerk of the ironworks at Rievaulx. The Receiver-General lived at Belvoir and handled all receipts from Lincolnshire, Leicestershire, and Nottinghamshire; there was a northern receiver for Yorkshire rents at Helmsley; and there was an agent in London.[1] The interlocking of these separate accounts was bewildering in its

---

[1] Between 1597 and 1599 there was a single receiver for Yorkshire and midlands rents.

complexity. The northern receiver collected Yorkshire rents and profits, the net profits of the Helmsley bailiff and some of the profits from the Rievaulx ironworks; after paying local overheads, including, when necessary, money for the running of the Rievaulx works and the Helmsley demesnes, the rest was sent in fluctuating proportions to the Receiver-General at Belvoir and to the London agent. The Receiver-General at Belvoir collected the midlands rents and profits, the profits paid over by the Belvoir bailiff, and the sums sent down by the northern receiver. After paying necessary advances to the Belvoir bailiff and covering the cost of the household and establishment at Belvoir, the remainder was sent down to London. The London agent thus drew money from both the northern receiver and the Receiver-General, part of the money from the latter coming originally from the former. He also received the profits of all Rievaulx iron sold to Londoners, of the Kentish lands of the Countess, and of the Garendon demesnes and farms, and on one occasion he directly intercepted the profits from the Belvoir bailiff. He also received extraordinary income from loans, sales of land, or payments by the Crown. With this money collected from so many different sources, he paid for the various expenses of the Earl in London.[1]

Thirty years later, in 1627–30, for which years another little group of the final rolls has survived, no fundamental change in the system had occurred. There was still a Yorkshire receiver, a Receiver-General at Belvoir, and a London agent, with the same interlocking sets of accounts. There was still a clerk of the ironworks at Rievaulx, whose profits were paid either to the Yorkshire or the Belvoir receiver, although the bulk of the production was sent to London and appeared in the London agent's accounts. There was now a western receiver for the lands of the Countess, and bailiffs for demesnes at Helmsley, Garendon, and Bestwood Park. There was still no central accounting system and, though evidence *ex silentio* is always dangerous, no indication that calculations of annual profit and loss were ever made.[2]

Because of this decentralization, and because of the 'charge and discharge' system of accounting, it is very difficult to get an accurate picture of the Earl's total income. And even when it is possible to work it out for a given year, the use of beneficial leases caused such enormous fluctuations from year to year that it is dangerous

[1] B/A 278, 309, 310, 312.   [2] B/A 315, 316, 382.

to regard it as an average. Nor is it possible to trace the changes in mere rental with any certainty. The total absence of surveys, lease-books, and individual leases, and the extreme rarity of rentals, make comparison difficult, while the constant and considerable fluctuations in the property held by the Earls owing to transfers to and fro under family settlements make it hard to trace a continuous picture of any considerable block of property. The issue is further obscured by purchase not so much of altogether new property as of small parcels of land adjacent to existing holdings.

Owing to the uncertainty of how far the royal survey of the estate in 1563 provides a realistic figure for the rental, it is impossible to prove conclusively that Earl Edward's recorded zeal in estate management succeeded in keeping his income abreast of the price revolution. Since the 1563 figures differ suspiciously little from those given in the first Earl's will in 1543, they are probably far too low. The next figures with which they may be compared are a 'clear net revenue' for 1608–9, which gives the sum due by the bailiffs for this year after deduction of £138 for fees and expenses of keeping courts. This certainly includes fines in certain instances and represents the amount actually due this year. It is thus not truly comparable with the 1563 valuations. Nevertheless, when we find that after deducting fines those items which occur in both documents show an increase of 300 per cent, one may perhaps conclude that the Manners were more successful than most of their fellow peers in keeping pace with the Elizabethan price revolution. The credit for this should go to Earl Edward, for the receivers' accounts show clearly that the increases had mostly occurred before 1597, when Earl Roger came of age and took charge of his estates.[1]

The next document which gives a set of figures directly comparable to this is a rental for 1636–7. Identical properties in both documents show an increase by 1636–7 of about 66 per cent over 1608 rentals, while a similar document for 1658 shows an increase of 100 per cent over the rentals fifty years before. This does not necessarily mean, however, that average annual returns from the estate increased to this degree. Though Earl Roger claimed in 1601 that most of his property was 'to the uttermost improved' the fact that he had just raised in fines for new twenty-one-year leases no less than £14,600, the equivalent of over four years' rent of the whole estate, suggests that he was still taking much of the increased

[1] Rentals and Surveys, Portfolio 22/36. B/A 481, 309.

value of the property in fines rather than rents. When these leases fell due for renewal in 1618, his brother apparently received only about £11,000 in fines, the equivalent in real terms of well under two-thirds of the sum levied twenty years before. This would suggest that part of the increase in rents was due to a reduction in the irregular windfalls of large fines, which was itself a most uneconomic method of anticipating landed revenue. Even allowing for this factor, however, the evidence, inadequate though it is, would suggest that the income per acre from the estates of the Earl of Rutland in the early Stuart period was rising rather faster than the value of money was deteriorating.

Owing to the loss of lease-books and surveys we have no idea of the administrative methods by which these increases were brought about. It may have been entirely due to careful surveys, which enabled the Earls to take advantage of the pressure of population on land and the tremendous rise in the price of agricultural produce to extract realistic rents from their tenants. The only hint that they might on occasions have employed more drastic methods of reorganization is the grant of a royal pardon in 1619 for having converted tillage to pasture at Pillarton, Warwickshire.[1]

Demesne lands were kept under direct agricultural management by the Earl's agents at Belvoir and Helmsley throughout the whole period. The figures for net receipts from the bailiffs are, however, deceptive. In the first place it is necessary on occasions to subtract the advances made by the receivers to the bailiffs for running expenses. Secondly, at Helmsley part of the park was joisted (let for pasture) and not grazed by the Lord's own beasts, while at Belvoir a good deal of the receipts came from the sale of corn received not from the demesnes but in rent-corn paid by neighbouring farmers. On the other hand, the profits shown by the Belvoir bailiff would drop sharply whenever the Earl came into residence, since much of the produce was at once diverted to supplying the kitchen and stables.

It is fairly clear that up to the death of Earl Edward the demesnes were on a considerable scale. The sale of cattle after the Earl's death in 1587–8 may have been exceptional, amounting as it did to £1,461, but the £818 from sale of corn and £312 from sale of wool suggest substantial agricultural activity. Gross receipts for sale of cattle and corn during the late 1590s were running at nearly £900 a year, the net profits being more like £700. After 1598 some

[1] B/G 186.

of Helmsley Park was being leased and the stock sold off, and it looks as if a further contraction of demesne took place soon afterwards. Certainly payments to receivers by the bailiffs were down to £560 in 1613–14 and below £250 during the years 1616–21. Later still, in 1635, orders were issued to survey and lease Helmsley Castle itself, which presumably meant the disappearance of the whole of the demesne pasture in the surrounding parks.[1] Stock accounts which survive for 1596–8 and 1627–9 confirm this trend. In the Helmsley pastures at the year's end in 1596–8 there had been about 100 steers of various ages and between 480 and 700 wethers, but in 1627–9 there were only between 40 and 50 oxen and no sheep; wethers were merely bought, perhaps fattened, and sent down to Belvoir. At Belvoir grazing activity seems to have expanded, both for cattle and sheep, and arable farming to have diminished, or possibly disappeared altogether, the receipts of corn being perhaps all now derived from corn-rents. There were also very small demesnes attached to the house at Garendon, and in 1627–9 a sheep farm of about 400 to 500 sheep in Bestwood Park, which was held on lease from the Crown.

Before 1600 the net profits of demesne farming contributed perhaps as much as 15 or 20 per cent of the total landed income of the Earl of Rutland, but it seems likely that after 1600 they never came to more than about 10 per cent, and that by 1613 they were below 5 per cent. The reason for the change of policy, which is to be found in many families at just this period, must lie in the shrinkage of wool profits, and the rise in rents obtainable from tenants. It should be remembered, however, that a large proportion of the produce was now being absorbed by the Belvoir household, so that the figures probably exaggerate the extent of the shrinkage. The 1658 figures, which probably represent the value of the whole of the produce, show that the Belvoir tithes and desmesnes amounted to about 7 per cent of the rental of the old estate. But by now the addition of the great Haddon property of the cadet branch substantially changed the over-all picture, for the net profits of the Haddon demesnes and tithes came to no less than one-third of the Haddon rental. If we ignore fines, net receipts from all the demesnes and tithes now amounted to 17 per cent of the total.[2]

It seems clear, therefore, that demesne farming occupied an unusually important place in the calculations of the Earls of Rutland

---

[1] B/G 699.   [2] B/A 1244.

during the Elizabethan period, but that thereafter it shrank in size and changed in character. By 1611 the main function of the demesnes was not to produce a cash income but to supply the household. Cattle, and sometimes sheep, were sent down to Belvoir from Helmsley and were mainly devoted to obtaining for the kitchen its annual quota of 70 beeves, 400 sheep, and 40 lambs. The 2,400 rabbits consumed each year were supplied by warrens at Belvoir, Bestwood Park, and Garendon. Nearly all the 400-odd quarters of corn of various kinds, materials for the 160 quarters of malt, and the 400 lb. of hops came from rent-corn, tithes, and the produce of farms near Belvoir.[1] It was to maintain this flow of produce into the kitchen and stables, not commercial farming for the market, that was now the real purpose of the demesnes.

VI. THE RIEVAULX IRONWORKS, 1530–1641

Of far greater significance is the story of the development of the family ironworks. Before the Dissolution the monks of Rievaulx Abbey in Yorkshire had begun to exploit the local supplies of iron ore and wood fuel, and in the 1530s there were already a couple of small bloomeries, valued at £20 a year. As soon as he got possession, the first Earl began to modernize the works, beginning with a water-powered hammer in 1540, installed with the aid of Lambert Symart, a Frenchman, who over forty years before had set up the first English water-driven hammer for Henry VII. It is symptomatic of the prudent management of the Earl and his agents that plans were made so that the works would be supplied with charcoal fuel from twenty separate areas, one for each year, thus allowing for regular cropping and so preventing permanent destruction of the woodlands.[2] In 1563 the works were valued at £55, though they were said to have been 'modo vastata'. Shortly before 1577 the third Earl erected near the rere-dorter of the old abbey the first recorded blast furnace in the north of England, and in that year he extended the casting floor, built a new forge, and hired a refiner out of Staffordshire, which apparently was the centre of technological innovation at this period. Water power both for the forge hammer and for the furnace bellows was easily available in the canals built by the monks in the twelfth and thirteenth centuries to transport

[1] H.M.C. Rutland MSS. iv, pp. 480–6.
[2] H. R. Shubert, *History of the British Iron and Steel Industry*, London, 1957, pp. 221, 395–6.

their building stone.[1] Production was now running at about 70 tons of bar iron a year, all sold locally. Earl Edward was still not content, however, for he sent an expert north to build a new furnace in 1582, and he modified the hearth in 1587. Between then and 1603 further improvement in the furnace took place, which certainly included the use of larger bellows.

As a result, whereas in 1582 production was 3·6 tons of pig-iron a week, and still only 4·7 in 1587, in 1591–2 it was over 7 and by 1603 had risen to over 12. Already it was, so far as we know, the most up-to-date plant in the north of England, and it remained in the lead at least up to the Civil War. The first English reference to the use of forge slag in a furnace comes from Rievaulx in 1605. In 1616 a completely new furnace was built at a cost of £104, and in 1623 there is the first reference anywhere to the arching over of the apertures in the furnace. All this technological innovation paid dividends in higher production, rising in some years to over 16 tons a week. As a result of this rising furnace output, the forge had to be expanded to keep pace, and shortly before 1613 a third finery and a second hammer were built, making it into a double forge, and a new hammerman was imported from Staffordshire. Right up to the Civil War experiment continued, and in 1636 an expert with the appropriate name of Blow Harder was sent up from Staffordshire to work a trial with the Rievaulx iron. The improvement in productivity of the forge, however, was less than that of the furnace, the amount of pig-iron needed to produce a ton of bar iron falling only very slowly from 1·65 to 1 to an average of about 1·4. On the fuel side, charcoal was made more economically, the ratio of wood to coal falling from three cords to a dozen in the 1580s to between 2·3 and 2·5 after 1615. Whether or not there were also economics in the use of fuel at the works, the accounts do not allow us to judge.

To maintain these operations in the second decade of the century required a labour force of about 80 persons. Most of the work was done on piece rates by casual labour which could be stood off at will. For some parts of the year there were employed about 30 woodcutters, 8 general labourers on day wages, 12 miners for the ore, 9 carriers of ore and charcoal, 6 carriers of wood, and 4 to 6 colliers. Permanent salaried staff, many of whom were also paid extra or piece rates, included the Clerk of the Works, the storekeeper and

---

[1] H. A. Rye, 'Rievaulx Abbey', *Archaeological Journal*, lvii, 1900, pp. 76–7.

overseer, the founder, the chafery man, the three finers, and the woodward. The auditor was also paid a fee for his intermittent services, and the colliers had 10s. a year each for liveries.

Since both the iron ore and most of the charcoal fuel came from the Earl's own estate, and since the capital value of the works themselves was not very great once the initial cost of making the dam and mill pond and streams had been covered, the main running expenses were on wages. The annual overheads were therefore only about £500 before 1614, though they rose to between £1,200 and £1,500 in the 1620s, due to the need to purchase some of the wood, and fell back again to about £1,100 in the 1630s.

The main hindrance to expanding production was the limited consumption in the locality. The output was nearly all in crude bar iron, though a little was in the form of finished articles. There was a small but regular trade in window bars, and after 1583 there is evidence of occasional production of fire-backs, for which a mould was made in 1603. In the 1580s two-thirds of the sale was by retail to farmers and small tradesmen in the neighbourhood, and it was not till the turn of the century that the wholesale trade outstripped the retail. Judging by later accounts this was principally due to the expansion of the cutlery trade at Sheffield. But this was precarious support for so efficient a works, as was shown in the late 1590s, when profits fell rapidly from over £1,000 in 1595 to a net loss in 1598. This contraction of the market was presumably due to a sharp fall in surplus purchasing power caused by the famine conditions of 1596–8.

It was clear that the only hope of selling the full potential output of the modernized works was to break into the great consumer market of London. This was first achieved in 1601, when a contract was made with some London merchants to take delivery of a fixed annual amount of iron at Hull for shipment south. Thereafter the Londoners bought some 80 to 100 tons a year and sometimes even larger quantities, the fairly static local sales being used to pay production costs. Output by 1602–3 was as high as 155 tons of bar iron a year, and the net profits amounted to over £1,000, while in 1605–6 the Londoners paid the Earl no less than £4,201 for his iron. This sort of output could not be maintained solely by the Earl's woods and in 1602–3 one-third of the total fuel had to be bought. This is not surprising when it is realized that between 3,500 and 5,000 cords of wood were cut each year in the early seventeenth century. If we reckon that there were about sixteen statutory cords of coppice wood to an acre, this meant cropping between 200 and 300 acres a year, which could not be cut again for at least fifteen years. To maintain this output indefinitely therefore required between 3,000 and 4,500 acres of wood, which was evidently more than the Earl possessed. From 1613 onwards production was maintained at a high, though fairly static level, and between 1616 and 1621 the Earl made a net average profit of £1,540 a year. Indeed the highest recorded production figures are for 1615–17, when 220 tons of bar iron a year issued from the forge. Throughout the 1620s and 1630s production fluctuated between 150 and 210 tons, but at any rate between 1627 and 1630 profits were reduced by the need to buy very nearly half the fuel. For the time being, at any rate, fuel from the Earl's own estate was running short. In 1636–8, however, hardly any wood was bought, although production remained high. This may be due either to a recovery of the coppices in the previous decade or to a deliberately improvident policy of cutting down all the woods on the Earl's own land, in the knowledge that at his death the property would pass to the Villiers family.

   Precise figures for production costs are not possible, firstly because fuel from the Earl's woods only cost the expense of cutting, cording, and coaling, and secondly because of the problem of stocks carried over from year to year. Bearing in mind the serious limitations and qualifications imposed by these factors, it is nevertheless possible to offer some figures which at any rate may serve to indicate rough trends. Presumably as a result of the technological improvements of the late sixteenth century, nominal costs per ton of bar iron fell from £7. 6s. in 1577–8 to £5. 16s. in 1602–6, although wholesale prices were static at about £10 to £11 a ton. Thereafter costs rose to a peak of £8. 12s. a ton in 1627–30 owing to the heavy purchase of wood, but dropped again to £5. 12s. in the 1630s when all the fuel was again being taken off the Earl's estates. But this rise in costs was more than offset by the rise in prices paid by the London merchants, which between 1606 and 1614 rose from £10. 11s. to £13. 14s. a ton. Though it fell off again to between £11 and £13 during the slump of the early 1620s, it soon rallied and reached its peak of £16 in 1637–8, a figure which suggests that Swedish competition had not yet begun seriously to affect the London market. As a result, between 1601 and 1640 the Earls of Rutland made an average net profit from these ironworks of between £1,000 and £1,500 a year. Although there is reason to suspect that this may only have been possible at the eventual cost of denuding the local woodlands, the achievement is none the less very impressive. Right up to the end, the Earls kept the works under direct management, and this entrepreneurial zeal paid handsome dividends. Very few of their contemporaries drew so much, over so long a period, from industrial undertakings on their estates.[1]

From the point of view of the history of the iron industry at this time, there are a number of important conclusions to be drawn from the study of the Rievaulx works. It is clear that the Elizabethan period witnessed a major technological revolution, introduced into the north mainly by experts from Staffordshire, and that as a result output rose rapidly. Thereafter development was limited not by any shortage of capital—the initial investment and the annual overheads were both on a limited scale—but by the appalling deficiencies of transport and the inelasticity of the local market. Cost of transport severely restricted the range from which fuel supplies could be drawn and this consequently limited output. The Sheffield cutlery industry was expanding, but not fast enough to absorb the output of the local works together with that of Rievaulx. The only hope of achieving large sales was by breaking through to the London market, and it was Rutland's success in doing this, thanks to ready water transport from Rievaulx to Hull and from Hull to London, which brought him his high profit in the early seventeenth century. It is significant, however, that output and sales did not increase after about 1600, which suggests either that the expansionist phase of the industry was now over, and the market was saturated, or else that the limiting factor was now an adequate fuel supply within a reasonable distance from the works.

---

[1] The accounts of the ironworks are to be found in B/M 106; B/A 527–39, 1155, 1300, 878, 431, 588, 881, 459, 315–16, 382, 858; B/BSA. They have been used extensively by Dr. H. R. Shubert, op. cit. I am unable to agree with Dr. Shubert in a number of important points. By confusing the terminal dates of the accounts with those of the blowing, errors have crept into Dr. Shubert's calculations of output between 1613 and 1623, which are in reality rather smaller than he alleges since his figures exclude the early and relatively unproductive weeks of blowing before the accounts begin (p. 349). He is similarly wrong in stating that the Rievaulx works blew for eight weeks in 1613–14, a figure produced merely because the accounts do not begin till 20 November of that year (p. 243 note 4). His figures for pig-iron/bar-iron ratios exaggerate the improvement by taking exceptional years rather than the average (p. 291 note 1). The argument that furnaces were operated in winter to take advantage of clear cold weather looks rather dubious when it is found that in every year but one blowing began in the heat of July or August, and stopped between November and January, that is before the period of cold dry weather normally arrives (p. 244). (The furnace at Oakamoor in Staffordshire also blew in the autumn, see Notts. University Library, Middleton MSS. 5/165.)

VII. THE SIXTH AND SEVENTH EARLS FRANCIS AND GEORGE, 1612–1641

Earl Roger, or his wife, suffered from a family tendency to sterility, and they produced no heir. He was therefore succeeded by his next younger brother, Francis, who also failed to produce a male heir, and was therefore in turn succeeded in 1632 by his younger brother George. Francis was the first in the family since the Reformation to have adopted Catholic religious beliefs, which was the main obstacle which prevented him from profiting by a lifetime spent at Court. The only bounty the family obtained from the Crown between 1612 and the Civil War was a grant made in 1628 to Francis's brother and heir George, the future seventh Earl, of £4,000 in old unpaid debts due to the Crown, which he was left to collect as best he could. He did not have much success, and in ten years he only managed to make a net profit of £1,200 from the grant.[1]

Although an active courtier, the sixth Earl thus owed little or nothing to the Court, but his mounting income from lands and ironworks exceeded his expenditure, and left him with a considerable surplus for the purchase of additional property. In his years of retirement just before his death, the fifth Earl Roger had bought two manors for £4,000. His brother the sixth Earl bought Minting Park in Lancashire from Lord Willoughby's executors for £5,000 in 1618.[2] He also made other minor purchases of small parcels of land, bought Sir George Manners's leasehold interest in Uffington and Tallington for £2,650 in 1615, and at an unknown date the extent held by the Viscountess Campden on some of his nephew's Tyrwhit's estates. This last must have been an expensive investment, since the rental in 1636 was £611.[3] In all, therefore, between 1610 and 1630 the Earls added a rental of over £1,000 to their estates, at a cost which can hardly have been less than £18,000, to say nothing of the leasehold interest purchased from Sir George Manners.

Although for any other noble family these substantial additions to the estate would be of the greatest importance, they pale into insignificance in comparison with the changes brought about by biological accident. We have seen how in 1587 the failure of the

---

[1] B/G 169. B/A 789.   [2] B/A 122, 127, 129, 130, 121, 125. B/C 6953, 3740.
[3] B/A 121, 126, 130A, 315. B/M 144. B/BSA.

Earl Edward to produce an heir male had resulted in the loss to a daughter of about a third of the estates. Thereafter the longevity of widows had seriously reduced the present income of Earl Roger, who at one time was deprived of the three jointures of his mother, his aunt, and his grandmother. Moreover Roger had three younger brothers, all of whom were left by their father life interests in some of the family estates in order to provide them with a decent livelihood. The result of all this was a bewildering series of changes in the composition of the property actually enjoyed by Earl Roger. In 1595 his mother died and he came into her jointure; in 1599 he married Sir Philip Sidney's heiress and so obtained temporary possession of her estates; in 1601 his grandmother at last died, and her jointure returned to the Earls of Rutland after an absence of nearly forty years; in 1606 his aunt died and he inherited her jointure; and in 1613 his brother Oliver died leaving him successor to his estates.

But against these accretions must be set certain losses. The prolonged lawsuit with Lord Roos and the Cecils eventually resulted in the cession of two more properties, and the marriage of his younger brother George in 1605 made it necessary to grant him an annuity of £180 a year and settle an estate on him for the lives of himself and his wife as jointure.[1] Meanwhile, the persistent sterility of Countess Elizabeth made it likely that Earl Roger would have no heirs, and that the title would pass to his brother Francis. Francis had made what seemed like a very advantageous marriage in 1602 to the coheiress of Sir Francis Knyvett of Charlton and widow of Sir William Bevill, but she had died of smallpox in 1605 leaving an only daughter, so that the great prize of the Knyvett estates had been lost. In 1608 Francis brought off a second marriage with Cecily, daughter of Sir John Tufton of Hothfield, and widow of Sir Edward Hungerford. Sir Edward had recently died without issue, leaving her a life interest in his estate, which amounted to about £2,000 a year. She was therefore a rich prize, but the cost of catching her was not small. In the first place the two did not get on at all well, and the Earl was told by the poet Beaumont that

> Marriage was to thee
> Naught but a sacrament of misery.

Secondly, she was a notorious Catholic recusant, which added to the Earl's political troubles. And thirdly she was expensive, since it

---

[1] B/S 101, 106. The estates brought in £47 in 1598–9 and £201 in 1636 (B/A 95; B/BSA).

demanded a substantial additional settlement on Francis by Earl Roger, who assured lands worth £666 a year for present maintenance and future jointure.[1]

With the death without heirs of Earl Roger in 1612, swiftly followed by his widow, his brother Francis succeeded to the family estates, adding to them those that had been settled on him and those in temporary possession of his wife. His first wife had given him a daughter, Katherine, and his second, the Countess Cecily, had provided him with two sons. But one died very young indeed in 1613, and the other while still a boy in March 1620. It was the mysterious death of the one son in 1613, and the mysterious wasting sickness of the other and the daughter in 1619, which stimulated the family to look for some supernatural cause for their misfortunes. Having decided that the family had been bewitched, the Earl and Countess picked on a discharged female servant as the likely suspect. The servant was tried, condemned, and executed for witchcraft, a drastic remedy which failed to prevent the death a year later of the last of the two sons.[2] As a result, the Manners family was faced for the second time within half a century with the prospect of a division of the estates between the heirs general and the heirs male. The Earl's brother George would now inherit the title and as he was still childless after fourteen years of marriage it looked very much as if Katherine would take away with her large sections of the family estates. By virtue of her rank and her expectations, she was now the greatest heiress in England.

For years Earl Francis had haunted the Court, he was made a Privy Councillor in 1617, and he was evidently consumed with ambition to obtain high office. It is therefore not surprising that in 1619 negotiations were opened to marry Katherine to the great Court favourite, the Marquis of Buckingham. According to Chamberlain, Buckingham's demands were so exorbitant that Rutland could not bring himself to accept them: he wanted £20,000 in cash and land worth £4,000 a year, to increase to £8,000 a year if the young heir died (as he did a few months later). A further difficulty was that Katherine had been educated in her parents' faith as a Catholic, and the marriage was therefore linked with the country's foreign policy and the prospect of the Spanish match for Prince

---

[1] W. Notestein, *Studies in Local History*, p. 93. *H.M.C. Rutland MSS.* i, p. 413. B/M 144. B/A 130A.

[2] *The Wonderful Discoverie of the Witchcrafts of Margaret and Phillip Flower*, London, 1619.

Charles, which would involve toleration or even favour for Catholic recusants.[1] After the death of her step-brother in 1620, Katherine became an even more desirable prize, and Buckingham's mother intrigued actively, if somewhat unorthodoxly, to bring the union about. There is reason to believe that the families had been friends ten years before when the Villiers were merely unimportant Leicestershire squires, for in his will Earl Roger left Mr. Villiers 'all my hounds for the hare'.[2] This previous friendship makes the conduct of the Villiers clan still more discreditable. Katherine was by now devoted to her brilliant young suitor—indeed she remained in love with him all her life, despite continual evidence of his indifference and infidelity—and the Villiers exploited this passion to force her to change her religion and to obtain the marriage on their own terms. The old Countess Buckingham, the favourite's mother, invited Katherine to her house, where she then spent the night without her father's leave. When she returned the next morning Earl Francis, rightly or wrongly suspecting the worst, refused to receive her, and she had to take refuge with her uncle, Lord Knyvett.

Buckingham took a very lofty line, claiming that he had received the King's full pardon for what had happened, denying that Katherine had received any 'blemish' from him that night, and stating that in view of Earl Francis's attitude, he was giving up the marriage. He concluded with characteristic arrogance: 'I never thought before to have seen the time that I should need to come within the compass of the law by stealing a wife against the consent of the parents, considering of the favour it pleaseth His Majesty, though undeservedly, to bestow upon me.' In fact, of course, as the Villiers family had calculated, things had now gone too far to be stopped, Katherine finally agreed to be accepted into the Anglican communion, and although Earl Francis and the Marquis of Buckingham were still hardly on speaking terms, the marriage took place in May.[3]

The price was a heavy one. The Marquis obtained £10,000 in cash—raised partly by borrowing and partly from fines for new leases—and the reversion of lands that had a rental of about £3,700

[1] N. E. McClure, *Letters of John Chamberlain*, ii, pp. 284, 293. *Cal. S.P. Dom.*, *1619–23*, p. 71.
[2] P.C.C. 64 Fenner.
[3] B.M., Harl. MSS. 1581, f. 134. McClure, op. cit. ii, pp. 297, 301, 306. *Cal. S.P. Dom.*, *1619–23*, p. 133. S. R. Gardiner, *Prince Charles and the Spanish Marriage*, i, London, 1869, pp. 328–32.

a year in the 1630s. The annual income this land produced was of course much larger—a later calculation suggested £4,600—to which must be added the profits of the Rievaulx ironworks of about £1,500 a year.[1] Nor was this the only sacrifice that Earl Francis had to make, for he was also obliged to patch up his quarrel with Buckingham. But he was under no illusions about his son-in-law's character, as is shown by the extraordinary letter he wrote to Buckingham after the latter had left with Prince Charles for Madrid in 1623.

> I know you are in a hot country, therefore take heed of your self, and if you court ladies of honor you will be in danger of poisoning or killing, and if you desire whores you will be in danger of burning. Therefore good my Lord take heed, and so praying sweet Jesus to bless you and send you safe here, I rest, your Lordship's father and friend, F. Rutland.[2]

If contemporary gossip is to be believed, the warning went unheeded, but the prospect of the Spanish marriage and this laboured affability to Buckingham brought Earl Francis the only reward he received from his daughter's brilliant and costly marriage: at the Duke's request he was appointed Admiral of the Fleet sent to bring back Prince Charles and his bride in triumph from Spain.[3] But in the event the scheme collapsed, Charles and Buckingham returned to England bent on war with Spain, all thought of toleration for Catholics was abandoned, and Rutland's hopes of a political career were destroyed before it had begun.

In 1632 Earl Francis died, no doubt a deeply disappointed man, to be succeeded by his childless brother George. Already the estate was much shrunken. Of Earl Francis's rental of £9,344, £2,144 passed to the dowager Countess Cecily as jointure; fee-farm rents, rents for leasehold property, and fixed annuities took another £1,323, and annuities left by Earl Francis by will a further £820. Of the remaining £5,057 a year Katherine, the dowager Duchess of Buckingham, had an immediate right to £615 and the reversion after Earl George's death to a very great deal more. To make matters worse Earl Francis left debts of £9,500 and legacies to Katherine and her daughter Mary of £10,000, while his funeral cost

---

[1] B/A 130A. B/C 2729. This is a document drawn up in 1666 on the basis of rent books of 1632, 1634, and 1640, and presents the situation after the agreement of 1634. The figures have been recalculated against the 1636 rental.

[2] Bodl., Tanner MSS. 73, f. 289.

[3] B.M., Harl. MSS. 1581, ff. 127–31.

the phenomenal sum of over £3,500. Although Earl Francis claimed to have been 'loving and kind' to his brother, Earl George did not see it that way. On the other hand, it is hard to see that he had much to complain of. After the inevitable litigation that almost always accompanied the division of an estate, agreement was reached in 1634 as to the extent of Duchess Katherine's claims, and though the evidence is fragmentary, Earl George's rental in the late 1630s was over £6,600 and his gross income probably about £8,000 a year or more.[1]

VIII. THE EIGHTH EARL JOHN, 1641–1660

It was only on the death of Earl George in 1641 that the full consequences of the Villiers marriage made themselves felt. Overnight nearly half the Manners property, including most of the Yorkshire estate and the Rievaulx ironworks, passed through the heir general, the Duchess Katherine, into the hands of the Villiers family. In addition a further huge jointure was taken temporarily out of the estate for the dowager Countess Frances, the improved rent of which came to over £3,000 a year. But against this must be set an addition of property about equal in value to what was lost to the Villiers. The total failure of the male line in the last three generations threw the title back to the descendants of John, the second son of the first Earl Thomas. This son John had married (reputedly after an elopement) the coheiress of Sir George Vernon of Haddon Hall in Derbyshire, one of the richest men in the north midlands, whose wealth and standing were certainly equal to those of many peers.[2] The grandson of this marriage now succeeded to the title as Earl John and brought with him all the Haddon estates. Earl John, who as squire of Haddon had had no court connections, spent the Civil War as a lukewarm Parliamentarian. Although this did not prevent the occupation of Belvoir by a Royalist garrison and its subsequent destruction by Parliamentary forces, his attitude saved Haddon and avoided sequestration of property and a fine for Royalist delinquency. After the death of John's mother Grace in 1650 and the two dowager Countesses Cecily and Frances in 1653 and 1656 respectively, it is possible to see the new shape of the Manners estates, without the distortions created by the omission

[1] B/A 807, 317, 318, 166. B/M 144. B/C 7624. B/BSA.
[2] In fact he was offered a peerage by Henry VIII (*Acts of Privy Council 1547–50*, p. 16).

of jointures. In 1656 the rents and demesne profits of the old Manners estate came to about £7,000 and those of the new Haddon estate to about £4,500. Since the bare rental lost to the Villiers was about £3,700 together with a probably diminishing asset of about £1,500 a year in ironworks profits, it would appear that the loss and the gain approximately cancelled out.[1]

IX. CONCLUSION

There can be no doubt that the most important changes in the fortunes of the Manners family between 1560 and 1660 were those wrought by birth, marriage, and death. It had been the Roos and St. Leger marriages, followed by royal favour and offices under Henry VIII, that had raised the family from the gentry to the higher aristocracy; it was the failure of male heirs which led to the loss of about a third of the estate to the Cecils in 1587 and nearly half of what remained to the Villiers in 1641. But it was the Vernon marriage and the consequences of this failure which brought in the huge Haddon estate in 1641, while the inheritance of the title by a succession of brothers meant the return to the main line of the property of the younger sons. Owing to these frequent failures of male heirs, there were very few periods when the Earls were faced with an unbreakable entail. They were very largely free to dispose of the property between heirs male and heirs general as they wished, and only Earl George in the 1630s found himself with no more than a life interest in the bulk of his estates.

It seems possible that the infertility that governed the family fortunes during this period was due in part at least to a single-minded search for wealthy rather than fruitful brides, for it is known that infertility and a tendency to female children can both be inherited. And yet Earl Roger married the only daughter and heiress of Sir Philip Sidney, and Earl Francis two childless widows one after the other. Earl George also married a widow, although admittedly one who had already borne her first husband two sons.[2] Up to a point, therefore, the Manners brought their troubles on themselves by their lack of discretion in the choice of brides. Their single-minded pursuit of heiresses was ultimately self-defeating,

---

[1] See Appendix IIA.

[2] J. L. Vivian, *Visitations of Cornwall*, London, 1887, p. 31. E. M. Oliver, *Memoirs of the Hungerford . . . Families*, London, 1930, p. 15. J. E. Cussons, *History of Hertfordshire*, London, 1870, I, i, p. 31.

since by failing to produce a male heir these women caused a dispersion of the properties they brought with them. Between the mid fifteenth and the mid seventeenth centuries the Manners gained more on the marriage swings then they lost on the roundabouts, but throughout the whole of this period they were peculiarly at the mercy of biological accident.

Furthermore, the family also suffered badly from the extreme longevity of these childless women. In the 100 years from 1560 to 1660 six Earls died, all of whom left widows, one of whom died the same year. The remaining five survived their husbands for a total of 100 years, an average of twenty years each, during all of which time they enjoyed very large jointures out of the main estate. For thirteen years from 1588 to 1601 there were three jointures in being and for twelve years from 1641 to 1653 there were two, to say nothing of a further jointure out of the Haddon estate until 1650. No aristocratic family in England was harder hit by the longevity of widows.

The third disadvantageous factor was the conspicuous extravagance and overspending of Earl Roger in the 1590s. Many peers and greater gentry were affected by the collapse of a sense of family responsibility in the 1580s and 1590s, but few, if any, contrived to spend more recklessly than Earl Roger. If the consequences in the long run were not very serious, this was due merely to the great size of the annual income, and still more to the windfall of fines for re-leasing the bulk of the estate. Apart from this isolated outburst, the Earls of Rutland acted with prudence. They were not heavy gamblers, and although a new south front was added to Belvoir Castle in 1625–6, they managed to avoid the competition in extravagant building that undermined the finances of so many families at this period.

The experience of the Earls of Rutland in politics is as unusual as everything else about them. For the first hundred years, until 1543, they had played the political game with conspicuous success, picking up by virtue of their contacts two heiresses who made the fortune of the family, and also a huge quantity of ex-monastic property. For the next hundred years they remained in Court, assiduously pursuing office and reward, but they never obtained satisfaction on either count. No more rich gifts came their way, and although they sometimes held minor positions, on the two occasions, in 1587 and 1623, when they seemed on the threshold of high office and royal favour, their hopes were blighted by unexpected death and a sudden shift in foreign policy.

Although their failure to obtain substantial rewards or favours meant that they had to maintain themselves on their own resources, on the whole they were remarkably successful in keeping the burden of debt within manageable proportions. By 1600 Earl Roger's debts had risen to nearly £5,000; Earl Francis's unrequited incursion into Court life after 1612 soon ran him into debt, but never on such a scale as to be really troublesome. Including unpaid tradesmen's bills, the total stood at £7,113 in July 1616, and rose sharply in 1619–20 when a further £7,000 was borrowed to help pay for Lady Katherine's portion. When he died in 1632 Earl Francis's debts came to about £9,500.[1] At no time therefore did the debt load exceed one year's income, and only Earl Roger was forced to sell land. Since Earl Francis spent far more than £10,000 in the purchase of land, and since the debt was rapidly cleared off by his executors without any sales, he cannot be regarded as having acted imprudently. More serious debts were incurred by Earl John, who by 1658 owed no less than £13,300, with an annual interest burden of £798. This was probably caused by excess of expenditure during the previous fifteen years, when income had been much reduced by the ravages of Civil War and by three jointures. Yet even this burden was rapidly reduced by the receipt of £12,200 as the bride's portion on the marriage of his eldest son.[2]

It is of course hardly surprising that the Earls of Rutland found it easier than most to live within their income, since it was so much larger than that of others. In 1560 the estates covered a tremendous area and their value was maintained or increased in the years to follow. Although the evidence is extremely tentative, it looks as if Earl Edward succeeded in keeping income abreast of inflation during the Elizabethan period, while in the early Stuart period there is fairly firm evidence of a rapid increase in money receipts. This was not achieved by drastic reorganization through enclosure or eviction, nor by large-scale sheep farming or arable cultivation, but merely by careful management and progressive increase of rents at each new letting. During the great price rise of the Elizabethan period the Earls retained substantial demesnes, from which they

[1] B/A 317, 318. B/C 252. B/BSA. P.R.O. L.C. 4/197, p. 439; 198, pp. 35, 36; 199, pp. 197, 210, 333, 398.
[2] B/A 1244. B/BSA.

drew profits which may have amounted to as much as 15 or 20 per cent of their total landed income. Thereafter they switched to a policy of leasing, using what was left of the demesnes mainly to supply the household. They now turned their attention to the management of their ironworks, and succeeded over a period of forty years in drawing profit from them that usually amounted to between 12 and 15 per cent of their gross income. In this, as in so many other ways, they were exceptional in that they maintained these high profits over so long a period, and that they kept the works under direct management.

In almost every feature the history of the Manners family is unusual, but in none more than the fact that between the accession of Elizabeth and the Civil War their purchases of land exceeded their sales. There is some uncertainty about one or two items, but it would appear that the Earls sold seven manors and bought seventeen, as well as the huge addition of Minting Park. Purchases were made mostly by Earl Edward in the late 1570s and early 1580s and by Earls Roger and Francis in the 1610s. The only sales after 1560 were three to clear off Earl Henry's debts after 1563, one in 1575, and three in the early years of the seventeenth century in order to pay off the debts incurred by Earl Roger.

But this favourable balance was more than offset by the losses of property to the heirs general, and on balance there can be little doubt that the Earl of Rutland in 1660 was a considerably smaller landowner than his great-uncle had been a hundred years before. About one-third of the estate passed to the heirs general in 1587, and this loss was never made good. Manorial counts are extremely difficult for this family, but, very approximately, it possessed about seventy to seventy-five manors in 1560 and about forty-five in 1660. These figures evidently grossly exaggerate the decline in acreage and value, for some of the new manors of the Haddon estate were very valuable indeed. We are not in a position to compare gross incomes, nor even bare rentals, owing to the paucity of material from 1543 to 1587, although there is reason to think that the family may actually have increased its purchasing power. On the other hand, the social and political position of the Earls as gigantic territorial magnates had certainly been reduced to more modest proportions, and other families had moved ahead of them. Although still one of the ten or so richest and most powerful families of England in 1660, it is doubtful whether the Manners could now be ranked among the first five. Primarily because of bad genetic luck, they had failed to maintain the commanding position achieved in the 1550s after the monastic spoils had been digested, and they had been overtaken by other ex-gentry families thrusting up in their turn by way of politics, business, marriage, or the law.

APPENDIX I

Income from Land

	Rents, court profits, and wood sales[1]	Fines and wardships	Net profits of demesne farming[2]	Net profits of Rievaulx ironworks	Total income	Ref.
	£	£	£	£	£	
1587–8	3,546	535	2,866*[3]	78	7,025	B/A 77
1594–7 (av. p.a.)	3,241[4]	200	1,012*[5]	530	4,983	B/A 378, 90 309
1597–9 (av. p.a.)	3,391	4,971[6]	994*[7]	. .[8]	9,056	B/A 310, 95
1603–4	4,443[9]	213[10]	321	860	5,837	B/A 374
1608–9	5,151[11]					B/A 481
1612	4,893[11]					B/B.S.A.
1613–14	9,258[12]	60[13]	559*[13]	2,240	12,117	B/A 129, 130, 130A
1616–18 (av. p.a.)	8,511[14]	. .[13]	247*[13]	650	9,408	B/A 130A
1618–21 (av. p.a.)	12,259[15]		205*[13]	2,132	14,596	B/A 130A
1627–30 (av. p.a.)	9,168[16]	1,833	c. 166[17]	1,583	c. 12,750	B/A 315, 316, 382
1632	9,344[18]					B/A 807
1636–7	6,676[19]					B/B.S.A.
1650	5,579[20]			*Sale of wood*		B/B.S.A.
1653–6 (av. p.a.)	2,898[21]	576	518*[22]	742	4,733	B/B.S.A.
1657–60 (av. p.a.)	9,161[23]		1,997		11,158	B/B.S.A.

[1] Unless otherwise stated, these are the sums due from the bailiffs and farmers, after the deduction of expense of court keeping, etc. They include a small amount of land held by the Earls on lease. The rents of these leaseholds and also the fixed fee-farm rents due to the Crown should be deducted from these figures in order to obtain the net receipts. The fee-farm rents came to £553 in 1593 (Rentals and Surveys, Portfolio 22/36); to £424 in 1601 and 1612 (Hatfield House, Salis. MSS. 77 f. 68; B.S.A.); and to £310 in 1658 (B/A 1244). The gross income from leasehold property was £123 in 1608–9, and £111 in 1628–9 (B/A 481, 316).

[2] The figures in this column are neither entirely reliable nor entirely consistent. They usually represent the sums paid over by the bailiffs to the receivers. From this figure must be deducted any imprests made by the receivers to the bailiffs earlier in the year to pay for running costs. Unfortunately the imprests are available only for a small number of years. Where they are not known and no deduction has been made, an asterisk has been put against the figure. These figures also include receipts of joist of grounds, and the large profits from the sale of corn delivered by neighbouring farmers at Belvoir in lieu of rent. They do not, therefore, indicate the true scale of the demesne farming. Occasionally they include some of the profits from the sale of wood, most of which are included by the bailiffs in their payment and therefore appear in the rent column. The amount paid to the receiver varied widely year by year according to the scale of purchases of cattle, and the amount of produce sent directly to the Earl's kitchen instead of being sold.

³ This figure is unusually large, £1,461 being received for the sale of cattle and sheep alone. This was probably due to the sale of the personal estate of the late Earl.

⁴ Since 1588 there had gone out of the estate life interests in several properties bequeathed by Earl John to his three younger sons (P.C.C. 1 Rutland).

⁵ In 1597–8, £232 was advanced in imprest and should be deducted.

⁶ This includes part of the sums received for re-leasing the estate for twenty-one years.

⁷ In 1598–9 £407 was advanced in imprest and should be deducted.

⁸ If the records are complete, as they seem to be, there is nothing paid into the account, and £298 paid out in imprests to the Clerk of the Ironworks.

⁹ £4,182 came from the Rutland estates, now swollen by the death of the dowager Countess Bridget in 1601. The remaining £261 was a half-year rent of the estate of the Countess, daughter and heir to Sir Philip Sidney. In a full year the rents should therefore have been about £4,700.

¹⁰ In addition, there was £145 received from the lands of two wards. But these were probably royal wards given to the Earl, not wards on his own estate.

¹¹ These are statements of the year's revenue. They exclude the lands of the Countess, but now include the jointure of the dowager Countess Isabel, who died in 1606.

¹² Of this sum £2,040 came from the western lands of Countess Cecily as jointure from her first husband, Sir Edward Hungerford; £502 from the estate formerly settled on the Earl's younger brother Oliver, who had just died, leaving it to his brother; about £700 previously held by the present Earl when he was a younger brother; and about £100 from newly purchased land.

¹³ These figures seem very low. Some fines, and perhaps some demesne profits, may be included in the figure for rents.

¹⁴ Only about half the Yorkshire rents came in during 1617–18, so the full amount would be about the same as in 1613–14.

¹⁵ This includes the huge fines for renewing the twenty-one-year leases made by Earl Roger in 1598.

¹⁶ This is the full amount due. £1,836 of it came from the lands of the Countess.

¹⁷ It is not possible to calculate the exact figure, since the husbandry expenses at Belvoir are included with those for repairs to the Castle in 1628–30. But judging by the first year, this would appear to be the approximate net figure.

¹⁸ This is a note of 1632 rental.

¹⁹ This is a rental.

²⁰ This is a rental. £2,201 came from the Haddon property and £3,378 from what was left of the old Rutland estate.

²¹ This only covers the old Rutland estate.

²² This is the gross figure, from which overheads should be deducted.

²³ This now includes the Haddon estate, and the jointure of the late dowager Countess Frances.

APPENDIX II

The Estate in 1656–1659

A. *A summary of the estate on the death of the dowager Countess Frances in 1656* (B/B.S.A.)

(1) Belvoir Estate: gross rents   £3,434
        demesnes: gross receipts   544 (overheads £22)
                                              Total   £3,978

(2) Belvoir Estate, late jointure of Countess Frances
        value at improved rent   £3,036 (old rent £2,200)
                                              Total   £3,036

(3) Haddon Estate: gross rents   £2,042
               demesnes   1,348
                                              Total   £3,390

(4) Haddon Estate, jointure of Lady Grace Manners   £1,143

                                        Gross total   £11,547

      Net total, after deduction of fixed charges   £10,189

B. *A summary of the estate, dated 31 January 1659* (B/A 1244)

Belvoir rental   £6,558
Haddon rental   3,067
                                 Total rental   £9,625

Belvoir tithes and demesne profits   £461
Haddon tithes and demesne profits   1,197
                             Total demesne profits   £1,658

            Total rental and demesne profits   £11,283

Fixed charges:
    Bailiff's fees, allowances, and quit rents   £   366
    Fee-farm rents to Crown   310
    Annuities to members of the family, etc.   718
    6 per cent interest on debts of £13,300   798
                       Total   £2,192

VII

THE WRIOTHESLEYS
EARLS OF SOUTHAMPTON
1530–1667

I. ACQUISITION AND CONSOLIDATION, 1530–1581

THOMAS WRIOTHESLEY, first Earl of Southampton, is one of
that fairly small but very important group who rose from humble
origins to great wealth and social eminence during the 1530s and
1540s. His family was of plebeian stock, the first members of any
distinction being his grandfather, who rose to be Garter King of
Arms, and his father, who was York Herald.[1] Thomas, who was
the eldest son, was educated in the civil law at Trinity Hall, Cambridge, whence he passed into government service under Thomas
Cromwell. By 1529 he held a position of some responsibility, and
therefore found himself launched on a career in the royal administration at the precise moment when it was undergoing rapid expansion
and when the rewards of office were greater than at almost any
other period of English history. His tenure of the Clerkship of the
Signet and of the Secretaryship coincided with a redistribution of
land on a larger scale than any since Duke William of Normandy
had shared out his English conquests among his followers. So
favourably placed in direct contact with the King, Wriothesley's
fortunes rose as the monasteries fell. In 1537–8 the great abbey of
Titchfield came into the hands of this devout Catholic, and ex-
monastic property in Hampshire continued to shower upon him
by grant or purchase in a steady stream for the next decade, culminating in a huge grant in 1547, allegedly in posthumous fulfil-
ment of the intentions of Henry VIII. He reached the peak of his
career in the last hectic years of the old king from 1544 to 1547,
when he held the office of Lord Chancellor and was raised to the
peerage, first as Lord Wriothesley, and later as Earl of Southampton.
When he died in 1550 he had made himself one of the two largest

---

[1] See genealogical table no. 4.

landowners in Hampshire. By far the most important unit was the
eleven manors and three absorbed 'ghost' manors, some of them
of very little value, which together made up the huge Titchfield
estate of nearly 5,000 acres. In addition, he held eighteen other
manors in the county as well as three in Devon, three in Dorset, one
in Somerset, and two houses and one manor in or near London.[1]

The basis of his great accumulation was the extensive grants and
purchases of land from the Crown, the consequence of the king's
favour and of shrewd investment of the profits of office. Precisely
how large those profits were, we have no means of telling. But we
know enough to be certain that the official fees and salary formed
only a proportion of the whole, the rest being made up of gratuities
from suitors, private fees from clients, sale of offices, and New Year
gifts from officials below him.[2] Then as now, the Lord Chancellorship was one of the most lucrative offices at the disposal of the
Crown, and Wriothesley's income during the years 1544–7 must
have been enormous, quite apart from his annuities of £100 a year
for life as Secretary and £400 a year as Chancellor.[3] In addition to
these central offices, he also accumulated a number of local titles
which conferred dignity and political influence rather than financial
reward. The Borough of Andover made him its High Steward,
Southampton a free burgess, Winchester College Steward of its
lands, and the Bishop of Winchester Master of his Game.[4]

In the 1540s these profits were nearly all immediately invested
in land, partly as speculation for prompt resale, and partly to round
off his already extensive Hampshire possessions. The full record of
these purchases has not survived, but in 1548–9 alone he can be
shown to have spent about £2,700 on buying land.[5] He was also
a more direct beneficiary of the onslaught upon ecclesiastical property. As the inevitable end drew near, the monastic authorities

---

[1] These were: *Hants:* Titchfield, Chark, Lee Britten, Segenworth, Bromwich, Crofton, Hook Mortimer, Hook Valence, Lee Markes, Mirabel, Swanwick, and the three 'ghosts' of Meon, Posbrook, and Funtley (all in Titchfield); Soberton, Flexland, Abbots Worthy, Micheldever, West Stratton, East Stratton, Beaulieu, North Stoneham, Walsworth, Dogmersfield, Newland, West Meon, Botley, Faringdon Episcopi, Portsea, Copnor, Corhampton, Bighton; *Devon:* Broadhembury, Wolveston, Wembury; *Dorset:* Stower Westover, Stower Eastover, Iwerne; *Somerset:* Long Sutton; *London:* Bloomsbury.

[2] W. R. Emerson, 'The Petre Estates' (Oxford D.Phil. thesis, 1951), p. 51 n. 3; p. 52 n. 1.

[3] Hampshire Record Office, Wriothesley Deeds (hereafter referred to as W.D.), 220, 242.

[4] W.D. 158, 58, 59, 132.

[5] W.D. 209, 211, 77, 78, 105, 517. *Letters and Papers of Henry VIII*, 19, i, 278 (74), 442 (34), 812 (114), 1035 (159); 20, i, 1081 (24, 58), 1335 (35); 20, ii, 226 (36), 496 (28), 1068 (52); 21, i, 1166 (39, 73). *Cal. Patent Rolls, 1547–8*, pp. 268, 335; *1549–51*, pp. 4, 358. *V.C.H. Hants*, iv, pp. 493–4.

all over the country tried to secure favourable personal terms by lavish grants to well-placed politicians. Thus in 1536 Hyde Abbey, Winchester, gave Wriothesley a 40-year lease of East Stratton manor and the tithes of East and West Stratton; a year later it granted him a 99-year lease of Micheldever rectory, a reversion of 99 years after that, and a promise—for what it was worth—of a third successive term of 99 years thereafter.[1] From the Dean and Chapter of Winchester he extracted a lease of Barton farm in 1542 and of Titchfield rectory in 1545, while in 1543 Gardiner, Bishop of Winchester, gave him a 99-year lease of Fareham Park at a rent in cash and kind of under £5 per annum, presumably in return for valuable political support in the struggle of the factions at Court.[2] Finally, like so many of his contemporaries, he had acquired a large town house for himself at the expense of the bishops. In 1547 the Earl of Warwick had extorted a grant from the Bishop of Lincoln of his house in Holborn, and two years later Southampton acquired it from Warwick.[3] At Titchfield, Wriothesley had no sooner obtained possession of the Priory than he began an ingenious conversion of the monastic buildings, including the church, to turn them into a large and handsome country seat, while in London he may also have done some building in Bloomsbury.[4]

When he died in 1550, the first Earl had securely laid the foundations of a great landed family. What income the estate brought in at this time is uncertain, since all we have is a valuation for the wardship of the Earl's son and heir, Henry, who was only four years old at his father's death. These valuations are invariably underestimates, sometimes scandalously so, and the official figure of £1,300 should be regarded as a bare minimum.[5] At best this would represent the mere rental of the property, and since it was all either leasehold or copyhold let for years or lives at old rent, the tenants paying substantial fines at each renewal, this figure would be far below the average gross annual income. We should probably not be far wrong in guessing that the estate was in fact bringing in a gross income of between £2,000 and £3,000.

[1] W.D. 168, 143.

[2] Hampshire Record Office, Wriothesley Books (hereafter referred to as W.B.), 128; W.D., 516.

[3] E. Williams, *Early Holborn*, London, 1927, nos. 359, 1236, 1230.

[4] W. H. St. John Hope, 'The Making of Place House at Titchfield', *Archaeological Journal*, lxiii, 1906. J. Parton, *Some Account of the Hospital and Parish of Saint Giles in the Fields, Middlesex*, London, 1822, pp. 244, 345.

[5] Hatfield House, P. 2138.

Against this must be set the charges on the estate. Every successful politician and landowner owed much to the honesty and
devotion of his servants, and it was both common form and very
understandable that Earl Thomas should have burdened his successors with handsome life annuities for some of his old retainers.
Ranging from £60 to £2, and including one of £20 for his physician, Dr. Fryer, these totalled £193.[1] In addition he died owing
£993 to the Crown, either arrears of fee-farm rents or money due
for land purchases. Five years later, about half the Hampshire
estate was extended by the Sheriff to secure the repayment of this
money at a rate of £400 a year.[2] However, since Earl Henry was
still a child and therefore not keeping up a great establishment or
otherwise spending the income, this can have been no very great
hardship.

More serious was the burden of wardship. The official annual
value of the Crown's third of the estate, which included Beaulieu
and many other Hampshire manors, was £322, which was paid into
the Court of Wards for some sixteen years. The custody of the child
himself was sold for £1,000 to the rising courtier William Herbert,
Earl of Pembroke. But King Edward agreed to remit £600 of this,
and to add an extra £100 a year for the better maintenance of the
child.[3] Pembroke seems immediately to have resold the wardship
of the young Henry to his mother, the dowager Countess Jane,[4]
and he was therefore brought up in the unwavering Catholic faith
of his parents. And so when the accession of Elizabeth saw yet
another turn of the religious wheel, the Wriothesleys were left
stranded in their devotion to Catholicism.

In 1565 Countess Jane followed what was to become the
standard practice in recusant circles, and married her son into
another family of similar views. Her choice fell upon Mary,
daughter of the great Surrey and Sussex landowner, Anthony
Browne, Viscount Montagu. A summary draft of the marriage
contract bears a personal endorsement by the Countess: 'by God's
grace, a note of the covenants of marriage between my son Southampton and mistress Mary Browne, my Lord Montague's daughter,
if they so like by God's grace.' The two did so like—or at least

---

[1] W.D., 288. One for £60 was given to Richard Cox, clerk, who was to be an exile for
religion under Mary and Bishop of Ely under Elizabeth. Why the Earl should have patronized
this zealous Protestant is a mystery (V.C.H. Hants, iv, p. 651).
[2] W.D. 222.   [3] W.D. 293. Hatfield House, p. 2138.
[4] C. C. Stopes, The Third Earl of Southampton, Cambridge, 1922, p. 500.

showed no signs of violent antipathy, which was all that was required in the sixteenth century—and they were married in February 1566. During the interval the young Earl had lived in the Viscount's house at the latter's expense, except for his clothes.[1]

So in 1566 the Earl both came of age, and got married. He therefore obtained his wife's portion of £1,333, extinguished the rent of £322 per annum due to the Crown for his wardship lands since his father's death,[2] and became liable to the last financial consequence of his minority, the payment to the Crown of a fine for suing his livery. This came to about £700 and was stalled over a period of nine years at £79 per annum.[3] The total wardship cost to the Earl's estate was therefore well over £6,200: the £400 or more which Countess Jane paid the Earl of Pembroke for the wardship (and the Earl is unlikely to have sold it at a loss); sixteen years' custody of the land at £322 per annum, making £5,152; and the £700 odd for livery. On the other hand, the long minority meant a prolonged period of severely reduced expenditure, and the estate may well have gained rather than suffered between 1550 and 1566.

The next fifteen years, however, were a time of increasing troubles. Earl Henry's ardent Catholicism led him to complicity in the Duke of Norfolk's schemes to marry Mary, Queen of Scots— he was foolish enough to hold a secret meeting in Lambeth Marsh with Mary's agent the Bishop of Roos—and as a result he spent the next three years, from 1571 to 1573, under restraint.

In 1574 his mother died, and her jointure lands therefore returned to the Earl's estate. But in spite of this accession of income, he soon ran into debt. One reason seems to have been excessive hospitality and the maintenance of a huge retinue on a scale that his income from land alone was unable to support. According to Gervase Markham 'his muster roll never consisted of four lackeys and a coachman, but of a whole troup of at least a hundred well-mounted gentlemen and yeomen'.[4] This is but one of several instances of a correlation of the old religion with the old aristocratic household and life-style.

[1] W.D. 198.

[2] Actually the Crown had granted them to Viscount Montagu the year before (W.D. 293).

[3] W.D. 199. The records of the Court of Wards are incomplete for this early Elizabethan period, and I cannot trace the precise figure in the official files. The valuation for livery of the estate, in possession and reversion, came to £1,272 (B.M., Lansd. MSS. 75/29).

[4] *Cabala sive Scrinia Sacra*, London, 1663, p. 178. Gervase Markham, *Honour in his Perfection*, London, 1624, p. 20.

In 1579-80 the Earl carried out a very sensible concentration of his estates. He sold Wembury manor in Devon and lands in East and West Stour, Dorset, for a total of £4,532,[1] and spent part of the money in buying the manors of Itchell and Ewshott in Hampshire.[2] But it seems likely that this was not enough. At any rate he had to borrow £500 on bond from William Denham, a London goldsmith, and a further £3,600 by Statute Staple from William Hodges, 'gent', of Weston under Edge.[3] When he died in 1581 it was discovered that his debts and legacies far exceeded his personal assets. Among the legacies he left £2,000 as a marriage portion for his only daughter Mary, £1,000 for his funeral, and £1,000 for his tomb, and also ordered the completion of his minor house at Dogmersfield.[4]

II. DECLINE, 1581-1624

The Earl's son and heir Henry was only eight years old, so once again the estate became subject to wardship. It was assessed, at the usual gross undervalue, at £1,097 per annum, of which £363 had been settled on the widow for her jointure,[5] £363 was devised to the executors for the payment of debts and legacies, and £371 came to the Crown for its thirds.[6] This last was let, at this very low rental and with a fine of only £250, to Lord Howard of Effingham, the Lord Admiral.[7] But the wardship and marriage of the young Earl himself were not sold. From the point of view of the government the important thing was to ensure his religious, and therefore political, conformity, and so he was taken away from his mother and put into the charge of Lord Treasurer Burghley. In defence of this practice, it should be pointed out that the late Earl had been on very bad terms with his wife in recent years, and the Countess claimed that she had not seen her son for two years before her husband's death. She therefore denied all responsibility for the little boy's somewhat precocious refusal to attend Anglican service. But her efforts, via the Earl of Leicester, to recover custody of the child and the administration of the estate were unavailing.[8]

---

[1] W.D. 286, 346-8. Most of the Dorset estate at Iwerne was sold at about this time, though the remaining manorial rights were not parted with until 1614 (W.D. 111).

[2] *V.C.H. Hants*, iv, pp. 8, 9. W.D., 436.

[3] W.D. 559, 259-61.   [4] Stopes, op. cit., pp. 525-6.

[5] W.D. 184.   [6] B.M., Lansd. MSS. 37/30.   [7] W.D. 273, 128.

[8] Rousham, Oxon., Cottrell-Dormer MSS., Correspondence 1570-1630. G. E. Cokayne, *Complete Peerage*, xii, pt. i, p. 127, note c.

It was therefore in Burghley's house, and under his personal care, that Earl Henry was brought up in the company of a number of other aristocratic wards, including his future intimate friend the Earl of Rutland. The atmosphere was one of Protestant piety, material austerity, sententious moralizing, and diligent application to book learning. The system was fairly successful in producing anti-Catholics, and although Southampton's religious orthodoxy was somewhat uncertain before 1605,[1] he was in the end the first of the family to break with Catholicism and conform to the national religion. This was a very important achievement, but Burghley's educational programme was far less effective in forming stability of character. The Earls of Oxford and Essex, the fifth Earl of Rutland, the third Earl of Southampton, and Lord Zouche were none of them a credit to their guardian in their early years of manhood, nor did they exhibit much gratitude for the undoubted care bestowed upon their education. It is unlikely that this subsequent instability and ingratitude can be explained by the psychological shock of early separation from their mothers. It was probably attributable partly to the reaction of high-spirited and fairly intelligent young men against the unimaginative academic discipline provided by Burghley, and partly to the realization of the latter's self-interest in undertaking the charge. One of Lord Burghley's dominant characteristics was an intense snobbery which made him a passionate student of heraldry and a complacent recipient of genealogical trees that traced the Cecil pedigree back to the Conquest. The same weakness led him to sacrifice his children's happiness for the sake of aristocratic alliances. As he had the marriage of these young wards at his disposal, he naturally tried to secure them for his children. He tried to unite his daughter Anne with the Earl of Rutland, but finally had to be content with the Earl of Oxford. He pressed the hand of his granddaughter Elizabeth Vere upon Southampton, who refused and is reported to have been forced to pay his guardian £5,000 to obtain his freedom.[2]

When he came of age in 1594 the third Earl's financial position was not unfavourable. Eleven years before it had been said that the true value of the estate, less his mother's jointure lands, would when out of lease be worth £4,000 per annum. Since the estate was

1 Stopes, op. cit., pp. 270, 295, 360.
2 Ibid., pp. 36–8. H. Foley, *Records of the English Province of the Society of Jesus*, iv, 1878, p. 49. For Burghley's role as aristocratic guardian see J. Hurstfield, 'Lord Burghley as Master of the Court of Wards', *T.R.H.S.*, xxxi, 1949, pp. 103—7.

mostly let on the system of large fines and small rents, the average annual income must have been well below this, and was probably not more than about £3,000. In addition there was leasehold property worth about £400 per annum gross, and there was about £2,000 in cash to come in from fines for re-leasing the estate.[1] With an annual income of well over £3,000 a year, a young man of the 1590s could live in considerable style. But life at Court was very expensive and Elizabeth in her old age became increasingly sparing with financial favours. She had always been chary of giving office and rewards to wild young men, unless, as with Essex, she was in love with them, and the irresponsible behaviour of the South-ampton–Rutland set met with no favour in her eyes.[2] When she ordered Southampton's dismissal from the post of General of the Horse with Essex in Ireland, she described him cruelly as 'such a one whose counsel can be of little, and experience of less, use'.[3]

Even among the young ladies at court, Southampton enjoyed the reputation of being too 'fantasticall'. What with his quarrelling, his wenching, and his gambling, he was a typical example of the fashionable young rake. He challenged the Earl of Northumberland to a duel; he struck Ambrose Willoughby in a quarrel over a game of cards in the Presence Chamber, and got some of his hair pulled out in the subsequent unseemly brawl; he was accomplice after, and possibly before, the act in the killing of Henry Long by the Danvers brothers; he went over to Holland in 1600 to fight a duel with Lord Grey of Wilton, who retaliated a few months later by attacking him in force in the Strand.[4] In 1597 he went off with his cronies, Rutland, Cromwell, and the rest, to follow their leader Essex on the unprofitable Islands Voyage. No sooner was he back at Court than he seduced a maid of honour, Elizabeth Vernon, got her with child, and was obliged to marry her in haste and secrecy.[5] To escape the royal anger he then fled back to Paris, where he had been staying, and plunged into a crazy orgy of gambling. His friend and patron Essex was warned that

il fait des parties de 2, 3, et 4000ᶜ a la paulone. Même le Maréchal de Biron dans peu de jours lui gagna 3000ᶜ, et chaqu'un se moque de lui,

---

[1] B.M., Lansd. MSS. 37/30. ·

[2] The young Earl of Rutland was living above his income at at least as great a rate as Southampton in these last few years before Essex Revolt (see above, pp. 178–82).

[3] *Cal. S.P. Ireland, 1599–1600*, pp. 61–2, 100–2. *H.M.C. Rutland MSS.* i, p. 321.

[4] Stopes, op. cit., pp. 102–3, 114–15; 69, 80–4; 163–70. N. E. McClure, *Letters of John Chamberlain*, i, 107, 115.   [5] Ibid., p. 44; Stopes, op. cit., pp. 122–4.

tellement que le Comte d'Essex faira un grand coup pour le dit Comte de le retirer de bonne heure, car autrement il perdra tout son bien et reputation, tant en France qu'en Angleterre, dont j'en suis bien marré, sachant que Monseigneur le Comte l'aime.[1]

In November, three months after the marriage, the news of the day was that 'The new Countess of Southampton is brought a bed of a daughter, and to mend her portion the Earl her father hath lately lost 18,000 crowns at tennis in Paris.'[2]

Soon afterwards the Earl returned to England to encounter the sharp but brief anger of the Queen, followed Essex to Ireland as General of the Horse, and then ended this roystering career in that absurd fiasco of gang-warfare and semi-rebellion, the Essex Revolt of 8 February 1601. For the next two years he cooled his heels and his passions in the Tower, until release came with the accession of King James.

The hectic six years (1595–1600) had eaten deeply into the Earl's estate. He had richly rewarded his servants for their loyalty during his minority with leases on favourable terms, he was soon involved with money-lenders, and by 1597 his position was becoming serious.[3] In February of that year he assigned six manors in Hampshire and one in Somerset to three trustees, a lawyer, a cousin, and a personal servant, to administer at their own discretion in order to raise money both to satisfy his debtors and to pay the fines for renewing his church leases, some of which were about to expire. The trustees were given complete control over stewards and bailiffs, including powers of dismissal, and were authorized to cut down woods, to compound with copyholders for fines, and to mortgage the property. A year later things were worse still, and the trustees' powers were extended to an absolute right to sell whatever they thought fit, an earlier deed of entail being revoked.[4] As he explained from Paris to his friend Essex: 'I scarce know what course to take to live, having at my departure let to farm that poor estate I had left for the satisfying my creditors and payment of those debts which I came to owe by following her [Majesty's] court.'[5] And so in these years a good deal of the Wriothesley estate was sold off. In 1595 the last two Devon manors had been sold for

---

[1] H.M.C. Salis. MSS. viii, pp. 358–9.   [2] N. E. McClure, op. cit. i, p. 52.
[3] W.D. 1, 79, 443. P.R.O., L.C. 4/193, p. 49.
[4] W.D. 581, 582, 169. P.R.O., Close Rolls, 40 Eliz., pt. 14.
[5] H.M.C. Salis. MSS. viii, p. 357.

£5,000 to Thomas, son and heir of Sir Matthew Arundel of Wardour. Next year the Hampshire manor and rectory of Faringdon Episcopi went to Robert Cage, a Middle Temple lawyer, for £4,100. Two years later still the trustees sold Portsea and Copnor manors to Robert Bold, a future mayor of Portsmouth, for £1,500, and in 1599 the Solicitor-General, Sir Thomas Fleming, bought North Stoneham manor for £5,000. Finally in December 1600, on the eve of the Essex Revolt, the Somerset manor of Long Sutton was sold to the great London money-lender, Alderman Sir John Spencer, for £4,900.[1] Thus in five years the Earl had raised the huge sum of £20,500 from the sale of these seven manors, in addition to the unknown price for which two other Hampshire manors of Bighton and Corhampton had been sold.[2] Assuming that the sale price was twenty years' purchase of the net annual return— and very often it was as low as fifteen or sixteen years, particularly when the seller was desperate—this must have meant a loss of landed income of over £1,100 per annum, or more than one-third of the whole estate in possession.

Besides such portion as the Earl may have obtained from his belated marriage with Elizabeth Vernon, there are hints that he was also raising money by demanding large fines for renewing leases at the old rents, sometimes for very long periods. For example, in 1595 he let Micheldever manor for the lives of three young children for a fine of £650 and in 1599 he gave a thirty-three-year lease of some pasture grounds at Beaulieu.[3] A year later he leased the house, rectory, and mills of Beaulieu for no less than sixty years, no doubt in return for a very large fine indeed.[4] Finally, as security for the loans and the fines for renewals of his church leases advanced by his trustees, he was obliged in 1597 to convey the unexpired leases to them as security. They then obtained fresh leases in their own names, part of the money being raised on mortgages.[5]

---

[1] W.D., 283, 442, 430, 441. Castle Ashby, Compton MSS. F.D. 362. P.R.O., Close Rolls, 40 Eliz., pt. 15; 43 Eliz., pt. 11.

[2] *V.C.H. Hants*, iii, pp. 39, 248.   [3] W.D. 416, 364.

[4] W.D. 382. It appears that this was an assignment, by way of portion on the marriage of John Chamberlain to Anne Oglander, of a lease granted to Sir John Oglander some years before (C. Aspinall-Oglander, *Nunwell Symphony*, London, 1945, pp. 34, 157). In 1604 Chamberlain married Priscilla, daughter of Sir Edward Monins of Waldershare, Kent, and settled the lease on her as part of her jointure, in return for a portion of £800 (W.D. 382; Bodl., North MSS. C 20 ff. 49, 50).

[5] P.R.O., S.P. Dom. Eliz. 278/133.

Yet for all these sacrifices his position on the day of his arrest in 1601 was as serious as ever it had been. His debts were 'near 8000 li' and he had little enough to spare with which to pay them. His mother was still alive, so that her jointure lands had not yet come to him. The estate was burdened with £395 in fixed annuities, £80 in rents and fees, and a £312 allowance to his wife Elizabeth. According to his trustees the rental of his landed property in possession in Hampshire by a recent survey was now only £1,146 per annum, so that fixed charges left the Earl a disposable income of only £319.[1] However, this was perhaps a deliberately gloomy assessment of the situation, as it took no account of the £400 per annum worth of church leases which were in the hands of the trustees as security for the debts for which they were responsible. A document, which on internal evidence can be dated to 1599, gives a 'value of the manors and lands . . . of rents only above charge' as £1,873 in all. This includes £161 for North Stoneham and £77 for Long Sutton, which were about to be sold, and the gross income from the leases.[2] This tallies very well with the 1601 report and provides striking evidence of the serious diminution of the Earl's income as a result of his six years of youthful dissipation. His receipts from land in possession, including sale of woods and casual profits and fines, but after deduction of the rents for leasehold property, were now probably under £2,000 per annum.

But when he emerged from the Tower in 1603 the Earl's prospects were not altogether unfavourable. He was by all accounts an agreeable and attractive young man, and was likely to catch King James's eye. Moreover he was a friend of the late Earl of Essex and a personal enemy of Lord Grey of Wilton, who was almost immediately to be involved in the Main Plot. As such he had strong claims upon the King, and in the flood of largesse with which James celebrated his acquisition of the throne and wealth of England, the Earl was not forgotten. His titles of lands were restored, he was made Captain of the Isle of Wight, Vice-Admiral of Hampshire, and Master of the Queen's Forests, he obtained a grant of fee-farm lands worth £247 per annum in old rent, and he was given a lease of the Sweet Wine customs that had been a mainstay of the fortunes of two Elizabethan royal favourites, first of the Earl of Leicester and then of the Earl of Essex.[3] Papers survive

[1] P.R.O., S.P. Dom. Eliz. 278/132.   [2] Hatfield House, G55/21.
[3] *Cal. S.P. Dom., 1603–10*, pp. 19, 34, 137, 162. W.D. 122.

concerning Essex's administration of this customs farm, but not sufficient to be able to assess its true net value to him.[1] But it was certainly worth £2,500 a year to Leicester,[2] and when Southampton surrendered it to the Crown in 1611 he was given a pension of £2,000 a year in compensation.[3] It seems clear, therefore, that by this one grant alone he succeeded in doubling his income.

The grant of fee-farm lands he used to secure the manors of Great Compton in Somerset, Romsey Extra, Longstock, and Widley in Hampshire, probably Nettleton in Lincolnshire, and lands in Gloucestershire and Essex.[4] In 1607 he was granted the Keepership of the New Forest, and with it a life tenure of Lyndhurst manor and park; in 1610 he obtained a sixty-year lease from the Crown of Bowcombe manor, Carisbrooke; and before 1619 he was compensated for the damage caused by an increase of deer in the New Forest by a further £1,200 a year annuity from King James.[5] In addition to all this he obtained a cash gift of £3,714 from the Exchequer for unknown reasons in 1617.[6]

Throughout the reign of James the Earl lived an active life in attendance at one of the most extravagant courts in Europe.[7] He was still impetuous and hot-headed, but apart from a brisk exchange of tennis racket blows with the Earl of Montgomery in 1610 he seems to have avoided further violence.[8] And if he still lived in the grand manner, he was no longer notorious for his dissipation. Like his friend Rutland, he had been sobered by the aftermath of the Essex Revolt. But he still had a reputation as a gambler, and to the local gentry his principal achievement as Captain of the Isle of Wight was the gay social life which he encouraged. Years later Sir John Oglander recalled with nostalgia the good old days when one could see 'with my Lord of Southampton on St. Georges Down at bowls, from 30 to 40 knights and gentlemen, where our meeting was then twice every week, Tuesdays and Thursdays, and we had an ordinary there, and cards, and tables'.[9] In addition to

---

[1] Hatfield House, S204 ff. 101–3; 214, ff. 31, 32. Longleat, Devereux MSS., vol. vi.

[2] Longleat, Dudley MSS., Box iii/50; vol. xx, f. 48. B.M., Harl. Charters, D. 35/14. B.M., Harl. MSS. 167 ff. 135–7.

[3] *Cal. S.P. Dom., 1611–18*, pp. 40, 154. W.D., 577.

[4] *H.M.C. Salis. MSS.* xvi, p. 187. W.D. 297. *V.C.H. Hants*, iv, pp. 450, 454; iii, p. 171.

[5] W.D. 544, 197, 289.

[6] B.M., Lansd. MSS. 169/52. This may, of course, have been for arrears of the annuity of £2,000 per annum.

[7] For frequent mentions of his activities at court see N. E. McClure, op. cit., *passim*.

[8] Ibid. i, p. 297.

[9] Bodl., Rawl. MSS., Poet. 26/2. W. H. Long, *The Oglander Memoirs*, London, 1888, p. 23.

bearing the cost of this handsome style of living in Court and country, he had married off at least two of his three daughters, the eldest to the son and heir of Lord Spencer with a portion of £4,000.[1]

How far he managed to balance income against expenditure in these years is not clear. On the one hand he could lend an odd £1,000 for a few months to oblige a friend like Lord Knollys and could buy out the Earl of Salisbury's rival claims on his manor of Hook Mortimer. He could even afford to purchase the manors of Fairthorne in Hampshire and Saint Giles in the Fields in Middlesex, the price of which must have been not far short of £2,000.[2] On the other hand, it took him some years to clear off the initial debt. He was successfully prosecuted in King's Bench for the repayment of £300 in 1605,[3] and had still to repay the trustees the large sums they had advanced on his behalf. So in 1605-6 he sold Great Compton for £2,000, Romsey Extra for more than £450, and Widley for an unknown sum. He also made a life grant to Sir William Hervey of Soberton manor, presumably in return for a large fine, and assigned his manor of Itchell to Sir Richard White, probably by way of mortgage, which he only redeemed ten years later in return for £400 in cash and an annuity of £120 per annum.[4] Finally in 1611 he conveyed five Hampshire manors, including the newly purchased Fairthorne, to two trustees, probably to provide a fund to pay off debts and raise marriage portions for his daughters.[5] Although the evidence is ambiguous for the first eighteen years of James's reign, there can be no doubt that things changed abruptly for the worse towards the end of his life, when he must have started running up very heavy debts indeed.[6] This was almost certainly due to the suspension of his two pensions of £3,200 a year in the summer of 1621, a financial catastrophe that he had brought upon himself

---

[1] Althorp, Spencer MSS., Cupboard K, shelf 2. The £2,000 portion of the third daughter, Elizabeth, who married a Master in Chancery, Sir Thomas Estcourt, was still unpaid in 1646 (P.R.O., S.P. 23/192, pp. 201-5).

[2] P.R.O., L.C. 4/196, p. 110. Close Rolls, 7 Jas. I, pt. 26; 13 Jas. I, pt. 25. Hook Mortimer formed part of the grant to the Earl of Salisbury in exchange for Theobalds in 1607, although it had been in the hands of the Wriothesleys since the reign of Edward VI. The deeds and accounts do not supply the amount paid, but it could not have been very much as both Hook Mortimer and Hook Valence together only produced an old rent of £5 per annum in 1624 (W.D. 117; Hatfield House, D 133/9; G 2/194; Close Rolls, 9 Jas. I, pt. 11/15).

[3] Stopes, op. cit., p. 292.

[4] V.C.H. Hants, iv, p. 454; iii, p. 171. W.D. 297, 510, 439. Close Rolls, 3 Jas. I, pt. 31; 4 Jas. I, pt. 21. Widley belonged to the recusant family of Uvedale, and may have been freely restored by the Earl. The Essex and Gloucestershire lands were probably also sold up at this time. They were certainly gone by 1624 (W.B. 128).

[5] W.D. 216.

[6] e.g. W.D. 562, 563, 564.

by his leadership of the war party and anti-Buckingham group in the House of Lords.[1] This act of political bravado is a striking example of the subordination of monetary factors to consideration of power and politics; it was to cost his family dear.

III. SOURCES OF INCOME, 1600–1624

A very large, if not the largest, part of the Earl's income during the years before 1621 was derived from royal favours. Old rents on Crown lands were usually valued at at least forty years' purchase, so that the £247 per annum which he was given in 1603 had a capital value of about £10,000. It was by the sale of most of this land that he cleared off the initial debt. Thereafter it was first the Sweet Wine Farm, then the annuities of £2,000 and £1,200 that kept him going. In about 1607 he had referred to the Sweet Wine Farm, as 'the best means I have to subsist, . . . which if it should be overthrown, I should be enforced to live in a very mean fashion'.[2] To this must be added the unknown profits of the Keepership of the New Forest, the Vice-Admiralty of Hampshire, and the Governorship of the Isle of Wight,[3] and the pay that he drew in 1624 as Colonel in the volunteer English force in Holland. Before the suspension of the pensions in 1621, his annual income from official sources was probably well over £3,500 per annum and was possibly even as high as £4,000.

There were also other ways in which this active courtier increased his income. Deprived till 1619 of a place on the Privy Council, he turned his restless energies and intelligence to participation in overseas trade and settlement. As early as 1593 he was investing in privateering expeditions, and while he was still in the Tower in 1602 he was the patron of a fresh attempt to colonize Virginia.[4] He was a leading promoter of the Virginia Company in the first decade of the reign and of the Somers Island Company in 1614–15, invested in the East India Company of 1609, was elected Treasurer of the Virginia Company in 1620 as the head of one of the two factions into which the Company was rent, and in the same

---

[1] Stopes, op. cit., pp. 404–9, 413. McClure, op. cit. ii, pp. 384–5. *Cal. S.P. Dom. 1619–23*, p. 269. Bodl. MSS., Add. D. 111, f. 152.

[2] Stopes, op. cit., p. 309.

[3] In 1603 the Venetian ambassador, no doubt with his usual exaggeration, reported the Captaincy to be worth 6,000 crown (*Cal. S.P. Venetian, 1603–7*, p. 56). The Vice-Admiralty brought in the profits of pirates goods and wrecks (*Cal. S.P. Dom., 1603–10*, p. 453).

[4] *Acts of the Privy Council, 1592–3*, pp. 109, 159. Stopes, op. cit., p. 319.

year became a foundation member of the Council for the Plantation of New England. How much all this was worth to him we have no means of knowing. But he was certainly granted twenty shares of land in the Old Adventure in Virginia in 1623, a reward for his services as Treasurer.[1] The impression remains, however, that all this activity was as much the result of an inquiring mind and an overflow of energies as of a calculated desire for profit.

Of this intellectual energy there is evidence in many spheres. The Earl's greatest claim upon the attention of posterity is in his role as a patron of Shakespeare and other playwrights and littérateurs of the day. But he also took a leading part in politics, and in 1621 frustration at exclusion from high office, contempt for the succession of unworthy favourites, and dislike of the pro-Spanish peace policy of James drove him into open opposition to the Crown.[2]

How far, and in what ways, did this energy show itself in the administration of his estates? In 1624 the gross rental from the Earl's property, both freehold and leasehold, was £2,384 per annum. The surveyor's estimate of its total gross value if out of lease was rather over £5,900.[3] Neither of these figures, however, represents the true annual receipts at the time. The same document shows that most of the estate was let on twenty-one-year leases, with a fine equivalent to about five and a half times the difference between the actual rent and the surveyor's valuation. The difference between the rental and the valuation is about £3,500. If a five and a half year fine was charged for each twenty-one-year renewal, this would make the *average* income from this source about £900 per annum. In addition there were the profits from sale of fuel and timber from the extensive woodland area round Beaulieu and Titchfield, which are known to have brought in at least £270 per annum. It is likely therefore that the Earl's gross income from the land, after deduction of leasehold rents and charges of about £125, was about £3,500. Although prices had risen sharply in the previous thirty years, the Earl's sales of land had caused the income from his estates to remain virtually static. To an increasing degree he now depended for the maintenance of his status and standard of living upon his pensions from the Crown, which in 1620 were about equal to his landed income. His assertion of political independence in 1621, which resulted in the cutting off of all payment on his pensions, was thus a very remarkable act of courage, or folly, or both.

[1] W.D. 312.   [2] See Stopes, *passim*.   [3] W.B. 128.

The Wriothesley property was almost entirely confined to Hampshire, and was therefore a fairly homogeneous unit to administer. Like most landlords of his class the Earl was affected by the prevailing moral pressure against radical change in the agricultural and social system. He was therefore no encloser, and no oppressor of the tenantry. He was content to jog along, renewing leases and copyholds on the old basis, the increased fines doing no more than keep pace with the general monetary inflation. Apart from the parks and woods kept in the lord's hands, the Earl's landed estates fell into two groups, copyhold and leasehold. With the exception of all at Dogmersfield and some at Titchfield, where they were fixed, all fines for renewal of copyholds were negotiable, and could therefore be raised as prices rose. As on most estates, copyholds were renewed at the old rents for ninety-nine years or three lives, whichever was the shorter. The result of this antiquated system was to create ever more serious fluctuations in both landlord's income and tenant's obligations. Thus a copyholder with a rent of £2 might pay £100 for a new entry[1] and on occasions the difference was greater still. Where fines were fixed, the landlord's position became less and less advantageous as prices rose, and it is not surprising that shortly before 1615 the Earl made some effort to overthrow the legal position of his Dogmersfield copyholders. But the tenants banded together, alleging ancient custom for a fixed fine of 11s. 6d. and a heriot of 5s. per yardland. In the face of this defence the Earl agreed to a fictitious suit in Chancery to register the tenants' customary rights, merely adding that under modern condition he thought them rather unreasonable—as indeed they were.[2] But his ready agreement with the tenants once the legal position was established shows that the episode is not part of an attempt by the Earl to flout the law or oppress the tenantry.

Elsewhere the situation adversely affected both parties, and on some estates there were moves—sometimes, but not always, resisted by the tenants—to convert copyholds to leaseholds. Thus in 1616-17 the Earl converted five copyholds at Beaulieu into leaseholds. In only one case did he let at a rack-rent, in the other cases contenting himself with renewal at the old rent with a large fine. Nevertheless, the way was now open for a massive rent increase and a consequent reduction of the fine at the next lease.[3]

[1] W.D. 596. At Beaulieu, in 1618.
[2] P.R.O., Chancery Proc., Ser. i, Jas. I, G 5/63.   [3] W.B. 128.

That this was not a very deliberate policy is proved by looking at the administration of the leasehold property. There have survived a large number of individual leases, and a valuation made in 1624, which together prove beyond doubt that the system was both haphazard and inefficient. The rents established at the last leasings in the 1590s tended to be preserved, and the Earl's immediate income was boosted by heavy fines. For example, Saint Leonard's farm at Beaulieu was leased for twenty-one years in 1616 at the old 1595 rent of £48, but with a fine of £667. It was valued in 1624 at £120 per annum, which means that this was a very profitable lease, the fine being 9·4 years' purchase of the difference in value. But it was not till the next lease in 1639 that the system was altered and the farm let at a rack-rent of £200 per annum.[1]

As a result of this policy it is clear that rents tended to remain fairly steady, though the immediate cash profits from the land were swollen at irregular intervals by the sudden flood of fines for new leases. For example there was a very heavy crop of new twenty-one-year leases in 1614–16, by which even the extremely incomplete series of surviving deeds shows the Earl to have gained over £1,700. The total profits from fines for these three years must have been very much greater than this, and may well have approached £3,000. The most remarkable feature of these new leases is not the system by which they were renewed, for this was normal practice everywhere, but the extremely variable rating of the fines, as revealed by the valuation of 1624. It is clear that the Earl's steward had no up-to-date valuation upon which to rely, as a result of which some tenants were getting very much more profitable bargains than others. Taking twenty-one-year leases made between 1616 and 1624, the fines of six were between three and five years' purchase of the difference between rent and the 1624 valuation, ten were between five and seven, and two between nine and eleven. This was, as competent surveyors of the day were arguing, a very uneconomic system. At the current interest rate of 10 per cent, the fine for a twenty-one-year lease should have been rather over eight and a half years' purchase,[2] and yet the Earl of Southampton was letting at an average of only five and a half years. It should perhaps be pointed out that this was not abnormal. For example, Lord Saint John at precisely the same period of the 1620s was working on a basis of

---

[1] W.D. 363, 390, 377.
[2] T. Clay, *Briefe, Easie and Necessary Tables*, London, 1622, p. 1.

six years' purchase for the leases of his Bedfordshire estates.[1] Nevertheless, quite apart from the long-term consequences of making full repairing leases at small rents and large fines in starving the land of capital for improvements, it is clear that the Earl was not getting anything approaching the full economic return on his property.

It would seem that the Earl did not take much interest in the humdrum routine of administering his agricultural property. This does not mean, however, that he confined his efforts at increasing his income to lobbying the Crown for monopolies, grants of land, and pensions. He was very probably encouraged to develop the industrial resources of his estate by the experience of his father-in-law Viscount Montagu, who had for years been working an iron furnace in Surrey,[2] and still more by the remarkable achievements of his intimate friend the Earl of Rutland at his ironworks at Rievaulx.[3] There was iron-ore at Titchfield and an abundance of wood for fuel both on the Earl of Southampton's nearby estates, and still more across the estuary at Beaulieu; it is not surprising, therefore, if he attempted to imitate Rutland. The works must have been started immediately after his release from the Tower in 1603, for by 1605 they were causing local complaints. The Corporation of Southampton protested to the government that the Earl's 'new erected iron works at Beaulieu and Titchfield' managed by Mr. Chamberlain, were insatiable in their demands for wood, and were causing a local fuel shortage.[4] But King James was not the man to interfere with the legitimate private interests of a highly placed courtier, and the works continued uninterrupted. At this early stage the Earl was clearly hopeful of expanding his operations, for in 1608 he inserted a clause in a lease of corn-mills at Botley giving him an option of cancellation if at any time he should decide to pull down the mills and erect an ironworks.[5]

But things did not work out according to plan, and these dreams of expansion had to be abandoned in the face of contracting markets. Like other industrialists, the Earl must have been hard hit by the 1621 economic depression, and the option at Botley was

---

[1] Beds. R.O., Dd/Dy, 2/15.   [2] *H.M.C. 7th Rep.*, App., pp. 622, 645.

[3] See above, pp. 190–94.

[4] F. J. C. and D. M. Hearnshaw, *Southampton Court Leet Records, 1603–24* Southampton, 1907, p. 430.

[5] W.D. 401. The clauses of this lease form a curious mixture of old and new. One gives the landlord the right of re-entry if the tenant becomes a retainer of anyone save the King or the Earl himself.

never taken up. In the 1620s, ironmasters were obliged to seek new markets amid increasing competition. The Earl of Cork tried to break into Southampton's monopoly of the Hampshire market at Poole, and the latter tried to sell his iron to forges near Bristol.[1] It was no doubt this problem of shrinking markets and profits that led the Earl in 1622 to abandon direct management of the works, and to make a seven-year lease of his furnaces at Titchfield and Beaulieu for £103 per annum, the lessee engaging to buy from the Earl's estate 1,600 cords of wood a year at 3s. 6d. a cord.[2] After this, the Titchfield works probably continued to be let to contractors, for they were certainly still under lease the next and the last time we hear of them, in 1662.[3] The Beaulieu works, on the other hand, seem to have returned to direct control, and by 1642 must have been operating on a substantial scale. At any rate the Earl claimed that 140 tons of iron valued at £980 were seized by the Parliamentarians at his Beaulieu furnace.[4]

Soon after the Earl gave up direct operation of his ironworks he was tempted into a fresh and far more revolutionary entrepreneurial venture. In 1623 a manufacturer called John Tilte wrote from London to his uncle in Bromsgrove, explaining to him how he and a business partner had been suffering from a growing shortage of tin-plates from Bohemia owing to the destruction of the works and the interruption of trade by the Thirty Years War. He explained that they had mastered the technical secrets of tin-plating and added that 'The mill which batters the iron is the Earl's of Southampton, he hath been at a thousand pounds charge to build it and to fit it for this work.'[5] They jointly agreed to raise a stock of £500 to get the mill started, the Earl providing £200 and the two partners £150 each. In return for this capital investment and the use of the mill, the Earl was to receive 50 per cent of the profits.

This is far and away the earliest recorded mill for tin-plate in England, and it would therefore be very interesting to know more about it. The only reference to it among the family papers is a document of 1647 which mentions a twenty-one-year lease made in 1628 by Sir William Uvedale of his plate-mill at Wickham to Arthur Bromfield, who was an agent regularly employed by the Earls of Southampton as trustee for conveyancing, and to a London

[1] A. B. Grosart, *The Lismore Papers*, 2nd ser., iii, p. 29. Also information given me by Professor W. O. Ranger.

[2] W.B. 128.   [3] W.D. 447.   [4] P.R.O., S.P. 23/192, pp. 201–5.

[5] Kidderminster Public Library, Knight MSS. 6443.

girdler Thomas Jupp.[1] By 1647 this lease had been assigned to the
Earl himself. This strongly suggests that Jupp was John Tilte's
unnamed partner, and it is clear that the mill was powered by the
River Meon and built on land leased from Sir William Uvedale
at Wickham, immediately up-river from the Earl's furnace at
Titchfield.

It seems likely that this plate-mill was still in operation after the
Restoration, and it may provide an explanation of a mysterious and
unfortunate episode in the history of the industry in England. In
1661 a patent for the English manufacture of tin-plate was granted
to the ironmaster Dud Dudley and to a William Chamberlain, and
when about four years later Andrew Yarranton tried to introduce
into England the more advanced manufacturing techniques practised at Dresden, his project was thwarted by the Chamberlain
patent. Yarranton remarks that his backers were 'afraid to offend
great men in power who had their eye upon us', and as a result the
scheme collapsed. Now the master of the Earl's ironworks in 1605
was William Chamberlain, whose son John was a tenant of Lyndhurst manor under the third Earl. Whether the Chamberlains were
the lessees of the ironworks in the 1620s we do not know, though it
does not seem improbable. John Chamberlain had a son William
who may well have been the post-Restoration lessee of the ironworks and plate-mill and the mysterious patentee who blocked
Yarranton's schemes. If this is so, 'the great men in power' who
supported Chamberlain would be chiefly the Lord Treasurer, the
Earl of Southampton himself.[2]

How far these bold industrial ventures were financially profitable
we cannot say. Evidently by 1624 the ironworks brought in only
a modest return of £100 a year together with a guaranteed market
for some £290 worth of wood a year. Whether the tin-plate mill
repaid its investment we do not know. It seems improbable, however, that the Earl or his successor succeeded by these means in
increasing their income by more than £400 or £500 a year.

The second major effort by the Earl to improve his income was
directed towards the development of his London property. By the
end of the sixteenth century the growth of the Court, the central

[1] W.D. 511.
[2] Andrew Yarranton, *England's Improvement by Sea and Land*, London, 1681, pt. ii, pp. 148–58.
F. W. Gibbs, 'The Rise of the Tin-Plate Industry', *Annals of Science*, vi, 1948–50, p. 400;
vii, 1951, p. 34. F. J. C. and D. N. Hearnshaw, op. cit., p. 430. W.D. 349, 444. *Visitation of
Hampshire* (Harleian Soc., lxiv), 1913, p. 218.

administration, and the law-courts at Westminster, and the expansion of the City of London had made the fields between the two ripe for development. More and more of the gentry were tending to take a London house, and the area today bounded by the Charing Cross Road, New Oxford Street, Chancery Lane, and the Strand was obviously suitable for high-class residential building to satisfy the rising demand of the professional and landed classes. Those peers who happened to possess or contrived to acquire property in this area, the Earls of Bedford, Salisbury, Clare, and Southampton, all enjoyed a tremendous increase in income during the early seventeenth century.

It was in the 1540s that the first Earl obtained the suburban manor of Bloomsbury, which had been the property of the Charterhouse priory. In 1547 he also acquired, by exchange with the Earl of Warwick, a large house and grounds fronting onto Holborn to the north and Chancery Lane to the west, together with part of the Holborn frontage along the west side of the Lane.[1] Until two years before, the house had formed the town residence of the Bishops of Lincoln, so that both London properties came ultimately from the Church. Nothing much was done to this property until towards the end of the sixteenth century. Already before 1594 building had begun on the south side of Holborn to the north of Lincoln's Inn, and in that year major development was started all along the frontage. The Earl adopted the normal device of the thirty-one-year building lease, but on this occasion he employed a single contractor. When the leases ran out, they were renewed to individual lessees for twenty-one years or less, at a fairly stiff rent and a moderate fine, while precautions were taken to maintain the value of the property by inserting clauses in the leases prohibiting artificers from practising their trade.[2] During the first two decades of the century more and more of the Southampton House grounds and outbuildings were absorbed, even the tennis-court and the chapel giving way to shops and houses.[3] Nor was this all, for the expansion of London had now begun to push northward as far as Bloomsbury, where in 1613 the Earl began leasing plots for building. Realizing the potentialities of the area, three years later he made a very shrewd investment, and bought for £600 part of the manor of

[1] E. J. Davis, 'The University Site of Bloomsbury', *London Topographical Record*, xviii, 1936, pp. 49–51. E. Williams, *Early Holborn*, nos. 359, 1236, 1230.

[2] W.D. 266, 267, 269, 298–306.

[3] J. Stow, *Survey of London*, London, 1755, ii, p. 67. W.D. 299, 266, 305, 128.

St. Giles in the Fields, which gave him a long frontage along Holborn. And finally in 1617 he obtained a confirmation that the liberties of Southampton House extended well down the east side of Chancery Lane.[1] If the third Earl had not achieved any dramatic increase in his income from London rents during his lifetime, he had prepared the ground for rapid expansion in the future.

IV. RECOVERY, 1624–1667

In 1624 Earl Henry, now aged fifty-one, set out to take over his military command in Holland, taking with him his son and heir James. Within a few weeks both were dead of an epidemic disease that was ravaging the camp. The effects on the family fortunes of the double blow were very serious indeed. Overnight were terminated the two suspended life annuities of £3,200, the life interest in Lyndhurst manor, and all the profits of office.[2] Secondly, the death of the eldest son James left a young child as the heir, with the result that the dowager Countess had to pay £2,000 to the Crown for his wardship and marriage in 1625, a further £334 for his livery four years later, and £400 a year for the King's third for wardship in the meantime. Even so, the Countess did not regain custody of the child, whose education was entrusted by the King to his father's old enemy, the Duke of Buckingham, to whom all the profits of the wardship were assigned.[3]

In addition to these burdens provision had also to be made for the maintenance of the dowager Countess Elizabeth. Owing to the circumstances surrounding the hasty marriage of the pregnant bride in 1598, no jointure settlement had ever been made, although at Common Law the Countess had a right to one-third of the estate. Fortunately, however, she did not claim her full due and continued to live modestly at Titchfield, so that this burden was temporarily reduced.[4] Another piece of good fortune was the legacy from a great-aunt in 1626 of two manors at East Horsley, Surrey.[5]

[1] J. Parton, *Some Account of the Hospital and Parish of Saint Giles in the Fields, Middlesex*, London, 1822, pp. 331–3; P.R.O., Close Rolls, 14 Jas. I, pt. 52. S.P. Dom. Jas. I, 94/93. G. Scott Thompson, *The Russells in Bloomsbury*, London, 1940, p. 24.

[2] The Earl apparently recovered favour with Buckingham in 1622–3, and vigorously supported the war-policy in 1624, but it is not certain whether or not the payment of the pensions was resumed. In view of Cranfield's economy drive at this time, it seems unlikely (N. E. McClure, op. cit. ii, p. 438; W.D. 227). After the Earl's death, Elizabeth, Queen of Bohemia, tried to get them renewed for his son, but without success (*H.M.C. Bath MSS.* ii, p. 73).

[3] W.D. 201, 549. *Cal. S.P. Dom. 1625–6*, p. 549. P.R.O., Court of Wards, Misc. Books, 207, f. 192ᵛ.   [4] S.P. 23/192, pp. 201–5.   [5] *V.C.H. Surrey*, iii, pp. 350, 351.

But this was no compensation for the loss of official income, and the moment he came of age in 1629 the young Earl had to sell off a good deal of the Wriothesley estate to pay off the debts, most of which were certainly inherited from his father. This is proved by some notes of his brother-in-law Lord Spencer, who shows great anxiety lest Lady Elizabeth's rights to a third of the property should be endangered by the need to pay off the heavy debts incurred by her late husband.[1] In an attempt to reduce the burden, the young Earl sold the manor of Walsworth to Sir Daniel Norton of Southwick for £1,900, the house, manor, and rectory of Dogmersfield to John Godson for £3,600, and Itchell and Ewshott manors to Robert Mason, M.P. and Chancellor of the diocese of Winchester, for a figure which must have been over £3,000.[2] In addition he also sold to Carew Ralegh, son and heir of Sir Walter, the two Surrey manors that he had just inherited.[3] Both Nettleton manor in Lincolnshire and the very valuable manor of West Meon were probably sold at this time, for they do not appear in any document after this date.[4] If this is so, the price he received for these eight manors must have been about £19,000, for six of them were reckoned in the 1624 document to be worth no less than £1,427 per annum, or over one-quarter of the total value of the estate.

With this money he redeemed for £20,000 the property that had been conveyed as long ago as 1611 to Arthur Bromfield and other trustees as security for payment of debts and other charges.[5] But a heavy load of debt continued to weigh on the estate despite these massive sales of 1629. In 1633 things had got so bad that he was obliged to empower trustees to sell Beaulieu if the debts were not paid off within the year.[6] Fortunately, however, this desperate measure did not become necessary (possibly thanks to the sale to the Navy for £2,295 of over 2,000 trees in Titchfield great park). Even so, mortgages for £3,000 which were made in 1630–1 could not be paid off till 1640, and in about 1641 he had to sell his interest in the manors of Soberton and Flexland to Bishop Curll of Winchester.[7]

Things were not easy for the Earl in the 1630s. At any rate up to 1634 he had something of his father's reputation as a gambler,

---

[1] Althorp, Early Spencer Papers, 10.

[2] W.D. 639, 505. *V.C.H. Hants*, iv, p. 8. The sale price of Walsworth and Dogmersfield was between thirteen and fourteen times the theoretical gross valuation (W.B. 128). Thirteen times the Itchell and Ewshott valuation is about £3,100.

[3] *V.C.H. Surrey*, loc. cit.   [4] W.D. 239, 279.   [5] W.D. 216.

[6] W.D. 292, 350.

[7] W.D. 534, 412–13, 247, 634–5. *V.C.H. Hants*, iii, p. 259. *Cal. S.P. Dom.*, *1635*, p. 388.

although it was said in that year that as a result of a run of minor
losses at Newmarket he was selling his stud, giving up all heavy
play, and going abroad.[1] So off he went to France, where he finally
ruined his political and financial chances by marrying a well-born
but poorly endowed Huguenot beauty. George Garrard commented that 'My Lord is a very happy man in her, yet would he
have hearkened to a match offered unto him in England, it had
been much better for his estate.' According to Garrard, Sir Thomas
Thynne of Longleat had taken a fancy to the young Earl, and
would have given him his blue-stocking daughter with a marriage
portion of £40,000—a gigantic sum for that time—and would have
married his son and heir to Elizabeth Wriothesley without asking
for any portion at all.[2] If the story is true, and Garrard was usually
well informed, the Earl's sacrifice for love was very great indeed,
for Sir Thomas was probably the richest commoner in England.

A further consequence of his marriage was that some permanent
provision had now to be made for his mother in lieu of dower, and
so Southampton House in London and four manors in Hampshire
were settled on her for life. In 1640, however, presumably because
of the death of his wife, this settlement was changed to an annuity
of £800 a year, and the dowager Countess again took up residence
at Titchfield.[3]

From his father the Earl inherited a position as a leader of the
moderate aristocratic opposition to royal policies. Moreover, his
marriage to a French Huguenot was not calculated to win the
favour of Henrietta Maria, so that the Earl was deprived of all hope
of favour at Court leading to office or rewards. On the contrary, he
was singled out as one of the victims of royal fiscal exactions. One
of the quasi-legal methods of raising money adopted by Charles's
government in the 1630s was the recovery of ancient boundaries of
the royal forests, which had been shrinking for some 300 years. As
a result of its antiquarian researches, the Crown suddenly laid claim
to some 2,236 acres of the Earl's land at Beaulieu. It was reported
that the Earl complained bitterly of this measure, and it was
rumoured that it, coupled with the smallness of his wife's dowry,

---

[1] W. Knowler, *Strafforde's Letters*, i, p. 225.

[2] Ibid., pp. 337–8. For her appearance, see R. W. Boulding, 'Wriothesley Portraits', *Walpole Soc.* viii, 1920.

[3] W.D. 292, 294, 414, 126. The Earl concealed this agreement from the Commissioners for Compounding, and claimed a deduction for his mother's dower of a full one-third of the estate (S.P. 23/192, pp. 201–5).

would ruin him.[1] But despite his protests the Forest Court held in 1635 declared the land to be ancient royal forest, thus depriving the Earl of much of his extensive woodlands. As an act of grace the King freed the abbey itself and certain lands the next year, but much continued to remain under royal control. In 1638–9 the Earl was reduced to the humiliating position of having to ask royal permission to cut wood in his own coppices.[2]

In addition to a political position antagonistic to the Crown, the Earl also inherited from his father a taste for risky entrepreneurial ventures. In 1639 he organized a group of investors and prepared a ship for the colonization of the remote island of Mauritius. The scheme was blocked by the Crown, however, in response to protests by the East India Company that the venture infringed its monopoly.[3]

In view of this treatment and the position earlier adopted by his father, it is not surprising that Southampton emerged in 1640 as a leader of those constitutional reformers who were determined to place limited restrictions upon royal power in the future. But his hopes for a compromise settlement were illusory. Although he was made a Privy Councillor, the King never trusted him and went his own way; and, on the other hand, he was gradually alienated by the extremist policies of the leaders of the House of Commons. Like so many of his kind who found themselves trapped between two groups of extremists, he changed from a moderate Parliamentarian in 1640 to a reluctant Royalist in 1642.[4]

There are always severe financial penalties for backing the losing side in a civil war, and in 1646 the Earl of Southampton was faced with the reckoning. He was ordered by the Parliamentary Commissioners to draw up a statement of his pre-war finances to form a basis for assessing his fine for royalist 'delinquency'.[5] The main conclusion to be drawn from the document is the striking success achieved in increasing income from the estate since the death of

---

[1] Northants. R.O., Finch-Hatton MSS. 1737. W. Knowler, op. cit. i, pp. 463, 467. It was reported that the profits of Beaulieu were likely to be reduced from £2,500 per annum to £500 per annum. But this was a gross exaggeration since the valuation of the Beaulieu estate in 1624 was under £1,500 per annum (W.B. 128).

[2] *V.C.H. Hants*, iv, p. 651. *Cal. S.P. Dom.*, *1638–9*, p. 167. W.D. 73.

[3] E. B. Sainsbury, *Cal. of Court Minutes of the East India Company*, *1635–39*, pp. 317, 344, 350; *1640–43*, pp. 8, 25, 296.

[4] Clarendon gives a measured eulogy of Southampton's intelligence and honesty, and a description of the evolution of his political opinions, in his *History of the Rebellion* Oxford, 1732, p. 302.

[5] P.R.O., S.P. 23/192, pp. 201–5.

his father in 1624, despite the total absence of royal gifts or favours, and indeed in the face of royal harassment.

In the first place his income from his London property had increased enormously. He had further encroached upon Southampton House and grounds in Holborn for new building, and in 1636 he had petitioned King Charles for leave to demolish the house altogether and build tenements, since 'his fortune hath need of some helps'. Permission was granted two years later and eighty dwellings and a tavern were erected on the site, the whole forming a housing project known as Southampton Buildings. At the same time houses had spread right along the Holborn frontage of the Bloomsbury estate, behind which lay orchards and specialized market-gardens.[1] It seems very unlikely that the Earl was in a position to finance these buildings himself, and they appear to have been erected by contractors or lessees on the usual thirty-one-year leases from 1640. In 1640 he had obtained royal permission to build himself a big new town house on his Bloomsbury estate to replace the house that had been pulled down in Holborn, and a beginning had certainly been made before the outbreak of war two years later.[2] As a result of all this activity on his urban properties, the Earl had to admit a rental of £536 from Bloomsbury and £434 from Holborn, and to add that when the leases ran out the rental would improve by a further £300 a year. By 1642, in fact, one-quarter of his stated rental was coming from his London properties.

In addition to this, the Earl greatly improved the rental of his Hampshire estates by making substantial increases in leasehold rents and reducing the fines to more reasonable proportions. In some cases he began making twenty-one-year leases of large farms at rack-rents without an entry fine at all. For example, a farm at Beaulieu which was valued at £20 per annum in 1624 and had been let for twenty-one years at £10 per annum and a £50 fine in 1616, was let at £20 per annum without a fine in 1639.[3] And so although he had sold over one-quarter of the estate in 1629 to pay off his father's debts, his admitted Hampshire rental in 1642 of £2,700 was over £300 more than it had been in 1624.[4]

To estimate the total income of the Earl's estate in 1642, we must resort to a good deal of guess-work. The stated gross rental in all

[1] W.D. 306, 307. W. Knowler, op. cit. ii, p. 57. E. Williams, op. cit. ii, no. 1230. *Cal. S.P. Dom.*, *1639-40*, p. 501; *1640*, p. 91. G. Scott Thomson, op. cit., pp. 26-33.

[2] S.P. 23/192, pp. 201-5.   [3] W.D. 593, 599.

[4] P.R.O., S.P. 23/192, pp. 201-5. W.B. 128.

counties of £3,733 in any case is very probably an underestimate, and to it must be added the profits from fines, sales of wood, and sales of iron. It is likely, therefore, that the average gross annual income from his estate was between £5,000 and £6,000 a year. A result of this increase in income, combined with prudent living away from the expensive temptations of life at Court, was that the Earl's debts in 1642 were within reasonable bounds. They were £3,000 at interest, £2,000 still due to his sister as a legacy from their father, and £1,000 to a certain Mrs. Turvile.

The 1640s and 1650s were a sad time for the Earl. The death in childbed of his first wife in 1640 served to increase his natural melancholy, particularly as she had not provided him with a surviving male heir. Moreover his next wife, daughter of Francis, Earl of Chichester, died in 1654, still without providing a male heir. His hope of a moderate political settlement was shattered by the Civil War, from which he also suffered financially. The Parliamentary Commissioners fined him £6,466 for his royalism and made him settle £250 a year on the clergy serving those churches of which he was lay rector. According to the Earl, he also suffered more directly from the ravages of war. The big new house he had been building on the Bloomsbury estate had received £1,000 worth of damage. Moreover, one of the forts built for the defence of London in 1642–3 ran right across this property,[1] resulting in the destruction of a number of houses, and a loss of rental of over £100 per annum and a capital loss of £1,600. In Hampshire £980 worth of iron was seized at the Beaulieu furnace, £235 worth of woods were cut down and sold, and the rental of Titchfield fell by £50 a year as a result of encroachments by the sea.[2]

In addition to all these disasters there was the burden of war taxation, which now for the first time was hitting the landowning class very hard. Tenants were suffering severely from compulsory billeting of troops and some allowance had to be made both for this and for the monthly assessments and other parliamentary taxes on land, for which the landlord was legally responsible. The Earl did what he could to shift part of these burdens on to the tenants, though no doubt he was obliged to make corresponding reductions in rent. For example, clauses in a lease of a farm at Micheldever in 1649 stipulated that the tenant was to pay a share of contributions,

[1] W. Maitland, *History of London*, London, 1756, i, p. 369.
[2] P.R.O., S.P. 23/192, pp. 201–5.

etc. for the army, and was to give the Earl all money he received from soldiers towards the cost of their quarter. In return the Earl was to allow the tenant rebates of 2s. 6d. a day for each man and horse billeted on him, and 1s. 3d. for each foot-soldier. Another lease of 1655 allowed rebates of only 2s. and 1s. By a Beaulieu lease of 1652 the tenant agreed to pay all ordinary taxes and 'such part of contributions and other military taxes as other tenants bear in regard of their stocks'. One of the tenants at Fareham agreed to pay one-third of the monthly assessment and of the cost of quartering soldiers, others to pay all ordinary and a quarter, a third, a half, or two-thirds of all extraordinary taxes. It is evident from these leases that the tenants were very far from helpless in bargaining with their lord, and that each contract was the result of tough individual negotiation. Occasionally the Earl was obliged to make allowances for the burden of indirect taxation, as when a ten-year lease of Botley mills in 1660 at £10 per annum granted a remission of rent of £1 a year so long as the excise continued.[1]

For all these variations in leases, it is clear that there was a continuance of that policy of obtaining the maximum possible profit from the land that was already in full swing in the 1630s. Further evidence of this is the increased control the Earl now exercised over agricultural practices. A lease of a farm at Droxford of 1650 forbade the tenant to turf up and burn his land 'because that kind of husbandry will cause future weakness and barrenness in the land', and another lease ten years later only permitted it if the tenants agreed to chalk, marl, or lime the ground. A lease at East Stratton laid down that the tenant was only to plough the land two years in three, others in 1651-2 that no corn was to be sown in the last two or three years, and in 1660 that a proportion of the arable land was to be sown in the last year with peas and vetches to get it ready for wheat.[2] Like so many aristocrats, Southampton was a zealous and efficient *rentier* rather than a progressive landlord; he carefully avoided putting capital into his estate, preferring to leave the cost both of development and of repairs to his tenants.

The Earl's fortunes changed abruptly with the Restoration, when Charles gave him the very important and very lucrative office of Lord Treasurer. Though temperamentally unsuited to Charles's easy ways, the Earl held the office until his death. In the hope of

[1] W.D. 421, 424, 387, 397, 446, 598, 599, 602, 604.
[2] W.D. 507, 380, 419, 387, 397, 598.

begetting an heir to his estate, he had married yet again in 1659, this time Frances, daughter of the Duke of Somerset, and widow of Richard Viscount Molyneux.[1] But there was no issue from the marriage, and it was now clear that the Wriothesley estate would be dispersed, since of the nine children by the first two marriages, only three daughters had survived. Consequently the Earl neither sought nor obtained great favours, and appears to have spent his time playing cards and the profits of office—reputed to be about £8,000 a year[2]—on maintaining himself at Court. The evidence for this is that he seems to have purchased no land, and sold none.

One of his chief interests, and sources of income, was his property, whose value had increased enormously by the time of his death. Already in 1657 he had begun to repair the damage of the war years, and by 1660 his great Bloomsbury house was at last finished. Since 1640 a mass of ramshackle wooden houses had sprung up to fill almost the whole area between Holborn and his new house, so that by now the property had degenerated into a near slum. In 1661 he therefore got permission from Charles II to tear down all these mean tenements and to build a high-class residential suburb, the most attractive in its semi-rural setting, and the most up to date in its planning, in the whole of Restoration London. Opposite his house he laid out a great open square flanked by uniform terrace housing; other, even grander, houses were built on either side of Southampton House, further elegant streets were laid out, and a market was established and built nearby to serve the new suburb.[3]

Together with the St. James's Square complex, which was slower to develop, this was the first planned, economically self-contained, residential suburb in London, and the largest single project in urban development that had so far been undertaken. It comprised the present Bloomsbury Square, Great and Little Russell Street, Bloomsbury Market, and Southampton Street. It would appear that architectural design and layout were planned and controlled by the Earl, to whom certainly went the glory of the enterprise. Pepys, who visited the site in 1664, called it 'a very great and noble

---

[1] The marriage contract left the Countess in free possession of her jointure estate from her former husband, and relieved the Earl of all obligation to provide a jointure for her after his death. In other words, the Earl neither gained nor lost financially by the marriage (W.D. 160).

[2] *Diary of Samuel Pepys*, ed. H. B. Wheatley, London, 1913, v, p. 67. H. C. Foxcroft, *A Supplement to Burnet's History*, Oxford, 1902, p. 57. (I owe this reference to Professor G. Aylmer.)

[3] *Cal. S.P. Dom., 1661–2*, pp. 118, 142, 189, 191. G. Scott Thomson, op. cit., ch. iii, *passim*.

work', and Evelyn a few months later repeated the adjective: 'a noble square or piazza, a little town'.[1] We cannot be absolutely sure that the regular terraced appearance of the square in the mid eighteenth century was part of the original design rather than later reconstruction (Pl. VI). On balance the former seems the more likely, in view of the Earl's obvious interest in planning and the admiring comments of virtuosi like Pepys and Evelyn. But if the Earl can—and did—take the credit, he skilfully avoided shouldering the costs. Building was financed not by the Earl himself but by the tenants and by speculators on building leases, now for the longer term of forty-two years. The leases were snapped up at once, and new buildings sprang up all over the site with extraordinary rapidity. Thanks to this development, and the pre-war building on the Holborn site, by 1669 the Earl owned some 450 houses, 40 cottages, and 30 shops on both London estates, although there still were a few acres of arable and pasture.[2]

Early in 1667 the fourth Earl fell ill of the stone and, after lingering in agony for some weeks, died on 16 May.[3] With him the house of Wriothesley came to an end and the property was split between the three heiresses. The Earl merely ordered the property to be divided equally, and it was the pure hazard of a drawing of lots which determined who should get which parts of the estate. Elizabeth, wife of Lord Noel, son and heir of Viscount Camden, inherited Titchfield and much of the Hampshire property; Elizabeth, the only surviving daughter of the second marriage, brought Beaulieu first to Lord Percy and eventually to the Earl of Montagu; and Rachel, the second daughter, took Bloomsbury to the Russells Earls of Bedford.[4] In the early nineteenth century Bedford was among the richest noblemen in England, in no small measure because of the income derived from his Bloomsbury and Covent Garden properties. As we have seen, he owed the one to the luck of the draw in 1667, and the other to his ancestor's fortunate inability to sell out to the Earls of Salisbury in 1608.

The transfer of the Bloomsbury property to the Russells did nothing to arrest the vigorous development of the area, which for

---

[1] *Diary of Samuel Pepys*, iv, p. 240. *Diary of John Evelyn*, ed. W. Bray and H. B. Wheatley, p. 177.

[2] W.D. 279.

[3] The post-mortem revealed a stone in the bladder measuring $2\frac{1}{2}'' \times 1\frac{1}{2}'' \times \frac{1}{2}''$, which had caused a stoppage of urine and acute inflammation (B.M., Sloane MSS. 1116, f. 46).

[4] G. Scott Thomson, op. cit., pp. 58, 16–17.

another half-century remained one of the healthiest and pleasantest of London suburbs. The same upper-class clientele continued to be attracted to the area and induced to settle all along Great Russell Street, Southampton Row, and King Street. The number of tenants on the rent-roll grew from 150 in 1668 to 450 in 1732, by which time a church had been built and an independent parish created. Like Covent Garden before it, the Bloomsbury community was now complete, with its own market and its own church.[1]

Certain general conclusions can be drawn from the study of the Wriothesley family fortunes over 140 years. The period falls into three distinct phases, those of rapid accumulation, slow decline, and stabilization or even recovery. The history of the first Earl shows the extraordinary speed with which a courtier-administrator who had the good fortune to serve between 1530 and 1550 could build up a huge estate. Starting with nothing, the first Earl died holding thirty-six manors (and three 'ghost' manors) in the country and one in London. The history of the family for the next eighty years until 1626 was of intermittent but relentless decline, the cause of which was a persistent inability to keep expenditure in line with income. It was their persistent incapacity to live within their revenues that drove the Earls further and further down the ranks of noble fortunes. The maintenance of a semi-feudal state by the second Earl caused the first great spate of sales of 1579–80, in which most of four manors were sold. The reckless gambling of the third Earl in 1595–1600 caused the second wave of sales during which nine manors were sold before 1600 and a further three to clear off debts in 1603–5. For about fifteen years lavish favours from the Crown enabled the Earl to live in a princely style probably more or less within his income. With the withdrawal of that favour and the suspension of his annuities in 1621, the Earl once again plunged into debt because of his refusal to reduce his style of living accordingly. The ultimate result was the third great wave of sales in 1629, when probably another eight manors were disposed of, while another two went in about 1641. The thirty-seven genuine manors of 1550 had increased by five by grant, four by purchase, and two by inheritance, making eleven in all, and had decreased by sale by twenty-six; by 1642 there were only eleven left besides the Titchfield group of eleven.

[1] Ibid., pp. 171–85.

It is not until the late 1630s that rising revenue began to set the pace instead of rising expenditure. The combination of increasing agricultural rents, developing urban building, and industrial activity undoubtedly played a most important part in increasing the Earl's income in the years before the Civil War. Thereafter enforced seclusion during the Commonwealth and Protectorate kept expenditure low, while after 1660 there was the huge official income of a Lord Treasurer to be drawn upon. But what really saved the situation after 1640 was the phenomenal development of the value of the London property, which by the Earl's death in 1667 was amply compensating for the hundred years' shrinkage of the agricultural holdings. To estimate the total income of the Earl in 1668 we have to make some extrapolations. In 1668 the Bloomsbury estate was bringing in almost £2,000 and ten years later the Holborn property rental alone was about £1,000, so that we can be confident that the annual income of the London estate was over £3,000 at the time of the Earl's death. In 1668 the Micheldever property was bringing in about £1,000, ten years later the Beaulieu rental was £1,458, and in 1714 the rents and profits of the Titchfield estate amounted to £3,720.[1] It is therefore reasonable to suppose that the gross annual income of the estate in 1668 amounted to between £8,000 and £9,000, over a third of which derived from the London estate.

If this recovery after 1640 was due to exceptional and in a way accidental factors, neither the nature of the previous long decline nor its causes are at all unusual during this period, for they arise out of certain general conditions that affected the class as a whole. The only exceptional feature of the case is the absence of any attempt to apply the usual remedy of marriage with a rich heiress. The two love-matches of the third and fourth Earls were both unusual in their character and unfortunate in their financial consequences, or lack of them. Apart from two manors bequeathed by a great-aunt in 1626, no windfalls from inheritance came the Wriothesleys' way throughout the whole 140 years. For most of the period the Earls were either in Court but outside the charmed circle of richly rewarded favourites, or were positive opponents of the Crown. Moreover, in the 1640s they concluded this long period of royal neglect by supporting the Royalist cause, which cost them about

---

[1] G. Scott Thomson, op. cit., p. 58. Boughton House, Buccleuch MSS., North Colonnade, Shelf 3, parcel G. Badminton House, Beaufort MSS. 300.2.5.

one year's income in fines and other losses. Without help from marriage with heiresses or from rewards from the Crown, attempts to live the life of a great courtier, or of a heavy gambler, or even of a semi-feudal local potentate, were bound to lead to trouble. This was particularly the case with a family like the Wriothesleys whose estate was free from the burden of provision for widows for only twenty-four out of the 100 years between 1550 and 1650. With the standard interest rate at 10 per cent until 1624, debt servicing soon placed a crippling burden on the estate and the ease with which entails could be broken at this period made the sale of lands a tempting solution. Furthermore, rental income from agricultural land was at best only keeping pace with the price-rise, and at worst, particularly before about 1600, tended to lag behind it. Owing to a refusal to face up to this situation, especially by the third Earl, the fortunes of the Wriothesleys underwent a long decline. They rose again thanks to urban development, and were then dispersed by biological accident.

APPENDIX

London Rentals of the Earls of Southampton

	London rental		Total London rental	Total gross landed rental	London rental as per cent of total	Reference
	Holborn	Bloomsbury				
	£	£	£	£		
c. 1601	113	..	113	1,873	6	(1)
1624	126	22	148	2,524	6	(2)
1642	550	434	984	3,733	26	(3)
1668	997	1,980	2,977	*c.* 8,500	35	(4)
1701	?	2,097	..	..	..	(5)
1732	?	3,700	..	..	..	(6)
1765	?	7,800	..	..	..	(6)

(1) Hatfield House, G 55/21.

(2) Hants. R.O., W.B. 128.

(3) P.R.O., S.P. 23/192, pp. 26–33.

(4) G. Scott Thomson, op. cit., p. 58. Boughton House, Buccleuch MSS., North Colonnade, shelf 3, parcel G. Badminton House, Beaufort MSS., 300.2.5.

(5) G. Scott Thomson, op. cit., p. 101.

(6) Ibid., p. 355.

VIII

THE BERKELEYS LORDS BERKELEY
1500–1680[1]

IN 1534, nine weeks after the death of his father, there came into the world Henry, eleventh Lord Berkeley.[2] Though the title was one of the oldest in the country to descend in continuous male line, the eccentricities and vagaries of his ancestors had left the infant with a somewhat confused inheritance. The root of the trouble went back to 1417 when Thomas, fourth Lord Berkeley, died leaving considerable uncertainty about the partition of his estates between his daughter Elizabeth, the heir general, and his nephew James, the heir male.[3] The result was a protracted fight for the disputed lands, both in the field and in Westminster Hall, between the Berkeleys and the Beauchamps, Nevilles, and Talbots. The situation was further complicated by the behaviour at the end of the century of William, sixth Lord Berkeley. He had no children and was consumed with two driving passions: a lust for honours, and a hatred of Maurice, his brother and heir. He therefore traded his lands for titles and died in 1492 as a Marquis, leaving to Henry VII and his heirs male most of his vast estates, which included well over seventy English manors and other estates in Ireland inherited from his mother as her share of the vast Mowbray property.[4]

The Marquis therefore left his brother Maurice to start from scratch, without an acre of land or even a recognized right to the title of baron. By the time the latter died in 1507, however, legal chicanery and influence in high places had enabled him, after fourteen years of intensive effort, to recover some forty-one manors.[5] His son Maurice, an active military figure in the early years of

---

[1] See genealogical table no. 5.

[2] This account of the Berkeleys is based principally on J. Smyth, *The Berkeley Manuscripts*, ed. J. Maclean, Gloucester, 1883–5, the Smith (Smyth) of Nibley MSS. in Gloucester Public Library, and microfilms of the Berkeley MSS. from Berkeley Castle. These three authorities will be referred to as 'Smyth', 'Smith MSS.', and 'Berkeley MSS.'. For permission to use the last I am indebted to the trustees of the will of the Right Hon. Randal Thomas Mowbray, Earl of Berkeley, deceased.

[3] Smyth, ii, p. 36.

[4] Ibid., pp. 121–4, 128–30, 147–8.

[5] Ibid., pp. 156–72, 188–9.

Henry VIII, carried out some consolidation of the inheritance in Gloucestershire, but also sold some outlying property and settled others on his brothers. As a result, when he died in 1523 the family estate still amounted to no more than some thirty-six manors.[1] He was succeeded in quick succession by his brother Thomas and the latter's son, Thomas, who died in 1534 leaving his wife *enceinte* with the future Lord Henry.

The first misfortune that befell the Berkeleys in the sixteenth century was the accident that, during the late 1530s and 1540s when the huge monastic properties were being redistributed to courtiers, noblemen, and others, Lord Berkeley was a child living in the country in charge of his mother, a follower of the now discredited Boleyn family. The Berkeleys are thus among the few older peerage families which obtained absolutely nothing from the Dissolution. Indeed they lost severely; for the numerous monasteries and chantries of which the Lords Berkeley had been patrons had been a fruitful source not merely of prestige, influence, and power but also, to a more limited extent, of money. Moreover, lack of favour at Court meant that no influence could be brought to bear to save the family estates in Ireland from confiscation under the Statute of Absentees of 1536, by which Henry VIII seized to himself the estates of absentee landlords.[2]

During these years the principal concern of Henry's mother, Lady Anne, must have been to watch the matrimonial vagaries of the King. Not merely had they ruined her chances of influence at Court, but the failure of the royal male line should by the entail of Marquis William bring the rest of the ancient Berkeley estates and Berkeley Castle back again into the possession of the family.[3] With the death of Edward VI in 1553 the crisis arose, and it became necessary to persuade Queen Mary to concede a substantial estate that the Tudors had enjoyed for over half a century. To achieve this, Lady Anne married the young Henry, on generous terms, to Katherine, daughter of the executed Earl of Surrey and granddaughter of the Duke of Norfolk. This secured the support of the great Howard family, now high in favour at Court with the Catholic Queen. At the time the manœuvre was clearly advantageous, for it obtained the uncontested return of some fifteen manors in the vale of Berkeley and elsewhere, of which the old rents alone were

[1] Smyth, ii, pp. 215–18.   [2] Ibid., pp. 252, 250, 270.
[3] Ibid., p. 261.

officially reckoned at £687 per annum.[1] But quite apart from Katherine's personal defects, the marriage hitched the fortunes of the Berkeleys to those of the Howards, with disastrous consequences for the future.

The day Queen Mary died, young Henry might reasonably have been regarded as one of the most fortunate young men in the kingdom, 'of as great note and hope as any of his age and of that time'.[2] His grandmother died in 1558 and his mother in 1564, so he was soon in full enjoyment of his fifty-odd manors. What gross annual income these brought in we do not know, but it is unlikely to have been less than £4,500, and may well have been over £5,000. In 1579–80, after some losses of property to the Dudleys had already occurred, and after £17,000 had been raised by the sale of land, Lord Henry's gross income from rents, fines, and wood-sales (in an average year) was still around £4,000. He could certainly be counted among the ten richest landowners in England, and possibly among the top five.[3]

The seeds of decline, however, were already apparent. He was a lazy, weak-willed, unintelligent man, without ambition or vigour of mind. Gentle, friendly, and affable, he was well named by his biographer 'Henry the Harmless'. But stern qualities were needed to weather the reign of Elizabeth. Without personal supervision the administration of so huge an estate could easily fall a prey to laxity, muddle, and worse. Moreover, the continuous rise in prices made necessary a vigorous and forward policy if income from land was to keep pace with the change. But young Henry was not the man for such dreary desk-work. Instead, he settled in London and 'spent all his time at tenys, bowles, cards, dice, and in the company of his huntsmen and faulkeners, delights that drew on greater totalls in his Accompts at the years end then his revenue would support'. Occasional bursts of retrenchment like going to live with his mother-in-law at 17s. a week did little to remedy matters, particularly as his wife was as prodigal as himself.[4] A forceful woman, Lady Katherine dominated her weaker husband. At first she helped herself freely from his income without account; later, she made herself his Receiver-General; and it was only after many years that she was curbed within an allowance of £300 a year for

---

[1] Ibid., pp. 275–7, 282, 381–2.   [2] Ibid., p. 282.
[3] Berkeley MSS., Books 55, 56, 58, 59. L. Stone, *The Crisis of the Aristocracy, 1558–1641*, p. 760.
[4] Smyth, ii, pp. 281, 284, 376–7.

personal expenses—secretly augmented by the levy of a 10 to 15 per cent rake-off on all her husband's fines and land sales. Observing her recklessness, the dowager Countess Anne used to prophecy to her attendants 'by God's blessed sacrament, this gay girle will begger my son Henry'.[1]

But Henry needed little encouragement. Even without the urging of his haughty Howard wife, he would probably have tried to keep up the state of his medieval ancestors. Always on the move from house to house, the pair hunted and hawked their way about the country, 'seldom or never attended with fewer then one hundred and fifty servants in their tawny cloth coats in summer, with the badge of the white Lyon rampant imbroidered on the left sleeve; And in coats of white frize lined with crimsen taffety in the winter'.[2] For nearly twenty years Lord Henry kept up this style of living. Smith observed that 'his chiefe delights wherein he spent near three parts of the yeare, were, to his great charges, in hunting the hare, fox, and deere, red and fallowe . . . ; And in hawking both at river and at land'.[3] His household hospitality was on an equally generous scale and his cooks were as cherished as his huntsmen. The keeping of open house on such a scale could be ruinous, particularly if he frequently indulged in curious extravagances such as the 'whole bore inclosed in pale workmanly guilt by a Cooke hired from Bristoll', with which he entertained his friends and neighbours one Christmas.[4] So lavish and so disorderly an establishment naturally attached to it a host of parasites, and Lord Henry soon found himself supporting a crowd of indigent hangers-on, 'Captaines, Schollers, Poetts, cast courtiers and the like'. When not rumbling round the countryside with this vast train, Lord Henry was savouring the gambling resources of the metropolis. 'His longe and slender lady-like-hand knew a dye as well and how to handle it as any of his ranke and time.' Dice-throwing was, indeed, the only accomplishment with which his biographer could credit him.[5]

This splendid, carefree existence lasted for eighteen years, from Lord Henry's marriage in 1554 till 1572. In that year his brother-in-law the Duke of Norfolk was finally caught in the toils of his intrigues with Mary Queen of Scots, was convicted of treason, and beheaded. The fall of the Duke marked the end of Court influence for the Howards for thirty years, and Lady Katherine took it hard.

---

[1] Smyth, ii, pp. 387, 254.   [2] Ibid., pp. 285–6.   [3] Ibid., p. 363.
[4] Ibid., pp. 364, 287.   [5] Ibid., pp. 286, 363.

But worse was to follow. A little before this the royal favourite, the Earl of Leicester, and his brother Warwick had offered a double marriage alliance for Lord Berkeley's daughters with their two nephews, Philip and Robert Sidney. This was an important offer, and, given the critical situation of the House of Norfolk, with the Duke in prison on a treason charge, it was not ungenerous. Leicester was evidently making an attempt to patch up a feud that had divided the Howards and Dudleys since the beginning of the century, and which had already cost the lives on the scaffold of several generations on both sides. But Lady Katherine made the fatal mistake of rejecting the proposal with aristocratic scorn, and so earned the lasting hatred of the Dudleys. Smith insinuates that this repulse was partly responsible for the execution of Lady Katherine's brother, the Duke; and it was certainly connected with the great legal assault launched a week or two later by the Dudleys upon an important part of the Berkeley inheritance.[1]

The property recovered from Queen Mary in 1553 had been acquired by the Crown in two ways: part of it by the will of Marquis William in 1492; and part escheated to the Crown on the attainder for the Duke of Northumberland, which had come to the Dudleys as their share of the disputed Berkeley inheritance of 1417. Owing to the avarice of Lord Henry's mother, who had wished to cancel the tenants' leases and raise money from fines for new leases, the grant had not been made as a free gift from the Crown, but as a restoration of rightful inheritance.[2] Unfortunately this left open the question whether or not the Berkeleys could lawfully claim the inheritance of the lands, including the very important manors of Wotton and Simondshall, which had belonged to Northumberland.

As early as 1558 certain courtiers had seen the weakness of the Berkeley title and were preparing to challenge it, in the hope of rich rewards from the Crown. Sir Thomas Parry, Treasurer of the Household, promoted an action against Lord Berkeley, and had to be bought off with a reversionary lease for sixty years after 1578 of the two key manors of Wotton and Simondshall for a derisory rent of £2. 10s. However, Parry died two years later, and the lease never came into force.[3] But with the rise of the Dudleys to high royal favour, the spurning of their offer of a marriage alliance, and the fall of the Duke of Norfolk, the way was open for a fresh assault on the Berkeleys. The title was tried at law and adjudged to the

[1] Ibid., pp. 335–6.   [2] Ibid., pp. 277–8.   [3] Ibid., pp. 288–9, 374.

Crown, who also claimed £5,024 for rents and profits illegally levied by the Berkeleys in the past eighteen years. As soon as Elizabeth's title was established, she granted the manors to Warwick and Leicester. Even now Lord Berkeley had a chance of escape. The Dudleys were evidently reluctant to fight to a finish, and with the blackmail card of Wotton and Simondshall up their sleeves, they renewed the offer for a marriage treaty. Lord Berkeley's relatives and allies solemnly advised him to accept, but Lady Katherine would not hear of it. The offer was again rejected and the fight went on.[1]

Meanwhile Lord Henry had further weakened his position by another act of folly. If he insisted on fighting the Dudleys, it was essential for him not to make the Queen his open enemy. Already he had behaved tactlessly by outbidding the economical Elizabeth for a lute of mother-of-pearl that she and Lady Berkeley had both coveted.[2] After the execution of the Duke, the Queen was convinced that the Berkeleys were henceforth irreconcilable. When Lady Katherine was suing for remission of the royal claim for the £5,024 arrears of rent of Wotton and Simondshall, Elizabeth replied: 'Noe, noe, my Lady Berkeley, wee know you will never love us for the death of your brother.'[3] And yet this critical moment in 1573 was chosen by Lord Henry openly to affront the Queen and turn her wary suspicion into frank hostility. That summer the Queen came to Berkeley Castle, and indulged in one of her usual barbarous and unsporting battues of trapped deer in Lord Berkeley's park nearby. When Lord Henry heard of the slaughter of his favourite game he flew into a rage and ordered the ground to be disparked. Naturally enough the Dudleys saw to it that his words and actions were reported to the Queen, and his friends warned him lest he allow himself to be provoked into anything that could be construed as treason.[4]

Hated by the Dudleys, disliked by the Queen, and burdened with the liability of an arrogant papist wife and former friendship and dependence on the late Duke of Norfolk, Lord Berkeley's position was precarious indeed. Not surprisingly, his prolonged and costly lawsuits with the Dudleys availed him nothing in the face of royal favour, packed juries, and stolen evidences, and in 1580 a fresh attack was begun by which the Queen sued Lord Henry in the

[1] Smyth, ii, pp. 289–90, 336.   [2] Ibid., p. 337.   [3] Ibid., p. 291.
[4] Ibid., p. 378.

Exchequer Court for two more manors and a third of three others. Leicester again exerted his enormous influence to rig the jury, the evidence for which are a letter from the Sheriff of Gloucester to Leicester assuring him of the reliability of the men he had picked, and another from Leicester to one of the jurors urging him to be sure to be present on the day. Moreover, many years before in 1570, when he was making friendly overtures to Lord Henry, Leicester had succeeded in getting an agent granted admission to the muniment room at Berkeley Castle, where he had stolen some of the vital medieval documents. What with purloined evidence and a rigged jury, he was in an all but invincible position. As a result of these exertions, the verdict was in favour of the Queen, who immediately granted the property to the Dudleys, and charged Lord Berkeley with £3,954 for rents and profits wrongly received since the beginning of the reign.[1]

And so by 1584 Lord Berkeley had lost property, the bare rental of which came to £390 per annum.[2] Since most of it was old rent, the gross annual income was considerably higher, and must have amounted to about 15 per cent of his total revenues. It was not until the accession of King James that any prospect opened of recovering these lost estates. With the renewed political influence of the Howard clan, and with the deaths of Warwick, Leicester, and Warwick's widow, the Countess Anne, there seemed some hope of forcing their heir Robert, Viscount Lisle, to come to terms. And indeed, in 1609, thanks to this changed political atmosphere and to the prolonged legal and antiquarian researches of John Smith of Nibley, Viscount Lisle found it prudent to surrender the property in return for the immediate cash payment of £7,320.[3]

This prolonged dispute with the Dudleys was the second great cause of the decay of the Berkeleys. In both cases for the grossly extravagant manner of their life and for this quarrel, Lord Henry's wife Katherine must bear a considerable share of responsibility. Not merely did the latter result in the loss for about thirty years of some very valuable property, but it also involved Lord Henry in ceaseless and very expensive litigation, besides the bribes and gratuities at

---

[1] Ibid., pp. 300–1. Berkeley MSS., Letter Book II, ff. 66–7. The fact that the incriminating letters are at Berkeley Castle suggests that the Dudleys were not the only ones to steal documents.

[2] Belvoir Castle, Rutland MSS., unsorted.

[3] Smyth, ii, p. 331. No doubt his urgent need for ready cash was also a factor in persuading Lord Lisle to this agreement (H.M.C. De Lisle and Dudley MSS. iii, pp. 412, 429, 431–2).

Court needed to evade the Crown claims for arrears of rent. To settle the first claim for £5,025, he paid £1,800 in gratuities and £500 into the Exchequer.[1] The only benefit derived from the quarrel is that it deprived Lord Henry of his peace of mind and brought about a curtailment of that happy-go-lucky way of life in which he had hitherto indulged. After 1584 he was making do with a checkroll of seventy servants instead of the 150 he retained before 1572.[2]

The third set-back to the family fortunes arose out of the character of the only surviving son and heir, Sir Thomas Berkeley, who proved to be as improvident as his father. Married in 1595 to Elizabeth the only daughter and heir general of George, Lord Hunsdon, in the next fourteen years he contrived to spend about £1,500 a year in excess of his allowance of £600 per annum. He was, as John Smith sadly observed, 'profuse in expence beyond his ordinary means'. When he was not gallivanting about Europe, as was his periodic habit, he ran up huge debts in England. On an income of £600 a year, he was cheerfully paying £100 for a jewel, £200 for a clock, or £200 for a horse.[3]

For some years he lived on selling his reversionary interest to his father's property, by which he raised £7,150 in the first eight or nine years of marriage. In 1606–7 things came to a head as his debts grew to intolerable dimensions. His capable wife took over the management of his affairs and the receipt of his annuity, sold her inheritance at Tunbridge and Hadlow, Kent, for £8,450 and set about reducing both his annual expenditure and his debts.[4] How large were the latter we do not know, but it is evident that they were substantial. In 1602 his creditors were mostly Coventry tailors, but by 1606 they were a group of London scriveners who had arranged a series of small loans, usually of £100, for other investors.[5]

This reorganization and retrenchment was not at all to the taste of Sir Thomas, who spent most of the few remaining years of his life on the Continent. During one spell in England in 1609, he was obliged to sign a contract handing over all responsibility for

[1] Smyth, ii, p. 291.   [2] Ibid., pp. 282, 364.
[3] Ibid., pp. 394–9. Smith MSS., 3/2, 3.
[4] Smyth, ii, p. 397; Smith MSS. 2/38–9. Berkeley MSS., Letter Book II, f. 36.
[5] For example: 'Mr. Daniel and Mr. Elkins, taken up by Mr. Fylkens at 10%: 131 li' (Smith MSS. 3/3). Smith says that the debt exceeded 'the greatest part' of the £8,450 received for the sale of the Kent estates (Smyth, ii, p. 397).

managing his household to his wife and John Smith. In return for £400 they promised to maintain an establishment suitable for a knight, with up to eighteen servants and six couple of hounds for hunting. In return Sir Thomas promised 'on the word of a true gent.' to allow Smith to discharge drunken or unruly servants, and not to keep more than four horses in the stable.[1] Smith and Lady Elizabeth evidently distrusted Sir Thomas's weaknesses for horse-flesh and roistering servants. In addition to his extravagance, he got into continual domestic quarrels when he was in England. On one occasion in 1609, he made all preparations to spend a splendid Christmas at home, laid in huge stocks of food and drink, instructed the servants, and invited the guests. Then on 23 December he suddenly left home without a word of warning, leaving orders that everything was to be cancelled and his wife to be removed from the house on Christmas day. This was more than John Smith could bear, and he wrote Sir Thomas an indignant letter, upbraiding him for deserting his wife and family in this manner at a moment's notice 'out of a humorous passion' in order 'to runne for Italy or some other unknowne country', without money in his purse or friends to accompany him. Smith flatly refused to arrange to supply him with funds, and concluded with the rhetorical question: 'What bees carry you in your braynes that should singe you to the distruction of your credit and estimation?'[2] This outspokenness served its purpose, but the respite was only temporary. On the whole, it was clearly lucky for the Berkeleys that Sir Thomas died in 1611 at the early age of thirty-seven.

The fourth and last cause of his troubles Lord Henry brought upon himself. In 1596 Lady Katherine died, leaving him a sixty-two-year-old widower. Two years later he married again, this time a middle-aged lady, Jane, daughter of Sir Michael Stanhope and widow of Sir Roger Townshend of Raynham. Whatever were Lord Henry's objectives in this second marriage they were sadly disappointed. If it was sex, they never slept together; if companionship, they usually lived apart; if money, it cost him dear in the end. We do not know for certain what were the terms of the marriage contract, but on his side Lord Berkeley is reported to have promised her £300 a year during his life-time, and a jointure of £1,000 a year after his death.[3] If these were in fact the terms they were very

---

[1] Smith MSS. ii, pp. 398 note 1, 399.   [2] Smith MSS. 3/6.
[3] A. Collins, *Sydney Letters*, 1746, ii, p. 92.

onerous, and it is not surprising that Lord Berkeley tried to evade them. And so in 1600 Lady Jane brutally enforced her rights by extending all his Gloucester estate on a statute of £6,000 that he had given as guarantee for performance of his obligations. This brought Lord Berkeley to terms, and in his will he declared that his wife's dower and jointure was already fully delivered, to the value of 'nigh 4000 li.'[1] He had evidently bought her out with a cash payment.

It seems unlikely that progressive estate management did much to offset the effect of these many financial disasters. His steward, John Smith of Nibley, tells us that before about 1580 the accounting system was chaotic and that Lord Berkeley had no idea of the true state of his affairs. Thereafter Smith claims to have introduced method into the accounts, which no doubt served to reduce peculation and slackness. But more than this was needed if income was to keep pace with prices. Leasehold rents needed to be raised sharply to prevent the ratio of rent to fine from sinking to too small a proportion; small holdings needed to be consolidated and leased out as large compact farms; such mineral wealth as existed needed to be exploited; and so far as possible copyholders needed to be bullied or persuaded into becoming leaseholders. But there were three factors militating against such a forward policy. The first was the character of Smith himself. Antiquarian by taste and temperament, his efforts lay more in exploiting and enforcing the surviving remnants of ancient feudal obligations than in developing estate management on modern lines. He took pride in enforcing right of wardship by actions of 'Ravishment del gard', in levying an 'Aid per faire filz chevaler, according to the Statutes of 3 E. I and 25 E. III', or in claiming a composition in lieu of obsolete villein works not performed for over 100 years.[2] Such a combination of paternalism, deference, loyalty, and antiquarianism was hardly compatible with ruthless modernization of estate management or much of a shift to a more crassly commercial relationship with the tenants. Even so, it is astonishing to discover that in 1614 Smyth could blandly announce that although the bare rental of the Gloucestershire property was less than £1,500 a year, he estimated that the true value over the rent amounted to another £8,500 a year.[3]

---

[1] Smyth, ii, pp. 392–3, 359–60; Smith is wrong in alleging that the statute was for £10,000 (P.R.O., L.C. 4/193/360). P.C.C., 11 Lawe.

[2] Smith MSS. 3/80; Smyth ii, pp. 412, 333, 433; iii, p. 202.

[3] Gloucester Public Library, 16059, 16062–3.

His estimate of the true value is scarcely credible, and the income from fines and casualties, so far as we can tell, never amounted to anything remotely like this sum. But what is striking is Smith's acceptance of a system of three-life leases under inflationary conditions in which annual rent had got so far out of line with real value.

On the other hand, Smith was by no means entirely to blame, for this conservative approach fitted in only too well with the attitude of mind of Lord Henry, who clearly tried to behave very much as his feudal ancestors had done before him. Land to him was as much a source of manpower as of profit. He trailed about the country with his 150 servants at his back. When he visited Berkeley he liked to be escorted into the town by 300 to 500 respectful tenantry on horseback; and when he was involved in disputes with his neighbours it seemed natural for armed violence to be used by his servants and supporters. In his early days, Smith gives us to understand, church bells were rung as he travelled through each village, and men doffed their caps when his letters were read out in public gatherings. Smith records the local saying: 'Hee is a hughy proud man, hee thinkes himselfe as great as my Lord Berkeley', and adds the comment 'our simple ancient honesties knewe not a greater to make comparison by, when this proverbe first arose'.[1] In financial terms this meant, on the one hand, that food was distributed to the poor of the surrounding district three times a week with great regularity, and that when he died Lord Henry's tenants accompanied the body with tears in their eyes, well knowing that 'they had lost the best landlord that England had, whose like might not after bee by them expected'. On the other hand, Lord Berkeley demanded a similar personal sympathy with his own difficulties. Encouraged by Smith, he insisted on the enforcement of the obsolescent practice of private wardship, and three times he requested a benevolence or free gift from his tenantry to help him out of his financial troubles. Many tenants were loyal or deferential enough to comply, because of 'the dewtie or love wee bere unto his Lordship'.[2]

Optimum economic exploitation of the Berkeley estates was further hindered by the pressing needs of Lord Henry. Always

[1] Smyth, ii, pp. 282, 370, 267-9, 313, 343; i, p. 308; iii, p. 26.
[2] Ibid. ii, pp. 368, 408, 333, 373; iii, p. 411. I. H. Jeayes, *Catalogue of the Muniments of Berkeley Castle*, 1892, pp. 307, 312. Smith MSS. 1/25.

haunted by debt, again and again he was forced into the ultimately uneconomic practices of cutting down woods and making long leases at low rent in return for immediate cash fines. In 1598 he ordered the Berkeley demesne to be let for twenty-one years with fines, reducing the existing improved rents where necessary. In 1610, in order to find money to pay for the settlement with Viscount Lisle, he ordered £4,000 to be raised in fines from new leases for lives in reversion and £5,500 from the sale of wood.[1] This system of long leases at low rents with large initial fines was admittedly traditional in the west of England. But it was very disadvantageous to the landlords in the long run, and the more far-sighted of them were already moving towards a system of higher rents, lower fines, and shorter leases.[2]

Selling woods and making long leases at low rents were devices for mortgaging the future which lacked the finality of actual sale of land. This last expedient was one, however, in which Lord Henry indulged with a reckless prodigality only exceeded among his contemporaries by the seventeenth Earl of Oxford. On the day of his marriage in 1554 he was owner, in possession or reversion after the death of his mother and grandmother, of fifty-nine manors. One more was recovered after a protracted lawsuit in 1563, a second, worth under £6 a year, was bought in 1571, and a third was redeemed from a relative in 1579. On the death of George, Lord Hunsdon, in 1603, Lord Henry's son and heir, Sir Thomas Berkeley, inherited through his wife a reversionary interest in two large estates in Kent.[3] Against these modest acquisitions is to be set the sale by Lord Henry and Sir Thomas of no fewer than thirty-eight manors, and the alienation to a branch of the family of one, besides the sale of a good deal of other miscellaneous property. The sales can be seen to fall into groups, caused by the various factors already described.[4] The first phase from 1561 to 1569 raised over £8,000 merely to pay for current expenditure on port and jollity. Next there was over £4,300 received from sales in 1572, no doubt to pay for past extravagance and to compensate for the sudden expenses and loss of income due to the lawsuit with the Dudleys. Thereafter from 1573 to 1580 there was a steady trickle of sales to pay for the lawsuit and current expenditure, which

---

[1] Smith MSS. 1/29; 2/45–6.
[2] L. Stone, *The Crisis of the Aristocracy, 1558–1641*, pp. 303–22.
[3] Smyth, ii, pp. 261, 282, 361, 396; P.R.O., Chancery Proc., Series I, Eliz. B 28/9.
[4] Smyth, ii, pp. 356–61, *passim*.

raised £4,666. In 1581 he incurred the one and only expenditure of his life in the service of the state, when Elizabeth obliged him to spend £2,500 in thirteen weeks in waiting on the royal suitor, the Duc d'Anjou. In 1584–6 he married off his two daughters at a cost in portions and clothes of £3,000 each, and it is not surprising that this produced a crisis in his affairs. He gave up housekeeping for the time being and went to live with his cousin Sir John Savage at Baraper, Hampshire, while £8,260 was raised by the sale of lands.[1] For the next ten years or so the increasing age and illness of his wife, the constant supervision of John Smith, and Lord Henry's preoccupation with his lawsuits caused a considerable curtailment of needless expenditure, and income would seem more or less to have balanced expenditure.

After his son's marriage in 1595, however, a new phase opened. As an heiress, Elizabeth Carey's portion was mostly a reversionary interest in her father's land, and she only brought £1,000 with her in cash. In return Lord Berkeley had to settle the substantial annuity of £600 per annum on the young couple for maintenance. This in itself was a severe drain on his resources, aggravated a few years later by the need to fulfil the obligations to the Stanhopes over his second marriage. This precipitated a fresh crisis in 1600 when three Huntingdon manors were sold to Alderman Sir John Spencer for £7,000. Thereafter there was a lull until 1610–11 when fresh sales raised £4,800 to help pay the composition money due to Viscount Lisle for the restoration of the property lost to the Dudleys in the great lawsuit.

Meanwhile Sir Thomas Berkeley had been treading the same primrose path as Lord Henry. He joined his father in 1600 in selling the fourth and last Huntingdonshire manor to Sir John Spencer for £3,000; he sold Daglingworth manor for £1,320 two years later, and the reversionary interest in other manors for a further £2,830. Then in 1606 he sold his reversionary interest in his wife's inheritance in Kent for £8,450.[2] Lastly in 1613 the marriage portion of Sir Thomas's daughter, Theophila, was paid for by the surrender by Lord Henry of the manor of Portbury, Somerset, which was valued at £6,000.[3] Thus in the fifty-three years from 1561 to 1613 Lord Henry and Sir Thomas had raised about £58,700 by the sale

---

[1] Ibid., pp. 314, 402–3, 376.   [2] Ibid., p. 397.
[3] The manor was worth £8,000, and Sir Edward Coke, the father of the bridegroom, was to pay £2,000 for it; in fact, however, little or none of the money was ever paid (ibid., pp. 405–6).

of land.[1] Thirty-nine manors had been sold, and as a result the family estates were reduced from about fifty-nine manors to twenty-five.[2] All of the outlying property in eight counties had gone, and even in Gloucestershire itself eight manors had been dispersed. Smith tells us that during sixty years from 1553 to 1613 Lord Henry's gross receipts from all sources totalled about £260,500,[3] of which about £37,100 came from land sales. If we add to this last figure the £21,600 from Sir Thomas's sales and for Theophila's marriage portion, we may calculate that Lord Henry and Sir Thomas derived about one-fifth of their income over this prolonged period from the sale of capital, quite apart from the use of other methods of mortgaging the future like the cutting down of woods and the raising of large fines for new leases. To put it another way, for decades the pair had managed to spend about a quarter as much again as their regular annual income from their property.

At last, in 1613, poor 'Henry the Harmless' passed away. Characteristically enough, when he died he had not revised his will as he intended, and his debts exceeded the value of his personal estate. What income he was drawing from his twenty-five surviving manors we do not know for certain. His *average* income from rents and casual profits over the previous sixty years had been about £3,700 per annum,[4] but this figure needs interpretation in the light of three changing circumstances. Some of the property had been enjoyed by the Dudleys and Sydneys for twenty-five years, from 1584 to 1609. Secondly, some increase of annual value is bound to have occurred in this inflationary period; and thirdly the massive sales of land must have caused a progressive reduction in the

---

[1] This includes £37,100 received by Lord Berkeley, £15,600 by Sir Thomas, and the £6,000 worth of land given as a marriage portion with Theophila. Smith gives the receipts by Lord Berkeley from land sales as £41,400, but this includes £4,320 that in fact went to Sir Thomas (ibid., pp. 361, 397).

[2] The following table of manors summarizes the result:

	Manors owned in 1553	Acquired 1553-1613	Sold, etc. 1553-1613	Manors owned in 1613
Total	59	5	39	25

It should be emphasized that this table minimizes the true situation, for much non-manorial land was sold which realized over £13,000.   [3] Smyth, ii, p. 373.

[4] $\dfrac{£260,500 - £37,100}{60}$.

sources of income. The only fairly firm evidence we have is that the bare rental of the whole estate after his death in 1614 came to under £2,600.[1]

After weighing all this fragmentary evidence, it is fairly safe to conclude that the gross average landed income of the estate for the next few years was probably less than £3,500 a year and perhaps a good deal less. Now even if we assume that the lands were sold at the highest possible figure of twenty years' purchase, the 1613 income of the land sold must have been distinctly over £3,000 a year, since many of the sales took place before 1580 and so before land values began moving substantially upwards. There can be no doubt, therefore, that during Lord Henry's lifetime not far short of one-half of the original value of the estate had been sold.

On the death of Lord Henry this truncated inheritance descended to his twelve-year-old grandson George. The first problem facing his mother, the Lady Elizabeth, was to secure from the Crown the wardship and marriage of her son. Before Lord Henry had died he had obtained a promise of the wardship from that unctuous and treacherous courtier, his brother-in-law, the Earl of Northampton. Indeed Northampton was as good as his word in obtaining the wardship for himself, possibly free of charge, and Elizabeth assumed that the letters of affection and devotion of a wealthy bachelor brother-in-law could be trusted.[2] However, when he died in 1614 he left instructions for the executors to sell the wardship to the Berkeleys for the £1,500 which he alleged it cost him.[3] Elizabeth jibbed at this burden, and a lawsuit followed, but eventually she agreed to pay the money. When in 1614 she obtained a lease, without fine, of the King's thirds of her son's lands during the minority at a rent of £450 per annum, she was again in full control of the estate.[4]

Meanwhile, she had traded on the Earl of Northampton's promise to assure her the wardship and marriage to arrange a most advantageous match for young George. Smith writes that: 'It was the

---

[1] Gloucester Public Library, 16062-3. To this rental has been added Worthy Park. Lady Elizabeth also enjoyed what was left of her own Hunsdon inheritance, at Cranford in Middlesex, which was worth £400 a year thirty years later, and which she eventually left to her younger son.

[2] No payment for the wardship and marriage is recorded in P.R.O., Court of Wards, Misc. Books, 204 or 255. On the other hand, in a letter of 1612, the Earl suggests that the cost of the wardship be taken out of the £8,000 he was owed by the Crown for arrears of a pension of £4,000 per annum (S.P. Dom., Jas. I, 70/55 [1]).

[3] P.C.C. 55 Lawe.

[4] Smyth, ii, pp. 405, 427, 430-1. Court of Wards, Misc. Books, 204 f. 150.

prudent observation of this lady that in the five last descents her son's family had not received into it the warmth of any other influence save what their ancestors left to shine on them.' She realized, in fact, that the only quick way to retrieve the family fortunes was by marriage with an heiress, a method of advancement not practised by the Berkeleys since the fifteenth century (if we except her own patrimony, which was already sold). And so in April 1614 there took place the marriage of the thirteen-and-a-half-year-old George with a little girl of nine, Elizabeth, daughter and coheiress of Sir Michael Stanhope, and granddaughter and prospective coheiress of Sir William Reade of Osterley. According to Smith, Sir Michael settled on her the reversion of property rented at £1,503, and she might reasonably hope for a half-share in the £3,000 a year Reade estate, making £3,000 a year in all.[1] It seemed a very successful *coup* to have caught an heiress to property which with luck might almost be as valuable as the total remains of the Berkeley inheritance.

As yet, however, these broad acres were only a distant prospect, and could do nothing to help the immediate financial situation. There was charged upon the estate both the jointure of Lady Elizabeth and the £450 a year rent due to the Crown for the wardship lands. Jane, the dowager Lady Berkeley and widow of Lord Henry, lived on until 1618, but as has been seen she had no claim to any jointure out of the estate. She enjoyed an income of about £2,700 a year, but this must have come mostly from her first husband, Sir Roger Townshend. Her principal interest was in her Townshend connection—she paid for her grandson's baronetcy in 1617— though she was on sufficiently good terms with the Berkeley's to play a major part in arranging George's marriage with her niece, Elizabeth Stanhope.[2]

Lady Elizabeth, however, certainly took a large slice out of the estate as jointure. The base rental of her jointure came to £1,169 in 1613 and £1,300 in 1622, while her gross receipts for three-quarters of the year in 1618–19 amounted to over £1,200. In 1622 she was

---

[1] Smyth, ii, p. 428. Before the marriage Sir Michael Stanhope settled the reversion of some twelve manors in Suffolk and Middlesex on Elizabeth and her heirs male (Middx. R.O., Acc. 530, Bdle 10). In fact the income of the Stanhope property in about 1645 was £1,643 and of the Reade inheritance £859 in possession and £160 in reversion (Smith MSS. 3/20–1). That this is the approximate figure is supported by the report that in 1614 Elizabeth's sister's inheritance was £700 a year in possession and £700 in reversion (*Letters of Philip Gawdy*, ed. J. H. Jeayes, Roxburghe Club, 1906, p. 176).

[2] Gloucester Public Library, 19382. B.M., Add. MSS. 45902. Smyth, ii, p. 428.

married again, to Sir Thomas Chamberlain, a Judge of the King's Bench, from whom she extorted terms which show her to have been a very rich and very independent woman.[1] This remarriage did not affect the jointure (though she did agree to release Lord George of a debt of £1,500), and so till her death in 1635 she continued to draw an income of about £1,500 a year from the Berkeley estates.[2]

During the first years of their married life the children almost certainly lived apart, and it is uncertain when they began to cohabit. Smith calls the young Lord 'George the traveller or George the linguist' and he seems early to have qualified for the title. In 1621 he was in Paris, drawing large sums on letters of credit of the two government financiers Calandrini and Burlamachi. He was certainly back in England by 1625, when his wife was reported to be 'distracted' from jealousy, but the next year he went off on another foreign tour that lasted three years and took him down into Italy.[3]

Although before, between, and after these tours the couple lived together sufficiently long to beget three children, it is fairly clear that the household was not a happy one. Smith insinuates that Elizabeth was of a masterful disposition, and Lord George evidently resented the fate that had indissolubly linked him with this woman while he was still a child. Like his father, he tended to seek refuge from domestic tyranny in flight abroad. When at home, he seems to have lived a life of jollity and dissipation, although possibly redeemed by a open-handed patronage of the theatre. In his dedication of the *Renegade* in 1630, Massinger was so carried away by his enthusiasm that he told Lord Berkeley that 'with a full vote and suffrage it is acknowledged that the patronage and protection of the dramatic poem is yours, and almost without a rival'. These associations were not well received in the family, and an undated letter, probably from Smith, urges Lord George's mother to plead with him to avoid the company of those roistering blades, Lords Morley and Cromwell, and to avoid being drawn by them into

---

[1] Smith MSS. 2/19, 25, 26; 3/10. The contract allowed her to live where she pleased and and not where it pleased her husband, and to dispose of her money and property without restraint.

[2] Smith MSS. 2/22, 30. In six months in 1634 her gross receipts from the jointure lands were £735. When she died in 1635 her personal goods were valued at £4,500 and recoverable debts due at £3,400 (Berkeley MSS., Roll 77).

[3] Smyth, ii, p. 423; Smith MSS. 1/91-6; Gloucester Public Library, SF 2/5/2; N. E. McClure, *Letters of John Chamberlain*, ii, p. 610. *Cal. S.P. Dom., 1627-8*, p. 169.

bonds for debt or into 'intemperancy'.[1] The chance survival of a letter shows that by December 1630, eighteen months after his return home, things had come to a head. His wife flatly refused to comply with an order of his, perhaps about the placing of her inheritance at his disposal to clear his debts. 'My lord,' she wrote, 'you are pleased to prove my obedience to you (above reason) which I beseech you not to make long trial of; when you have considered the years of sorrow I lived in, in your first absence, with the pains of childbirth, your Lordship will know none can plead that merit of you but the wife of your affections.' On the back of this letter is what is presumably the draft of Lord George's furious reply:

> You do now so much provoke my patience as not being sensible of that I have desired both by my own requests and letters for that which is the good of your self & your posterity, which you will not understand. That since I find you have neither obedience nor love, but that you will be the overthrow of both me & my posterity, I hold you to be so unworthy a wife, that I am determined for many years not to come near you, but seek my fortune in other places, & whatsoever becomes of me, I will let the world know you are the cause of it in being so undutiful a wife, so fare well.[2]

Whether or not this brisk exchange precipitated a separation we do not know, although Lord George had certainly gone off to France again in 1631.[3] But two years later there was evidently a fresh crisis. On Christmas eve 1633 Lady Elizabeth arrived at the house of Sir Henry Berkeley of Wymondham, to be kept, apparently under some restraint, on the orders of the King. There can be little doubt that the two subsequently lived apart.[4]

Other troubles followed thick and fast. Lord George was a violent young man, and a later anecdote had it that he was made to pay for his temper. Sir Michael Stanhope had left his property to be divided between his two daughters, Jane and Elizabeth, the latter of whom was married to Lord Berkeley. But shortly before her death Lady Stanhope had given birth to a third daughter, Bridget, the paternity of whom her husband Sir Michael had

---

[1] Smith MSS. 3/12; Smyth, ii, p. 229. For an idea of Lord Cromwell's character, see his obscene letter in S.P. 16/275/23. For Lord Morley's drunken frolics, see W. Knowler, *Strafforde's Letters*, i, p. 225.

[2] Smith MSS. 2/58.   [3] Smyth, iii, p. 407-8.

[4] *Cal. S.P. Dom., 1633-34*, p. 336. She was living with her daughter Mrs. Coke in about 1643 (Gloucester Public Library, SF 2/11).

refused to recognize. According to Lady Betty Germaine, Lord George lost his temper one day and hit his Steward over the ear. The Steward 'told him it should cost him dear, and carried Mrs. Bridget to the Duke of Buckingham, who married her to a near relation of his & went to Law with the Lord Berkeley whose wives sister shee was proved'.[1] There is circumstantial evidence that tends to support the story. Sir Michael certainly left none of his property to Bridget, either by settlement or in his will, though he acknowledged her right to a third part of the Reade estate that came to her via her mother.[2] In his will he asked that the wardship of the child be given to her two sisters and their husbands, and it may well be that the sisters conspired to keep Bridget out of her share in the Reade inheritance until her marriage in 1630 with the late Duke of Buckingham's nephew, George Fielding Earl of Desmond, gave her the necessary backing. In this case her successful challenge would have reduced Lady Berkeley's share from the £1,500 a year quoted by Smith to £850, which is the figure at which it is put in a memorandum of about 1645.[3]

Meanwhile Lord Berkeley's income was proving grossly insufficient for his needs. During his three years' travel, 1626–9, his receiver obtained from all his Gloucester and Leicestershire lands only about £2,000 a year, a figure which excludes the Warwickshire, Somerset, and Sussex property in the hands of his mother. Out of this there was a £150 annuity due to the Countess of Leicester, and £30 a year for ever to Chenies Hospital, charged by the Dudleys and Sidneys on the Gloucestershire property returned in 1609.[4] The cost of Lord George's foreign travel and of his reckless way of life seems greatly to have exceeded his income. He was heavily in debt to the first Viscount Bayning, a most successful city merchant and financier who died in 1629. In 1634 he had raised £1,000 on a fine of Simondshall; he had sold the three Gloucestershire manors of Tetbury, Hannam, and Bitton, and yet at the end of the year he still owed the staggering sum of £18,767. Of this sum, £3,500 plus £2,000 interest was due to Viscount Bayning's executors on the mortgage of Wotton, and £6,250 to a Mr. Mynne on

[1] Smyth, ii, p. 429 n. 1.   [2] P.C.C., 10 Savile.

[3] Smith MSS. 3/20–1. £859 a year had already come to Lady Berkeley, and another £160 was to come on the death of her mother, the widow of Sir William Reade.

[4] Gloucester Public Library, SF 2/5/2; Smith MSS. 2/32. This fits in well with the later statement that the Gloucestershire lands, without improvement, were worth £1,500 per annum, and with Smith's receipts for Gloucestershire in 1634–5. These came to £1,879, including £300 for sale of land and £800 for a fine (SF 2/10/2; Smith MSS. 2/32).

a mortgage of Hame and Alkington, while there was a £200 per annum rent-charge for ten years secured on the lands in Leicestershire. There were numerous small loans arranged by various scriveners, and £2,500 due to tradesmen, of which £716 were for 'the young lady', presumably his daughter Elizabeth.[1]

How Lord Berkeley lived during the next few years we do not know. He was certainly in England in the late 1630s, and when war came he played a fairly passive role among the peers who stayed in London with the Parliament. Thanks to this prudent course he both avoided the financial burdens of royalist delinquency and prevented the destruction and mitigated the looting of Berkeley Castle.[2] But it would appear that Lord Berkeley's financial difficulties were as great as ever. In 1637 he had sold the £800 a year manor of Bosham for £8,700 to trustees for his younger son George, who had inherited the Cranford estate and a large sum of money from his grandmother Lady Elizabeth two years before.[3] It was no doubt with the money raised from this sale that he cleared off the Bayning mortgage in the same year.[4] Nor was there any sign of efforts to compensate for these losses. Admittedly in or before 1630 he had invested a little money in obtaining from Attorney General Heath a grant of land in the Carolinas. But he lacked the capital to develop it, and sold his rights to a merchant syndicate in return for 5 per cent of the profits of settlement.[5] It is unlikely that he had reaped much advantage from this before the war broke out in 1642.

As the first Civil War drew to a close in 1645, Lord Berkeley's personal affairs had reached a critical point, even if the long-term prospect for the family as a whole was quite promising.[6] Thanks to the accidental death by drowning of his eldest son Charles in 1641, his younger son George had become the heir, and therefore brought back with him to the title the money and estates which he had inherited from his Hunsdon grandmother. These included the

---

[1] T. D. Fosbrook, *History of Gloucestershire*, 1807, i, p. 397 and corr.; ii, p. 94 and corr., P.R.O., Wards, 9/359. Smith MSS. 2/32, 3/14. He had also sold a small manor for £1,500 in 1631 (Smyth, iii, p. 407).

[2] *Cal. S.P. Dom.*, *1636-7*, p. 115; *1638-9*, p. 478; *1645-7*, pp. 154, 156, 236.

[3] Smyth, iii, pp. 408, 412. C. W. James, *Chief Justice Coke . . .*, 1929, p. 83.

[4] P.R.O., Wards 9/359.   [5] *Cal. S.P. Colonial, 1574-1660*, p. 115.

[6] Smith MSS. 3/20-1. These documents are certainly dated after Lady Elizabeth Berkeley's death in 1635, as her estate at Cranford was now in the hands of her grandson, and before Lady Spencer's death in 1658. It refers to 'these bad times' during which the raising of money by fines and sales of wood is impossible, which clearly refers to the Civil War and dates the document to after mid-1642 and before mid-1645. It is probably connected with the opening of the marriage negotiations in the latter year.

Bosham estate that he had bought from his father in 1637, and the manor of Cranford, Middlesex, left him by his grandmother, which together amounted to £1,200 a year.[1] As a result, young George would eventually become heir to the Berkeley, Hunsdon, Stanhope, and Reade estates all rolled into one. In 1645 his father Lord Berkeley's present rental in Leicestershire, Gloucestershire, and elsewhere came to over £2,600 a year, and at the end of the war there was a prospect of large capital gains from sale of woods and fines for new leases. The Stanhope property, which had a rental of over £1,600, would almost all go to his eldest son when his wife died, and she seems already to have obtained control of it. Owing to the unfortunate blow Lord Berkeley gave his Steward so many years before, some of the Reade inheritance had been lost to the third sister, now Countess of Desmond. Nevertheless, by the most optimistic calculations one could therefore reckon the gross family rental in temporary or permanent possession or reversion, owned by father, mother, and son, to be about £6,700, to which should be added fines and wood sales, which would bring a hypothetical total of annual receipts up to perhaps £8,000 a year in all.[2]

In contrast to these castles in Spain, was the bleak reality of 1645. Some of the Reade and Stanhope property could not be sold or mortgaged until his wife died and his son became of age. Lord Berkeley was obliged to pay £300 a year to his estranged wife, and £1,200 a year to Sir Henry Berkeley, presumably as trustee for the children out of the Stanhope–Reade estate. He owed his daughter Elizabeth £5,000 for her marriage portion with Edward Coke, for which he was paying £400 a year in interest at 8 per cent, and he had charged the estate with miscellaneous pensions amounting to £340 a year. How much he owed we do not know, but there is reason to believe that the £18,000 debt of 1635 had increased rather than diminished over the years since, as we shall see, it was to take a massive injection of ready money and the ultimate sale of nearly all the Reade and Stanhope inheritance to clear them off. Lord

[1] Lady Elizabeth had bought Cranford in 1618 for £7,000 (Smyth, ii, p. 435. Some of the deeds of sale are in Middx. R.O., Acc. 530, Bdle 15). It is here put at £400 per annum. Bosham was an ancient Berkeley estate inherited from the Mowbrays. Smith gave its rental in 1623 as £756, and it is here put at £800 per annum (J. Dalloway, *History of the Western Division of the County of Sussex*, 1815, ii, p. 87 note b).

[2] Since the figures printed by Mr. Cooper in his appendix to Professor Trevor-Roper's article on *The Gentry* (*Econ. Hist. Rev.*, Supplement I, p. 54) are still referred to from time to time, it should be pointed out that the £8,000 per annum figure for Lord Berkeley in 1635 (*sic*) in that table is based on the same 1645 document and ancillary materials that are used here. Readers can draw their own conclusions about how meaningful the figure of £8,000 really is.

Berkeley was still living beyond the available income, and he had so incumbered his estate that he lacked security for further loans; he was therefore at the end of his tether.

In this predicament he took the only possible way out, and married his son and heir to a wealthy commercial heiress. His choice fell on the daughter and coheiress of one of his creditors, John Massingberd, a successful London merchant and Treasurer of the East India Company. In return for the social prestige which the marriage would bring to the Massingberds, Lord Berkeley must have obtained a cash windfall as the marriage portion—how much we do not know—and a line of credit for the prolongation of the debt. But Mr. Massingberd drove a hard bargain.[1] Now that old John Smith was dead and buried, he insisted on taking over full responsibility for estate management, all rents and fines being paid directly to him at East India House. He promised an annual audit of accounts, with statements of profit and loss, and accompanied by searching inquiry for the elimination of waste and fraud by agents and bailiffs, 'the want whereof hath much prejudiced the estate'. He ordered the dispatch of a commission into Gloucestershire to sell woods and to dispark parks, and he ruthlessly extruded Lord Berkeley's son-in-law Edward Coke and the estranged heiress and wife Lady Elizabeth from any control whatever over the management of the estates. Lady Elizabeth was peremptorily removed from the house of her son-in-law Mr. Coke, and housed as economically as possible elsewhere, and an attempt was made to get her to surrender her rights of dower and her inheritance, which were reckoned to be worth £2,000 a year, in return for an annuity of £800 or £1,000. Lord Berkeley was reduced to the condition of a remittance man on a fixed allowance of £800 a year, and was ordered to reduce his household immediately in order to live within his now straightened means. It seems to have been anticipated that he would withdraw abroad again and stay there. As for the young couple, they were to have a present allowance of £600 a year, while Miss Massingberd was to be assured a jointure after Mr. Berkeley's death of £700 a year from the Berkeley estate alone, together with more from the Hunsdon and Stanhope inheritances. These heroic measures were apparently necessary in order to increase the income from the estate, and to devote a large part of it to the repayment of what was described as 'that great debt'.

[1] Gloucester Public Library, SF 2/5/2; SF 2/11.

A further cause for anxiety was that there was as yet no guarantee that the huge Stanhope–Reade inheritance of Lady Elizabeth would remain with the Berkeleys. Unless Lord and Lady Berkeley could be persuaded to join with their son George when the latter came of age to suffer a recovery and so bar the entail, the deaths of George and his sister without male issue would mean that their daughters would not inherit the estate.[1] Steps were therefore taken to prevent such an eventuality.

There is an air of cold-blooded ruthlessness, remorseless efficiency, and even of financial duplicity about the document setting out Mr. Massingberd's terms, which forms a most striking contrast both to Smith's scrupulous honesty and cautious conservatism, and to the happy-go-lucky spendthrift ways of the last three generations of Berkeleys. Its acceptance may have been the only way to salvage the family fortunes and to redeem the debt, but it clearly marked the end of feudal paternalism, and a shift to the commercialization of landlord-tenant and even intra-familial relationships. It is proof of how desperately serious the situation was, despite the apparently rosy long-term prospect, that as soon as Lady Elizabeth died, most of the Stanhope lands were sold to clear off the debt, presumably in addition to the residue of the Reade lands which had already been allocated to this purpose.[2] For the second time running most of the property acquired by marriage with an heiress had been sold to pay off current debts, instead of going to swell the permanent family patrimony.

The history of the Berkeleys during the late Tudor and early Stuart period is one of imperfectly arrested decline, the main causes of which were twofold. The primary factor was undoubtedly the personal behaviour-patterns of Lord Henry, Sir Thomas, and Lord George. For three successive generations the heir to the title was without the ambition or intellect to cut an important political or even courtly figure; worse still, he was recklessly improvident. Three generations of wastrels lived on their capital by selling land in large quantities. The first two reduced the ancient Berkeley heritage by over half and absorbed all the property of the Hunsdon

---

[1] Ibid., SF 2/11.

[2] Land in Suffolk rented at about £800 a year in 1645 was sold to Sir Henry Wood, Treasurer of the Household of Henrietta Maria (W. A. Copinger, *The Manors of Suffolk*, London, 1905–11, ii, p. 19; iv, p. 91; v, pp. 124, 187; vii, pp. 249, 253). On the other hand, one of the Reade properties in Norfolk, which was rented at £267 in about 1645, was certainly retained (F. Blomefield, *Topographical History of Norfolk*, 1805–10, iv, p. 522), and only part of the Middlesex estate was sold (Middx. R.O., Acc. 530, Bdle 10).

heiress; and the third ran up debts that before the end absorbed most of the great Stanhope–Reade inheritance. The second cause of the Berkeleys' troubles was the prolonged loss of court favour, due to bad luck or bad judgement in the choice of wives. Anne Savage had been a Boleyn adherent, which lost the Berkeleys any prospect of royal favour during the great distribution of monastic property. Katherine Howard involved the Berkeleys in the fall from favour of the house of Norfolk in 1572, while her family hatred of the Dudleys precipitated the disastrous lawsuit and the prolonged loss of much Gloucestershire property.

To compensate for these two adverse factors there can be set the diligent estate management of the family's devoted Steward, John Smith of Nibley, and the marriages with the Carey and the Stanhope–Reade heiresses. But as has been seen, Smith's turn of mind was more conservative and antiquarian than radical, and the pressure for immediate cash windfalls to meet current expenditure made increases of income by improvement of rents rather than fines virtually impossible. In any case Smith's control over estate management only lasted for a limited period. It was not till about 1580 that Lord Henry adopted a careful and sensible accounting system, and it would appear that Lord George let things slide again in the 1630s.[1]

The Carey heiress certainly brought with her substantial property in Kent and elsewhere, but the reversion of most of this was sold long before it fell in, at a consequently low figure. Against this is to be set the twenty-four years that Lady Elizabeth lived after the death of her husband, during all of which time she was drawing about £1,500 a year from the estate in jointure. On balance, the Berkeleys probably lost by the marriage.[2] Though the Stanhope match promised eventually almost to double the family income, it did not quite turn out that way, and it had severe psychological costs. The instability and dissipation of Lord George can no doubt be partly attributed to his indissoluble union when still a child to a little girl of nine. Moreover Lord George's quarrel with his wife, and her longevity, meant that the Berkeleys did not gain full control of the Stanhope estate till after the Restoration.

The third marriage to an heiress, the Massingberd girl, certainly

---

[1] Smyth, ii, p. 412. Gloucester City Library, SF 2/11.

[2] They gained £1,000 portion in 1595 and £8,450 from the sale of the Carey estate in 1606. From 1612 to 1635 they paid out about £1,500 a year, that is to say about £36,000 in all.

saved the family from a major crisis due to an intolerable load of debt, and in the end Mr. Massingberd's ruthless management must have resulted in a significant increase in annual income. But most of the Stanhope–Reade inheritance eventually had to be sold in the 1670s, so that it is unlikely that the gross family income in 1680 was much more than £5,000 or perhaps £6,000 a year. This story points to the danger of using crude figures for total income, in possession and reversion, held by various members of a family, as a reliable indicator of current financial standing. In the case of the Berkeleys, the long-term estimates of 1645 were wholly misleading as an indicator of the short-term situation.

In the end, therefore, three generations of reckless dissipation and political ostracism outweighed the benefits of marriage with three heiresses. Deprived of any share in the profits of office or the benefits of royal favour, without any dramatic increase of income from the development of urban property or mineral wealth, the Berkeleys sank quietly from a position as one of the five or ten wealthiest landowners in England, with very strong claims to promotion to an earldom if the political winds had been favourable, to a more modest place among the wealthier of the barons. They remained one of England's great county families, but they were no longer in the first rank.

The history of the Berkeleys over this period is almost entirely dominated by chance. It was the unpredictable accident of bio-chemistry, aided no doubt by unfortunate upbringing, which saddled the family with three generations of unambitious wastrels; it was the lottery of marriage which had hitched the fortunes of the family to serious political liabilities like the Boleyns in the early sixteenth century and the Howards in the late sixteenth century; it was biological accident which caused the death of the eldest son Charles and so reunited the title with the estates of the younger brother George; it was also biological accident which kept the family going in the male line and so saved the Stanhope inheritance. The only significant elements of calculation in the story are the deliberate marriages with heiresses, which provided the only important injections of new wealth, and to a secondary degree the very different kinds of attention paid to estate management by John Smith and Mr. Massingberd. But the determining factor was luck.

IX

THE HOWARDS EARLS OF SUFFOLK
1574–1745

THOMAS HOWARD was the second son, by a second marriage, of Thomas, fourth Duke of Norfolk, one of the most powerful and richest noblemen in England.[1] He was only eleven years old when disaster overcame his family in 1572 with the conviction and execution of his father on a charge of treason. Queen Elizabeth and her advisers evidently thought, not without reason, that the accumulation of landed property and family connections of the late Duke, both in possession and expectation, was more than was good for the safety of the state. Although there was no desire wholly to ruin the family, there was equally clearly a determination substantially to reduce the size of their land-holdings.

The huge Howard estates in East Anglia were therefore retained in the hands of the Crown, thus destroying the traditional political influence of the Dukes of Norfolk in that area. This was far from leaving the children destitute, however, since the late Duke's eldest son by his first marriage was heir to the estates and title of the Earls of Arundel, mainly in Sussex, to which his mother was the sole heiress. Similarly, his second son by his second marriage, Thomas, was the heir to the estates of the Lords Audley, mainly in Essex, to which *his* mother was the sole heiress. Nor was this all, for the late Duke had acquired the wardship of the three young daughters and heiresses of the last Lord Dacre (the first husband of his second wife), and had been planning to absorb their northern property into the family by a triple marriage with his three surviving sons. The eldest son, Philip Earl of Arundel, had already married one Dacre daughter in 1569 and the eleven-year-old Thomas received the following letter from his father shortly before the latter's execution three years later; 'Tom, you have ever from your infancy been given to be stubborn,—if you buy your wardship, then if you have a liking to my daughter-in-law Mary Dacre I hope you shall

---

[1] See genealogical table no. 6.

have it in your own choice.'[1] Some time in the next five years Thomas went through with the marriage, but Mary died childless soon after in 1578 at the age of fifteen, and with her went his share of the Dacre inheritance. In view of the age of the bride and groom, it is very unlikely that the marriage had even been consummated. Five years later, however, Thomas Howard tried again, still pursuing the family obsession with heiresses. This time his choice was Katherine, daughter and coheiress of Sir Henry Knyvett of Charlton in Wiltshire, and niece and eventually heiress of Thomas, future Lord Knyvett of Escrick.

Despite his high ancestry and wealthy marriage, in the 1580s Thomas was nonetheless a young man whose prospects of a successful career depended largely on his own abilities. The Audley inheritance from his mother gave him an income of about £1,000,[2] which was very substantial for a commoner, but barely sufficient for someone of his birth and aspirations. His way in the world was not smoothed by his elder step-brother, the Earl of Arundel, who maintained an obstinate Catholicism and aroused such suspicion of disloyalty that he ended his days in the Tower of London in 1595. Like all the Howard children, Thomas had received a careful education, including a spell at Cambridge University, but he never pretended to be an intellectual or a scholar. Indeed when James I made him Lord Treasurer in 1614, he explicitly stressed the contrast with his predecessor in office, Robert Cecil Earl of Salisbury, telling him that 'he had made choice of him not for his learning in Greek and Latin, or for that he could make epigrams and orations, but for his approved fidelity and integrity, etcetera'.[3] Lacking intellectual distinction, young Thomas Howard's best hope of recovering political favour, and with it the lost family estates, was to make his career partly at Court but mainly in the field. The distinction he sought was as a man of action in the prolonged naval war against Spain. He did outstanding service at sea in the Armada campaign of 1588, for which he was knighted by his cousin the Lord Admiral, Charles Earl of Nottingham. He commanded a naval squadron to the Azores in 1591, and another to Cadiz in 1596, in recompense for which Queen Elizabeth summoned him to rejoin the House of Lords as Lord Howard of Walden, and made him a Knight of the Garter.

[1] G. E. Cokayne, *Complete Peerage*, xii (i), p. 465 note b.
[2] Essex R.O., D/DBy, M 157, 158.
[3] N. E. McClure, *Letters of John Chamberlain*, 1939, i, p. 548.

Lord Thomas's professional career was built on the sea, and it was as a privateer, as a diligent hunter after Spanish prizes in the Atlantic and the Caribbean, that his reputation was made.[1] He was no armchair investor in privateering like his political ally Sir Robert Cecil or his cousin the Lord Admiral, but a leader of men on the high seas. He was no doubt partly driven to the sea by a love of adventure for its own sake, but partly also by that reckless gambler's instinct that he was to display throughout his life. He personally invested heavily in these risky enterprises, few of which paid off after one or two minor successes in 1591-2. For a decade he pursued the chimaera of the capture of a Spanish treasure ship, but like those other Elizabethan adventurers he was doomed to disappointment. Consequently his apparently dazzling political and naval career was built on a quicksand of mounting debts and mortgages.

As he came increasingly into political favour in the 1590s, so Elizabeth grudgingly released to him small parcels of the old Howard estates. These were not enough to keep him going, and throughout the 1580s and 1590s he was steadily running down his capital by sale of land and running up his obligations by borrowing money on credit. Between 1583 and 1595 he must have raised getting on for £15,000 by sale of land,[2] and for the next five years his troubles increased rapidly. Between 1596 and 1600 he raised a further £1,000 by sale of land, borrowed nearly £13,000 on mortgage,[3] and piled up another £7,500 worth of debts on statute staple. He was borrowing from all the leading moneylenders of London, including the greatest of them all, Sir John Spencer, and especially from Thomas Sutton, the latter of whom he was careful to address as 'my very loving and assured good friend'. He was also borrowing from one of the tellers in the Exchequer, Robert Taylor. The latter was turning a dishonest penny by using official money lying in his hands to put out at interest, and in order to postpone repayment to him Howard was obliged to have recourse

---

[1] K. R. Andrews, *Elizabethan Privateering, 1585-1603*, pp. 28, 37, 79, 89, 165-7, 264.

[2] Tilty manor in Essex was sold to Henry Maynard, Lord Burghley's secretary, for £5,000 in 1587 (P. Morant, *History of Essex*, Chelmsford, 1768, ii, p. 436; P.C.C., 1 Alan); a group of manors in Suffolk was also sold in 1586 for £4,700 (J. Gage, *Thingoe Hundred*, London, 1838, p. 344; W. A. Copinger, *The Manors of Suffolk*, v, pp. 235, 239; iv, pp. 145, 165); almost all the Hertfordshire property, including seven manors, went between 1583 and 1592 (*V.C.H. Hertfordshire*, iii, pp. 309, 360, 399; iv, pp. 75, 84, 116).

[3] P.R.O., Close Rolls, 38 Eliz., pt. 7; 40 pts. 14, 19, 20; 41 pts. 22, 28, 29; 42 pt. 19; 1 Jas. I. pt. 9; 3 Jas. I, pt. 30.

to his friend Sir Robert Cecil to smooth things over in the Ex-chequer.[1]

As his political career improved, his economic position became more desperate, so that in the end it became a close race between ruin and salvation. By 1596 he claimed to have spent £20,000 of his own money in the Queen's service in expeditions at sea, and was hoping to recoup with the loot of Cadiz. This was a vain hope, and the next year he set out to sea again, telling his friend Cecil 'I would we might put it out of question by possessing them [the Spanish treasure ships], without which I come home bankrupt.' The expedition failed, and ruin stared him in the face. In 1598 he had to throw himself on the good offices of Queen Elizabeth—not the most generous of sovereigns—to save him from losing pro-perty mortgaged for £12,000 and forfeit within twelve days unless he could raise the money to redeem it.[2]

Somehow or other he staggered on through the hectic years of the late 1590s, but, unlike the other young rakehells of the age, he avoided the fatal mistake of joining the anti-Cecil party of malcon-tents around the Earl of Essex. Despite his commitment to aggres-sive naval action against Spain, he none the less sided with Cecil, Ralegh, and his scheming uncle Henry Howard. When the crisis came with the Essex Revolt of 1601, he was one of the leaders of the royal forces besieging Essex's house, and one of the peers who condemned Essex to death for treason. The second stroke of good luck, or good judgement, was to allow himself to be carried along in the wake of his uncle Henry as the latter conspired with Cecil first to put James I on the throne upon the death of the old Queen, and then to destroy their old allies against Essex, Sir Walter Ralegh and Lord Cobham. With James's accession in 1603, Cecil and the Howards were on top of the world, and a new epoch began.

The rewards of backing the winning side were immediate and enormous: elevation to the Earldom of Suffolk; appointment to the office of Lord Chamberlain of the Household, which was one of the most important and profitable positions in the court, since it offered almost daily contact with the King; and the grant to him and his uncle of a very substantial part of the old Howard estate in

[1] P.R.O., Lord Chamberlain's Office, Recognizances for Debt, 193-5 *passim*. Charterhouse MSS., F. 3/409. P.R.O., Lord Chamberlain's Office, Recognizances for Debt, 193/42. *H.M.C. Salis. MSS.* vii, p. 283.

[2] T. Birch, *Memoirs of the Reign of Queen Elizabeth*, London, 1754, ii, p. 115. *H.M.C. Salis. MSS.* vii, p. 346. *Cal. S.P. Dom. 1598-1601*, p. 16.

East Anglia and Shropshire, some of which could be immediately sold off to reduce the debts owed, and the rest could be restored again to the family patrimony.¹ What was left of the old Audley inheritance, together with this new grant of ex-Norfolk property brought in about £5,000 a year in the later 1630s, after some portions had been sold and others bought. It was therefore probably bringing in at least £3,800 in 1605. To this should be added his wife's inheritance in Wiltshire worth at least £2,500 a year in 1652 and therefore probably about £2,000 a year in the early 1600s.² Moreover this was a time when for once the Earl imagined— wrongly as it turned out—that he could afford to buy land. Between 1604 and 1608 he spent at least £13,000 on land purchases in East Anglia and the West Country.³

The reason for this optimism was the staggering quantity of the fruits of office which were also being showered upon him. In the last years of Queen Elizabeth's reign, Lord Howard had been granted the customs on gold and silver thread imported from Venice, from which in 1612 he was reckoned to be drawing a clear profit of £800 a year by subcontracting with a group of merchant financiers. Six years later a £500 annuity from this customs farm was being used to pay for the maintenance of his second son Thomas.⁴ Far more important, however, was the farm of the customs and impositions on currants, which Suffolk obtained in 1604 and which was eventually to play as large a part in his finances as the farm of the silk customs was to play in those of his friend and ally Robert Cecil, now Earl of Salisbury. The farm was let to Suffolk for ten years at a rate which was £500 a year more than the average profits for 1594–1603. Suffolk subcontracted for two years for £6,000 a year, which left him a clear profit of £678 a year over the rent due to the Crown. More efficient management, however, and the growth of Mediterranean imports, allowed the contractors to make very large profits indeed.⁵ A leading contractor was Arthur Ingram, a shady but energetic promoter and financier whose career was to remain closely interlocked with the Suffolks for another

¹ P.R.O., Close Rolls, 2 Jas. I, pt. 1; Land Revenue Office 1/313, ff. 232–3.

² Essex R.O., D/DBy, M 159, 162. House of Lords MSS. 1652 (particular of the Earl of Berkshire). At the time of the marriage in 1614 the estate was rumoured to have been worth £3,000 a year, but this was probably an exaggeration (McClure, op. cit. i, p. 516).

³ P.R.O., Close Rolls, 2 Jas. I, pt. 1; 3 Jas. I, pt. 21; 4 Jas. I, pt. 2; 5 Jas. I, pts. 21, 27, 35.

⁴ Cal. S.P. Dom., 1598–1601, p. 517. H.M.C. Sackville MSS. i, p. 290. H.M.C. 3rd Rep., App., p. 15.

⁵ S.P. 14/7/15. H.M.C. Salis. MSS xviii, pp. 305, 306.

thirty years. In 1609 political opposition from the Levant Company made it prudent to reduce the rates on currents, and a new farm had therefore to be arranged. By this time the Lord Treasurer was Robert Cecil, Earl of Salisbury, Suffolk's close friend and ally and now a relative through the marriage of their children. This opened the way for a regranting of the farm on terms so favourable to the Earl as to be scandalous. Suffolk reached a prior agreement with four subcontractors to obtain from the Exchequer a twenty-one-year lease of the farm to them at a rent of £2,800 a year. As a bribe for arranging this lease, the contractors promised to pay Suffolk the gigantic sum of £20,000. The grant from the Crown was certainly made on these terms, but an annuity to the Earl over and above the annual rent to the Crown was eventually substituted for the £20,000 in cash. By 1610 Suffolk was receiving an annuity of £3,000 a year from the farmers, while in 1612 it was alleged that he was receiving £5,000 a year. Whichever is the correct figure, there can be no doubt that the profit was at least equal to, and possibly a good deal more than, the total income from his landed estates.

But in 1613 Salisbury was dead, the Crown's financial situation was desperate, and Parliament seemed the only recourse. It was therefore thought prudent to comply with the scheme of the Crown's new financial expert, Lionel Cranfield, to anticipate parliamentary criticism by redeeming for cash the most blatantly corrupt of the customs farms. By a series of complicated calculations Cranfield fixed Suffolk's recompense for the surrender of the remainder of his lease at £10,000. But the Exchequer was empty, and so the money was advanced—or promised—to the Crown by the ubiquitous and indispensable Ingram in return for the transfer of some Crown land, and was used by Suffolk and his Countess as a drawing account for current cash needs.[1]

Another small but socially highly obnoxious grant, which was obtained in 1608 by Suffolk, was of the surplus value of land sold by Queen Elizabeth at untrue valuations. Exploitation of the grant demanded long and tedious searches in the official records, but there is scattered evidence that there were profits to be made out of such fishing expeditions. In 1610 Suffolk extracted £520 from a Northumberland gentleman for an old and apparently fraudulent

[1] Leeds Public Library, Temple Newsam MSS., English Customs vii, 2. *H.M.C. Sackville MSS.* i, pp. 268–9. Hatfield House, S. 129/8. A. F. Upton, *Sir Arthur Ingram, 1565–1642,* Oxford, 1961, pp. 7–8. He is incorrect in stating that the 1609 proposal for a twenty-one-year lease at £2,800 a year was rejected.

purchase, and as late as 1633 Suffolk's heir was still busy mining the same vein. In that year the second Earl prosecuted Wadham College, Oxford, over a forty-two-year-old sale by the Crown of a rectory, which had been resold to the foundress of the College in 1610. It was alleged, apparently correctly, that forty-two years ago the fee-farm rent payable to the Crown had been set £3. 16s. 8d. a year too low.[1]

These Crown grants were not the only extraordinary windfalls that came Suffolk's way, for he and his son and heir were also the residuary legatees of a number of relatives. 'Daily fortune doth strive to overwhelm him with wealth', an observer remarked in 1611 about his son and heir Theophilus Lord Howard of Walden.[2] The first of these relatives to die was his cousin Thomas Howard Viscount Bindon, the owner of a great estate in the West Country. Suffolk had long had his eye on this inheritance, and in 1600 was reported to have been negotiating to marry Theophilus to Bindon's only granddaughter and heiress, for whom he was prepared to pay £10,000. But he saved his money since the young girl died before the marriage arrangements had been completed, which left Theophilus as the heir to the estate. And so when Bindon died in 1611, Theophilus inherited property worth £3,100 a year in possession and a further £270 in reversion.[3]

In the end Suffolk married Theophilus to another heiress, the only daughter of the Scottish courtier Lord Hume. The marriage contract was drawn up when the girl was only six years old, and the marriage took place the moment she reached the minimum legal age of twelve. When her father died in 1612 Theophilus and his wife inherited another substantial estate in the North Country, worth about £1,600 a year.[4] Three years later, in 1614, came the death of Suffolk's uncle Henry Earl of Northampton. He left the bulk of his estate to the head of the Howard family, the Earl of Arundel, but Suffolk inherited his great town house at Charing Cross and some East Anglian property, said to have been worth some £800 a year.[5] If one includes the estates of the father and son,

---

[1] Cal. S.P. Dom., 1603-10, p. 421. A History of Northumberland, v, p. 233. Wadham College MSS. 47/5-12.

[2] H.M.C. Rutland MSS., i, p. 429.

[3] McClure, op. cit. i, p. 109. Wilts. R.O., Suffolk and Berkshire MSS., Moore's Boxes S/21 (this is the gross income in 1619).

[4] J. Raine, History of North Durham, London, 1852, p. 43. Lord Braybrooke, Audley End, London, 1836, pp. 42-3.

[5] McClure, op. cit. i, p. 541.

the total landed income of the family between 1614 and 1620 cannot have been far short of £8,000 or £9,000 a year.

These great accretions of property were in a sense incidental to Suffolk's political career, which for fifteen years from 1603 to 1618 pursued a consistently upward path. To the Lord Chamberlainship of the Household of 1603, he added the Captainship of the Gentlemen Pensioners in 1605. With the death of Salisbury in 1612, the Howards, allied with Robert Carr, Earl of Somerset, were left in full control, and Suffolk's uncle Henry Earl of Northampton became the leading figure in the government. With the latter's death in 1614, Suffolk was awarded the highest and most lucrative prize of all, the Lord Treasurership, which he held for four years.

The year 1615 saw him at the peak of his prosperity and political power. Sir Roger Wilbraham described the situation as follows:

Himself Lord Treasurer; his son-in-law, the Earl of Somerset, Lord High Chamberlain and the most potent favorite in my time; Lord Knollys, another son-in-law, Treasurer of the Household and by his favor made Master of Wards; the Earl of Salisbury another son-in-law; the Lord Walden, his eldest son, married to the heir of the Earl of Dunbar, another of the chief favorites of King James; all the younger sons married to livings of £1,000 and more; the Chancellor of Exchequer and many other officers placed by his means and his son-in-law Somerset's, that great favorite.

But 1615 was the turning-point. The anti-Somerset and anti-Howard faction were scheming to overthrow Somerset, and to this end they introduced into Court a potential rival for King James's attentions, a young man called George Villiers.

The fall of Somerset and the rise of Villiers were brought about that same year through the unexpected disclosure of the former's complicity in a particularly unsavoury murder. After that the only question was whether the Howards could either come to terms with the new favourite, or could supplant him. It was a miracle that they survived the fall of Somerset, and they made frantic efforts to maintain their power, by trying to supply King James with an alternative homosexual attachment to Villiers, who might be more favourably disposed to themselves. They went so far as to pick out a handsome young man with a fine complexion, 'washing his face every day with posset curd' to improve his appearance.[1] But it was no good, for King James did not take to him at all, and

[1] *Journal of Sir Roger Wilbraham, Camden Miscellany*, x, 1902, p. 115. McClure, op. cit. ii, p. 144.

the only consequence was that Villiers, who was more and more securely established in the King's affections, found it necessary to destroy them politically. And so in 1618 the Suffolks were put on trial on a charge of corruption in office. They had lasted at the top of the greasy pole exactly four years.

Lack of documentation makes it impossible to guess what were the total profits derived from official fees attached to all the offices held by Suffolk, from bribes from clients from the sale of offices under him, and from the various patents and annuities which he obtained from the Crown. Before 1608 he was sharing a £500 annuity out of the Court of Wards with the Earls of Worcester and Northampton; in 1611 he is reported to have had a £1,000 a year annuity out of the Exchequer renewed for ten years; and in 1614 he was certainly drawing pensions from both the Irish and the English customs.[1] The unofficial rewards, however, were far greater. For one thing, he hastened to continue the corrupt relationship with the customs farmers which had been begun by his predecessor the Earl of Salisbury.[2] Previous to becoming Lord Treasurer he had been the patron of a rival group of farmers, and the existing farmers had to offer a powerful inducement to get him to switch his allegiance to themselves. It is not surprising, therefore, to find the farmers advanced Suffolk a personal loan of £10,418 exactly one month after he became Lord Treasurer. He had also borrowed £6,000 from one of them, Nicholas Salter, which he paid off by selling him a Dorset manor, and in 1616 he borrowed a further £1,000 from the farmers.[3] Like Salisbury before him, Suffolk's personal financial obligations to the custom farmers were so enormous that it would be wholly unreasonable to expect him to have exercised judicial objectivity in his official negotiations with them. One way or another one must conclude that Suffolk's conduct in—and therefore his income from—high office was very similar to that of the Earl of Salisbury before him. He inherited a bad system, and he exploited it for all it was worth.

These corrupt financial entanglements with the customs farmers were not the end of Suffolk's subordination of the public interest

---

[1] S.P. 14/34/39. T. D. Whitaker, *Deanery of Craven*, Leeds, 1878, p. 362. Upton, op. cit., p. 69. Leeds Public Library, Temple Newsam MSS., Irish Customs III/33, 34.

[2] A. P. Keep, 'Star Chamber Proceedings against the Earl of Suffolk and Others', *Eng. Hist. Rev.*, xiii, 1898, pp. 726-7.

[3] Leeds Public Library, Temple Newsam MSS., Family Papers 9. P.R.O., Chancery Proc., Series I, Jas. I, G 14/34.

to private gain. Recently discovered evidence proves that he became even more dependent than Salisbury himself upon the charity
of King Philip of Spain. He may or may not have been a sincere
supporter of a pro-Spanish foreign policy on its merits, but we
now know that he was lavishly rewarded for his attitude. In 1609
the Countess of Suffolk reminded the Spanish ambassador 'about
the amounts of money for her and Cecil for what they had striven
to do' over the truce negotiations between Spain and the Dutch.
Later in that year Cecil had an extraordinary interview with the
ambassador, in which he explained that the Earl and Countess of
Suffolk were on the verge of bankruptcy, and brazenly asked for
the staggering sum of £25,000. The bulk of the money was to go
to the Suffolks, but he was to have a share. The ambassador agreed
to the extent of paying £11,000, which was sufficiently large a
sum to keep the Howards afloat and in a friendly mood. Subsequently the Countess was the recipient of further sums paid by
Spain for services rendered.[1]

Suffolk's character is something of an enigma. On the one hand
he had the external appearance of a bluff sea captain—'a plain honest
gentleman' as James I described him[2]—but on the other he was
surrounded with a pack of dishonest and rapacious scoundrels, and
it is impossible to believe that he was not aware of what was going
on. The leader of the pack until his death in 1614 was his hypo-
critical and malicious uncle, the Earl of Northampton. All the most
corrupt of the transactions were handled by his ambitious and
scheming wife, Katherine, and by the Teller of the Tallies under
him in the Exchequer, Sir John Bingley. And lastly there was his
indispensable and ever-ready creditor, the devious and untrustworthy financier, Arthur Ingram. Of the last he once wrote, 'There
is nothing that I shall think too much for Sir Arthur Ingram that
I may safely do.'[3] In the end he was better than his word and helped
to accelerate his own destruction in doing so. It is virtually impossible to believe that Suffolk was not aware that his wife was
demanding and getting gigantic bribes from the Spanish ambassador, and was involved in a host of shady deals and bargains; or that
the favours he bestowed as Lord Treasurer upon his friend Ingram

[1] A. J. Loomie, 'Sir Robert Cecil and the Spanish Embassy', *Bulletin of the Institute of Historical Research*, xlii, 1969, pp. 55–7. S. R. Gardner, *History of England, 1603–16*, London, 1863, ii, p. 362.

[2] T. Birch, *Court and Times of James I*, London, 1848, p. 336.

[3] Upton, op. cit., p. 69.

were highly improper; or that Sir John Bingley was in the habit of issuing, for a price, a host of official licences and grants in his name; or that his own personal financial dependence upon the customs farmers was directly contrary to the best interests of the Crown.

A few scattered lawsuits, and the revelations disclosed at his trial for corruption in 1618, give some idea of the kind of transactions in which he, his wife, and his associates were involved. For example, there was the ancient claim on the Exchequer of the war loan made by Queen Elizabeth to the Dutch rebels in 1578, the capital for which had been advanced by Sir Horatio Palavicino. Palavicino's heir by marriage was Sir Oliver Cromwell of Hinchinbrook, and when the Dutch at last in 1616 cleared off their debts by a cash payment to the Crown of £210,000, Sir Oliver naturally demanded a settlement. In this effort he enlisted the support of the Countess of Suffolk, who agreed to get her husband to grant £21,000 worth of Crown land to him. According to Sir Oliver, his part of the bargain was to sell the lands immediately to the Countess at the gross under-valuation at which she had arranged for them to be rated in the Exchequer. As a result, Sir Oliver would receive from her the rated value of the property, and the Countess the difference between the rated and the real value. The lands were granted and resold as arranged, but in the end, as so often happened, the Countess cheated on her own corrupt bargain, and Cromwell was obliged to sue her in Chancery for a missing £2,000.[1] This was not the only part of the Dutch war loan repayment which came the way of the Suffolks, for it emerged in the trial that they had contrived to 'borrow' £3,000 of the cash, which they did not repay until eight days before the trial opened.[2]

In a second case, the Royal Jeweller, Sir John Spilman, claimed in 1624 that Suffolk had been running up bills since 1603. As an example of the latter's chaotic finances, he had on one occasion in 1611 bought—on credit—a diamond ring for £1,000, and immediately pawned it for £500. When Suffolk became Lord Treasurer in 1612, Spilman, who was owed £3,700 by the Crown, promptly obtained from him a warrant for payment so as to satisfy him. But the Countess borrowed £1,000 of this on bond for a month and never paid it back. Instead she suggested Spilman think up some

---

[1] F. C. Dietz, *English Public Finance, 1558-1641*, New York, 1932, p. 162. L. Stone, *An Elizabethan: Sir Horatio Palavicino*, pp. 93-4, 308. P.R.O. Chancery Proc., Series I, Jas. I, C 23/83.

[2] Wilts. R.O., Suffolk and Berkshire MSS., Moore's Boxes, S/21.

profitable grant from the Crown as a means to recover his money. He did so, but the grant went to someone else. The Countess then suggested the debt be liquidated by sale of land, but after the documents had been perused by Sir Arthur Ingram, and the total amount agreed upon, the Countess refused to go through with the sale. Meanwhile the bonds had been deposited with Sir John Bingley for safe keeping, but the Countess got them from him and refused to surrender them. In 1624 Sir John Spilman was still suing in Chancery for his money.[1]

At the trial itself other scabrous stories came to light. One of them concerned the £10,000 borrowed in 1614 at interest from the customs farmers on mortgage of the Earl's Shropshire estate at Oswestry. Soon after he became Lord Treasurer, the farmers sent him a New Year's gift of £500 for his good will—a present which was rejected as inadequate. The Earl and Countess first asked for £520 a year and then stepped up the demands to £2,000. When the customs farmers refused, they began a policy of harassment, obstructing the farmers in the execution of their duties. Moreover, an agent of the Suffolks, Sir John Townshend, borrowed the mortgage documents on the pretext of showing them in court, and then refused to return them, leaving the unfortunate farmers without proper legal security for their money. When the latter sued for their return, Townshend did not deny the fact, but merely alleged that he had never promised to return the documents. Under these pressures the farmers finally gave way and promised the Earl £1,500 a year for seven years, provided the Earl was still Lord Treasurer and they still retained the farm that long. The £1,500 was to be used to pay the interest and to reduce the capital of Suffolk's private debts to them.[2] Here was a situation in which the financial connection between the farmers and the Lord Treasurer was so close and so substantial that the public interest was inevitably lost sight of. Once again, Suffolk was merely continuing a practice begun by his predecessor the Earl of Salisbury—or possibly by the Earl of Dorset before that. But his ruthless enforcement of bribes in return for administrative favours on this extensive scale shows how deeply the canker of corruption had eaten into the highest offices of the State. Governmental efficiency, and indeed the

---

[1] P.R.O., Chancery Proc., Series I, Jas. I, S 32/27.
[2] Ibid., G 14/34. *H.M.C. Cowper MSS.* i, p. 142. This document puts the gratuity at £2,500 a year, not £1,500. A. P. Keep, op. cit., pp. 726–7.

very stability of government finances, were endangered by such practices.

It is clear that the Earl and his Countess, assisted by Sir John Bingley, had been conspiring on a huge scale to abuse their power to award royal contracts and to allocate payment of Crown debts and cash assignments. The Exchequer never had enough money to pay all its creditors, and to meet current expenditure for the maintenance of the Court, the pension list, and the armed forces. In such a situation, the Lord Treasurer was in a position to allocate scarce resources as he pleased; if he was corrupt, he tended to satisfy friends and clients rather than those who should have had priority. The Suffolks went to extreme lengths, at great expense to the State, to conceal the corrupt practices of their family clients such as Sir Roger Dallison as Master of the Ordnance, and Sir Arthur Ingram as contractor for the royal alum works. Moreover, case after case was cited in which creditors of the Crown could only get payment by giving a substantial bribe to the Countess, often 10 per cent or more of the sum due. The most astonishing example of this process that came to light at the trial was the trouble experienced by the military forces in Ireland in getting paid. By 1617 things had got so serious that the Treasurer at War in Ireland and the leading military commanders and captains held a meeting and decided to make a collective bribe of £1,000 a year to the Earl and Countess, and £200 a year to Sir John Bingley, in order to expedite the transfer of moneys officially appropriated to them for maintenance. The bribes were to be deducted at source from the sums appropriated. And yet it was alleged at the trial that, despite this bribe, the payments were still delayed and diverted for private purposes.[1]

It is indicative of the moral climate of the day that most of the judges took these revelations of corruption very coolly indeed, and expressed little serious indignation. Most of the minority who voted for the higher fine of £100,000 did so explicitly in the expectation that it would be largely pardoned by the King. Even more remarkable is Suffolk's subsequent attempt to collect his £1,500 annuity from the customs farmers for the two years after he was dismissed from office, on the grounds that the bargain was still in force since no successor as Lord Treasurer had yet been appointed. In 1623 the farmers appealed indignantly to the King,

---

[1] Keep, op. cit., pp. 721, 724–5. A. B. Grosart, *Lismore Papers*, 2nd ser. ii, London, 1887, pp. 168–80. Wilts. R.O., Suffolk and Berkshire MSS., Moore's Boxes, S/21.

claiming that it was outrageous that they should be obliged by law to pay a gratuity to a royal official after he had been prosecuted, convicted, and dismissed from office for taking such gratuities.[1]

Suffolk practised corruption on a gross scale; he enjoyed the legitimate profits of the highest offices of the land; he gained enormous rewards from his customs farms and from Crown annuities; he inherited one windfall of property from his uncle the Earl of Northampton, and his son inherited two others from his cousin Viscount Bindon and his father-in-law Lord Hume. By 1618 the gross landed income of father and son must have been between £8,000 and £9,000, while the official and unofficial must have amounted to a further £4,000 to £5,000, making £12,000 to £15,000 in all. The fact is, however, that at the time of his fall his finances were in a very precarious condition. Despite this huge income, and despite considerable sales of land over the years, the load of debt had risen to dizzy heights. There had been a spate of sales soon after the accession of James I, in order to liquidate the debts accumulated in the last year of Elizabeth, but for the first few years after Suffolk had risen to high favour at Court, he for once became a purchaser. In 1609, however, he began to sell land again. In that year a Cambridgeshire manor was sold to Chief Justice Coke, and in 1611 his great town house of the Charterhouse, where King James had stayed on his first arrival in London, went to his old creditor Thomas Sutton for £13,000. In 1616 one of the Bindon estates went to one of the customs farmers, Nicholas Salter, for £6,000, in an effort to reduce the debt. Then finally, in 1618, just at the time of his fall, he sold more of the Bindon estates to the London goldsmith John Williams for £15,000.[2]

Despite receipts of £34,000 from these sales in seven years, the Earl's financial condition in 1618 remained as serious as ever. In July he told King James and the Marquis of Buckingham that he still owed £40,000 in bonds and mortgages.[3] He was therefore in no position to give up his official income without a fight, and he

[1] H.M.C. Cowper MSS. i, p. 142.

[2] C. W. James, *Chief Justice Coke*, London, 1929, p. 305. Coke had bought four other manors from Suffolk in 1602, so this was not the first time they had done business together (Norwich Central Library, Flitcham MSS. 408, 410, 413; P.R.O., Close Rolls, 44 Eliz., pt. 15). P. Bearcroft, *Thomas Sutton and his Foundation in Charterhouse*, London, 1727, pp. 229–30. Leeds Public Library, Temple Newsam MSS., Family Papers 9. P.R.O., Close Rolls, 14 Jas. I, 22/28; 16 Jas. I, 22/33.

[3] Bodl. MS. Add. D. 110 ff. 59, 189. *Cabala Sive Scrinia Sacra*, London, 1663, p. 359. B.M. Harl. MSS. 1581, f. 146.

defended every inch of the way. As a result King James and his
enemies were obliged to bring him before the Star Chamber in
1619, where he was fined £30,000 and imprisoned in the Tower
during pleasure.[1] This crushing fine added on top of his debt load
of over £40,000 was more than the estate could bear. Suffolk
hastened to protect himself by transferring all his estate to his son
Lord William Howard and his creditor and friend, Sir Arthur
Ingram, and by stripping his country house at Audley End and his
town house at Northampton House of all their movables. When the
bailiffs came the Earl ostensibly possessed no landed property which
could be extended to enforce payment of the fine, and no rich plate
or jewels or furniture which could be seized. Moreover, his two
sons, who were supposed to resign their offices in return for their
father's prompt release from the Tower, were refusing to do so,
arguing that they could not legally be removed. James was initially
furious at this sharp practice, but he retained a good deal of affection
for the old rogue, despite his proven dishonesty. Apart from the
fine, Suffolk's private debts had now run up to £50,000 plus interest,
but a half-hour's personal interview with King James sufficed to
save him. James agreed to remit all of the fine except £7,000 which
had already been promised to a Scottish favourite, Lord Haddington.
Thanks to this interview, and to the continuing pressure of the
Spanish ambassador in favour of a man who had been a leading
advocate of the pro-Spanish foreign policy, Suffolk seemed to be
back on the road to political favour.[2]

The question must now be asked how it was possible that a man
so generously endowed with landed property, so lavishly rewarded
by the Crown, so fortunate in inheriting property from relatives,
and so morally unrestricted in the pursuit of corrupt gains could
have contrived to run so heavily into debt. The short answer is that
generalized extravagance was one of the hallmarks of one of the
most opulent courts in Europe. 'The fault of the expense was my
folly', as Suffolk succinctly put it after his fall.[3] In every possible
way he was living beyond his means, while there is reason to think
that his accounting system was far less efficient than that of Salisbury. But beyond this vague and unhelpful generalization two
prime causes stand out: excessive building and excessive children.

[1] McClure, op. cit. ii, p. 274.
[2] Ibid., pp. 207, 251, 272-3, 277, 281, 283, 313, 321. Bodl. MSS. D. 110, f. 63. *Cabala*,
pp. 362-3.
[3] Bodl. MS., Add. D. 110, f. 189.

Hatfield House had cost Salisbury about £40,000, but Audley End was on an even larger scale, and was built in stone not brick. Begun in 1603 and completed in 1616, it was said by a contemporary to have cost at least £80,000, while there is a fairly well-authenticated story that Suffolk told King James that including all the furniture it had cost him £200,000.[1] This latter figure must be exaggerated, but the former is certainly credible. This gigantic edifice was easily the largest private house in England, so large indeed that within a half a century the family was obliged to sell it to the Crown, since its upkeep was too great for a private purse to endure. Just as Hatfield House imposed corruption on the Earl of Salisbury, so Audley End imposed corruption on the Earl of Suffolk.

The second major cause of heavy expenditure was the children. Although a high birth-rate was common among the upper classes at this time, a high death-rate usually considerably reduced the number surviving into expensive adulthood. In the case of Suffolk, however, all but four of the children lived, and he found himself with three adult daughters and seven adult sons to be provided for. As has been seen, the marriages of these children were valuable tools in the construction of a political connection with wide ramifications in early Stuart Court society. But the cost of bringing them up and marrying them off was very substantial indeed. At least two sons were sent off on one of those expensive tours of the Continent which were just becoming fashionable.[2] The eldest son, Theophilus, had been married to the heiress of the Scottish favourite, the Earl of Dunbar,[3] to obtain which his father would have had to provide the couple with a substantial allowance. The second son was the heir of the Knyvett estate in Wiltshire, belonging to his mother, which was settled on him in 1615. This property, worth between £1,500 and £2,500 in 1652, thus passed from the main line of the family to found a secondary peerage and dynasty as the Earls of Berkshire. The seventh surviving son was given the Escrick estate inherited from his mother, was married to a co-heiress of Lord Boteler, and went on to found a secondary peerage and dynasty as Lords Howard of Escrick. The third son, Henry, inherited after his father's death the £800 a year estate left by his great-uncle the Earl of Northampton, and was married to the only daughter of William Bassett of Blore, an heiress to property worth

<hr />

[1] *Journal of Sir Roger Wilbraham, Camden Misc.* x, p. 115. Lord Braybrooke, *Audley End*, p. 82.
[2] McClure, op. cit. i, p. 273.   [3] Lord Braybrooke, op. cit., p. 43.

£2,400 a year. The fourth son, Charles, was married to the twice-widowed heiress of Sir John Fitz of Fitzford, later described by Clarendon as the greatest match in the west, to obtain whom Suffolk had to settle on the pair an annuity of £600 for their two lives for maintenance and jointure.[1] All these were highly successful marriages by the strictly financial standards of the day, but they involved a considerable sacrifice on the part of Suffolk, who settled substantial properties on his sons to match their brides' fortunes, but got no cash reward in return since these fortunes were in land not monetary portions.

The fifth son, Robert, was the only one who did not marry an heiress, although his wife was the daughter of a peer. He was also the only one whose marriage notoriously collapsed, when he created a major scandal by taking the Countess of Purbeck as his mistress. Although the sixth son, William, remained a bachelor, both he and Robert must have cost their father a good deal to maintain them at Court, since they were frequent participants in masques and other festivities, and were both made K.B., which was always an expensive honour. William's father had got him his office as Lieutenant of the Gentlemen Pensioners, with an income of £300 a year, but this could not have been enough to maintain him. As for the three daughters, all were married, at very great cost, to prominent members of the very high Court nobility. One was matched with the Earl of Salisbury with a portion of £4,000, and the other two to the Earls of Essex and Banbury with portions of £6,000 each. Thus these three marriages alone, not counting the cost of the marriage ceremonies and feasts, demanded an expenditure by Suffolk of some £16,000.[2] Since he had married most of his sons to landed heiresses, he had settled substantial landed properties or annuities on them but had not received any compensatory inflow of immediate cash from portions of their wives at the time of their marriages. Suffolk had therefore deliberately sacrificed his own advantage in order to enhance the long-term financial prospects of his children, who had all made socially and financially advantageous matches.

This aspect of his devotion to his children was not the only cause of Suffolk's financial troubles, for he was lavish to a degree in

[1] Margaret Duchess of Newcastle, *Life of the Duke of Newcastle*, ed. C. H. Firth, London, n.d., p. 72. Edward Earl of Clarendon, *History of the Rebellion*, ed. W. D. Macray, Oxford, 1888, iii, p. 419. *Cal. S.P. Dom., 1639–40*, p. 415.
[2] S.P. 16/443/86. Hatfield House D. 114/6; A. 8/24. P.R.O., Close Rolls, 3 Jas. I, pt. 32.

his encouragement of them to take part in the most expensive extravaganzas of the Court. As one of his daughters told King James after his father's fall, 'My lord has spent in running at tilt, in masques and following the Court about £20,000.' For a considerable period he had no fewer than four sons taking a prominent part, at his expense, in Court festivities. In 1606 two sons and a daughter performed in the masques to celebrate the marriage of his daughter Frances to the Earl of Essex. In 1613 four sons participated in a most expensive masque for Queen Anne at Lord Knollys's house at Caversham, and in an even more costly one to celebrate the second marriage of their sister Frances to the Earl of Somerset. All four took part in the tilt at Court at the New Year of 1614, while three sons performed again in 1616.[1] Another heavy source of expenditure was on entertaining King James, at Audley End in 1614, at Chesterford Park in 1616, and on a five-day visit to Cambridge in 1615 which was reported to have cost Suffolk £1,000 a day.[2]

There is no reason to suppose that Earl Thomas did anything very significant to reduce the burden of debt before his death in 1626. The only effort he made in this direction was the sale in 1622 of a Yorkshire manor for £4,400 to his old friend Sir Arthur Ingram, the latter being expected to use the money to pay off creditors. As usual, Ingram failed to fulfil his side of the bargain, and had to be sued by the indignant creditors. But Ingram's relations with Suffolk were not shaken even by the most obvious evidence of deceit, and he continued to act as the latter's creditor, advancing him sums in petty cash to meet tailors' bills and the like.[3] The death of Earl Thomas in 1626 and the succession of Theophilus did little to alter the fortunes of the family. The second Earl, like his father, was a life-long courtier, saddled with all the expenses that that way of life entailed, and for thirty years he served first as Lieutenant and then as Captain of the Gentlemen Pensioners. Worse still, he inherited not only his father's debts and his father's unfortunate choice in friends, like Sir Arthur Ingram, but also to an even higher degree his father's weakness for grotesque extravagance. For example, in two games of bowls in a three-day period in 1623 he is reported to have lost £2,000. He was only saved from

[1] *Cabala sive Scrinia Sacra*, p. 254. W. B. Devereux, *Lives of the Devereux*, London, 1853, ii, pp. 226–7. McClure, op. cit. i, pp. 446, 450, 487, 496, 498, 617.

[2] McClure, op. cit. i, pp. 502, 619, 587.   [3] Upton, op. cit., p. 83.

his own folly by increasing ill health, for by the early 1630s, although less than fifty years old, he was lame and crippled by intermittent stoppages of his urine.[1]

Apart from his two offices of Captain of the Gentlemen Pensioners and Warden of the Cinque Ports, which probably brought in about £1,700 a year between them,[2] the only rewards he obtained from a lifetime of attendance at Court were the Keepership of Greenwich Park in 1611, and a Privy Seal from King James for £5,000 just before the latter's death in 1625, a gift which had still not been fully converted into hard cash some eleven years later.[3]

Such was his extravagance that despite a gross landed income of about £11,000 and another £2,000 or so from offices and other perquisites, Earl Theophilus continued to run up even larger debts than before. As a result, the debt burden continued to press upon him as heavily as ever, and indeed got steadily worse. In 1633 a commentator reported that he showed no signs of taking care for 'paying his own debts, which will shortly eat up his inheritance'. In 1635 increasing ill health and political pressure forced him to surrender his office to his brother-in-law, the Earl of Salisbury, and to retire from the Court. He could not afford to live in the fantastic palace of Audley End, and instead retired to Lulworth Castle in Dorset, which he had inherited from the Viscount Bindon, and where he now devoted himself to gardening.[4]

His retirement exposed him to mounting pressure from his creditors, among whom was now the Crown, which began pressing him for over £600 in ancient arrears of fee-farm rents and of parliamentary subsidies which had been allowed to trail on unpaid as long as he was a prominent Court official. The financial regime of Juxon and Cottington was ruthless in its treatment of all save its own close adherents, and Earl Theophilus was infuriated to find his land extended to enforce payment of the royal debt.[5]

In these straitened circumstances, Earl Theophilus was in no position to fulfil the promises which had been made by his father to obtain those rich heiresses for his brothers. The main difficulty was over the £600 a year for two lives which Earl Thomas had

[1] McClure, op. cit. ii, p. 500. W. Knowler, *Strafforde Letters*, i, p. 412.

[2] See above, ch. iv. p. 117. The Wardenship appears to have been worth about £700 a year in 1624 (*Cal. S.P. Dom., 1623-5*, p. 304).

[3] *Cal. S.P. Dom., 1623-5*, pp. 439, 447; *1625-6*, p. 11. *H.M.C. Cowper MSS.* ii, pp. 123-4.

[4] W. Knowler, op. cit. i, pp. 167, 208, 412, 506. Dorset Record Office, Weld MSS., Box H/General 42.

[5] *Cal. S.P. Dom. 1635*, p. 37; *1637-8*, p. 281. Dorset R.O., Weld MSS., Box H/General 42.

promised to settle on his son Charles when he married the heiress of Sir John Fitz. Charles died unexpectedly in 1622, thus leaving the widow with a claim for a life annuity of £600 out of the Suffolk estate. But she soon found that the land assigned on lease for assurance of the annuity was inadequate to provide £600 a year. She therefore sued Earl Theophilus, and in 1629 obtained a judgement in Chancery for payment of £1,500 arrears and the full £600 a year in future. At this point she was persuaded to marry a military client of the late Duke of Buckingham, Sir Richard Grenville, with whom there promptly began a prolonged and vicious legal battle as he tried to enforce payment. Things were considerably complicated by the fact that the Fitz heiress soon quarrelled with her new husband for his brutal and avaricious behaviour and for begetting a bastard. She was separated from him in 1632 and re-allied herself with the Howards. Suits, counter-suits, and accusations flew to and fro. Lady Grenville sued her husband for £2,600 a year alimony, and Suffolk sued him for slander in Star Chamber. The latter was awarded a verdict of a fine of £4,000 and £4,000 damages, and Grenville was imprisoned in the Fleet until he gave bond not to molest his wife. But he escaped from prison and fled abroad, thus avoiding the necessity of paying Suffolk. Some years later, in 1639, he returned home, and again sued Suffolk for the arrears of the annuity plus interest, now amounting to £16,656. From this he generously agreed to deduct the £4,000 due in damages, leaving him with a claim to £12,656 in the right of his ex-wife.[1]

The burden of fulfilling his obligations to his brothers and sisters was serious enough, but what compounded Earl Theophilus's financial difficulties was the problem of disposing of his own children as well. Like his father before him, he found himself saddled with an excess of offspring to be maintained and to be disposed of in marriage, for no fewer than four sons and five daughters survived to adulthood. He apparently planned to settle £1,000 a year on the three younger sons out of the ex-Bindon land in the West Country, but there is considerable doubt whether they ever got the money. Financial pressure forced their elder brother to sell the whole estate in the early 1640s,[2] and it is noticeable that all three married into relatively obscure families. It looks as if the

[1] Clarendon, op. cit. iii, p. 419. S.P. 16/443/86. *Cal. S.P. Dom.*, *1633–4*, pp. 158, 379; *1639–40*, pp. 74, 414–15.

[2] *Cal. S.P. Dom.*, *1639–40*, p. 478. Essex R.O., D/DBy, A. 5.

younger sons were cheated out of their inheritance by the refusal of their elder brother to fulfil the promises of their father. But no such economies were possible for the girls, since both honour and the desire to extend connections among influencial families dictated that they should be married off at an appropriate high social level. Earl Theophilus consequently assured each of them a portion of £5,000, making a total liability of £25,000 in all.[1] With this money to back them, all five ostensibly married well, three to peers or heirs of peers, and two into distinguished gentry families. Even for the favoured daughters, however, things did not always turn out the way they were supposed. One husband, Lord Broghill, found his family estates and income suddenly wiped out by the Irish Rebellion of 1641, and it took him the best part of a decade to recover them. Another, Sir Thomas Walsingham of Scadbury in Kent, was a disappointed courtier who backed the winning side in the Civil War, but none the less was obliged to sell the ancestral seat and all the estates in the 1650s.[2]

The problem posed by the urgent necessity of both paying off the accumulated debts of himself and his father, and of raising the money for the daughters, who were now approaching marriageable age, forced Earl Theophilus in the last years of his life to plan a major reorganization of the family estates. The moment his wife died in 1633 the Earl had begun to sell off her northern inheritance in Northumberland and Durham, which had already realized about £22,000, with another £14,000 worth still to be sold. In addition, in 1635 he sold the ancient seat of his ancestors the Dukes of Norfolk at Framlingham in Suffolk to Sir Robert Hitcham for £14,000, so that before 1639 he had already raised about £36,000 by the sale of land.[3] And yet in that year he was forced to inform the Privy Council that his debts amounted to £55,000, which was more than the estate could bear. The problem was further complicated by the death in 1639 of the old dowager Countess, as a result of which a fresh series of family lawsuits broke out over the disposal of her

    [1] Essex R.O., D/DBy, A. 5.
    [2] A. Everitt, *The Community of Kent and the Great Rebellion, 1640–60*, Leicester, 1966, pp. 146, 181.
    [3] Cambridge University Library (C.U.L.), Ee 3/25 f. 75. *A History of Northumberland*, xi, p. 454; xv, pp. 239, 477. *Archaeologia Aeliana*, 3rd ser. iv, 1908, p. 120. J. Raine, *History of North Durham*, pp. 157, 200–3, 243, 283, 301. Essex R.O. D/DBy, A. 6. *Journal of the House of Lords*, iv, p. 695; vi, p. 299; vii, pp. 358, 492, 493. Among the properties sold was 'the stewhouse in Berwick', presumably the brothel that served the garrison, which realized £100.

personal estate.[1] All the landed property was entailed, the Howard and the Bindon estates by the first Earl Thomas and the Hume estate by the Countess's father the Earl of Dunbar. Theophilus was therefore obliged to get help from the Privy Council to permit his son and heir James, aged seventeen in 1637, to join him in breaking the entail and transferring large parts of the estate to feoffees as security for the liquidation of the debt. Immediately, however, the usual family dispute broke out, with different groups of trustees quarrelling with one another and with the young James, who was under pressure from various factions in the family to resist the dismemberment of his inheritance.[2]

Sales of land had already begun, despite the family quarrel, when in 1640 Earl Theophilus died, leaving his dismembered and heavily burdened inheritance to the young son and heir James. When the executors came to survey the situation, they must have been appalled at what they found. Including the unsecured £1,000 a year annuity to be shared by three younger brothers of the new Earl, the secured marriage portions of the five sisters, and the various annuities settled by the grandfather to his uncles, the obligations to relatives were capitalized at about £50,000, while the debts to others amounted to no less than £82,000, making a grand total of £132,000.[3] Many of the debts went back to the early 1630s and in most cases no interest had been paid on them for three years. In consequence, many of the creditors had sued and obtained judgement in the courts. It should be remembered that these enormous debts had piled up despite land sales throughout the previous seven years which had brought in about £36,000. Earl Theophilus must have been a spendthrift on a monumental scale.

As soon as he came into his inheritance in 1640, Earl James and his advisers and feoffees set about reducing the debt to manageable proportions. It has already been suggested that it is almost certain from the accounts that one economy measure was a refusal to pay the three younger brothers their promised annuity, which cut some £18,000 in capital value from the debt. This was not a good moment in which to sell land, since the political crisis had depressed the market, but Earl James had no option. The whole of the huge

---

[1] Essex R.O., D/DBy, A. 6. Hatfield House, A. 157/3.

[2] *Cal. S.P. Dom.*, *1637*, pp. 241, 500; *1639–40*, p. 252.

[3] Essex R.O. D/DBy, A. 5. The distribution between family and private debts given in L. Stone, *The Crisis of the Aristocracy, 1558–1641*, p. 779, is incorrect, since the capital value of the £1,000 annuities to the three sons was erroneously counted as a private debt.

Bindon estate in the west, including the great house of Lulworth Castle, was sold for some £69,000.[1] A rich Londoner, Humphrey Weld, was the principal purchaser, for £29,000, thus establishing a landed family at Lulworth Castle which has endured from that day to this. Other purchasers were local gentry anxious to expand their holdings in the area, such as Sir John Strangways and the M.P. Dennis Bond. And lastly there was the ubiquitous and indestructible Sir Arthur Ingram, who was as deeply involved in the family finances as ever, and was up to his usual tricks again. He bought four Dorset manors for £14,200, some £11,500 of which was to liquidate a debt of Suffolk to himself (part of it advanced to pay one of the married daughter's portions), and the rest to be used by Ingram to pay off other creditors. Earl James was as dependent upon Ingram as his father and grandfather had been, and he gratefully noted on one document 'I think it very reasonable that Sir Arthur Ingram should have a £100 abated of this contract.' But Earl James's confidence was misplaced, for Ingram failed to satisfy the creditors, and twenty years later, after the Restoration, the Earl was pursuing Ingram's heirs through the courts in order to enforce payment.[2]

At the same time, most of the last remnants of the northern estates of the Earl of Dunbar were sold for £6,500 to a local gentleman Sir Robert Widdrington.[3] And lastly the great town house at Charing Cross, which had been inherited from the Earl of Northampton, was sold to the Earl of Northumberland for £15,000, £5,000 of the purchase price being remitted in payment of the marriage portion of the latter's wife, who was one of Earl James's sisters.[4] In the two years before the outbreak of war, Earl James had raised nearly £100,000 by the sale of land, and saved himself another £18,000 by abandoning his brothers. He had now no town house, and no property outside the central estates in Essex and Cambridgeshire except a single large block of land at Oswestry in distant Shropshire and a few remnants in the north. In eight years between 1633 and 1641 Earls Theophilus and James had sold about half the family patrimony. The gross income in

[1] J. Hutchins, *History of Dorset*, London, 1861–70, i, pp. 343, 347–8, 360, 369–70, 378, 421, 441; ii, pp. 575, 619–20. C.U.L. Ee 3/25, ff. 5ᵛ–10. Essex R.O., D/DBy, A. 5.

[2] Leeds Public Library, Temple Newsam MSS., Family Papers 9. C.U.L. Ee 3/25, ff. 3ᵛ, 4, 5ᵛ.

[3] J. Hodgson and J. H. Hinde, *History of Northumberland*, i, pt. ii, p. 79. H. K. S. Causton, *Howard Papers*, London, 1862, p. 506.

[4] C.U.L., Ee 3/25, ff. 5ᵛ–10.

1630 was around £11,000 a year, which made the Suffolks one of the dozen wealthiest families in England, but it was now reduced to about £6,500.[1] This was still a respectable income by any standard, but it was on the modest side for an Earl, and was clearly insufficient to support a palace like Audley End.

When war came Earl James sided with Parliament, thus starting a 'Whig' tradition in the family that lasted throughout the rest of the seventeenth century. One can only guess at the motives behind his decision, but the opinions of his new brother-in-law, the Earl of Northumberland, and his uncle, the Earl of Salisbury, must presumably have been influential. He may also have inherited the resentment of his father at being ousted from Court office in 1635, and at being subsequently hounded for his debts to the Crown. A final consideration, which must have weighed heavily with him, was that if he joined the King he was likely to be almost penniless, since what was left of his estate was almost entirely in Parliamentary hands. Be that as it may, his choice of sides at least spared him a fine as a Royalist delinquent, although his disillusionment with the drift of Parliament into radicalism after 1646 led him to withdraw his support.

This negative triumph of avoiding a fine was not enough to solve Earl James's financial problems. In 1646 there was still £18,000 worth of his father's debts to be cleared off, and his own debts were mounting inexorably again.[2] Like all other landlords, he found that the pressures of war devastation and taxation meant that the tenants fell more and more behind in the payment of their rent. By 1650 the arrears, which had been under £500 in 1639–40, were running at £5,000, or almost the equivalent of a full year's gross income, while the burden of rates and taxes was now pressing very heavily indeed, absorbing over 10 per cent of total gross receipts.[3] The Earl was forced first to raise money on mortgages in order to carry on, and then to start selling land again. The valuable Cambridgeshire property at Haddenham, which was mostly old enclosed pasture and was worth about £600 a year, was sold off in the 1650s, presumably for about £10,000.[4]

[1] See Appendix. The Shropshire property was fully mortgaged to Lord Craven for £18,800 (C.U.L., Ee 3/25, ff. 72ᵛ, 76; Essex R.O. D/DBy, A. 6).

[2] C.U.L., Ee 3/25, f. 32ᵛ; 68ᵛ. Essex R.O. D/DBy, A. 6. National Register of Archives inventory, Wimpole Hall MSS., MTD 2/4.

[3] Essex R.O., D/DBy, M. 62. C.U.L., Ee 3/26, f. 6; 25 f. 39ᵛ.

[4] Essex R.O., D/DBy, M. 159, 165. Wimpole Hall MSS., MTD 6/8. V.C.H. Cambridgeshire, iv, p. 143. Bodl., Tanner MSS. 97, f. 137.

Although the Restoration saw Suffolk's re-entry into Court life, the highest office he could acquire was that of Gentleman of the Bed Chamber, and his financial difficulties consequently continued. In 1669 he managed to persuade King Charles II to relieve him of the incubus of Audley End—'cette grande maison, vaste et solitaire' as St. Evremond described it—which enabled him to withdraw to the less pretentious and more economical seat at Chesterford Park. The promised price was £50,000.[1] These further sales and the secular decline in rents had by 1687 reduced his gross landed income to between £3,300 and £4,300 a year, which was fortunately supplemented by an office he had picked up along the way during his period as an active courtier. Described as 'the Seal Office', it was presumably a sinecure in one of the courts of law, and was bringing in a handsome £2,100 a year.[2]

With Earl James, the biological fortunes of the Suffolks changed abruptly from an excess of children to a shortage. Despite three marriages Earl James was childless, as was the next brother and heir George, while the third brother and heir Henry had only one son. By 1687 Earl James was now very old, and was living in very modest circumstances. For the first time in the history of the Howard Earls of Suffolk they seem to have been free of debt, and were actually putting aside a surplus on the year's accounts. The old Earl was still treating his siblings with conspicuous shabbiness, his brother George, now the heir to the estate and title, being kept on an annuity of no more than £150 a year.[2]

The information is lacking for any detailed study of the estate administration of the Earls of Suffolk, since no more than scattered fragments of the accounts have survived the passage of time, the dismemberment of the estate, and the failure of the male line. A survey of the East Anglian estate in 1602 strongly suggests that the property was let on the usual pattern of leases with entry fines, but that an unusually large amount of property was kept in the Lords' hands around the house at Audley End. The ley grounds, meadows, parks, arable lands, and woods in hand were valued at £670 a year, while the great tithes of the parish of Walden, which were received in kind, amounted to a further £260.[3] Some accounts of the parsonage show how the big farmers, or the tithe holders, profited in a famine year. In the two fairly good harvest years of

[1] Lord Braybrooke, *Audley End*, pp. 89, 90.   [2] Essex R.O. D/DBy, A. 1.
[3] Ibid., M. 159.

1583–5, Lord Howard received an average of 320 quarters of corn, which he sold for £170. In the near famine year of 1585–6, however, the quantity fell by nearly 30 per cent to 23 quarters, but the receipts rose by 20 per cent to £205, since the price of wheat had doubled and that of barley risen by two-thirds.[1] By 1640 most of the land in hand had been leased, like the rest of the estate, and the home farm had been greatly reduced.[2]

In places the Earls achieved truly astonishing increases in rental income, presumably by putting the maximum pressure on the tenants, but possibly also by shifting increasingly from reliance on fines to reliance on rents. On the four main properties in Essex, the rental income between 1575 and 1641 increased fourfold, from £564 to £2,451, despite the fact that there had been only very trivial additional purchases to round out these particular estates in the interval.[3] Later still, in the 1660s and after, the leases tended to be shortened from the previously standard twenty-one years to twelve to fourteen years, the rents were raised, and the fines for new leasing were kept down to one or two years' rent. By the 1680s fines seem to have been largely eliminated, and the Earls had gone over to rack-renting.[4] This is very advanced estate practice, and suggests that whatever the financial shortcomings of the late seventeenth-century Earls of Suffolk, inept and improvident estate management was not one of them. As so often happened, extreme extravagance in expenditure and consequent financial pressure dictated ruthless efficiency in the handling of the income side.

During the early eighteenth century the family struggled on. It was now in much reduced circumstances and played no more than a relatively minor social and political role in the single county of Essex. In 1701 Audley End was handed back to them by the Crown, which had still not paid over the last £30,000 of the £50,000 purchase price, and no longer wanted the place. But the Earls could not afford to live in it and in 1721 a major demolition was carried out, which more than halved the size of the house. A series of childless marriages, some of them due to sterility, others to the early deaths of the children, meant a rapid succession to the Earldom of impoverished younger brothers. As the family fortunes declined, so the means adopted to supplement them became more squalid. One early eighteenth-century Earl got into

---

[1] Ibid., M. 158.   [2] Ibid., M. 162, 163.   [3] Ibid., M. 157, 163; E. 4.
[4] Ibid., E. 1, 2.

trouble with his peers in the House of Lords for selling protections from arrest for debt to anyone who was willing to pay; another accepted a royal pension in return for quietly allowing his wife to serve as the mistress of King George II. In 1745 the end came; on the death of the tenth Earl, the male line of the Howards Earls of Suffolk ran out, the title was extinguished, and the great house at Audley End was sold.

The Suffolks had risen in a single generation, as a result of political favour and a diligent pursuit of heiresses. But no sooner had they reached the peak of their prosperity than they began to fall. In the first place both the first and the second Earl were some of the more extravagant spenders in one of the most extravagant courts in Europe. The result was to saddle the family with a house which was so gigantic that no private individual could afford to live in it and maintain it, and with a burden of debt (partly caused by the cost of building the house) which was too great for the income to support. In the second place the family suffered for two generations from the biological accident of too many children surviving into adulthood, who cost too much to be successfully launched into the world. And in the third place it subsequently suffered for two generations from the biological accident of too few children surviving into adulthood, which finally led to the total extinction of the line. Pursuing an initial upward projectory almost identical to that of the Earls of Salisbury, the fortunes of the Howards Earls of Suffolk consequently began to decline very rapidly; without support from soaring urban rents and without the injection of new capital from marriage with rich heiresses, they reached their nadir within little more than a century of the peak of their wealth and power. The expiry of the male line was merely the *coup de grâce*.

APPENDIX

Summary of Gross Yearly Landed Income of the Earls of Suffolk and their Eldest Sons, 1575–1688

	1575–6	1615–19	1633	1639–40	1644–50	1687–8
	£	£	£	£	£	£
East Anglia	1,100[1]	[4,000]	[5,000]	5,100[4]	5,300[6]	3,500[7]
Shropshire	..	700[2]	[1,000]	[1,000]	[1,000]	?[8]
Dorset	..	3,100[2]	[3,000]	3,000[5]	..	..
The north	..	1,600[3]	[2,000]	[200]	200	..
Estimated total	1,100	9,400	11,000	9,300	6,500	3,500(+ ?)[8]

N.B. Figures in brackets are extrapolated from earlier or later accounts.

These figures are for rents and casualties received, but do not seem to include the fines for new leases.

[1] Essex R.O., D/DBy, M. 157, 158.
[2] Wilts. R.O., Suffolk and Berkshire MSS., Moore's Boxes S/21.
[3] J. Raine, *North Durham*, p. 43.   [4] Essex R.O., D/DBy, M. 162, 163.
[5] Dorset R.O., Weld MSS., Box H/General 42 (account for 1635–6).
[6] C.U.L., Ee 3/25, ff. 6–46.   [7] Essex R.O., D/DBy, A. 1.
[8] The Shropshire estate may have still been held, but accounted for separately. If so, the total would be about £4,300.

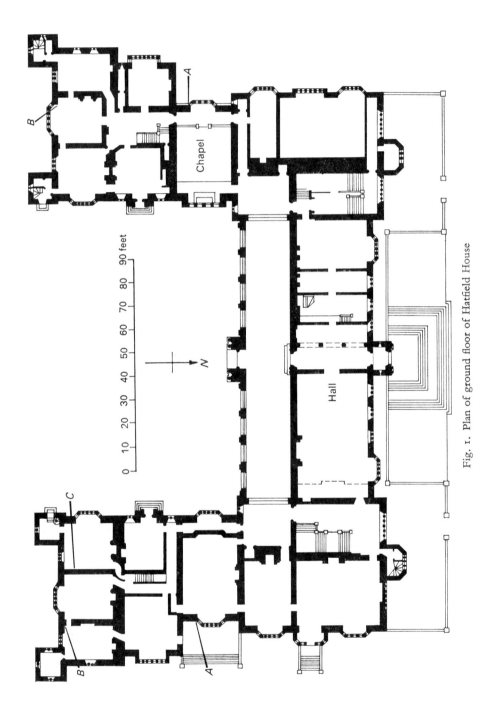

Fig. 1. Plan of ground floor of Hatfield House

APPENDIX

Summary of Gross Yearly Landed Income of the Earls of Suffolk and their Eldest Sons, 1575–1688

	1575–6	1615–19	1633	1639–40	1644–50	1687–8
	£	£	£	£	£	£
East Anglia	1,100[1]	[4,000]	[5,000]	5,100[4]	5,300[6]	3,500[7]
Shropshire	..	700[2]	[1,000]	[1,000]	[1,000]	?[8]
Dorset	..	3,100[2]	[3,000]	3,000[5]	..	..
The north	..	1,600[3]	[2,000]	[200]	200	..
Estimated total	1,100	9,400	11,000	9,300	6,500	3,500(+ ?)[8]

N.B. Figures in brackets are extrapolated from earlier or later accounts.

These figures are for rents and casualties received, but do not seem to include the fines for new leases.

[1] Essex R.O., D/DBy, M. 157, 158.
[2] Wilts. R.O., Suffolk and Berkshire MSS., Moore's Boxes S/21.
[3] J. Raine, *North Durham*, p. 43.   [4] Essex R.O., D/DBy, M. 162, 163.
[5] Dorset R.O., Weld MSS., Box H/General 42 (account for 1635–6).
[6] C.U.L., Ee 3/25, ff. 6–46.   [7] Essex R.O., D/DBy, A. 1.
[8] The Shropshire estate may have still been held, but accounted for separately. If so, the total would be about £4,300.

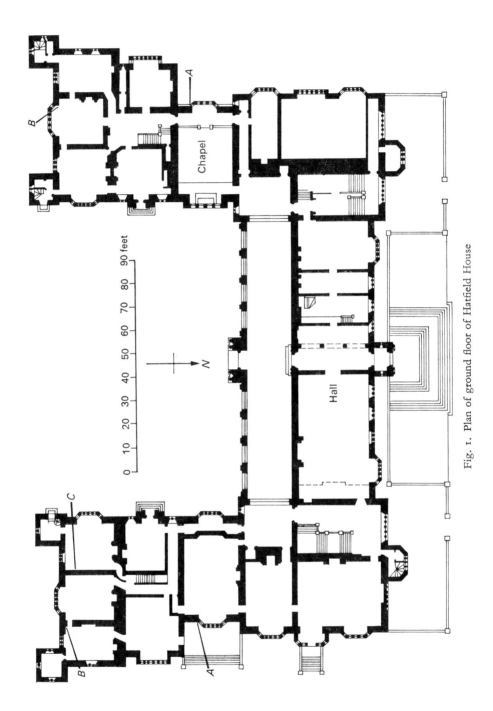

Fig. 1. Plan of ground floor of Hatfield House

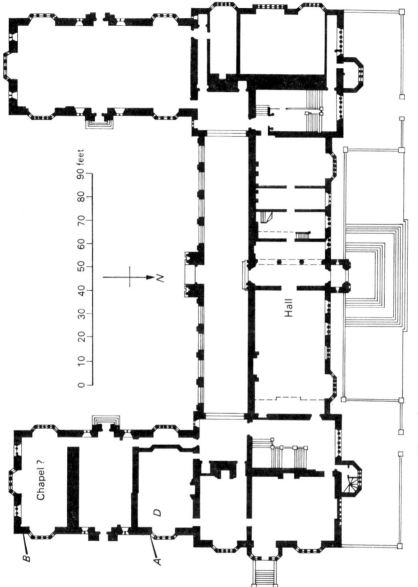

Fig. 2. Suggested original plan of ground floor of Hatfield House

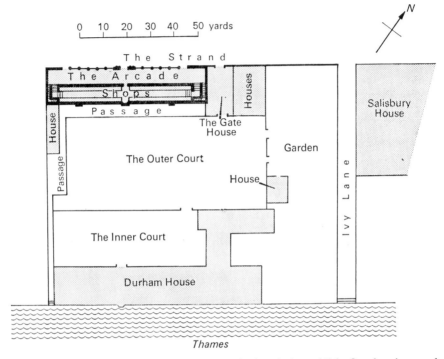

Fig. 3. The Durham House site, based on the sketch-plan of 1621 and John Smythson's ground-plan of the New Exchange, as illustrated in A. W. Clapham and W. H. Godfrey, *Some Famous Buildings and their Story*, figs. 67, 68

INDEX

Abbreviations: w. = wife; m. = married. Titles in brackets are those held subsequently to the events mentioned in the text.

PLATES

I. SOUTH FRONT OF HATFIELD HOUSE

II. SOUTH PORCH OF HATFIELD HOUSE

III. CLOCK TOWER OF HATFIELD HOUSE

IV. NORTH FRONT OF HATFIELD HOUSE

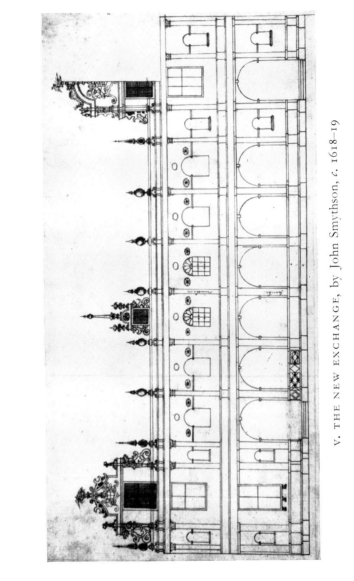

V. THE NEW EXCHANGE, by John Smythson, c. 1618–19

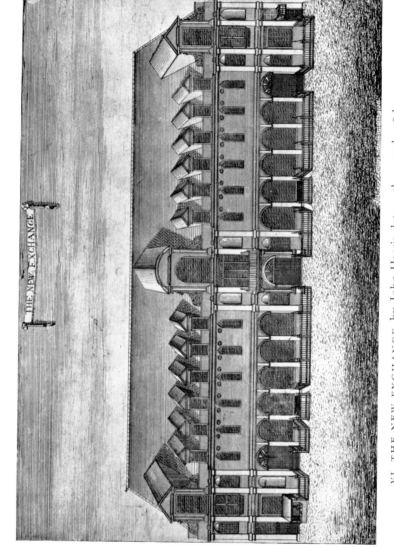

VI. THE NEW EXCHANGE, by John Harris, late 17th or early 18th century

Iilington

Southampton
Row

Allington Row

Southampton Row

18